CHESTERTON

MCI

The Making of the Christian Imagination

Stephen Prickett
general editor

OTHER BOOKS IN THIS SERIES

CHESTERTON

The Nightmare Goodness of God

Ralph C. Wood

BAYLOR UNIVERSITY PRESS

Jacket Design by Andrew Brozyna, AJB Design, Inc.
Cover Art: The Power of the Press: First With the News. G. K. Chesterton. Original artwork from Look and Learn no. 624 (29 December 1973). Gouache on paper. Used by permission of Bridgeman Art Library.

Library of Congress Cataloging-in-Publication Data

Wood, Ralph C.
  Chesterton : the nightmare goodness of God / Ralph C. Wood.
    358 p. cm.
  Includes bibliographical references and index.
  ISBN 978-1-60258-161-6 (alk. paper)
  1. Chesterton, G. K. (Gilbert Keith), 1874–1936—Religion. 2. Chesterton, G. K. (Gilbert Keith), 1874–1936—Themes, motives. 3. Theology in literature. I. Title.
  PR4453.C4Z885 2011
  828'.91209—dc22

                        2010053045

Printed in the United States of America on acid-free paper with a minimum of 30% pcw recycled content.

For Suzanne
my *sine qua non*

Behind the Johnsonian fancy-dress, so reassuring to the British public, he concealed the most serious and revolutionary designs—concealing them by exposure, as his anarchist conspirators chose to hold their meetings on a balcony in Leicester Square. . . . Even if Chesterton's social and economic ideas appear to be totally without effect, even if they should be demonstrated to be wrong—which would perhaps only mean that men have not the good will to carry them out—they were *the* ideas for his time that were fundamentally Christian and Catholic. He did more, I think, than any man of his time . . . to maintain the existence of the important minority in the modern world.

T. S. Eliot (1936)

Chesterton would not have tolerated the imputation of being a contriver of nightmares, a *monstrum artifex* . . . , but he tends inevitably to revert to atrocious observations. . . . Chesterton restrained himself from being Edgar Allan Poe or Franz Kafka, but something in the makeup of his personality leaned toward the nightmarish, something secret, and blind, and central.

Jorge Luis Borges (1946)

[T]he substructure of [Chesterton's] farce and fantasy—a concern with free will, Western civilization, and the ultimate mysteries of religion—is not less valid in the age of superstates and nuclear deterrents and brainwashing than it was in Chesterton's more innocent heyday.

Anthony Burgess (1969)

Chesterton's merits as a thinker are grossly neglected but are probably irrecoverable by the mainstream of modern criticism. He is the nearest thing to an English Nietzsche, but neither modern Nietzscheans nor modern Chestertonians are likely to welcome the comparison.

Nicholas Boyle (2005)

If there is a curious and fantastic art it is the business of the art critics to create a curious and fantastic expression for it; inferior to it, doubtless, but still akin to it. If they cannot do this, as they cannot; if there is nothing in their eulogies, as there is nothing except eulogy—then they are quacks or the high-priests of the unutterable.

G. K. Chesterton (1912)

SERIES INTRODUCTION
by Rowan Williams

The current rash of books hostile to religious faith will one day be an interesting subject for some sociological analysis. They consistently suggest a view of religion which, if taken seriously, would also evacuate a number of other human systems of meaning, including quite a lot of what we unreflectively think of as science. That is, they treat religious belief almost as a solitary aberration in a field of human rationality; a set of groundless beliefs about matters of fact, resting on—at best—faulty and weak argumentation. What they normally fail to do is to attend to what it is that religious people actually do and say—and also to attend to the general question of how systems of meaning, or "worldviews," work.

Systems of meaning—philosophies of life, if you must, though the term sounds immediately rather stale—seem to operate by allowing us to see phenomena in connected instead of arbitrary ways. But this means the capacity to see things in terms of other things: it means abandoning the idea that there is one basic and obvious way of seeing the world which any fool can get hold of (and which some people then insist on dressing up with unnecessary complications), and grasping that seeing the world and being able to talk about what it is that we encounter is something we have to learn, a set of skills that allows us to connect and to see one event or phenomenon through the lens of another. At the most severely pragmatic level, this leads to observational generalizations about laws; at a quite different but no less important level, it leads us into the world of metaphor. And in case anyone should think that these are radically separate, consider that "law" itself is a metaphor in the context of natural process. . . .

Metaphor is omnipresent, certainly in scientific discourse (selfish genes, computer modelings of brain processes, not to mention the magnificent extravagances of theoretical physics), and its omnipresence ought to warn us against the fiction that there is a language that is untainted and obvious for any discipline. We are bound to use words that have histories and associations; to see things in terms of more than their immediate appearance means that we are constantly using a language we do not fully control to respond to an environment in which things demand that we see more in them than any one set of perceptions can catch.

All of which is to say that no system of perceiving and receiving the world can fail to depend upon imagination, the capacity to see and speak into and out of a world that defies any final settlement as to how it shall be described. The most would-be reductive account of reality still reaches for metaphor, still depends on words that have been learned and that have been used elsewhere. So it should not be too difficult to see that a map that presents the intellectual world as a struggle between rival pictures, well-founded and ill-founded ways of describing things, literal and fanciful perspectives, or even natural and supernatural vision, is a poor one and one that threatens to devour itself in the long run, if the search is for the unadorned absolute. How shall we move the cultural discussion on from a situation in which religious perspectives are assumed to be bad descriptions of what can be better talked about in simpler terms?

This will involve the discipline of following through exactly what it is that the language of a particular religious tradition allows its believers to see—that is, what its imaginative resources are. When believers are engaged (as they routinely are, despite what may be assumed by the critics of faith) in society and politics and the arts in ways that are recognizable to nonbelievers, how are their perceptions actually and specifically molded by the resources of their tradition? This is not—*pace* any number of journalistic commentators—a matter of the imperatives supposedly derived from their religion. It is about what they see things and persons in terms of, what the metaphors are that propose further dimensions to the world they inhabit in common with nonbelievers.

Characteristically this repertoire of resources—in any religious tradition—is chaotically varied, not just a matter of a few leading ideas or doctrines. It includes the visual and the aural—what is sung and seen as well as said. It includes formative practices, rites, which leave their semantic traces in unexpected settings. And it includes the legacy of others who have engaged the world in the same ways, at various levels of sophistication. The forming of a corporate imagination is something that continues to be the more or less daily business of religious believers, and it needs to be acknowledged that this is a process immeasurably more sophisticated than the repetitive dogmatism so widely assumed to be the sole concern of those who employ religious language.

The way to demonstrate this is to lay out what it means in the practice of specific people; this series is an attempt to exhibit a common imagination at work—and in the process of further refinement and development—in the labors of a variety of creative minds. Because we are in danger of succumbing to a damaging cultural amnesia about what religious commitment looks like in practice, these books seek to show that belief "in practice" is a great deal more than following out abstract imperatives or general commitments. They look at creative minds that have a good claim to represent some of the most decisive and innovative cultural currents of the history of the West (and not only the West), in order to track the ways in which a distinctively Christian imagination makes possible their imaginative achievement. And in doing so, they offer a challenge to what one great thinker called the "cultured despisers" of Christian faith: in dismissing this faith, can an intellectually serious person accept confidently the simultaneous dismissal of the shifts, enlargements, and resources it has afforded the individual and collective imagination? What, finally, would a human world be like if it convinced itself that it had shaken off the legacy of the Christian imagination? The hope of the authors of these volumes is that the answer to that question will be constructively worrying— sufficiently so, perhaps, to make possible a more literate debate about faith and contemporary culture.

CONTENTS

PREFACE

"Of making many books there is no end," laments the Preacher with gloomy weariness (Eccl 12:12).[1] The making of this book has entailed no such weariness, no such gloom, because it has brought so many occasions of gratitude to so many aides in the long process of its gestation. These helpers rescued me at many points along my slow and winding path in the study of G. K. Chesterton. It began a quarter century ago when I reviewed Alzina Stone Dale's fine biography of Chesterton, *The Outline of Sanity*. I wanted to assess Dale's book, not because I was a veteran Chestertonian seeking to test her accuracy, but because I was a neophyte immensely impressed with *Orthodoxy* yet knowing little about the great man's life and work. I had read Chesterton's most famous book with riveted interest but also with considerable puzzlement. About its penetrating insight and coruscating wit, I had no doubt. But concerning Chesterton's basic premises, his theological assumptions, his ecclesial commitments, his moral judgments, his place in British letters, his friends and foes—of these, I knew virtually nothing. And so I determined to learn.

I learned by way of a method acquired from a friend. When asked whether she has read this or that book, she answers, "*Read* it? I haven't even *taught* it!" Thus it was with me. First at Samford and then at Baylor, I began teaching Chesterton books in order to read and comprehend them more carefully. I taught *Orthodoxy* to my seminarians, *The Everlasting Man* to my doctoral students, and *The Ball and the Cross* to my undergraduates. (I remain convinced that this last is the best book for beginners, since it embodies almost all of Chesterton's concerns in a context at once hilarious and serious.) To the dozens of students in these classes, I owe my immense gratitude for engaging these and other Chesterton texts in an invigorating way, especially two students who have taken up the Chestertonian cause: Don Shipley and Cameron Moore.

My opportunity to begin this book came in 2006 when, thanks to an invitation first suggested by Bill Reimer, I taught a course devoted entirely to Chesterton at Regent College in Vancouver. Due to the generosity of David Solomon and the Center for Ethics and Culture at the University of Notre Dame, I was then able to spend the academic year of 2007–2008 probing more deeply into Chesterton's work and its larger world, especially its Thomistic aspect. The editors of several journals have also welcomed earlier versions of chapters and sections: *First Things*, *Christian Century*, *Pro Ecclesia*, *Logos*, *VII*, and *First Principles*. In addition, various church and seminary and university audiences have attended my lectures on Chesterton in recent years: at Wheaton College in Illinois, Montreat Presbyterian Assembly in North Carolina, Wesley Biblical Seminary in Jackson, St. Charles Avenue Baptist in New Orleans, the Episcopal Church of the Holy Spirit in Waco, the Conference on Christianity and Literature at both Le Tourneau University and Wingate University, plus Saint Anselm College, the University of Notre Dame, and Providence College. Few things are more gratifying than to receive lively and critical responses to my lectures and essays.

I have incurred so many personal debts along the way that I can barely begin to enumerate them. Dale Ahlquist at the Chesterton Society has been unfailingly helpful with my many queries. The Interlibrary Loan workers at both Baylor University and Providence College have delivered all of my many requests. So have student assistants at both schools remained cheerful and steadfast in answering my many summons for help, especially Octavia Ratiu at Notre Dame, David Wilmington at Baylor, and Francesca Genova at Providence. Carey Newman, the director of Baylor University Press, has exhibited what the epistle of James dubiously calls "the patience of Job." Like his predecessor in suffering, Carey has rightly complained about the unjust distress that my many delays have caused him. Yet he has also resembled Job in never losing faith in this book that has been so long unfinished.

My greatest gratitude goes to various Baylor colleagues who have transformed my academic and theological life in recent years. Among many others, these stand out: Mike Beaty, Pete Candler, Phil Donnelly, Barry Harvey, Doug Henry, David Jeffrey, Bob Kruschwitz, Scott Moore, and Don Schmeltekopf. These friends are not bland yea-sayers but the keenest critics of my work. They often check my waywardness by maintaining that I am *phronesis* challenged and prudence deprived, so often do I blunder into territory that angels rightly fear but fools gladly tread. I am tempted to get revenge by blaming them for this book's many faults. Yet I cannot, for then I would be unable to credit them with its modest merits. Thanks largely to their friendship, my dozen years at Baylor have been the best years of my life. In word and deed, in worship and fellowship, they have shown me that we are meant to be awakened from the temporary nightmare of God's goodness into the permanent joy of the Beatific Vision.

INTRODUCTION

I think, if there were light enough, I could sit here and write some very
creditable creepy tale, about how I went up the crooked road beyond
the church and met Something—say a dog, a dog with one eye. Then
I should meet a horse, perhaps, a horse without a rider; the horse also
would have one eye. Then the inhuman silence would be broken;
I should meet a man (need I say, a one-eyed man?) who would ask me
the way to my own house. Or perhaps tell me that it was burnt to the
ground. I think I could tell a very cosy little tale along some such lines.
Or I might dream of climbing for ever the tall dark trees above me.
They are so tall that I feel as if I should find at their tops the nests of
the angels; but in this mood they would be dark and dreadful angels;
angels of death.

* * * *

That one-eyed universe, with its one-eyed men and beasts, was only
created with one universal wink. At the top of the tragic trees I should
not find the Angel's Nest. I should only find the Mare's Nest; the
dreamy and divine nest is not there. In the Mare's Nest I shall discover
that dim, enormous opalescent egg from which is hatched the
Nightmare. For there is nothing so delightful as a nightmare—
when you know it is a nightmare.

G. K. Chesterton, "The Nightmare" (1911)

*N*ightmare is a word that recurs throughout the work of G. K. Chesterton. "I was still oppressed with the metaphysical nightmare of negations about mind and matter," he writes in his *Autobiography*, "with the morbid imagery of evil, with the burden of my own mysterious brain and body; but by this time I was in revolt against them; and trying to construct a healthier conception of cosmic life, even if it were one that should err on the side of health. I even called myself an optimist, because I was so horribly near to being a pessimist."[1] Originally referring to a witch or goblin, a nightmare was once understood as "a female spirit or monster supposed to beset animals and people at night, settling on them when they are asleep, and producing a feeling of suffocation by its weight."

Chesterton retains only the latter sense of the word—a smothering or stifling or strangling—but now with even greater terror: it is a distress "from which the sleeper vainly endeavours to free himself."[2] In *Sartor Resartus*, Thomas Carlyle precisely defines Chesterton's use of the word, as his narrator records Dr. Teufelsdröckh's own tenebrous encounters with

> . . . "fever-paroxysms of Doubt;" his Inquiries concerning Miracles, and the Evidences of religious Faith; and how "in the silent night-watches, still darker in his heart than over sky and earth, he has cast himself before the All-seeing, and with audible prayers cried vehemently for Light, for deliverance from Death and the Grave. Not till after long years, and unspeakable agonies, did the believing heart surrender; sink into spell-bound sleep, *under the nightmare*, *Unbelief*; and, in this hag-ridden dream, mistake God's fair living world for a pallid, vacant Hades and extinct Pandemonium."[3]

The chief contention of this book is that Chesterton makes his deepest affirmations about God and man and the world in the face of nightmarish unbelief—the abiding fear that God's seemingly wondrous universe is, instead, devoid of divinity, that it is in fact a well-populated Hell unrecognized as such. There is, of course, the cheerier Chesterton—the beef and ale believer, the fat *jongleur de Dieu*, the merry tumbler of the Lord. Hence his delight in reversing the motto over Dante's portal to Hell by jauntily inviting readers to enter Dickens' joyous world: "Abandon hopelessness, all ye who enter here."[4] There is no denying this comic and yea-saying Chesterton. I contend, however, that there is another darker, more complex Chesterton, and that his daytime confidence about Christian things becomes fully persuasive only when examined in relation to his night-haunted terrors.

This examination of Chesterton's awakenings from the various nightmares of our time seeks to avoid two typical errors. Uncritical enthusiasts have approached Chesterton in virtually hagiographical terms. They continue to regard the great man as an unassailable titan, an argufier who was as persuasive in his ideas as he was gargantuan in his girth. For these Chesterton acolytes, he is the quintessential Christian apologist, slaying all enemies of the Faith with his penetrating wit and his staggering paradoxes. They find him the perfect exemplar of his own aphorism: "Christianity has not been tried and found wanting; it has been found difficult and not tried." These encomiasts hold that Chesterton has tested and been satisfied by the difficult Christian challenge. They contend that, if only we would examine Chesterton's work—his gnomic sayings and knotty aperçus, his outrageous turning of everything upside down—we would eagerly embrace the perfect case that he makes for Christianity in his fiction and poetry, his plays and essays.

Yet Chesterton also has his detractors, those who dismiss him as an impossible throwback to an earlier and allegedly easier age of belief. They regard him as a reactionary antimodern, as a thoroughly illiberal writer—indeed, as an antediluvian. He did, in fact, advocate nearly all things ancestral, describing tradition as "the democracy of the dead"—a proper granting of the franchise to the largest of all majorities, the deceased. Chesterton's view of the Protestant Reformation was almost entirely negative. He held it accountable for producing two of modernity's chief curses: individualism and capitalism. Calvinism and Puritanism were among the vilest words in his lexicon. The doctrine of predestination was, for him, a monstrous and freedom-denying dogma. He admired most things medieval and scorned many things modern: women's suffrage, divorce on all grounds, and birth control in every form. His love of chivalry prompted him to saunter about with a swordstick and to reject dueling only because it settles no arguments, not because it leaves someone wounded or dead. Such retrograde belligerence provokes Chesterton's despisers to damn him not with faint bleats of praise but with loud shouts of derision.

I do not seek to divide the difference between these extremes, as if truth were somehow to lie in a vague *via media*. I seek, instead, to be "critical" in the etymological sense: *krisis* entails discrimination and decision, the reaching of turning points, whether for good or ill. Alasdair MacIntyre brought this truth home to me in our very first meeting, when I declared my desire to write a book on Chesterton. With his typical indirection, he warned that "It simply won't do to repeat Chesterton. He wrote for his age and thus cannot speak for ours." Evelyn Waugh offered a similarly sour rejoinder to all secondary criticism of Chesterton: "[I]t is a grave reproach to suppose that his work needs elucidation. A writer who cannot make his meaning clear to his own generation and their successors is a bad writer. Chesterton, of all men of our times, wrote especially for the common man, repeating in clear language his simple, valuable messages."[5] MacIntyre and Waugh are both correct but not altogether silencing. This book is premised on the conviction that Chesterton's "messages" are indeed valuable but not at all simple. For reasons not attributable entirely to Chesterton himself, his work has been at least partially misunderstood. The keenness and complexity of his vision and voice need to be both discovered and recovered, so that they may indeed speak *to* our time. Hence this critical retrieval of Chesterton's work for the life of the academy, the Church, and the circumambient world—precisely as his texts become pivotal points of discernment and decision concerning the vexing questions of our age.

Such a task requires its own self-critical point of view. As we shall discover, Chesterton understood the limits of so-called impartial reason. Experience and imagination and well-grounded conviction are required for discerning the real. I happily confess that this project makes no pretense to neutrality, as if it were possible to occupy an eagle-eyrie view from nowhere in order to inspect Chesterton's work. Quite simply put, this is a theological investigation as much as an academic treatise, a work of argument and advocacy rather than disinterested description. In this regard I follow the command of St. Augustine to "take the spoils of the Egyptians"—that is, to make use of everything in the pagan world that accords with the gospel, except that in this case the Egyptian is a Christian residing in Battersea and Beaconsfield during the early years of the twentieth century, and the "spoils" are found in a Chestertonian trove of bright humor and dark wit.

In thus reclaiming what is useful in Chesterton both *urbi et orbi*, for both the Church and the world, I do not hold him to standards that are completely foreign to him. Smug extrinsic criticism would do violence to both Chesterton and the Christianity that he advocated. Insofar as possible, I seek to measure Chesterton's work against his own excellence when such internal criteria are available. When they are not, I offer evaluations based almost entirely on fellow Christian thinkers and writers who are not intrinsically alien to Chesterton. I remain convinced that ours is an age wherein believers across all the Christian traditions will be ever more strongly united by the convictions they hold in common.[6] My interpretation of GKC is rooted, therefore, in the creeds and confessions, in the habits and practices, in the liturgical worship and the prophetic preaching of all who regard Jesus Christ and his Church not as one among other roads to be taken but as "the way, the truth, and the life" (John 14:6). That the tiny article remains definite rather than indeterminate will serve, I hope, to invite non-Christian readers of Chesterton to consider the nightmare goodness of God as the Reality meant not only for Christians but also, perhaps even chiefly, for others who have not yet perceived and embraced it. "The next best thing to being really inside Christendom," Chesterton declared, "is to be really outside it."[7] Unbelievers entering the Faith often discern its riches and depths as veteran disciples do not. In any case, the hour is much too late for an insular book intended "for Christians only." I seek, instead, to address those whom the Book of Common Prayer calls "all sorts and conditions of men," including especially the audience that Chesterton himself sought to address: "the ordinary modern man, sympathetic but skeptical."[8]

A further confession is required. It is exceedingly difficult to write about comic matters lightly, despite Chesterton's warning that heaviness is the essence of arrogance:

> Pride is the downward drag of all things into an easy solemnity. . . . Seriousness is not a virtue. It would be a heresy, but a . . . sensible heresy, to say that seriousness is a vice. It is really a natural trend or lapse into taking one's self gravely, because it is the easiest thing to do. . . . For solemnity flows out of men naturally; but laughter is a leap. It is easy to be heavy: hard to be light. Satan fell by the force of gravity.[9]

If my argument fails to fly with the levitation of the unfallen angels—who still soar because they take themselves so lightly—I hope that my descent will not be due to an "easy solemnity." I trust also that it will not meet the response of a Peter De Vries character named Dr. Didisheim. After giving a lecture on comedy, the professor is confronted by a lady from the audience who smacks him in the face with a *recipe* for custard pie.

To speak of God's goodness as nightmarish is not to indulge in wanton and idle use of paradox. On the contrary, it is an effort to overcome the mistake of regarding the grace and mercy of God as something always cheering and comforting. Thomas Merton once lamented that the command to "Love God" has little more force in our culture than the commercial injunction to "Eat Wheaties." So does Binx Bolling, the narrator of Walker Percy's novel *The Moviegoer*, confess that whenever the word *God* is mentioned, a curtain is lowered in his head. Like *love*, such words as *God* and *Gospel* and *grace* and *judgment* have become coins worn almost faceless by glib overuse. They often fail to signify, to register with any real import. However mistaken he can sometimes be, Chesterton remains the enemy of glibness. He wrestles with the hard counterclaims of modern paganism, even as he reckons with the far more troublous claims of the Christian faith. This book seeks, therefore, to reveal Chesterton's often nightmarish and Jacob-like encounter with the living One, so that we too might receive a blessing from this great fat Jester of God whose work, like that of the angel at the River Jabbok, both wounds and blesses.

MAN AS HOLY MONSTER
Christian Humanism, Evolution, and *Orthodoxy*

Anyone who has read any of Chesterton's work is likely to have read *Orthodoxy*. First published in London by John Lane Press in 1908, it has never gone into dormancy; there are more than two dozen printings still available. How to account for such enduring interest? Graham Greene described *Orthodoxy* as "among the great books of the age," calling Chesterton "a man of colossal genius." Dorothy L. Sayers was inspired to reclaim her natal Christianity mainly by reading *Orthodoxy*.[1] Etienne Gilson saluted Chesterton for having a philosophical mind of the first rank. Hugh Kenner claimed that the only other twentieth-century author to whom Chesterton should be compared, in sheer originality of style and vision, is James Joyce.[2] Even H. L. Mencken, perhaps the most antithetical figure imaginable, praised *Orthodoxy* as "indeed, the best argument for Christianity I have ever read—and I have gone through, I suppose, fully a hundred."[3] Yet such encomia threaten to obscure the subtle truth about Chesterton's most celebrated work. Far from being a sunny and bouncy book, *Orthodoxy* offers an extremely dark diagnosis of the ailments that dominate modern life, while prescribing an astringent version of Christianity as their cure.

Chesterton as a *Nouvelle* Christian Humanist

Because Chesterton's work fits within the broad scope of Christian humanism, it is instructive to define the basic terms and tenets of this tradition. The primary maxims of Christian humanism were famously formulated in the fifth century by St. Augustine of Hippo: *credo ut intelligam* ("I believe so that I may understand") and in the eleventh century by St. Anselm of Canterbury: *fides quaerens intellectum* ("faith seeking understanding").[4] In both cases, Christian humanism holds that God has instilled in every person a natural desire for a happiness that can be completely satisfied by nothing else than the final, indeed the eternal and Beatific Vision of God.[5] He has also implanted the natural law of conscience within every human being. Even though we have violated this inward law, thus becoming fallen no less than finite creatures, we remain capable of understanding ourselves and our cosmos. Rightly used, the mind discloses that we are not self-sufficient but dependent and broken beings. It also discerns that we can only partially repair our damaged lives and disordered world. Above all, the intellect can detect the need for what it cannot supply—namely, the divine grace that alone can heal ourselves and our world—imperfectly here and now, perfectly in the life to come.

In the Christian humanist view, God provides us the immense freedom both to receive such an incomparable gift—or else, alas, to reject it with the entirety of our being.[6] Our cooperative grace (i.e., human assent) is essential to the operative grace of God. The maker of heaven and earth is no bully, even if he remains the One whom Francis Thompson called the Hound of Heaven, pursuing his prey down all the alleys of our lives, even to the uttermost parts of the earth, even to the depths of Sheol. There is thus a fundamental though complicated synergism between the human and the divine; for, while complementary, they remain immensely and qualitatively different. St. Thomas Aquinas gave classic expression to the synergistic character of Christian humanism in his well-known formula: *Gratia non tollit sed perficit naturam* ("Grace does not destroy but perfects nature"). This proposition is much more complex than it appears, since each of these words is edged with theological nuance. We can nonetheless affirm with confidence the prime Christian humanist claim: human life does not begin with a blank slate in Lockean fashion, for God has freely graced it from the outset, making us capable of magnificently accomplished goods if also maleficently produced horrors. Man is indeed a monster, though a holy one. The God who in Christ creates all things, and who in the Spirit sustains them in their very existence, seeks also to transform their perverted character so as to bring them fully to participate in the divine life itself.[7]

There is immensely more to be said about Christian humanism, but suffice it here to declare that it understands salvation as the happy, though still scandalous and difficult, participation of human life in the life of the triune God. In our always and already God-graced humanity, we are called to pursue our natural desire for the Holy to its completion by grasping the divine hand that has been extended to us in Christ through his Church. All gifts—and this is supremely true of the ultimate Gift—become true benefactions only when they are received and enjoyed. This way of summing up Christian humanism is also a way of setting Chesterton's work in relation to a theological movement represented by Henri de Lubac, Hans Urs von Balthasar, and Pope Benedict XVI.[8]

La nouvelle théologie flourished from the late 1930s through the early 1990s. Its advocates sought to correct the neo-scholastic Thomism that had, in their estimate, largely removed the theology of the Church from the concerns of the world by speaking not of one but of two final destinies for human life—the purely natural end of human flourishing and the truly supernatural end of the Beatific Vision. Neo-scholastics worried that human nature would be too highly exalted and made sufficient unto itself if it contains its own natural desire for the supernatural Life. God's grace must be given in pure gratuity—as sheer "superaddition"—to overcome human finitude and fallenness. And without humanity's having a purely natural end, how to account for the many human accomplishments that seem to have no eternal consequence? And did not Thomas himself teach that human reason is capable of knowing God, at least in a preliminary way, without the aid of supernatural revelation, even if it remains incapable of achieving salvation apart from his grace?

Henri de Lubac, among others, answered that such sixteenth- and seventeenth-century commentators as Cajetan and Suarez had introduced this concept of two human finalities when such an idea is to be found in neither the ancient Church Fathers nor in Aquinas himself. Humanity's singular end, replied de Lubac, has always lain in the desire to behold God face to face. Human freedom, it follows, is not extrinsically "invaded" by divine grace, as if it had to be wrestled into an alien supernatural end—as if, in sum, the house of grace were some-what crudely constructed on the foundation of nature, without their having any *intrinsic* relation. This rather coarse extrinsicism, a layer-cake theology of two separable and essentially impermeable realms, was first unmasked by Pierre Rousselot (1878–1915). "Accepting Thom-as's view of the unity between love of desire and love of friendship," writes Hans Boersma, "Rousselot emphasized the continuity between nature and the supernatural. Furthermore, his insistence that rational judgements of credibility were powerless without corresponding 'eyes of faith' implied a sacramental view of the natural order as pointing to the supernatural end of the beatific vision."[9]

The core claim of *la nouvelle théologie* lies in the contention that, while nature and grace must be distinguished, they must not be sepa-rated. Their intrinsic relation gives the Gospel an abiding concern for the natural realm, here understood primarily as the political and social order rather than the animal, plant, and mineral worlds alone. It can-not be contained within itself, consigned to a merely natural end of human happiness apart from God. Humanity, for these theologians, is supremely social, not because it has been forced to create a social con-tract to escape the brute state of nature, but because it is created in the image of the triune God. Human nature is not one thing here and another thing elsewhere. However twisted and tarnished, all human beings bear the imprint of God as the result of both their creation and their redemption. Humanity constitutes, in fact, a bodily no less than a spiritual whole. We cannot violate one without also dishonoring the other. To desecrate even a single person is to desecrate them all.[10] "The divine image," Henri de Lubac declares, "does not differ from one individual to another: in all it is the same image." Our embodied souls/ensouled bodies display our shared human dependence, our single-ness as a race, our commonality that makes us "so entirely one that we ought not speak of man in the plural any more than we speak of three Gods." Hence the teaching of St. Augustine that we are "one spiritual family intended to form the one city of God"[11] This is very much the fashion in which we shall hear Chesterton speaking. He stands in such radical solidarity with all sorts and conditions of men that he can speak to them in their own voice, without importing the Gospel as some-thing extrinsic to their condition.[12]

Salvation, it follows, is not an affair primarily of post-earthly salvation intended for solitary souls "getting to heaven" apart from their fellows. Christianity is not an inner and individual religion having to do with a hidden, invisible, and private relation to Jesus. Redemption is found in the public, visible, and social reality *already* present in Jesus Christ and his Church as the true human community. To be Christian, therefore, is to belong to the Body of Christ. Our restoration "is the recovery of lost unity," de Lubac writes, "—the recovery of supernatural unity of man with God, but equally of the unity of men among themselves." Hence de Lubac's remarkable declaration that "Christ the Redeemer does not offer salvation merely to each one; he is himself the salvation of the whole, and for each one salvation consists in a personal ratification of his original 'belonging' to Christ, so that he not be cast out, cut off from this Whole."[13] Though the *nouvelle* theologians did their main work after Chesterton's death, we will find that, like them, he has virtually no interest in so-called "private" salvation, but that his heroes always find their deliverance from evil in community with others, especially in marriage and domesticity.

Sin, in this reading of it, is nothing obvious. It can be properly defined only in relation to redemption. Just as salvation is the supremely social reality, so is evil a corporate before it is an individual thing. All particular sins are symptoms of the contagious and collective disease called Sin. The most deadly evils, as we shall discover in Chesterton, are social evils. He does not sermonize about individual immorality. Sin is to be defined, in fact, as the satanic attempt to break apart Christ's incorporation of himself within humanity, to sunder his uniting and enclosing of humanity within himself. Sin shatters our divinely constituted *unity* into mere individual and self-serving *units*. "*Ubi peccata,*" declared Origen of Alexandria in the third century, "*ibi multitudo.*" "Where there is sin," he insisted, "there is multiplicity."[14] Thus does Origen oppose the modern notion that division and plurality lie at the core of our existence. Humanity has been shattered into a thousand pieces, Maximus the Confessor lamented in the sixth century. Instead of constituting a harmonious whole, we have turned ourselves into a discordant multitude of mere individuals who, as Shakespeare said, prey upon one another like monsters of the deep. Saint Cyril of Alexandria put the matter even more memorably in the fifth century:

"Satan has broken us up."[15] We shall discover that, for Chesterton, the demonic seeks to sunder what was meant to be joined, to blinker the imagination, so that it fails to discern the superabundant presence of God in the natural no less than the supernatural order.

Such demonic deceptions reveal why Chesterton's Christian humanism does not envision an unflawed relation of nature and grace. His work deals, in fact, with the nightmarish disrelation between the human and the Holy.[16] Against the grain of a secular age bent on denying all signals of transcendence, he announced from the beginning that "mysticism keeps men sane." The young Chesterton had not yet developed an appropriate synonym for "mysticism," but it is clear that he meant something very much akin to what the *nouvelle* theologians call the natural desire for Ultimate Beatitude, an allurement that is divinely ensconced within every human being. God does not begin to operate in human life only when reason has reached its limits, so that grace is "superadded" to nature in a clumsy, two-storied fashion. *Humanity is always and already graced*, even as it is already but not always and forever disgraced.[17] This watchword belongs as fully to Chesterton as to Henri de Lubac, Hans Urs von Balthasar, and Pope Benedict XVI.[18]

Supernaturalizing the Natural

Like the *nouvelle* theologians, Chesterton seeks to supernaturalize the natural, principally in two ways, art and morality—though in neither case is such an undertaking an obvious and effortless enterprise. Chesterton himself succinctly defined the link when he declared that "[a]rt, like morality, consists of drawing the line somewhere."[19] Far from being a secular activity to be set over against the sacred, art is a human response to the divinely implanted desire for the beatific life. Properly embraced, it constitutes a summons to the constant re-formation of the primary world by means of imaginative acts that J. R. R. Tolkien called "sub-creation." Guarding against the romantic delusion that, like God, artists create *ex nihilo*—from nothing but their own imagination—Tolkien grounded the creative act in the concrete particulars of the world, i.e., the original creation that all makers are called to reorder into new and significant forms. As St. Paul declares in 1 Corinthians 3:9, we are divinely dependent creators, *synergoi*, coworkers with God in *all* the expressions of our salvation, especially in our many and varied acts of making. We shall find Chesterton arguing that art created under Christian aegis is not concerned primarily with balance and harmony and proportion of a strictly classical kind. Grace, it must be remembered, not only completes and perfects but also radically transforms and renovates the natural. Chesterton has repeated recourse to the grotesque and the burlesque, to mime and farce, radically revealing the always surprising goodness of God. It throws everything sinful off balance, often appearing more akin to macabre nightmare than to Beatific Vision. Chesterton is agreed with the "new theologians" (a term assigned to them by Reginald Garrigou-Lagrange in derision) that God is the risk-taking Deity. He is not remote from his creation like a distant observer, but actively working within it, primarily through humanity's own freely *cooperative* response to God's freely given *operative* grace.[20]

While Chesterton was suspicious of romantic pretensions to divinity, he often praised the revolution wrought by the English romantic poets. They taught him that we do not remain utterly passive before the world's external realities, as if we were inert receivers of already-completed truth. Our arrival at truth is indeed rooted in our sensate perception and discovery of what is already there. Yet the "thereness" of things also requires our imaginative engagement and creative involvement.[21] Hence Chesterton's early affirmation that "God did not give us a universe but rather the materials of a universe. The world is not a picture, it is a palette. [God] gave man a paint-box. He gave him the crude materials of something; the crude materials of everything."[22] Even in his later devotion to St. Thomas, Chesterton never abandoned his prime conviction that the juncture of mind and world reaches its highest pitch in the creative act. Aquinas taught him that the world remains magnificently surprising in its sheer objective otherness, its power to prompt the imagination to an encounter with the otherness of external realities:

> All their romance and glamour, so to speak, lies in the fact that they are real things; things *not* to be found by staring inwards at the mind. The flower is a vision because it is not only a vision. Or, if you will, because it is not a dream. This is for the poet the strangeness of stones and trees and solid things; they are strange because they are solid. . . . According to Aquinas, the object becomes part of the mind; nay, according to Aquinas, the mind

actually becomes the object. . . . And *therefore* it enlarges the mind of which it becomes a part.[23]

Chesterton's artistic concerns are intrinsic to his moral concerns. They resonate deeply with the social and communal character of *la nouvelle théologie*. Neo-scholastic Thomism had rendered the Church increasingly silent vis-à-vis secular affairs. If salvation is primarily an individual and spiritual matter having to do supremely with postworldly existence, and if reason operates according to its own autonomous agency until grace is superadded to it, then the world's political and intellectual life is left largely to its own devices, often self-destructively.[24] The Church might have resisted the horrors of the twentieth century more stoutly if it had not rigidly disjoined the sacred from the secular. De Lubac cites Philippe de Régis' claim that if the Church had stressed the centrality of communal life in the natural no less than the supernatural order, "perhaps Marxism and Leninism might not have arisen and been propagated with such terrible results."[25]

Perhaps the most profound connection between Chesterton and the *nouvelle* theologians concerns the nature of the Gospel itself. They are agreed that it is always the Good News of human transformation here and now, far more than the Ill Tidings of the wrath to come. They are not obsessed with Hell. This is not due to any fear of offending secular audiences. Chesterton, for example, is seriously convinced that there are souls who are indeed damned, and in *The Flying Inn* (as we shall see) he depicts one man's terrifying descent into final impenitence. There is no "cheap grace" in Chesterton. "Redemption," he declares, "should bring truth as well as peace. . . . Things must be faced, even in order to be forgiven; the great objection to 'letting sleeping dogs lie' is that they lie in more senses than one." Not to tell the nightmarish truth is to defraud and delude: "There is nothing very heroic in loving after you have been deceived. The heroic business is to love after you have been undeceived."[26]

Even so, Chesterton has no moralistic desire to damn and dismiss, least of all in the Father Brown stories. They all hinge on the priest's uncanny discernment of secretly murderous motives. Though readers and other detectives cannot plumb the hidden depth of sin, Father Brown enables them to locate it in their own hearts—and thus in the hearts of fictional malefactors as well.[27] Chesterton was much more troubled by his own sins than by the sins of others. Hence Father Brown's deeply Pauline confession to Flambeau that evil works its deceits far more subtly on the good than the evil:

> "Well, what you call 'the secret' is actually the opposite. I don't try to get outside the man. I try to get inside the murderer. . . . Indeed it's much more than that, don't you see. I *am* inside a man. I am always inside a man, moving his arms and legs; but I wait till I know I am inside a murderer, thinking his thoughts, wrestling with his passions; till I have bent myself into the posture of his hunched and peering hatred; till I see the world with his bloodshot and squinting eyes, looking between the blinkers of his half-witted concentration; looking up the short and sharp perspective of a straight road to a pool of blood. Till I am really a murderer."
>
> . . .
>
> "No man's really any good till he knows how bad he is, or might be; till he's realized exactly how much right he has to all this snobbery, and sneering, and talking about 'criminals,' as if they were apes in a forest ten thousand miles away; till he's got rid of all the dirty self-deception of talking about low types and deficient skulls; till he's squeezed out of his soul the last drop of the oil of the Pharisees; till his only hope is somehow or other to have captured one criminal, and kept him safe and sane under his own hat."[28]

Such statements reveal that Chesterton is much more than a moralist operating in the fashion, for instance, of George Orwell. Like Orwell, he is deeply concerned with the ethos and *mores* of his time and place, with the vagaries and vicissitudes of the human condition; yet the motives and resources of the two writers are essentially different. Orwell is a moralist *simpliciter*, a humanist who holds his fellow citizens accountable to their own highest standards of moral responsibility, without any recourse to transcendent revelation. Chesterton, by contrast, belongs in the line of biblical prophets for whom the justice of God rightly orders the relations of neighbor with neighbor and nation with nation—not by high ethical standards abstractly embraced so much as by the cardinal virtues taught and practiced in the true (if also flawed) community established for the sake of the world in Israel and Christ and the Church.

As a Christian humanist, Chesterton possesses a moral vision that is sacramental no less than prophetic. He understands that the ethical life is radically redirected to the love of God less by harsh adjuration than by the sacraments found only in the Company of the Crucified. In his sacrifice for the sins of the world, Christ brings something far more frightening than stern ethical injunction and dire penal retribution—namely, forgiveness and reconciliation with God and neighbor alike. Long before he was received into the Church, Chesterton went to the heart of the matter:

> The Christian Church can best be defined as an enormous private detective, correcting that official detective—the State. . . . [T]he real difference between the Church and State is huge and plain. The State, in all lands and ages, has created a machinery of punishment, more bloody and brutal in some places than others, but bloody and brutal everywhere. The Church is the only institution that ever attempted to create a machinery of pardon. The Church is the only thing that ever attempted by system to pursue and discover crimes, not in order to avenge, but in order to forgive them. The stake and the rack were merely the weaknesses of religion; its snobberies, its surrenders to the world. Its speciality—or, if you like, its oddity—was this merciless mercy; the unrelenting sleuthhound who seeks to save and not to slay.[29]

To offer such high praise of Chesterton's Christian humanism is not to claim that it is without fault. In fact, there is one glaring gap in the bridge that splendidly spans the natural and the supernatural in his work. His treatment of the vexed question of evolution is shaky indeed, and we must examine it before turning to *Orthodoxy* as the most convincing display of Chesterton's deft supernaturalizing of the natural.

Chesterton as the Parodist of Evolution

Chesterton was right to rail against the immoral uses to which Darwinism was being put in his time. Survival-of-the-fittest capitalists favored the competitive strong over the economically weak, while eugenicizing socialists sought to improve the species by eliminating the mentally inferior. As a result, Chesterton came to an almost wholly negative estimate of Darwin's discoveries and theories. This was not true in his early writings. There he declared Darwin to be one of the stellar figures of English national achievement. Already in his early book *The Defendant*, Chesterton was urging that "[t]he rebuilding of [a] bridge between science and human nature is one of the greatest needs of mankind."[30] During this first decade of the twentieth century, Chesterton was making similar affirmations in the *Daily News*, but with increased emphasis on what would become his consuming concern—namely, the uniqueness of the human species. To embrace evolution, he came to believe, is falsely to affirm that *Homo sapiens* differ from all other anthropoids only in continuous degree, not in discontinuous kind:

> Evolutionists cannot drive us, because of the nameless gradation in Nature, to deny the personality of God, for a personal God might as well work by gradations as in any other way; but they do drive themselves, through those gradations, to deny the existence of a personal Mr. Jones, because he is within the scope of evolution and his edges are rubbed away.[31]

"Man is the ape upside down," Chesterton trumpeted in a similar vein.[32] As the superprimate who is also the subangel, our human kind does not look down at the ground like the other beasts. We are *anthropoi*, the upward-looking creatures who seek transcendent beauty and truth and goodness. We live and move and have our being as the other animals do not—namely, as siblings of nature rather than her children:

> The essence of all pantheism, evolutionism, and modern cosmic religion is really in this proposition: that Nature is our mother. Unfortunately, if you regard Nature as a mother, you discover that she is a step-mother. The main point of Christianity [is] this: that Nature is not our mother: Nature is our sister. We can be proud of her beauty, since we have the same father; but she has no authority over us; we have to admire, but not to imitate. This gives to the typically Christian pleasure in this earth a strange touch of lightness that is almost frivolity. Nature was a solemn mother to worshippers of Isis and Cybele. Nature was a solemn mother to Wordsworth or to Emerson. But Nature is not solemn to Francis of Assisi or to George Herbert. To St. Francis, Nature is a sister, and even a younger sister: a little, dancing sister, to be laughed at as well as loved. (O, 119)[33]

Chesterton's basic intuition is correct: unless there is a fundamental distinction between our species and the other animals, we have little reason to regard humans as anything other than beasts—or even to treat beasts humanely. Yet Chesterton took a crucial further step. Despite his self-professed Christian humanism, he began to draw a hard line between biological evolution and divine revelation, and thus (at least in this matter) between nature and grace. He became convinced that it is utterly impossible to defend human distinctiveness if one concedes the evolutionist principle that man differs from the other animals relatively rather than absolutely. And so he came increasingly to parody evolution rather than seeking to comprehend it. Instead of insisting that the massive web of dependencies that constitute the natural realm point to the One who is not thus dependent, he offers witty burlesques of evolution:

> Who ever found an ant-hill decorated with the statues of celebrated ants? Who has seen a bee-hive carved with the images of gorgeous queens of old? No; the chasm between man and other creatures may have a natural explanation, but it is a chasm. We talk of wild animals; but man is the only wild animal. It is man that has broken out. All other animals are tame animals, following the rugged respectability of the tribe or type. . . . [M]an alone is ever undomestic, either as a profligate or a monk. . . . [I]t is exactly where biology leaves off that all religion begins. (O, 151)[34]

Ironic misgivings about evolution become increasingly unironic in the later Chesterton, as his pen drips with contempt for the Darwinist claim that humankind emerges in a manner that is gradual and quantitative, not in a sudden and qualitative leap. Having once been willing, given certain crucial limits, to admit evolutionary changes *within* but not *across* species, Chesterton came to regard science as unable to explain complex intraspecies developments, as in this 1920 essay on the rhinoceros' horn, where he is mocking the uncritical enthusiasm for evolution that H. G. Wells had heralded in *An Outline of History*:

> It is very far from obvious that the first rudimentary suggestion of a horn, the first faint thickening which might lead through countless generations to the growth of a horn, would be of any particular use as a horn. And we must suppose, on the Darwinian hypothesis, that the hornless animal reached his horn through unthinkable gradations of what were, for all practical purposes, [a] hornless animal. Why should one rhinoceros be so benevolent a Futurist as to start an improvement that could only help some much later rhinoceros to survive? And why on earth should its mere foreshadowing help the earlier rhinoceros to survive? This thesis can only explain variations when they discreetly refrain from varying very much. To the real riddles that arrest the eye,

it has no answer that can satisfy the intelligence. For any child or man with his eyes open, I imagine, there is no creature that really calls for an answer, like a living riddle, so clearly as the bat. But if you will call up the Darwinian vision, of thousands of intermediary creatures with webbed feet that are not yet wings, their survival will seem incredible. A mouse can run, and survive; and a flitter-mouse can fly, and survive. But a creature that cannot yet fly, and can no longer run, ought obviously to have perished, by the very Darwinian doctrine which has to assume that he survived.[35]

Again, Chesterton is partially correct in protesting Darwin's pretentious attempt to turn natural selection into a monocausal account of earthly life.[36] As the evangel of his brave new theory, Darwin had proclaimed that natural selection explains *everything*: "There is one general law, leading to the advancement of organic beings, namely, multiply, vary, let the strongest live and the weakest die."[37] Yet one error cannot be corrected by another. And in *The Everlasting Man*, Chesterton makes a serious error. He maintains that our species, as the sole speaking and art-making animal endowed with moral freedom, stands in *total discontinuity* with our alleged ancestors. In the cave paintings at Lascaux, Chesterton finds clinching evidence that "man [is] something separate from nature," that "every sane sort of history must begin with man as man, a thing standing absolute and alone," that "there is not a shadow of evidence that *this* thing was evolved at all," but that, instead, "something happened; and it has all the appearance of a transaction outside time":[38]

> It must surely strike [even a child] as strange that men so remote from him should be so near, and that beasts so near to him should be so remote. To his simplicity it must seem at least odd that he could not find any trace of the beginning of any arts among any animals. That is the simplest lesson to learn in the cavern of the coloured pictures; only it is too simple to be learnt. It is the simple truth that man does differ from brutes in kind and not in degree; and the proof of it is here. . . . Something of division and disproportion has appeared; and it is unique. Art is the signature of man. . . .
>
> It is not natural to see man as a natural product. . . . It is not seeing straight to see him as an animal. It is not sane. It sins against the light; against the broad daylight of proportion which is the principle of all reality. . . . The solid thing standing in the sunlight, the thing we can walk around and see from all sides,

is quite different. It is also quite extraordinary; and the more sides we see of it the more extraordinary it seems. *It is emphatically not a thing that follows or flows from anything else.*[39]

Chesterton's argument rings right only insofar as he claims that human consciousness, especially in creating such nonutilitarian things as art, reveals that *Homo sapiens* is a species radically unlike any other. Yet Chesterton goes much further. He accuses those who regard man as the product of natural processes *in any sense whatsoever* as committing the sin against the Holy Ghost, the one beyond all forgiveness. This is to commit a theological heresy of Chesterton's own: an ignorant and arrogant denial of his erstwhile Christian humanist refusal to make a complete disjunction between nature and grace. Nowhere is his invidious opposition made more evident than when, in the opening paragraph of *The Ball and the Cross*, the narrator likens the creations and discoveries of science to the work of a demonic succubus: "For the world of science and evolution is far more nameless and elusive and like a dream than the world of poetry and religion; since in the latter images and ideas remain themselves eternally, while it is the whole idea of evolution that identities melt into each other as they do in a nightmare."[40]

To avoid this goblin dream, Chesterton turns God into a deistic Supreme Being who operates on the world entirely from *outside* its own processes, in the rather crude extrinsicist fashion that we shall repeatedly find him denying in his fiction and poetry.[41] Here Chesterton would have done well to follow the splendid logic that we will hear him articulate in *Orthodoxy*, where he celebrates the wonder of the regular, rather than pining for the ecstasy of the exceptional:

[T]he repetition in Nature seemed sometimes to be an excited repetition. . . . The grass seemed signalling to me with all its fingers at once; the crowded stars seemed bent upon being understood. The sun would make me see him if he rose a thousand times. The recurrences of the universe rose to the maddening rhythm of an incantation, and I began to see an idea. . . . The thing I mean can be seen, for instance, in children, when they find some game or joke that they specially enjoy. A child kicks his legs rhythmically through excess, not absence, of life. Because children have abounding vitality, because they are in spirit fierce and free, therefore they want things repeated and unchanged. They always say, "Do it again"; and the grown-up person does it again until he is nearly dead. For grown-up people are not strong enough to exult in monotony. But perhaps God is strong enough to exult in monotony. It is possible that God says every morning, "Do it again," to the sun; and every evening "Do it again" to the moon. It may not be automatic necessity that makes all daisies alike; it may be that God makes every daisy separately, but has never got tired of making them. It may be that He has the eternal appetite of infancy; for we have sinned and grown old and our Father is younger than we. The repetition in Nature may not be a mere recurrence; it may be a theatrical encore. (O, 65–66)[42]

Since he is here speaking metaphorically and analogically, we need not literalize Chesterton's suggestion that God acts in time rather than beyond it. Yet the important difference must not be missed. For the early Chesterton, God's original and sustaining creative act is to be discerned in the astonishing vitality of nature's smooth regularities more than in its spike-like irregularities. The later Chesterton becomes obsessed, instead, with exorcizing the devil of evolution. Chesterton contends, therefore, that we must read biological evolution as either total and unguided randomness or else as step-by-step providential management. He thus approaches something akin to modern theories of "intelligent design" that deny the presence of chance in the natural order. "God's eye is on the sparrow" becomes a biological rather than a theological claim, though elsewhere Chesterton decried such wooden literalism:

> The member of a sort of mouse family, destined to found the bat family, could only have differed from his brother mice by some minute trace of membrane; and why should that enable him to escape out of a natural massacre of mice? Or even if we suppose it did serve some other purpose, it could only be by a coincidence; and this is to imagine a million coincidences accounting for every creature. A special providence watching over a bat would be a far more realistic notion than such a run of luck as that.[43]

Hence his conclusion that it is impermissible to admit any element of probability or chance whatsoever: "There is always a conscious or unconscious effort of selection. And it is by no means a Natural Selection. It is, in spite of the phrase that is their motto, a very unnatural selection."[44] Chesterton's intuitive Thomism might have taught him, instead, that God achieves his creative purposes in the world *intrinsically*—through efficient no less than formal, material, and final causes.

Teleological reasoning is thus the prime requisite when interpreting evolution.[45]

A Counterproposal: Teleological Evolutionism

There are far more scientifically valid and theologically faithful alternatives than this stark opposition between an interventionist, micromanaging providence on the one hand, and pure accident and fortuity on the other. As Keith Ward has demonstrated, arguments about the *telos* of the universe can elucidate the working of evolutionary processes more fully and satisfactorily than can strictly scientific explanations.[46] For instance, the astonishing results (i.e., human consciousness, unselfish sacrifice, scientific discovery, artistic creativity, religious awe and worship) of our probabilistic universe can be made intelligible only if there is a supracosmic creator sustaining and superintending the whole enterprise. Something so complex and free, so capable of both good and evil, so fully able to turn the terror-striking beauty of the earth into the ghoulish nightmare of nuclear holocaust—such a holy monster as self-conscious man can be the work only of the God who providentially orders but who does not coercively manipulate his cosmos.

David Bartholomew maintains that, far from controlling the universe microcosmically, God operates precisely by means of chance. He contends, in fact, that primeval chaos—something akin to the *tohu-wabohu* (desert ocean) that names the formless void in Genesis 1—"was the precondition of a lawful world." Bartholomew points out, for instance, that "Even when we specify a process which seems to be totally random, patterns emerge which display all the characteristics we associate with the idea of law." The most familiar of these statistical laws, the so-called Normal Distribution Law, traces the familiar bell-shape frequency that characterizes everything from the height of American males to the thickness of tree bark. Statistical law thus emerges, paradoxically, from chaos. "[O]rder and randomness are so closely tied together," Bartholomew adds, "that we can hardly speak of one without the other." Far from diminishing belief in God, the chanciness of the cosmos enhances the wonder that so often struck Chesterton with awe:

> It is on this borderland of chaos and order that the interesting things happen.
> There is just sufficient order to produce simple patterns which persist, but

not so as to render the result chaotic. Order on the edge of chaos seems to be a key characteristic necessary for the emergence of interesting phenomena.[47]

As we have seen, Chesterton was virtually obsessed with discontinuities in nature, as if they were evidence of a divinely "intelligent design"—as if God's creativity depended on his periodic disruptions of nature. Yet there is no need to deny that human beings become the crown of creation by affirming that our species seems to have emerged slowly, almost imperceptibly, until certain anthropoid creatures stopped hooting and screeching, grunting and gesturing—that is, until they gradually began to speak and sing and tell stories. With such a gradual supernaturalizing of the natural, man ceases to be a product of biological processes alone, as he becomes capable of self-consciousness and thus of remembering and anticipating, of partially grasping the meaning of life's totality, including its radical dependency. Indeed, man thus becomes a creature made in the image of God.

There is one passage in *Orthodoxy* where Chesterton rightly affirms that God may well have created human beings during immeasurable millennia: "If evolution simply means that a positive thing called an ape turned very slowly into a positive thing called a man, then it is stingless for most orthodox; for a personal God might just as well do things slowly than quickly, especially if, like the Christian God, *he were outside time*" (O, 39–40, emphasis added).[48] What Chesterton seems not to understand is that God not only exists but also *acts* "outside time." This distinction is the key to Pope John Paul II's argument that God implants the soul *immediately* in human beings. The soul is no mere epiphenomenon of nature, an unintended development wherein the human brain somehow leapt into reflexive self-awareness in spite of its animal nature. The word *immediately* is not a temporal term. The late pope's use of it does not place divine action *within* a measurable temporal moment. *Immediate* signifies that nothing "mediates"—i.e., nothing stands *between*—God and the soul's creation.

The Church's magisterium is directly concerned with the question of evolution, for it involves the conception of man: Revelation teaches us that he was created in the image and likeness of God (cf. Gn 1:27-29). The conciliar constitution *Gaudium et Spes* has magnificently explained this doctrine, which is pivotal to Christian thought. It recalled that man is "the only creature on earth that God has wanted for its own sake" (No. 24). In other terms, the human individual cannot be subordinated as a pure means or a pure instrument, either to the species or to society; he has value *per se*. . . . It is by virtue of his spiritual soul that the whole person possesses such a dignity even in his body. Pius XII stressed this essential point: If the human body take its origin from pre-existent living matter, the spiritual soul is immediately created by God ("animas enim a Deo immediate creari catholica fides nos retinere iubei"; "Humani Generis," 36).[49]

Michael Tkacz rightly observes that not to understand divine action as "immediate" and "outside time" is to take refuge in a "god of the gaps." Chesterton searched for this supposed shelter by seeking those discontinuities within nature that supposedly leave room for divine "intervention." As Tkacz makes clear, such a nature-interrupting "god" is not the triune God whose creative act is eternal rather than temporal:

> [C]reation is the result of the divine agency being totally responsible for the production, all at once and completely, of the whole of the universe. . . . To come to know the natural causes of natural beings is a different matter from knowing that all natural beings and operations radically depend on the ultimate cause for the existence of everything: God the Creator. Creation is not a change. Creation is a cause, but of a very different, indeed unique, kind. . . . God creates without taking any time to create: He creates eternally.[50] Creation is not a process with a beginning, a middle, and an end. It is simply a reality: the reality of the dependence of the universe on God's agency. . . . [Hence] the radical otherness of God's agency. God's productive causality is unlike that of any natural cause. . . . God is totally and immediately present as cause to any and all processes. . . . God causes natural beings to exist in such a way that they are the real agents of their own operations.[51]

Unlike Chesterton, most ancient Christian theologians were astonished at the seemingly infinite *continuities* of nature. They were not devoted to things naturally inexplicable but to nature's thoroughly comprehensible operations. "The emphasis in early Christian writings," declares Stephen Barr, "was not on complexity, irreducible or otherwise, but on the beauty, order, lawfulness, and harmony found in the world that God had made."[52] Such theologians would have perceived no diminution of our divine dignity and worth in affirming our close kinship with other anthropoid species. On the contrary, our uniqueness is *enhanced* by the confession that God's immediate creation of the human soul makes man his set-apart creature. Indeed, this humble admission frees us from relying on the fabled "missing link," as Chesterton seems to do. Even such a notion as "irreducible complexity" holds Christianity hostage to science. For if fossil records of a median creature existing between man and chimpanzee were discovered, or if probabilistic processes were found capable of producing so intricate an organ as the human eye, then Christian faith would presumably be jeopardized.

Convinced instead that we humans stand completely apart from nature, Chesterton makes the astonishing claim that it "has no authority over us; we have to admire, but not to imitate" (O, 119).[53] Among many other Christian thinkers, Alasdair MacIntyre has shown that the created order has immense moral sovereignty over us, not only because we are supremely dependent on it for our very existence, but also because we can learn from many of the other animals that we are not the sole creatures having a capacity for self-sacrifice and care for others. The differences remain gargantuan, of course. The other animals cannot reflectively transcend their environment so as to grasp the world as a whole, nor can they recollect the past and envision the future so as to put the present within a temporal context, nor can they acknowledge (or refuse to acknowledge) their own dependence. Even so, it is crucial to confess our animal similarities, as MacIntyre argues:

> [O]ur whole initial bodily comportment towards the world is originally an animal comportment and . . . when, through becoming language-users, we under the guidance of parents and others restructure that comportment, elaborate and in new ways correct our beliefs and redirect our activities, we never make ourselves independent of our animal nature and inheritance. . . . For it is of the first importance that what we thereby become are redirected and remade animals and not something else. Our second culturally formed language-using nature is a set of partial, but only partial, transformations of our first animal nature. We remain animal selves with animal identities.[54]

Yet while Chesterton may be wrong concerning the nature-and-grace relation in matters biological, he is exactly right about its operations in human life. In fact, his most famous book, *Orthodoxy*, remains an indispensable analytic tool for probing the modern sickness unto death as well for providing a surprising remedy for its healing—not by way of a disruptive providence but by means of an "always and already" graced nature.

Maniacal Modernist Rationalism

For Chesterton, the conviction of sin depends on an assumed metaphysical order, a transcendent hierarchy of goods over against which we can both identify vices and promote virtues. The collapse of this venerable Great Chain of Being, as it was once called, is precisely the condition and thus the curse of our age. Christian apologists can no longer assume that their audiences will credit this ancient model of the cosmos as a carefully ordered realm. From the remotest heavens to the lowest depths of the earth, everything from angels to minerals were once envisioned as being ranged according to their relative worth in relation both to each other and to the triune God who at once creates and governs this grand hierarchy. Nor was he understood as a distant and nameless architect but as the personal director of the cosmic pageant, having entered its drama to realize its proper End through the incarnate Lord and the sustaining Spirit. Human life could then be understood either as existing in sinful revolt against the very grain of the universe, or else as dwelling in faithful (though incomplete) obedience to it.

What tack, then, does Chesterton take in dealing with such an enormous collapse in the courts of heaven? He avoids conventional Christian apologetics if only because conventional atheist apologists, quite against their intention, had almost persuaded him to become a believer. Ironically, he was driven back to orthodox Christianity by such flaccid defenders of unbelief as Huxley and Spencer, Ingersoll and Bradlaugh. "They sowed in my mind," he wittily observes, "my first wild doubts of doubt" (O, 90). Chesterton fears that a traditional argument for Christianity—proceeding from human sinfulness to divine salvation via shopworn theological terms—might put off prospective Christian converts just as the old-fashioned atheists almost persuaded him to become a Christian.

> In this remarkable situation it is plainly not now possible (with any hope
> of a universal appeal) to start, as our fathers did, with the fact of sin. This

very fact which was to them (and is to me) as plain as a pikestaff, is the very fact that has been specially diluted or denied. But though moderns deny the existence of sin, I do not think that they have yet denied the existence of a lunatic asylum. (O, 19)

In an exceedingly shrewd ploy, Chesterton argues that our age, in its obliviousness to sin, must be regarded as *insane*. Perhaps sensing that the new vogue of psychology would come to dominate our Western mentality, he declares us to be morally and religiously unhinged. In so characterizing our age, GKC becomes the uncanny critic of both modernism and postmodernism.

Chesterton attends first to our insane modernist rationalism. Yet his attack on rationalism is not an attack on reason. Quite to the contrary: "Reason is itself a matter of faith," Chesterton observes. "It is an act of faith to assert that our thoughts have any relation to reality at all" (O, 38). We presuppose the rationality of the world as the fundamental postulate and axiom of our very existence. That the world is basically rational rather than irrational is the assumption that enables everyday life: we could not engage in the most elementary communications and relations if our words and concepts—our reason—did not have at least a partially truthful relation to reality. Alas, since the time of Descartes, we have come to believe that there is nothing *but* reason—"reason" of an increasingly reductive and calculating sort. The only real things are said to be those that can be demonstrated by either empirical science or mathematical logic.

For Chesterton, such modernist rationalism is maniacal. "The madman is not the man who has lost his reason," he wisely observes. "The madman is the man who has lost everything except his reason. He [dwells] in the clean and well-lit prison of one idea" (O, 24, 27). The mental jail cell of modernist rationalism is, for Chesterton, the monomaniacal notion that the universe consists of nothing but matter and energy. Though Chesterton identifies such madness as "materialism," it is perhaps more appropriate to call it *physicalism*. As believers in the triune God who has enfleshed himself amidst this human fray, taking human form for the sake of humanity's redemption, Christians are unabashed materialists, repudiating all Gnostic spite and scorn for the corporeal creation.[55]

What Chesterton rightly rejects is the deadly physicalism that attributes everything to mechanical and efficient causes *alone*, failing to ask also about material and formal and final causes—namely, what prime purposes bring things into being, what formal causes enable them to achieve their particular shape, what final objectives pull them toward perfection, indeed what ultimate goods do they serve? In refusing to ask such questions, physicalism attributes everything to inexorable forces. Its curious effect is to turn us in upon ourselves, convincing us that we could not be radically other than what our genetics and environment have decreed us to be. Insane rationalists are profound pessimists. Chesterton thus links modernist rationalism to ancient Stoicism. The Stoics were also pessimists who believed in a self-enclosed, self-repeating cosmos. Absent any belief in the transcendent God, their only recourse was to worship the god within, the deity who in later centuries would be called the Inner Light. As Chesterton wittily observes, this is the worst form of lighting. Hence his striking prophecy of the religious immanentism that would eventually give rise to the vague New Age spirituality of subjective inwardness:

> That Jones shall worship the god within him turns out ultimately to mean that Jones shall worship Jones. Let Jones worship the sun or moon, anything rather than the Inner Light; let Jones worship cats or crocodiles, if he can find any in his street, but not the god within. Christianity came into the world firstly in order to assert with violence that a man [has] not only to look inwards, but to look outwards, to behold with astonishment and enthusiasm a divine company and a divine captain. The only fun of being a Christian [is] that a man [is] not left alone with the Inner Light, but definitely [recognizes] an outer light, fair as the sun, clear as the moon, terrible as an army with banners. (O, 81)

The madness of modernist rationalism was also at work in the so-called natural religion of the Enlightenment. Yet the deist enthronement of nature as having no *telos* beyond itself proves to be unnatural and even demonic since, as Chesterton keenly notes, Pan is the god of the cloven hoof. The physical world is no less dark and cruel than innocent and amiable. There are good reasons for being responsible stewards of the environment, but they cannot be derived from the environment alone. Chesterton insists, as we have seen, that no satis-factory ethics can be deduced from the physical world. It cancels what it seems to affirm, as self-sacrificial acts are set at naught by rapacious acts. While democracy declares all men to be worthy, for example, and while aristocracy designates some men as worthier, Chesterton con-tends that "nature makes no remark on the subject" (O, 110). Animals are social creatures, but they have no politics. Revelation is required, therefore, to take a sane view of nature.

Chesterton does not deny the partial validity of physicalism. We are shaped by our cultural and bodily conditions. Yet the fundamental pattern of the physical world is circular rather than linear. It is alto-gether predictable, therefore, that most of the world's religions should be based upon some form of the Eternal Return—the notion, namely, that life repeats itself endlessly. Hence the need either to conform one-self to this eternal round (as in Stoicism) or else to escape it (as in cer-tain forms of Hinduism). For Chesterton, by contrast, the essence of the Christian faith lies not in its fatedness but its freedom. The funda-mental human problem is that we are insanely turned in on ourselves, nightmarishly employing our reason to encircle and thus to imprison ourselves. The Cross, by contrast, breaks all confines. It alone has the power to free us from the insane circle of physicalist rationalism:

> As we have taken the circle as the symbol of [physicalist] reason and mad-ness, we may very well take the cross as the symbol at once of mystery and of health. . . . For the circle is perfect and infinite in its nature; but it is fixed for ever in its size; it can never be larger or smaller. But the cross, though it has at its heart a collision and a contradiction, can extend its four arms for ever without altering its shape. Because it has a paradox in its centre it can grow without changing. The circle returns upon itself and is bound. The cross opens its arms to the four winds; it is a signpost for free travellers. (O, 33)

As the ultimate paradox of the worst embodying the best, the Cross is also the ultimate mystery. Its union of apparent contradictions prompts what Chesterton—not having yet learned to use the language of metaphysical vision—calls the "mysticism [that] keeps men sane." "The whole secret of mysticism is this: that man can understand every-thing by the help of what he does not understand."[56]

The Suicide of Mind in Postmodernist Irrationalism

If hyper-rationalist modernism is one symptom of our cultural madness, hyper-emotionalist postmodernism is the other. The former is filled with false pride, the latter with false humility. It's a false humility because, unlike lunatic rationalists who believe they know *everything*, mad emotivists deny that they know *anything*. This is what Chesterton calls "humility in the wrong place":

> Modesty has settled upon the organ of conviction; where it was never meant to be. A man was meant to be doubtful about himself, but undoubting about the truth; this has been exactly reversed. Nowadays the part of a man that a man does assert is exactly the part he ought not to assert—himself. The part he doubts is exactly the part he ought not to doubt—the Divine Reason. (O, 36–37)

We once had misgivings about the adequacy of our moral efforts, Chesterton notes, and were thus spurred to greater diligence. Our new irrationalists, by contrast, are loath to make ethical claims of any kind. Having no high purpose, they are tempted to cease striving altogether, sinking into moral lassitude or else plunging into frenetic hedonism. These various forms of emotivist antirationalism, Chesterton accurately prophesies, will produce a people too intellectually meek "even to claim their inheritance." We have become so suspicious of large truth claims that we are suspicious of even the smallest. "[M]adness may be defined," according to Chesterton, "as using mental activity so as to reach mental helplessness" (O, 48). "We are on the road," he wittily but alarmingly adds, "to producing a race of men too mentally modest to believe in the multiplication table" (O, 37).

Chesterton rightly discerned that Nietzsche would become the ultimate exemplar of the antirationalist "turn to the subject"—indeed, that he would be the philosophical father of the postmodern and irrationalist century to come. Though in 1908 Nietzsche had just recently been translated into English,[57] Chesterton saw immediately that he would inaugurate the triumph of will over reason. With remarkable acuity, Chesterton went to the heart of the matter, casting his argument in the third person plural, as if to signal the invasion of an enemy (and surely Prussian!) army: "Will, they say, creates. The ultimate authority, they say, is in will, not in reason. The supreme point is not *why* a man demands a thing, but the fact *that* he does demand it. . . . They say that choice is itself the divine thing" (O, 43, emphasis added). Whereas the real was once the objectively rational, it is now the subjectively chosen and the inwardly felt that alone can be credited.

Chesterton shrewdly notes Nietzsche's retreat from comparative to spatial metaphors taken "from acrobats or alpine climbers." To avoid the challenge of ethical judgment, Nietzsche transports us "beyond good and evil," rather than having the courage to declare whether our moral path should be determined by considerations of better and worse. In similar recourse to metaphors of extension rather than comparison, Nietzsche exalts the "over-man" as his hero, refusing to describe "the purer man" or "the happier man." Yet, as Chesterton notes, the will to power is not the strongest but the weakest of things:

> No human being of any imagination ever took the smallest interest in the victories of the strong. It is only the victories of the weak that can be interesting [Chesterton wrote in 1907]. And all the victories, almost literally without exception, which humanity has celebrated at all, have been the victories of the weak—the weak in size, as in Jack the Giant-Killer; or in numbers as at Marathon or Thermopylae; or in station and obvious chances, as in Cinderella or modern socialism; or in bodily defect, as in the blind Samson or the hump-backed Punch.[58]

"Nietzsche is truly a very timid thinker," Chesterton concludes (O, 111). To the philosopher whose brave motto was "Be hard," GKC replies with one of his most lapidary aphorisms:

> The stone must by its own nature go downward, because hardness is weakness. The bird can of its nature go upwards, because fragility is force. In perfect force there is a kind of frivolity, an airiness that can maintain itself in the air. Modern investigators of miraculous history have solemnly admitted that a characteristic of the great saints is their power of "levitation." They might go further; a characteristic of the great saints is their power of levity. Angels can fly because they can take themselves lightly. (O, 127)[59]

With stunning foresight, Chesterton already saw it all coming in 1908. Allegedly objective reason describes the madness of modernity, while the subjectivist denial of reason is an apt account of postmodernity. François Lyotard famously defined postmodernism as the suspicion of all metanarratives: the mistrust of all totalizing and exhaustive explanations, whether in the Copernican and Newtonian science of the Enlightenment, or in the Christian creeds that narrate the story of the entire cosmos. Postmodernists seek to dismantle such metanarratives, replacing them with aesthetic preferences and personal choices and thus to deny Truth in the uppercase. In such an emotivist and subjectivist world, the only putative good is diversity. The central postmodernist premise is that to affirm multiple viewpoints and multiple interests is to acknowledge the final incomprehensibility of the universe.

As with rationalist modernism, so with irrationalist postmodernism: there is much truth in it. All our seeing is indeed subjective and culture bound. We behold the world through the lenses of our own conceptions and assumptions. All truth is filtered and sieved, all understanding rooted in time and place and community. There is no view from nowhere, no godlike perch from which we can behold the world neutrally—as if that were God's own view. But from the valid premise that there is no such thing as bare-naked knowledge, postmodern relativists and emotivists reach invalid conclusions. They hold that we can make *no* comparative moral judgments, engage in *no* time-transcending religious arguments, allow *no* privileging of certain cultures—for example, cultures that dignify women over cultures that demean them, or even governments that enhance democratic freedoms over those that destroy them.

The Best of All Impossible Worlds

Where can we locate the moral and religious sanity that would answer our twin insanities of hyper-rationalism and hyper-emotivism? Like the *nouvelle* theologians, Chesterton believes the divine order to be so deeply ingrained in human existence that we acquire our most basic convictions from the fantasy books of our childhood, where the natural is already supernaturalized. Fairy stories reveal "the original instinct of man for adventure and romance," he declares. They embody the same "irregular equilibrium" that operates in the physical world. We have two eyes, two ears, two nostrils, two hands, two feet—but only one heart, and it is slightly to the left of center. "The Ethics of Elfland," as Chesterton calls the moral world of fairy tales, also constitutes a surprising analogue of the Gospel's own asymmetrical kind of sanity. Here we find parabolic answers to the most fundamental of questions: "How can we contrive to be at once astonished at the world and yet at home in it?" (O, 14). How can human life be made at once strange and startling because it is an unaccountable and undeserved gift, yet at the same time homely and familiar because it is to be embraced and enjoyed? How are we to love the world without regarding it as our final destiny? How, in sum, to be in the world but not of it?

Fairy stories answer by administering two indispensable tests, says Chesterton. The first elfin trial concerns the *imagination*: whether we are willing to see the world as multilayered and interstitial. The fantastic imagination does not envision the universe as consisting of separable realms—the visible and the invisible, the literal and the figurative, the necessary and the free, not even the natural and the supernatural. Fairy stories invite us to discern these spheres as mysteriously, even miraculously, overlapping and intersecting. Adam and Eve failed the test of imagination because they clung to a univocal understanding of the world, as if eating the forbidden fruit had but a single and uncomplicated consequence. They were the first fundamentalists and hyper-rationalists.

Certain kinds of modern scientists may have been the second. They operate, says Chesterton, "as if the connection of two strange things physically [also] connected them philosophically" (O, 57) Such physicalists thus speak philosophically of "laws" and "necessity," even of "mechanism" and "inevitability," when they have observed only physical events. Yet such a monocausal cosmos would permit no novelty, no creativity, whether natural or human or divine. Chesterton found the recent discoveries of Einstein and modern physics to be at work in fairy tales deriving from the primeval past. In their imaginative and surprising way, fairy stories credit a hidden and invisible logic that Chesterton would have done well to notice in his critique of evolution:

> There are certain sequences or developments (cases of one thing following another), which are, in the true sense of the word, reasonable. They are, in the true sense of the word, necessary. Such are mathematical and merely logical sequences. We in fairyland (who are the most reasonable of all creatures) admit that reason and that necessity. . . . You cannot *imagine* two and one

not making three. But you can easily imagine trees not growing fruit; you can imagine them growing golden candlesticks or tigers hanging on by the tail. . . . When we are asked why eggs turn to birds or fruits fall in autumn, we must answer exactly as the fairy godmother would answer if Cinderella asked her why mice turned to horses or her clothes fell from her at twelve o'clock. We must answer that it is *magic*. It is not a "law," for we do not understand its general formula. It is not a necessity, for though we can count on it happening practically, we have no right to say that it must always happen. It is no argument for unalterable law (as Huxley fancied) that we count on the ordinary course of things. We do not count on it; we bet on it. (O, 55–58, emphasis in original)

In the penetrating and humorous final sentence, Chesterton probes the crucial distinction between the necessary (what we take for granted) and the contingent (what we wager on).[60] The physical world is not only deterministic, he discerns, but also probabilistic—again, an insight that eluded him when dealing with evolution. For Chesterton, *magic* is a synonym for the mysterious, complex, and often unaccountable transformations of one thing into another. In the famous formula of the chaos theorists, a butterfly rippling its wings in India can cause a tornado in Texas. Unpredictability is not itself a cause for distress, however, for probability is at work even in chance events, as we have seen in investigating the evolutionary processes. So, Chesterton insists, do the physical and spiritual realms operate in a similarly paradoxical way. They converge and overlap in a manner that can be grasped in the magical, imaginative quality of many fairy stories.

Paradox is the ultimate expression of such thought. It is truth standing on its head, Chesterton said, waving its legs to get our attention. We usually regard such hand-walkers who use their legs as semaphores to be manifestly mad. Yet such drastic analogies are required to name the likeness often found in unlikeness, and thus to see that the world's seeming contraries are more complementary than contradictory. Only such a paradoxical and metaphysical vision of the intersecting realms of the supernatural and the natural can produce proper wonder and praise for the good creation.

If the analogical imagination of wonder and praise is Chesterton's remedy to the insane rationalism of modernity, then the "Doctrine of Conditional Joy" is his cure for our equally maddening irrationalism.

This doctrine deals with the drastic *if* upon which everything hangs, the singular decision that determines everything else.[61] Nothing akin to autonomous willpower is here entailed. Chesterton is no Pelagian. The act of obedience is itself enabled (though not enacted) by God. Our first parents were commanded to eat of every tree in Eden except one, the Tree of Life. From the very outset the utter priority of divine grace is established. God has already bestowed happiness on the primal couple by way of their Edenic bliss. Everything is theirs, if they meet the simple condition for keeping such joy: they must not eat from the Tree of the Knowledge of Good and Evil.[62]

This Hebrew doublet does not signify basic moral knowledge, as in the distinction between right and wrong. Such ethical differentiation has already been given to Adam and Eve in the divine command that they serve as keepers of the Garden and that they abstain from the forbidden fruit. The phrase "knowing good and evil" means something akin to "having godlike knowledge of all things." Not until the primal couple had been habituated to obedience—perhaps over many years, as their souls would have fully informed their bodies—might they have been permitted to live everlastingly as God's own companions. Such complete congruity between the divine image and the divine likeness is what Eastern Christianity calls *theosis*, or divinization. Though perhaps unaware of the term, Chesterton describes its fruition aptly: "an ultimate and absolute pleasure, not indirect or utilitarian, the intoxification of the spirit, the wine of the blood of God."[63]

Chesterton the Christian humanist descries analogies of the biblical story in classic myths and fairy stories.[64] They name the gift as well as both the prerequisite and the peril of not obeying the rule for enjoying it. "In the fairy tale an incomprehensible happiness rests upon an incomprehensible condition. A box is opened, and all evils fly out. A word is forgotten, and cities perish. A lamp is lit, and love flies away. A flower is plucked, and human lives are forfeited. An apple is eaten, and the hope of God is gone" (O, 61).[65] In most fairy stories, as in the myth of Eden, everything hinges on the proper response to an undeserved gift. Faithfully to receive such an unbidden offering entails not blind obedience but the right kind of thoughtfulness. "I would maintain that thanks are the highest form of thought," Chesterton argues, "and that gratitude is happiness doubled by wonder."[66] Such gratitude should be given not only for special gifts but also for things that we obliviously take for granted:

> The test of all happiness is gratitude. . . . Children are grateful when Santa Claus puts in their stocking gifts of toys or sweets. Could I not be grateful to Santa Claus when he put in my stockings the gift of two miraculous legs? We thank people for birthday presents of cigars and slippers. Can I thank no one for the birthday present of birth? (O, 60)[67]

Gratitude of this kind prevents the irrationalist madness that seeks ever more intense forms of subjective self-satisfaction. It plants the flag of loyal indebtedness to the world and its cornucopia of blessings, preventing the false presumption that we deserve such benefits and that we may exploit them heedlessly. The world, writes Chesterton, "is the fortress of our family, with the flag flying on the turret, and the more miserable it is the less we should leave it. The point is not that this world is too sad to love or too glad not to love; the point is that when you do love a thing, its gladness is a reason for loving it, and its sadness a reason for loving it more" (O, 72).

The condition of obedient and grateful joy serves as a worldly analogue of the Gospel in yet a third way. It helps us to order our loves and to govern our desires, so that our choices eventually become our habits—our convictions thus having chosen us rather than the other way around.[68] The ultimately free decision, Chesterton the master of paradox rightly declares, is "the liberty to bind myself" (O, 130). Discipline and fidelity, oaths and obligations, are means, not obstacles, to joy. The making and keeping of promises, especially in marriage, provide the key to happiness. "Love is not blind," Chesterton keenly observes. "Love is bound; and the more it is bound the less it is blind" (O, 76). Morality is like art, we have heard him saying: it consists in drawing the line. In humbly embraced limits, not in swaggering will to power, lies the only liberty:

> The worship of will is the negation of will. To admire mere choice is to refuse to choose. . . . Every act of will is an act of self-limitation. To desire action is to desire limitation. In that sense every act is an act of self-sacrifice. When you choose anything, you reject everything else. . . . Every act is an irrevocable selection and exclusion. Just as when you marry one woman you give up all others, so when you take one course of action you give up all the other

courses. . . . Art is limitation; the essence of every picture is the frame. . . . The moment you step into the world of facts, you step into a world of limits. You can free things from alien or accidental laws, but not from the laws of their own nature. You may, if you like, free a tiger from his bars; but do not free him from his stripes. Do not free a camel of the burden of his hump: you may be freeing him from being a camel. (O, 44–45)

In his splendid chapter on "The Paradoxes of Christianity," Chesterton turns from anticipations and echoes of the Gospel to be found in fairy tales and other works of art to address the nature of the Faith itself. Here he sanely balances the seeming contraries of gift and requirement, of grace and ethics. Their delicate equilibrium serves to differentiate suicide from martyrdom. A suicide is one who has given up on life and thus desires death; a martyr is one whose "strong desire to live [takes] the form of a readiness to die. 'He that will lose his life, the same shall save it'" (O, 99).[69] Not Christian martyrs alone but the whole of humanity lives within these drastic opposites: meekness and folly, love and wrath, forgiveness and sin. Christians are happy pessimists, says Chesterton. They do what is unthinkable according to the pagan: they choose to love the unlovable and to pardon the unpardonable. The soldier of the Cross, he argues, "must not merely cling to life, for then he will be a coward, and will not escape. He must not merely wait for death, for then he will be a suicide, and will not escape. He must seek his life in a spirit of furious indifference to it; he must desire life like water and yet drink death like wine" (O, 99).

* * *

Though Chesterton died when the twentieth century was barely a third finished, we still dwell in his epoch. Our age belongs to him because he was its true physician, both probing our illnesses and prescribing our cure. *Orthodoxy* remains his most prophetic book because it foresees both the insane rationalism and the lunatic irrationalism that engulf late modern life, with nightmarish results. They were instances, Chesterton would later confess, of the simplest claim made in the *Penny Catechism*—that pride and despair are the worst sins. Hyper-rationalism reeks with pride, hyper-emotivism with despair. Chesterton's Christian humanism is alive and well because it affirms—no matter where in the evolutionary process our distinctive species emerges—that humanity is a monstrosity, a wild and not a tame type. Sartre was oddly if unwittingly right in saying that we humans have broken out of the closed circle of animality. We do not fit smoothly into the world; we stick out like a spike from the rest of creation, because we are embodied souls and ensouled bodies. Yet rather than constituting a futile and "sorry project," as Sartre famously said, we are monsters in the splendid sense of the Old French word *mostre*: a horror, a wonder, a marvel, a thing of God's own making and remaking.[70]

2

PATRIOTISM AND THE TRUE *PATRIA*
Distributism, Hymns, and *Christendom in Dublin*

> It is the final sign of imbecility in a people that it calls cats dogs
> and describes the sun as the moon—and is very particular about the
> preciseness of these pseudonyms. To be wrong, and to be carefully
> wrong: that is the definition of decadence. The disease called aphasia,
> in which people begin by saying tea when they mean coffee, commonly
> ends in their silence. Silence of this stiff sort is the chief mark of the
> powerful parts of modern society. They all seem straining to keep
> things in rather than to let things out. . . . Even the newspaper editors
> and proprietors are more despotic and dangerous by what they do not
> utter than by what they do. We have all heard the expression "golden
> silence." The expression "brazen silence" is the only adequate phrase
> for our editors. If we wake out of this throttled, gaping, and wordless
> nightmare, we must awake with a yell.
> G. K. Chesterton, "The Nameless Man" (1912)

In her still unsurpassed biography of Chesterton published in 1943, Maisie Ward declared that the three great loves of the great man's life were "his wife, his country and his Faith."[1] Ward's capitalizing of the final word seems to make clear that Chesterton had rightly arranged his central loves, with his Christian convictions properly subordinating the other two. Yet Julia Stapleton's study of Chesterton's politics reveals, on the contrary, that Chesterton's patriotism was stitched inextricably together with his Christianity so as to form a seamless, virtually undifferentiated whole. Chesterton's "ancestral disposition toward patriotism was instrumental in guiding him to the Christian fold," she claims, "one that he then sought to justify and strengthen in Christian terms. Henceforth his patriotism, Englishness, and Christianity were mutually dependent and reinforcing."[2] In sum, Chesterton's religious belief and political practice were integral and inseparable. The aim of this chapter is to trace the sunny rise and nightmarish fall of Chesterton's Liberal politics. As he became increasingly disenchanted with the British electoral system, he became ever more devoted to his program for land allocation called Distributism. The darkest of Chesterton's disillusionments led to a more fully Christian understanding of the political sphere, especially the place of the Church within it. This change is revealed not only in his two great hymns but also in a much-neglected work titled *Christendom in Dublin*.

Chesterton the Radical Who Became a Liberal

Many of Chesterton's advocates and opponents will be surprised to learn that his essential political stance was neither right nor left but radical. As the word's etymology reveals, he wanted to delve down to the *radix*, the root of things, so as to fathom the antecedent causes of social evils and thus to propose consequent remedies that would result in real reform. He thus complained that early nineteenth-century Liberals failed to grasp the cockney radicalism that Dickens so powerfully embodied in his fiction and that, for Chesterton, was the essential English quality:

> That spirit of his was one of the things that we have had which were truly national. All other forces we have borrowed, especially those which flatter us the most. Imperialism is foreign, socialism is foreign, militarism is foreign, education is foreign, strictly [speaking] even Liberalism is foreign. But Radicalism was our own; as English as the hedge-rows.[3]

Chesterton could make perceptive links between ancient and current events because his knowledge of the world was as democratic as his politics. He was a veritable polymath, having read almost everything and forgotten almost nothing. Such wide and deep mastery of books and ideas made him a Liberal in the etymological sense of the Latin *liber*, or "free." Though it originally referred to those who were not slaves, *liberal* gradually came to mean, as the *Oxford English Dictionary* indicates, "free in bestowing; bountiful, generous, open-hearted." The Liberalism of Chesterton's parents decisively shaped his political convictions.[4] They were such free-spirited souls that Chesterton never became smug about his own Liberalism. Asked to contribute to a symposium whose aim was to answer the question "What's wrong with the world?" Chesterton replied, "I am." He regarded humility, along with the courage it enables and the joy it promotes, as the highest of the virtues.

Chesterton's self-ironizing humor endeared him to audiences when he sparred with such vigorous opponents as G. B. Shaw and H. G. Wells. He responded to these atheist, socialist, teetotalist, vegetarian, nonsmoking, anti-Christmas friends, for example, by extolling "the trinity of drinking, eating, and praying which to moderns appears [as an] irreverent [indulgence on] the holy day which is really a holiday."[5] Shaw, he said, wanted nothing so much as that everyone be required to eat grass. Yet GKC also declared that "in a sweeter and more solid civilization," GBS might have been a great saint:

> He would have been a saint of a sternly ascetic, perhaps of a sternly negative type. But he has this strange note of the saint in him: that he is literally unworldly. Worldliness has no human magic for him; he is not bewitched by rank nor drawn on by conviviality at all. He could not understand the intellectual surrender of the snob. He is perhaps a defective character; but he is not a mixed one. All the virtues he has are heroic virtues. Shaw is like the Venus of Milo; all that there is of him is admirable.[6]

Chesterton also proved to be the most irenic of debating partners in intellectual combat, chiefly because he sought sympathy more than victory. "In the end," he wrote, "it will not much matter whether we wrote ill or well; but it will matter greatly on which side we fought."[7] Chesterton wrote exceedingly well on behalf of the common man whom he thought Liberalism ought to defend. He never aspired to be anything other than a journalist, an unabashed tradesman who wrote for the day (*le jour*) in the conviction that he was also writing for eternity. As a Christian convinced that God has taken human form to redeem the world by human means, Chesterton believed that everyday concerns are transcendently important. He always wrote hurriedly, usually to a deadline, sometimes dictating his work to his secretary, often petitioning the postman to wait until he had finished. Though he eschewed all exalted claims for journalism, Chesterton fulfilled Max Weber's understanding of it as one of the most responsible modern vocations:

> Not everyone realizes that a really good journalistic accomplishment requires at least as much "genius" as any scholarly accomplishment, especially because of the necessity of producing at once and "on order," and because of the necessity of being effective . . . under quite different conditions of production. It is almost never acknowledged that the responsibility of the journalist is far greater, and that the sense of responsibility of every honorable journalist is, on the average, not a bit lower than that of the scholar, but rather, as [World War I] has shown, higher. This is because, in the very nature of the case, irresponsible journalistic accomplishments and their often terrible effects are remembered.[8]

Because he sought to be nothing other than an honorable journalist in the Liberal tradition, Chesterton was not in the least troubled at being called "a master without a masterpiece." On the contrary, he knew the terrible deceptions endemic to the printed word, though he published more than one hundred books—the false assumption, namely, that because something has been put into type, it must be true: "This great delusion of the prior claim of printed matter, as something anterior to experience and capable of contradicting it, is the main weakness of modern urban society. The chief mark of the modern man is that he has gone through a landscape with his eyes glued to a guidebook, and could actually deny in one anything that he could not find in the other."[9] Hence Chesterton's refusal to make a god of art. Instead, he decried the division of high and low culture, believing that common people are capable of comprehending uncommon things. His detective stories featuring Father Brown as the consummate sleuth are deliberately cast into a popular medium. "I have no feeling for immortality," Chesterton confessed. "I don't care for anything except to be in the present stress of life as it is. I would rather live now and die, from an artistic point of view, than keep aloof and write things that will remain in the world hundreds of years after my death. . . . What I value in my own work is what I may succeed in striking out of others."[10]

Chesterton sparks endless glints of light because his Liberalism enabled him to attend to what William Blake called life's "minute particulars." In his book on Browning, for example, Chesterton cites the celebrated Indian story of five blind men seriously seeking but grossly failing to name the grotesque animal known as an elephant. The conventional but mistaken interpretation of the parable is that we are all sightless creatures groping in the dark, feeling after but never finding the Mystery that no one could possibly grasp. All religions and philosophies, it is supposed to follow, are more or less equal attempts to name the Unnameable. Chesterton points out, to the contrary, that the analogy depends on two kinds of prior knowledge: we ourselves know that the five men are blind and that there exists an exceedingly odd creature called an elephant. The real teaching of the fine fable, says Chesterton, is not that there is no such thing as firmly apprehensible Truth but that *experience of the world* is required in order to grasp it.[11]

Chesterton was a Liberal in this precise existential sense. The acquisition of truth is the result of effort and struggle and engagement, of mistakes and wrong turns and dead ends—in sum, of *experience*. Easily achieved truth is a delusion. "A Liberal may be defined approximately as a man who, if he could by waving his hand in a dark room, stop the mouths of all the deceivers of mankind for ever, would not wave his hand."[12] Chesterton admired Browning because there is no convenient truth to be found anywhere in his work. His poetry is imbued, instead, with the conviction that every person has a story worth telling and hearing because it constitutes at least a fragment of the whole Story. While denying that all angles of vision and personal perceptions and subjective biases have equal value, Browning discerned that they may serve as at least partial glimpses of the truth. To say that there are many versions of the truth is not to say that none of them can be definitively and unsurpassably true. A diversity of beliefs often indicates, instead, that many are wretchedly wrong, and that our difficult task is to sift them properly. In a practice that Chesterton would come to imitate, Browning sought to join charity and truth so as to make the link not weak but strong: "Charity was his basic philosophy; but it was, as it were, a fierce charity, a charity that went man-hunting. He was a kind of cosmic detective who walked into the foulest thieves' kitchens and accused men of public virtue."[13]

Such unabashed liberality of spirit enabled Chesterton the future Catholic to hail, quite surprisingly, the most anti-Catholic of events, the French Revolution. It was for him the great shining example of a nationalism that could throw off the shackles of money and privilege in order to deliver common people from bondage, granting them a social and political liberty previously unknown. Military actions of allegedly righteous kinds were never a problem for Chesterton. Yet there is a troubling vagueness about his recourse to "somewhere" and "something" in his defense of Napoleon Bonaparte, as if jocular martial means justified sober political ends:

> [W]hile Napoleon was a despot like the rest, he was a despot who went somewhere and did something, and defied the pessimism of Europe, and erased the word "impossible." One does not need to be a Bonapartist to rejoice at the way in which the armies of the First Empire, shouting their songs and jesting with their colonels, smote and broke into pieces the armies of Prussia and Austria driven into battle with a cane.[14]

Despite the carnage and blasphemy of the Reign of Terror, Chesterton praised the French for recovering a fundamental teaching of the Church that its magisterium had often neglected—specifically, "the idea that man himself is a king in disguise." Concerning the Derby-obsessed aristocrats of his own time and place, he acidly observed that they "were not interested in the equality of men but in the inequality of horses."[15] By way of a triple theological, political, and visual pun—it occurs in his splendid book on his literary hero, Charles Dickens—Chesterton vividly states the Christian premise undergirding democracy: "[A]ll men are equal, as all pennies are equal, because the only value in any of them is that they bear the image of the King."[16] He had no patience with those who complained that democracy is "coarse and turbulent."

> Aristocracy is the thing that is always coarse and turbulent: for it means appealing to the self-confident people. Democracy means appealing to different people. Democracy means getting people to vote who would never have the cheek to govern: and (according to Christian ethics) the precise people who ought to govern are the people who have not the cheek to do it.[17]

Liberty and equality and fraternity are never, for Chesterton, to be confused with license or anarchy or indiscriminate unity. Freedom, he believed, is always realized within constraints. Thus have we heard him declaring, "Art, like morality, consists of drawing the line somewhere."

Edges and borders, like things local and limited, do not stifle liberty and personality so much as they enable them to flourish. Chesterton first acquired these sentiments from his native love of the English shires, the "merry England" of Chaucer and the Middle Ages. These loyalties were later reinforced by his conversion to Roman Catholicism. Dogmas provided the means for spiritual growth within salutary bounds, just as patriotic loyalty to his homeland overcame the imperialist impulse to conquer other nations and peoples. So did the sacraments enable him to resist the Puritan denial of the earth's earthiness. In similar fashion, a snug and toasty homeliness undergirding convention and routine helped him stanch any desire to dissolve thick English particularity into the bland broth of cosmopolitanism.[18] During the first decade of the twentieth century, it is fair to say, Chesterton espoused a modest and Liberal kind of Christian patriotism—a religious loyalty to England that, as Stapleton notes, was "best enhanced by consciousness of national weakness and vulnerability rather than strength."[19]

Chesterton the Disenchanted Liberal

Gradually, however, Chesterton found himself to be an outsider to British electoral politics—disenchanted with left and right alike, especially as the old Liberals devolved into the new Labourites and as the old Tories became new Conservatives. He believed that both parties increasingly ignored the real plight of the common people. Chesterton undertook his own journalistic campaign on behalf of this silent throng, the anonymous masses whom he hoped would rise up against their collectivist and capitalist overlords. In one of his most stirring poems, "The Secret People" (1908), he spoke vehemently in their stead:

Smile at us, pay us, pass us; but do not quite forget.
For we are the people of England, that never have spoken yet.

. . .

There are no folk in the whole world so helpless or so wise.
There is hunger in our bellies, there is laughter in our eyes;
You laugh at us and love us, and both mugs and eyes are wet:
Only you do not know us. For we have not spoken yet.[20]

Though Chesterton had a large following among the cultured readers of the various newspapers for which he wrote, there was never any groundswell of revolt among the industrialized masses. He supported their labor unions, but he became increasingly convinced that the higher wages that they bargained for were but a higher form of slavery to their employers.[21] Hence the increasing shrillness—indeed, the considerable unreality—of Chesterton's mystical ideal of Englishness:

> . . . England is not of this world. [The true patriot] is not obliged to cling to the imaginary merits of his country, for he did not take her on her merits. . . . He will not . . . swallow any such insanity as that England is politically more efficient than the Continent. . . . To him England will cry not any of the pompous appeals to lead the race or reform the world which she cried to Kipling and Henley; she will cry the words of that very old English song:
>
> > Love me still and know not why,
> > So hast thou the same reason still
> > To dote on me for ever.[22]

That this anonymous seventeenth-century ditty is intended for a woman and not a nation is nothing to the point. For Chesterton, our *patria*—no less than our family and our religion—should remain one of our tripartite loves. It was such love for his own native land that made Chesterton a fierce opponent of British imperialism. He opposed it on the grounds that English culture and politics were unique to the people who forged them, making them unsuitable for export to other milieux. Christianity alone, he argued, is able to produce such distinctively self-bounded cultures that are not predatory on other peoples, whether far or near. He regarded Muslims, by contrast, as homeless desert dwellers whose crescent moon seeks always to increase, encircling and enveloping other peoples, while Jews are perpetual exiles whose loyalty to their host nation always remains tentative. Neither Judaism nor Islam, he argued, can produce distinctive nations because they are not rooted in the salutary limits of time and place, of blood and soil.[23]

As we shall see, gross moral and theological errors lurk in these evocations of *Blut und Erde*. Yet there is nothing remotely totalitarian about Chesterton's politics. He forecast, with horror, the rise of Hitler. Nor was his momentary fascination with Mussolini in any way Fascist. And while modern Israel and certain Arab states prove Chesterton ludicrously wrong about Christianity as the sole source of true nationhood,[24] his scorn for imperialism was prophetically right, since British aggression against the Boer Republics was yet another instance of the omnivorous modern state seeking to expand its dominion. Chesterton believed that England had already made this mistake in India, just as other European nations had committed the same error—with far more horrible results—in Africa, South America, and Asia.

Chesterton upheld patriotism, like traditionalism, as a far healthier sentiment than cosmopolitanism and presentism. "Being proud of your country," he wrote, "is only like being proud of your father or your friend; it is not, in the spiritual and evil sense, really pride at all. But being proud of yourself for being a citizen of that country is really using something else as an excuse for being proud of yourself."[25] "The patriot," he also declared, "never under any circumstances boasts of the largeness of his country. I think always of the smallness of it."[26] True patriots and traditionalists are grounded not in a tempestuous jingoism but in the rooted particularities of their own time and place. They are not likely to aggrandize themselves at the expense of others—as in the imperialism that Chesterton so roundly deplored—since they dwell in grateful attachment to the local goods that have enabled them to flourish. Love of one's own kith is coeval with human life itself—"deep, continuous and unconquerable," as Chesterton said.[27] Tradition, in turn, roots us in history:

> Tradition may be defined as an extension of the franchise. Tradition means giving votes to the most obscure of all classes, our ancestors. It is the democracy of the dead. Tradition refuses to submit to the small and arrogant oligarchy of those who merely happen to be walking about. All democrats object to men being disqualified by the accident of birth; tradition objects to their being disqualified by the accident of death.[28]

Kindred loves are the source of the corporate identity and solidarity that become the basis for a common culture and heritage. "Through acknowledged obligations expressed in laws and institutions," Daniel Jenkins observes, a people "have been trained to live together and care for each other as, in effect, members of one extended family."[29] These family-like links give rise to the establishment of such common goods as social services and public education. Only as one has a tradition of one's own, moreover, can one respect and honor other traditions.

There is no loving and understanding the other whom one has not seen without loving and understanding the neighbor whom one sees virtually every day.

Yet patriotism and tradition are not unambiguous goods. Many things ancient are oppressive, and fealty to the fatherland can be the notorious hideout of miscreants. As Jenkins insists, unless a salutary attachment to one's own place and people is at once bounded and animated by faith in the triune God whose aims always transcend and often contradict the nation's interests, a recrudescent paganism is likely to be the result:

> Paganism originally arose as the worship of the gods of hearth and home, . . . because good hearths and homes deserve to be cherished and the natural piety of a religious people leads them to love them dearly. This is why, from Abraham onwards, the Bible reserves its sternest warnings for those who are in danger of surrendering to this particular temptation [of pagan idolatry].[30]

Not only must Christians vigilantly refuse any conflation of the well-being of their country and the Kingdom of God; they must also willingly concede the considerable "amount of justice . . . in the position of those who seem to stand in the way of [their own] nation's aim." "[T]here must always be a tension," Jenkins adds, "between national loyalty and religious commitment. Where there is no consciousness of tension, someone is being unfaithful."[31] To paraphrase Alasdair MacIntyre, we must ask *whose* tradition and *which* patriotism must be embraced in order not to idolize one's own tribe.

In extolling the medieval virtues of "little England," Chesterton sought to address precisely this problem—the idolatrous self-aggrandizement of imperial Britain. What he did not recognize is that the politics of medieval Christendom led, though inadvertently, to the rise of the modern nation-state that tends to subvert *all* deeply rooted tradition and religiously chastened patriotism. A distinctively Christian polity had already been compromised during the late Middle Ages. Prior to Charlemagne, St. Augustine's *temporal* division between the cities of God and Man—between the present Babylon and the Jerusalem that is yet to come—was reconfigured as a *functional* distinction between royal and priestly power. These two authorities were to rule conjointly, each according to its proper office, so as to form a single social order—albeit with the final weight tilting toward the sacerdotal rather than the civil. In the schema of the fifth-century Pope Gelasius, for example, the *potestas* of king and emperor lay outside the Empire, since all true *auctoritas* resided solely within the Body of Christ.³²

The Carolingian period marked a decided shift away from this early medieval distinction, as the two "swords" came to be redefined by analogy with the two-natures Christology of Chalcedon. No longer was the Church the sole Body of Christ. Instead, the dual offices of king and bishop were said to correspond to the two natures of Christ himself—human and divine, neither confused nor separated. Kingship and empire were thus fused together with the Church, as the temporal ruler was now endowed with such titles such as "Vicar of Christ" as well as "King and Priest." The papal anointing of the king acquired a sacramental significance comparable to that of baptism and ordination. In this Carolingian reconfiguration, the king "exercised his office of ruling wholly within the church, as a kind of lay ministry or charism," writes Oliver O'Donovan. "With this "change from 'world' to 'church,'" O'Donovan remarks, "the last consciousness of a notional distinction between the two societies had disappeared; one could no longer say that the ruler ruled Christians *qua* civil society but not *qua* heavenly city."³³

Ernst Kantorowicz traces this slow but fateful evolution by showing how the word *patria* shifted in meaning from classical Antiquity ("the aggregate of all the political, religious, ethical, and moral values for which a man might care to live and die") to the early Middle Ages, when it became "an almost obsolete political entity." Due to the emergence of more "personal" relations between lord and vassal, the force of *patria* was removed from the political realm, having its only real currency in poetry and in the diminished sense of "the native hamlet, village, township, or province"—something akin to "the French *pays* or the German *Heimat*." *Patria* lost its "broader politico-philosophic background," Kantorowicz argues, so that "patriotism" came to require a "private rather than a public sacrifice." Early medieval warriors still regarded themselves as making religious oblation in *fides* and *fidelitas*, but they offered up their lives in a fashion unrecognizable to the noble paganism of Horace—namely, "*pro domino*, not *pro patria*."³⁴

During these prime medieval centuries, the Church preserved the Roman notion of *patria* in order to name the "*communia patris* in heaven" for which "the martyrs had shed their blood." Kantorowicz interprets this ecclesial transformation of *patria* as a transfer of "the political notion of *polis* to the other world" and thus as its expansion into "a *regnum coelorum*." The Christian's true *patria* was understood as belonging to the Kingdom of God rather than earthly empires. One effect of this veritable reversal of the pagan order was that the Church "not only faithfully stored and preserved the political ideas of the ancient world, as so often it did, but also prepared new ideas for the time when the secular world began to recover its former peculiar [i.e., sub-Christian] values." By the time of Charlemagne, as we have seen, this pillaging of Church doctrine for state usage had already happened. Though the Church had sacralized *patria* as the Fatherland governed by God, the state gradually usurped the term for its own worldly politics, while still imbuing it with the aura of divinity.[35]

Kantorowicz tracks the consequences of this cataclysmic shift: the new justification of taxes (no longer for "holy" wars but for general defense), the new investing of the earthly fatherland with emotional and religious "sacredness," and above all the gradual emergence of a drastic new idea of glory. Having been attached to knights who sacrificed themselves for the cause of God, glory was altered in order to signify the honor won by knights dying for the sake of their feudal lord, until finally the late medieval warrior came to achieve renown by surrendering his life on behalf of the emerging nation-state. Thus, according to Kantorowicz, did "the Christian virtue of *caritas* become unmistakably political." The notion of *patria* was utterly transfigured in order "to sanctify and justify, ethically and morally, the death [suffered] for the political 'fatherland.'"[36]

The long-term result of this nightmarish change—since it would eventually produce our ghoulish culture of death—is the emergence of independent and sovereign states, each now identified with a particular nation, language, tradition, and culture. Stephen Toulmin observes that the chief aim of these new nation-states is not to enhance the flourishing of their citizens within communal relations so much as to express and protect a monolithic thing called the national will and the national interest.[37] Thus did Frederick the Great boast that his people were free to say what *they* liked, so long as he was free to do what *he* liked. Among other critics of the modern nation-state, Simon Oliver has shown that its politics is hagridden by the incubus of nominalism—the notion that universals exist only in name, not in reality. From Hobbes through the American Founders to Rousseau and the Utilitarians, society is often regarded as the supreme fiction, an essentially human construct, an imaginary social contract of self-interested individuals whose natural relation to each other is strife, and whose moral governance is thus remanded to the nation-state. As Oliver writes,

> Social contracts are established whereby individuals give over to the central State or the monarch the means of violence and coercion . . . in exchange for the State's guarantee of the safety and rights of individuals. . . . That sovereign authority promises to keep peace through coercion in the form of law and punishment. Social relations are now mediated through politics, the law and economics, all made possible by the contract with the central, sovereign power. Religion becomes an entirely private matter and, indeed, the Church becomes a department of state and subject to the regulative and jurisdictional power of the sovereign. Leviathan swallows the Church.[38]

Chesterton the Distributist

Chesterton did not fail to remark this gargantuan shift, even if he did not always protest against it. Alas, he often adopted the nominalist kind of nationalism that we have heard Kantorowicz lamenting: "It is the vice of any patriotism or religion depending on race," Chesterton wrote in 1920, "that the individual is himself the thing to be worshipped; the individual is his own ideal, and even his own idol. . . . This is not so when the nation is felt as a noble abstraction, of which the individual is proud in the abstract."[39] Gradually but ever more certainly, he came to recognize that the monolithic nation-state of his own Great Britain was becoming monstrous, most especially in its worship of economic profit and imperialist acquisition.

From William Cobbett, Chesterton acquired the conviction that the triumph of the profit motive reverses one of the most basic human relationships, turning cooperation into competition. Something fundamental was lost when actual goods and services ceased to be the communal means of exchange and were replaced by abstract and impersonal money.[40] Chesterton also saw that it is based on "the vast legal fiction that we call finance."[41] Modern commercial culture based on getting and spending lays waste to Britain's moral and spiritual powers, as Wordsworth famously complained. Unlike many other Liberals, Chesterton did not admire John Stuart Mill and Jeremy Bentham as the prophets of democratic freedom; instead, he scorned them as the grim Utilitarian successors to their grim Puritan forebears. They were advocates of the New Poor Law of 1834, for instance, that left men politically free but practically imprisoned in workhouses.[42] Like Adam Smith and David Ricardo before them, the Utilitarians were heralds of the Industrial Revolution, of Manchester and Birmingham and Leeds, and thus of the ugly new cities and factories that reduced men and women and even children to mere commercial units. Though living a century later, Chesterton agreed with Cobbett:

> What he saw was not an Eden that cannot exist but rather an Inferno that can exist, and even that does exist. What he saw was the perishing of the whole English power of self support, the growth of cities that drain and dry up the countryside, the growth of dense dependent populations incapable of finding their own food, the toppling triumph of machines over men, the sprawling omnipotence of finances over patriots, the herding of humanity in nomadic masses whose very homes are homeless, the terrible necessity of peace and the terrible probability of war, all the loading up of our little island like a sinking ship; the wealth that may mean famine and the culture that may mean despair; the bread of Midas and the sword of Damocles.[43]

In one of his most astute exercises in cultural criticism, *The Victorian Age in Literature*, Chesterton argued that, in the years following the Reform Bill of 1832, the British political establishment succeeded in staving off the radical social renewal that could have led to a larger realization of the freedom that God intends for every human being. Entrenched aristocrats joined the newly rich bourgeoisie to prevent the masses from gaining any real power of self-determination. The "cold Victorian compromise,"[44] as Chesterton called it, stifled what should have been a drastic reordering of British political life. This quiet "revolution of the rich" was characterized by a brazen silence, a mute collusion of the upper and middle classes to deafen themselves to the Luddite cry of the poor:

An atmosphere was being generated not exactly like anything else that had ever existed or perhaps will ever exist again. . . . It was not exactly a creed or a cause, or even a spirit; the nearest is to say that it was a silence. . . . There was a silent understanding in the aristocracy that it would not really resist the invasion of the middle class. There was a silent alliance between the two that neither would really think about that third thing which moved in the depths visible for instance in burning hayricks and broken machines.[45]

Chesterton's literary heroes were those morally passionate Victorian Liberals who shouted an awakening alarm to break the shameful silence. Browning and Stevenson, Ruskin and Carlyle, but especially Dickens—they all refused any stultifying rapprochement with the establishment. Such writers were unafraid to mount their political pulpits, there to proclaim their abiding concern for the poor. Like his literary champions, Chesterton himself regarded the destitute not as an abstract and "surplus" class, but as his own countrymen whom he encountered in the streets and lanes and shops of London. His friend W. R. Titterton reported that GKC scandalized Fabian socialists like himself in having a deep respect for,

nay, . . . a fiery affection for, the average sensual man, whom we democrats regarded as our bitterest and most contemptible enemy. He exalted cabbies and carpenters and charwomen and fishermen and farm labourers, and was on pally terms even with small shopkeepers, farmers, and country squires. He visited the slum, not slumming, but hob-nobbing; and he found everything there admirable except the slum. If he had kept this sort of stuff for his poems it wouldn't have been so bad; but he made it a fighting philosophy.[46]

Chesterton followed the practice of his literary Liberal forebears without apology—thundering, for example, against the imperialism of Cecil Rhodes and Rudyard Kipling,[47] the jingoism of the Boer War,[48] the eugenics attempt to prevent the "mentally defective" from marrying, and (perhaps most vehemently) the gross commercialism that sapped England's moral and spiritual strength.

Like Belloc, Chesterton regarded the Liberalism that had begun to emerge among the Edwardians as a deadly abandonment of his old Liberal ideals. In an alleged concern for the impoverished, these new Liberals were in fact oligarchs and plutocrats who formed a new governing class that held the poor in secret contempt. "A philanthropist," he acidly observed in 1923, "may be said to love anthropoids."[49] Like Shaw and Wells, the new Liberals began to look to the interventionist state for solutions to inveterate human ills. Their cures struck Chesterton as being worse than the disease; indeed, as symptoms of a phantasmagoric sickness unto death. Patronizing oppressors of impoverished commoners ignored the actual lives of those whom they sought to help.[50] These wretched objects of governmental largesse became pawns for realizing the putative goods promoted by the enlightened. Hence the explosive resentment of the poor: "If the barricades went up in our streets and the poor became masters, I think the priests would escape, I fear the gentlemen would; but I believe the gutters would be simply running with the blood of philanthropists."[51]

Chesterton's critique of the state-sponsored socialism of the Fabians must not to be mistaken as a rejection of socialist ideals *tout court*. Race Mathews has demonstrated that Chesterton and Belloc were unwavering communitarians. They were inveterately socialist in their morals, even if they were unyieldingly antistatist in their politics. Thus did they cast about for a new term to describe their own kind of socialism, and Distributism was the name they gave it. They regarded Distributism as the only distinctively Christian answer to what Belloc called the Servile State.[52] Belloc argued that both oligarchic capitalism and statist socialism were producing a new generation of *voluntary* slaves—unlike ancient pagan civilizations, where slaves had no choice but submission.[53] Hence Belloc's vision of the two economic schemes as equally collectivist and thus as equally oppressive:

> Collectivism promises employment to the great mass who think of production only in terms of employment. It promises to its workmen the security which a great and well-organized industrial capitalist (like one of our railways) can give through a system of pensions, regular promotions, etc., but that security [is] vastly increased through the fact that it is the state and not a mere unit of the state which guarantees it. Collectivism would administer, would pay wages, would promote, would pension off, would fine—all the rest of it—exactly as the capitalist does today. The proletarian, when the collectivist (or socialist) state is put before him, perceives nothing in the pictures save certain ameliorations of his present position.[54]

Such clear distinctions have often been muddied by a false reading of Belloc and Chesterton, as if they had sent plagues of equal virulence upon socialists and capitalists alike. And since, during the several decades following Chesterton's death, capitalism seems to have issued in a rebirth of economic opportunity for myriads, while socialism seems to have pauperized millions with its hugely expensive and oppressive bureaucracies, Chesterton is thought most surely to stand on the side of the capitalists. It is not so. Like Belloc, he regarded laissez-faire capitalism as an anti-Christian abomination.[55] Chesterton's critique of unbridled capitalism as a system that encourages greed—sanctioning not economic cooperation among neighbors but a competitive gouging of each by all—was unstinting from beginning to end. The radical claim he made in *Orthodoxy* (1908) he would never repudiate:

> The whole case for Christianity is that a man who is dependent upon the luxuries of this life is a corrupt man, spiritually corrupt, politically corrupt, financially corrupt. There is one thing that Christ and all the Christian saints have said with a sort of savage monotony. They have said simply that to be rich is to be in peculiar danger of moral wreck.[56]

As fellow Catholics, Chesterton and Belloc were inspired by the economic claims made in the encyclicals *Rerum Novarum* (1891) and *Quadregismo Anno* (1931), both of which insisted on the practices of solidarity and subsidiarity. They argued that the infused Christian virtue of justice must be understood, as Aquinas had taught, not only as "reciprocal or mutually exchanged" justice on the one hand, nor solely as "general or legal" justice on the other, but also as "distributive" justice in the sense specified by Josef Pieper:

> Nothing that belongs to [the individual is] exclusively his . . . ; all that belongs to him is a share of something common to everyone. . . . *Iustitia distributiva* means to let individual members of a nation share in the realization of a *bonum commune* that cannot be definitively delineated in concrete terms. Taking part in the realization of that good in accordance with the measure of *dignitas*, capacity, and ability that is distinctively his, this is the share which is "due to" the individual. . . . This suggests . . . that all the good things in creation (men's capacities and abilities) belong to the good of the community, and that *iustitia distributiva* entails the obligation of granting such abilities [the] protection, support, and fostering [that] they need.[57]

Joined by Cardinal Henry Edward Manning, who had converted to Catholicism and become Archbishop of Westminster, as well as the Dominican priest Vincent McNabb, the artist Eric Gill, and Chesterton's brother Cecil—among other kindred spirits—Belloc and GKC set themselves against the Fabian socialists led by Sidney and Beatrice Webb as well as by Shaw and Wells. The Fabians held that too much property belonged to too few individuals, that it should be increasingly put into the hands of the state, and that the large accumulation of capital deriving from such premises and estates should be allocated equitably within the populace. For Chesterton the Distributist, such a socialist scheme replaced one kind of incubus with another. Their grim communism was a grim reflection of capitalism. He thus lamented the Fabians' insistence on "the centralisation of wealth and, its corollary, the abolition of private property. It is immaterial that they differ on where they wish to centralise this wealth—Communism in the state, and Capitalism in the hands of the most powerful plutocrats; both succeed in crushing the small individual by taking his property from him."[58]

The Distributists agreed with authentic socialists that the right allocation of private property was the essential problem. "It is the negation of property," Chesterton wrote in 1910, "that the Duke of Sutherland should have all the farms in one estate; just as it would be the negation of marriage if he had all our wives in one harem."[59] Yet the Distributists rejected state-managed socialism as the solution to grossly unjust ownership. Resorting again to the metaphor of the seraglio, Chesterton wrote in 1924, "To say we must have Socialism or Capitalism is like saying we must choose between all men going into monasteries and a few men having harems."[60] He and Belloc and their fellow Distributists proposed, instead, to redistribute *property* rather than money, as well as restoring a modern version of the guild system whereby the workers would also be the possessors of their companies. They sought to apply the Catholic principle of subsidiarity to families and small communities via the free possession of small properties and the free management of modest work.

Distributism was a sacramental matter for Chesterton. As we have heard the *nouvelle* theologians declaring, Jesus Christ is the sacrament of humanity. "Man requires a sphere of action in which he can act creatively and freely," writes Ian Boyd. "Without property, he is unable to exercise his own will and control his own business. Property provides the incarnational character which is essential to human liberty."[61] Hence Chesterton's strong Distributist proclamation from 1911:

> Property is the sacramental solidification of liberty. Property is to liberty what arithmetic is to algebra, what art is to beauty or, if I may use the highest example what Christ is to God. It is an embodiment which is in some sense a limitation; as every Christmas carol contains the suggestion that the Incarnation itself is a sort of colossal limitation.... Liberty without property is aimlessness ... property is simply the achievement of its aim. It is narrow in the sense that all creation is narrow; as all art is limitation because it is selection. In this sense it is not unnatural that those Utopians who are communist in politics are generally pantheist in philosophy, while the Utopia of Christendom has been the Distributist State.[62]

That this radical renovation of British economic life would be as sweeping and stern as the changes wrought by the French Revolution, and that such a drastic reordering would require "awful and inhuman sacrifices" to overcome the macabre injustices of capitalism, Chesterton had no doubt. Yet a Distributist world would not be monochrome; on the contrary, it would have immense color and diversity:

> [D]ifferent things of different types [would be held] on different tenures: that as in a medieval state there were some peasants, some monasteries, some common land, some private land, some town guilds, and so on, so in my modern state there would be some things nationalized, some machines owned corporately, some guilds sharing common profits, and so on, as well as many absolute individual owners, where such individual owners are most possible. But with these latter it is well to begin, because they are meant to give, and nearly always do give, the standard and tone of the society.[63]

Against those who complained that the Distributists sought a naïve return to a simple agrarian past, and thus to an economic scheme impossible to achieve in an urbanized commercial culture, Chesterton replied, "Even while we remain industrial, we can work towards industrial distribution and away from industrial monopoly. Even while we live in town houses, we can own town houses. Even while we are a nation of shopkeepers, we can try to own our shops. Even while we are the workshop of the world, we can try to own our tools."[64]

Hence his attempt to deliver small families and communities from the monstrous double-headed Leviathan of monopolistic capitalism and statist socialism.

The Distributist summons to a sacrificial solidarity with others was not naïve about the fallenness of human nature. Chesterton famously declared, on the contrary, that original sin is the one empirically demonstrable Christian doctrine. As Catholic Christians, he and Belloc confessed that the burden of sin weighs heavily and selfishly on every human being. Aquinas gave a name to our ingrained self-regard. He called it the *fomes peccati*, the tinderbox of sin. It kindles our lack of generosity toward others and our refusal of friendship with God. Distributive justice is a summons, by contrast, to a new commonality that enables a friendly sharing of goods. As Herbert McCabe explains, it requires us to surrender our own merely private good for the sake of the common good understood as social friendship, a polity that values others for their specific virtues: "For Aristotle and Aquinas human society is based on something deeper than justice, the human solidarity we call *philia*, which is the necessary context of justice. To get a true perspective on our fellow-animals, what we need is not an analogue of social justice but of social *philia*."[65]

Many of Chesterton's strongest advocates decry his immense investment of time and money and talent in the largely failed Distributist project. They lament the loss of the allegedly more enduring works of fiction and poetry and cultural criticism that he might have otherwise written. What these laments ignore is that Distributism was a matter of Chesterton's Christian vocation. It was not one project among others but, in many ways, the central effort of his life. For him and his closest friends, Distributism was an indispensable means of maintaining the two Cities in their proper relation. Both socialism and capitalism—as worldly systems incapable of being ordered to the eternal virtues—seek to create a single and omnipotent City of Man. They inexorably reduce Christianity to a religious hobby, diminishing the City of God to a private realm entered mostly on Sundays if at all. This secular City, whether socialist or capitalist, is a totalizing regime that demands no religious interference. The nation-state tolerates the Church so long as the Body of Christ offers no drastic critique of government policy, especially in matters economic and military.

Distributism, by contrast, enables the Church to make its unique witness to the world by fostering what McCabe calls a "social *philia*," rather than being confined to a religious ghetto. It is a Christian kind of economics aimed at helping even non-Christians to recognize every other human being as the neighbor (etymologically "the nigh-one"), and thus as a creature worthy of our friendship, indeed as necessary to our own well-being.

Chesterton and the Distributists challenge the Church to supply the positive motives and the saving virtues that are notably absent from what Stephen Clark calls "the Laodicean mood that best defines modernity . . . that nothing is worth dying for but life is not worth living."[66] "There is but an inch of difference," as Chesterton observed, "between the cushioned chamber and the padded cell."[67] Our madness is socially no less than individually destructive:

> The modern problem is more and more the problem of keeping the company together at all. . . . [It is a] division of heart masked by a certain heartiness in the modern pursuit of mere games and pleasures; but you cannot in some dark hour of peril ask thousands to die for the Derby or even to be taxed to death for the International Golf Championship.[68]

The failure of the Distributist project to find long-term adherents cannot be made grounds for dismissing it, especially when noting its long-term accuracy about the coming cataclysm of European culture.[69] Chesterton's prophecy of the horrendous breakdown of modern industrialized society anticipated the work of such later twentieth-century critics as Marshall McLuhan and E. F. Schumacher, Ivan Illich and Jacques Ellul, as well as the American Agrarians and Wendell Berry. Nor is Distributism a dead article. John Médaille offers this updated version of it that remains faithful to its founders:

> Distributism posits that the economy works better when productive property—the land, tools, and education needed to produce things for the economy—[is] widely spread throughout the population. It is the theory of small property, rather than large accumulations of capital. Under such a system, a person would have the option of making his or her own way in the world, or joining with his neighbors in larger enterprises, or of working for somebody else. And since he always has the option of working for himself, any wage he negotiates to work for another is more likely to be a fair wage.[70]

Though the Distributists were at once radical and semianarchist in their roots, Jay Corrin argues that they were essentially conservative in their vision, since they "looked to the past for social and political models, recognized man as a fallen creature, and appreciated the practical necessity of hierarchy, social deference, religion, and strong family ties."[71] Yet "conservative" is not a synonym for "reactionary," as Chesterton himself had already announced in his 1903 essay on Tennyson: "He is only a very shallow critic who cannot see an eternal rebel in the heart of a conservative."[72] T. S. Eliot, despite his own devotion to Tory politics, also emphasized the nonreactionary character of Chesterton's Distributism in this summary judgment of GKC's entire career:

> [Even if Chesterton's] revolutionary designs appear to be totally without effect, even if they should be demonstrated to be wrong—which would perhaps only mean that men have not the good will to carry them out—they were *the* ideas for his time that were fundamentally Christian and Catholic. He did more, I think, than any man of his time . . . to maintain the existence of the important minority in the modern world.[73]

Chesterton as the Poet of Christian Patriotism

Chesterton achieved such a salutary enhancement of the Christian witness in the modern world—not one witness among others, as Eliot's definite article declares the Church to be *the* "important minority"—only because he underwent a drastic political change in the second and third decades of the new century. As he gradually lost faith in Liberalism as a parliamentary program that would achieve the common good through electoral politics, Chesterton's work became increasingly and unapologetically Christian—though no less political, as we have seen. His remarkable devotion to Distributism as a Christian project was presaged early in his career with the penning of his two great hymns. They are both centered on the question of the Church's relation to the state, and thus on the issue of divine justice as it is exercised through political and even military action. Yet they are utterly different in both tone and substance.

In 1906 Ralph Vaughan Williams set Chesterton's most celebrated religious lyric, titled simply "A Hymn," to the spirited tune of "King's Lynn." The drumbeat quality of these lines, together with their martial melody, makes for a theologically problematic work, though it is often extolled for expressing a properly Christian patriotism.[74] Chesterton pleads not on behalf of the Church so much as the nation, perhaps as he remembers the recently concluded Boer War:[75]

O God of earth and altar,
    Bow down and hear our cry,
Our earthly rulers falter,
    Our people drift and die;
The walls of gold entomb us,
    The swords of scorn divide,
Take not thy thunder from us,
    But take away our pride.

From all that terror teaches,
    From lies of tongue and pen,
From all the easy speeches
    That comfort cruel men,
For sale and profanation
    Of honour and the sword,
From sleep and from damnation,
    Deliver us, good Lord.

Tie us in a living tether
    The prince and priest and thrall,
Bind all our lives together,
    Smite us and save us all;
In ire and exultation
    Aflame with faith, and free,
Lift up a living nation,
    A single sword to thee.[76]

This vivid hymn is a poignant plea for divine deliverance, beseeching the one and only Help against stumbling political shepherds as well as their sheep-like followers.[77] Chesterton laments England's entombing riches as well as its schismatic strife, asking God to remove the nation's arrogance but not to blunt its divine urgency—the thunderous might that should be exercised, presumably, in defense of righteous causes. Herein lies the beginning of trouble: To what extent can any nation visit the fury of God upon other nations? The question goes unanswered. Instead, we hear a petition (in the second stanza) for rescue from false fear of enemies, from counterfeit orators and truth-trimming journalists, from soft comforts that are in fact hard cruelties. Again the monetary metaphor recurs, referring perhaps to the sale of military honors that desecrate men at arms, as the word *sword* is repeated. Even so, these first two stanzas could be sung on almost any national holiday, especially with their ringing penitential iteration of the litany from the Book of Common Prayer: "Deliver us, good Lord."

The final stanza seems to maintain the necessary tension between divine wrath and divine mercy, as God is implored to unite the nation by at once striking it down in righteous wrath but also lifting it up in divine glory. Yet the hymn moves steadily toward the wedding of religion and state and populace into an indivisible whole. Chesterton thus has deliberate recourse to the myth of a perfectly realized Christendom. He even resorts to the old word *thrall*, meaning "villein" or "serf," in order to make the hymn redolent of the Middle Ages and the Crusades. Hence his evocation of the three medieval estates: those who prayed, those who fought, those who "delved and span."[78] It is noteworthy that Chesterton reverses the ancient order of the first two, placing the ruler before the clergy, while summoning the obedient masses to put themselves in the service of both their realm and its Church. Knit inseparably together, the three constitute God's militant Company—fulminating at things despicable, delighting in things glorious, keeping alive the Faith that ensures human liberty. Yet again, unavoidable questions arise: How is such liberty to be defined—by rendering unto Caesar and Christ a virtually identical fealty? What dangers, indeed what heresies, are inherent in declaring any people—not only ancient and undispersed Israel, but especially a modern nation-state such as the United Kingdom—to be the instrument of God's own exalted, saber-thrusting Militancy?[79]

Faithful answers to these questions are to be found in "A Hymn for the Church Militant."

> Great God, that bowest sky and star,
> Bow down our towering thoughts to thee,
> And grant us in a faltering war
> The firm feet of humility.

Lord, we that snatch the swords of flame,
Lord, we that cry about Thy car,
We too are weak with pride and shame,
We too are as our foemen are.

Yea, we are mad as they are mad,
Yea, we are blind as they are blind,
Yea, we are very sick and sad
Who bring good news to all mankind.

The dreadful joy Thy Son has sent
Is heavier than any care.
We find, as Cain his punishment,
Our pardon more than we can bear.

Lord, when we cry Thee far and near
And thunder through all lands unknown
The gospel into every ear,
Lord, let us not forget our own.

Cleanse us from ire of creed or class,
The anger of the idle kings;
Sow in our souls, like living grass,
The laughter of all lowly things.[80]

This is surely one of Chesterton's noblest works. It grasps the precise relation of the *ecclesia militans* to the *ecclesia triumphans*. The former is the struggling rather than the conquering people of God; it is the suffering Body of Christ that remains *in via*. The "faltering war" perhaps refers again to the South African bloodshed in the British attack on the Boers, though it may also point to the perennial twilight battle against evil fought by all people of good will. Only in the life to come shall such wavering combat against the principalities and powers cease, as the Church will finally enjoy the victorious Beatific Vision. Chesterton pleads with the God to whom all knees shall bow, as even the planets and the Empyrean humble themselves before him, asking that the Deity might also bring low the Babel-like presumptions of men, replacing their crumbling ziggurats with the firmness of the *humus*, the common dirt from which we are made, to which we return, and through which we receive a summons to true humility.[81]

Instead of a righteous insistence that we are fighting on God's side, as if we were the mighty criers and forerunners of the Lord's own chariot ("car"), there is instead a confession of our own "pride and shame," our false self-assertion and true humiliation. No longer do we lift up our own sabers; instead, the angels guarding the eastern Gates of Eden wield the "swords of flame." They forbid our reentrance into the lost Paradise, lest in our fallenness we eat of the Tree of Life and thus become ever more monstrous, haughtily snatching at things for which we are unfit, wickedly seizing power that makes us no better than our worst enemies. On the contrary, we are as unseeing and deranged as our adversaries. We are purveyors of the ill tidings of our own moral sickness—we *English* (and by extension, *American*) Christians who are the very fount of the Protestant missionary movement that proclaimed the Gospel to those whom Kipling called "lesser breeds without the Law." Hence the startling reversal of Kipling's pseudo-humble cry of "Lest we forget." Whereas in "Recessional" the martial poet of the Empire calls for England to remember that the "Lord God of Hosts" guarantees the victory of his holy armies, Chesterton beseeches God to prevent the Church that so confidently propagates the Gospel in foreign lands from overlooking the extent of its own unconversion.[82]

Already in this early poem Chesterton had begun to envision the nightmare quality of the love of God, the glad tidings that bring a terrible fear and trembling, the deliverance from sin and guilt that remains so drastic that it makes Cain prefer condemnation and death to exoneration and life. As the one utterly undeserved and thus absolutely obligating Gift, it summons all men to the inexhaustible gratitude that turned the illustrious Francesco Bernardone into the lowly St. Francis of Assisi: "It is the highest and holiest of the paradoxes that the man who really knows he cannot pay his debt will be for ever paying it. He will be for ever giving back what he cannot give back, and cannot be expected to give back. He will be always throwing things away into the bottomless pit of unfathomable thanks."[83] Hence the joyful meekness of Chesterton's last stanza. To be purged of the false fury of condemnation as well as the false superiority of rank is also to be freed from false dogmas—that is, from those political and economic systems that, like oligarchic capitalism and statist socialism, serve to demean and diminish humankind.[84] "Idle kings" are our rulers, perhaps even our democratically elected leaders, who grow militarily restive because they and we have become spiritually indolent. In a comic reprise of Isaiah 40, Chesterton declares the one thing requisite that only the Church can offer the world: a discernment of our kinship with the lowliest of plants. We are like the grass whose greenness withers, whose beauty fades. Yet we are also unlike the herbs that can neither laugh nor weep. Much less can they join us in rejoicing at our own evanescence. As creatures made in the image of God, we have also been remade according to the one thing that will never wilt and die: "the word of our God [that] stands forever" (Isa 40:8).

The Church's Awakening Cry to the World

Chesterton's last books give overt theological expression to this early intimation of orthodoxy. They contain his most vigorous defenses (together with his confession of its manifold sins and wickedness) of the only Community that will prevail against all enemies and that thus serves as God's own politics. The *ecclesia militans* triumphs not by running roughshod over its opponents, but by offering them incorporation into its own life. Truly pluralistic in its economics and politics, its cultures and ethnicities, it also remains universal in its final unity: the Body of Christ. The best of Chesterton's late work is devoted to the City of God in its right relation to the City of Man. Though his imaginative work suffers a final falling off, some of GKC's best theological treatises come near the end: *The Catholic Church and Conversion* (1926), *The Thing: Why I Am a Catholic* (1929), *The Well and the Shallows* (1935).

Perhaps the most revealing of these late pieces is one of the least known, *Christendom in Dublin* (1932), a short account of his participation in the International Eucharistic Congress held in 1932. There he heard the awakening cry that shatters the brazen silence of a world tossing and thrashing amidst its own nightmare—a world that would soon be convulsed by a new and worse war, a war that would be global as the Great War was not. Chesterton was astonished that partisan politics played no part in this international celebration. The pageantry contained no emblems of "most of the civic rites of civilization." The great displays of color and light were also present in the slums no less than the thoroughfares. "It was like that celestial topsy-turvydom in which the first shall be last." "In that strange town [of Dublin]," he observes, "the poorer were the streets, the richer were the decorations." There were barely literate inscriptions and crudely drawn pictures hailing St. Patrick and praising Christ the King. Among all the flags from all the peoples and nations of the earth, one stood out above all others: the papal pennant.

> I looked again at the great gold-and-silver banner and suddenly forgot all the nonsense about national and political conquest; and the idiocy that imagines the Pope as landing on our shores with a pistol in each hand. I knew there was another Empire that has never declined nor fallen; and there rolled through the heavens of pure thought the thunder of the great Encyclicals, and the mind of the new Europe in which the new nations find that the Faith can make them free. The great flag began to flap and crackle in the freshening evening wind; and those who had been toiling on the little farm, those whose fathers had been hunted like vermin, those whose religion should have been burnt out like witchcraft, came back slowly through the twilight; walking like lords on their own land. . . . Whatever St. Dominic may have said in the irritation of the moment, I am not so sure that St. Peter has lost the power to say, "Rise and walk."[85]

Such a confession demonstrates that Chesterton had not turned the Church into an impossible ideal, a rarefied thing so pure that (like his lofty vision of England) it became more myth than reality. Quite to the contrary, Chesterton's radically reordered patriotism retains immense currency for our time. He has shown us, albeit by inadvertence, that dread brand of patriotic triumphalism toward which even the noblest ethnic and cultural patriotism will surely lead. Yet by way of a salutary directness, he has also pointed to the one universal Community that is meant not to poison men with pride but to heal them with humility. Because the Church militant will not become the Church triumphant until the End, true freedom always lies ahead. Chesterton had said it well in 1908: "[T]he mass of men always look backwards; . . . the only corner where they in any sense look forwards is the little continent where Christ has His Church."[86] The community of Christ casts its eye on the future, not only in eschatological expectation, but also in the conviction that the Kingdom already dwells in our midst, however sinfully and partially, via the struggling Church. For all its failings and contradictions, it remains the world's one truly revolutionary force. It constantly pushes the world forward toward a radical reordering of human desires. It alone has the power that is not weakness, the militancy that is not militarism, the awakening cry that is not a scream of desperation, the patriotism that gathers all people to their true *patria*.

As Chesterton slowly discerned the incapacity of the nation-state to be, even at best, anything more than the indirect bearer of the Kingdom's goods, he turned ever more surely toward his own true *patria*. His reconversion to the primacy and finality of the Church is made especially evident in the inscription that he chose for his and his wife's tombstone in Beaconsfield, a phrase from the final stanza of Thomas Aquinas' splendid Eucharistic hymn, "O Salutaris Hostia." The engraving asks those who visit the graves of Frances and Gilbert to pray, not for their earthly, but for their eternal vindication: *Vita sine termino nobis donet in Patria*, "Grant us life without end in the Fatherland."[87]

3

MILITARISM AND THE CHURCH MILITANT
Lepanto, Defense of World War I, and "The Truce of Christmas"

[I]t's vain to try to talk as if one weren't living in a nightmare of the
deepest dye. How can what is going on not be to one as a huge horror
of blackness? . . . The plunge of civilization into this abyss of blood
and darkness . . . is a thing that so gives away the whole long age during
which we have supposed the world to be, with whatever abatement,
gradually bettering, that to have to take it all now for what the
treacherous years were all the while really making for and *meaning*
is too tragic for words.
Henry James, in a letter dated August 4, 1914

Mute in the clamour of shells he watched them burst
Spouting the dark earth and wire with gusts from hell,
While posturing giants dissolved in drifts of smoke.
He crouched and flinched, dizzy with galloping fear,
Sick for escape, — loathing the strangled horror
And butchered, frantic gestures of the dead.
Siegfried Sassoon, "Counter-Attack" (1918)

We do not hold, no sane man has ever held, that war is a good thing. . . .
But we hold that occasion may arise when it is better for a man to fight
than to surrender. War is, in the main, a dirty, mean, inglorious business,
but it is not the direst calamity that can befall a people. There is one
worse state, at least: the state of slavery.
G. K. Chesterton, "On War and Peace" (1936)

"Of all the modern poets," Charles Williams declared in 1930, "there is only one whose verse is always full of the voice of battle, and that is Mr. Chesterton." "There are drawn swords from the first page to the last," Williams added, "material, intellectual, and spiritual. . . . Everything is spoken of in terms of war, either actual or potential. For even when there is no enemy the state of being described [by Chesterton] is a state where man is strung to a high pitch of expectation and his delight is already militant." In Chesterton's poetry as nowhere else in English verse, Williams concludes, man is a fighting animal who "must be either a hero or a coward."[1] What shall we make of so pugnacious a poet who is so Christian at the core? At his best, Chesterton's bellicosity marks him as a soldier in the army of the *ecclesia militans*. At his worst, it makes him the advocate of holy war. He believed that Christians must do armed battle—not only against heretics in defense of property and territory, of doctrines and beliefs—but also against other Christians who support allegedly heretical regimes. Any valid retrieval of Chesterton's work for our time must confront this troublous matter, not only as it is articulated in his fine militaristic poem, *Lepanto*, but also in his support of the Great War as a religious crusade, especially in *The Ballad of St. Barbara* as well as dozens of essays. Lest this critique of Chesterton's Christian militarism seem a smug recourse to convenient hindsight, I will also give careful attention to a remarkable Chesterton poem wherein he offers "a more excellent way" than holy war: "The Truce of Christmas." In this last instance, Chesterton envisions Christianity as a religion of peace and reconciliation rather than war and destruction—that is, as a militant but not a militaristic Faith.

Jesus and Francis as Embodiments of the "Pluckish" Ideal

Chesterton regarded St. Francis as the ultimate Christian, the perfect "Mirror of Christ." His book on the Little Poor Man of Assisi remains one of his finest accomplishments. Francis possessed the remarkable qualities, says Chesterton, "of gentle mockery of the very idea of possession; . . . of a hope of disarming the enemy by generosity; . . . of a humorous sense of bewildering the worldly with the unexpected; . . . of the joy of carrying an enthusiastic conviction to a logical extreme." Such unstinting peaceableness prompted the diminutive little mendicant from Umbria to embark on his own "bloodless crusade" in 1219, hoping to end the mutual slaughter of Christians and Muslims by attempting to convert the Egyptian sultan al-Kamil.[2]

Despite his salutary admiration of St. Francis, Chesterton regarded him, like Jesus, as the rare embodiment of an impossible ideal. Both the savior and the saint existed for him in a transcendent realm of almost complete otherness, serving as radical exceptions to the Church's necessary accommodations with worldly power, especially in the waging of war. Chesterton gladly affirmed that Jesus overturned many ancient and contemporary expectations—especially by calling his followers either to celibacy or else to monogamous marriage, and by engendering a mutuality among fellow believers that would eventually make slavery impossible. Yet in dealing with the single most destructive human activity, Chesterton insisted that Christ was utterly mute: "not a word about the wickedness of war, the wastefulness of war, the appalling scale of slaughter in war and all the rest of the familiar frenzy; indeed not a word about war at all."[3]

This argument from silence is so outrageous that it must be addressed, for neither did Jesus inveigh against child abuse, abortion, or incest. Some evils are too obvious to require reproof. Yet Chesterton is hardly the first to regard Jesus as upholding a set of impracticable ideals that he expects none of his disciples actually to achieve—for example, in his saying that Christians should turn the other cheek rather than striking back, and the command that his followers are to repay good (and not evil) for evil. The leading American Protestant theologian of the twentieth century, Reinhold Niebuhr, held this same conviction. He and Chesterton could not have been more antithetical in spirit and demeanor. Unlike the jovial and self-deflating GKC, Niebuhr was extremely serious, even dour. Yet his reading of Jesus concerning war was very much akin to Chesterton's.

"Christian realism" is the name Niebuhr gave to his notion that individuals may undergo drastic moral transformation but that large social groups cannot be so radically changed. Those whose lives are enmeshed in institutional nets cannot transfer their private morality into the public realm, Niebuhr taught. Christians must recognize, therefore, that the peacemaking commands of Christ have personal more than societal import, and that, in the political realm, Christians must support an impure use of violence in defense of causes that can never be wholly just. According to Niebuhr, it is both vain and irresponsible for the Church to abstain from such morally compromising complexity:

> [F]orces which are morally dangerous must be used despite their peril. Politics always aims at some kind of harmony or balance of interests, and such a harmony cannot be regarded as directly related to the final harmony of love of the Kingdom of God. . . . [T]he first duty of Christian faith is to preserve a certain distance between the sanctities of faith and the ambiguities of politics. This is to say that it is the duty of Christians in politics to have no specific "Christian politics."[4]

That there is no "politics" in Scripture is a highly contestable claim. As God's set-apart People, Israel is meant to be the *polis* through which Yahweh provides redemption for the whole world. Abraham is God's elect servant, called to sacrifice his strictly earthly future by placing his son Isaac on the altar of slaughter. Only in such willingness to surrender his tribal lineage could Abraham father the People who would embody the true future of all peoples. In reward for his willingness to yield his son over to Yahweh, even in death, Abraham establishes a priestly kingdom rather than a self-aggrandizing empire. Instead of devouring other nations while enslaving many of its own people, Israel is summoned to embody God's own redemptive and reconciling politics as set forth in his gracious commandments. Israel cannot fulfill this calling by dint of her own efforts but only by worshipful obedience to Yahweh. This Chosen People will provide a light and blessing to all the nations. The young Chesterton would thus have heard these words from Genesis 22 read in his Anglican parish:

> And the angel of the LORD called unto Abraham out of heaven the second time, And said, By myself have I sworn, saith the LORD, for because thou hast done this thing, and hast not withheld thy son, thine only son: That in blessing I will bless thee, and in multiplying I will multiply thy seed as the stars of the heaven, and as the sand which is upon the sea shore; and thy seed shall possess the gate of his enemies; And in thy seed shall all the nations of the earth be blessed; because thou hast obeyed my voice.

The Church, as the extension (rather than the replacement) of God's original election of Israel, thus inherits this Jewish summons to be "a light unto the nations." She does so by welcoming Gentiles into its Christ-centered, sacramental, prophetic, multiethnic Company. Like Israel, the Church is also God's public and communal People, so that her life and witness are inherently *political*—as one kind of *polis* is set in relation to quite another: the City of God and the City of Man. And so the political question of violence, especially military violence, remains crucial to Christian faith.

In his attraction to the metaphor of the sword, Chesterton was thoroughly biblical.[5] That the sword is one of the most recurrent scriptural images cannot be gainsaid: it appears more than four hundred times in the Bible. The name "Israel" means, in fact, "El does battle." The term "holy war" does not appear in the Old Testament, however; it is borrowed from the Arabic *jihad*.[6] Gerhard von Rad enumerates twenty divine oracles from the so-called "historical" books—oracles promising that, "by the sword," Yahweh will deliver the enemy into Israel's hands.[7] Nor is there any doubt that Israel attributed its military victories to Yahweh: "Happy are you, O Israel! Who is like you, a people saved by the LORD, the shield of your help, and the sword of your triumph" (Deut 33:29). Exodus 33 is nothing less than a conquest poem, as Yahweh promises to lead Israel into "a land flowing with milk and honey" by sending "an angel before thee; and I will drive out the Canaanite, the Amorite, and the Hittite, and the Perizzite, the Hivite, and the Jebusite."[8]

Recent biblical scholarship has discovered that many of these "triumphs" are poetic and liturgical narratives rather than historical accounts of actual battles. During its worship, Israel as a tribal confederacy would rehearse such conquest poems (e.g., Exod 15, Deut 33, Ps 68) as a reminder that holy war "was aimed at restoring peace." "These poems portray Yahweh as the divine warrior who battles against cosmic foes for the order of the world," argues Ben Ollenburger, "but in so doing, and at the same time, Yahweh battles on behalf of Israel against its historical enemies." More telling still is the scholarly conviction that Israel's later prophets used the holy war tradition *against* the religious and military ideology of Israel's own kings. These new oracles of God did not promise Yahweh's victories on behalf of Israel; instead, they championed his Covenant promises that the monarchs had replaced with their own military stratagems: "In their strong emphasis on Yahweh's sovereign action, these holy war narratives criticize political policies that locate sovereignty elsewhere" than in God.[9]

There is considerable cause for doubting that Israel was primarily the *warrior* people of God. For example, the Old Testament does not serve as the founding epic meant to provide a heroic account of Israel's establishment, as Vergil's *Aeneid* provides for Rome. Instead, it often laments Israel's failed obedience to Yahweh. She is repeatedly summoned, therefore, to enter combat against her own apostasy as much as against the idolatry of surrounding peoples. Quite unlike the deities of most pagan religions, therefore, Yahweh is depicted as metaphorically wielding the sword *against* his own Chosen:

> When God heard this [i.e., the apostasy of his people], he was wroth, and greatly abhorred Israel: So that he forsook the tabernacle of Shiloh, the tent which he placed among men; And delivered his strength into captivity, and his glory into the enemy's hand. He gave his people over also unto the sword; and was wroth with his inheritance. (Ps 78:59-62)[10]

Two of the most important Hebrew prophets look forward to the time when there shall be no slaughter at all, when peace shall triumph, when "they shall beat their swords into plowshares, and their spears into pruninghooks: [when] nation shall not lift up sword against nation, neither shall they learn war any more" (Isa 2:4; Mic 4:3). In the New Testament, the sword metaphor is used almost exclusively in this nonmilitarist sense. Though Jesus declares that he has come "not to send peace, but a sword" (Matt 10:34), he makes the weapon a metonym for dividing good and evil, not for wielding it against enemies. Hence Jesus' stern rebuke to his blade-swinging disciple who had sliced off the ear of Caiaphas' slave: "Put up again thy sword back into his place: for all they that take the sword shall perish with the sword" (Matt 26:52). Christians who embody the reconciling life of the Church will not eagerly kill others, it follows, so much as they will discipline themselves to live not by the potency of weapons but by the inverted sword called the Cross. It enables Christ's followers to be far more willing to suffer violence than to commit it.

This summons to self-denial even unto death as constituting the only way to Life (Mark 8:34-35) always threatens the powerful. Whenever the Kingdom of Heaven is truly proclaimed and enacted, Christians are likely to bring down savagery on themselves, as the history of the martyrs attests. In the Fourth Gospel, therefore, Jesus is adamant about not confusing the Reign of God with earthly empire. Only if the two were wrongly joined, he declares, "my servants would fight" (John 18:36). Paul also clarifies the nonmilitary character of his martial metaphors when he lists the spiritual weapons necessary for the arming of Christians, concluding with the most important of all: "the sword of the Spirit, which is the word of God" (Eph 6:17). So does the book of Hebrews proclaim the judicial authority and transfixing power of the divine Logos to be "sharper than any two-edged sword, piercing even to the dividing asunder of soul and spirit, of the joints and marrow, and [it] a discerner of the thoughts and intents of the heart" (Heb 4:12).[11]

In addition to its nonmilitarist use of military metaphors, the New Testament contains many other injunctions for Christians to live peaceably with their pagan neighbors and among themselves.[12] As one who exalted Tradition, Chesterton surprisingly fails to note that the Church's early teaching against Christian participation in military service was no "familiar frenzy." Though a goodly number of believers during the first centuries of the Church certainly served in the Roman army, however strongly their pastors may have inveighed against such defections, they were not the rule but a departure from it. Not until Christianity became a dominant force under Constantine was the Church's overwhelming *theological* rejection of war seriously challenged. There is simply no denying that from Arnobius to Lactantius, from Justin Martyr to Tertullian, from Ignatius of Antioch to Origen of Alexandria, almost all major Christian thinkers embraced the acerbic antimilitarist irony of Cyprian of Carthage: "[H]omicide is a crime when individuals commit it, [but] it is called a virtue, when it is carried on publicly," i.e., in warfare.[13]

Chesterton ignored such strong voices from the early Church. On the contrary, he eliminated pacifism from the outset as being both contradictory and naïve. He rejoiced that progressives such as H. G. Wells and Bertrand Russell were proven wrong in proclaiming that "war was an anachronism like the tournament and the gladiatorial show." That their rationalist prophecies about the end of human bellicosity were mistaken served to invalidate, in Chesterton's view, their arguments against war itself.[14] While disregarding Russell and Wells, Chesterton honored Tolstoy and his pacifist followers for having at least the virtue of a foolish consistency. Believing human nature to be essentially unfallen, the Tolstoyans sought to make it corrigible by persuasion rather than force: "In their mythology St. George did not conquer the dragon: he tied a pink ribbon around its neck and gave it a saucer of milk. According to them, a course of consistent kindness to Nero would have turned him into something only faintly represented by Alfred the Great."[15]

Chesterton might have better answered the twentieth-century Tolstoyans by seriously engaging those who would put Christian limits on war—namely, the proponents of "just war,"[16] many of whom were his fellow Catholics. The "just war" tradition was first formulated by St. Augustine and then given fuller elaboration by St. Thomas Aquinas and other teachers of the Church: war, waged for quite specific causes and within very distinct limits, is a necessary form of justice to be set over against injustice. Instead of joining other Christians in seeking to discern which, if any wars, they are willing to support, Chesterton offered witty dismissals of the Lord's "evangelical counsels" as impracticable ideals, indeed as otherworldly and unfeasible audacities:

> The command of Christ is impossible, but it is not insane; it is rather sanity preached to a planet of lunatics. If the whole world was suddenly stricken with a sense of humour it would find itself mechanically fulfilling the Sermon on the Mount. It is not the plain facts of the world which stand in the way of that consummation, but its passions of vanity and self-advertisement and morbid sensibility. It is true that we cannot turn the cheek to the smiter, and the sole and sufficient reason is that we have not the pluck.[17]

Chesterton's Vindication of Holy Slaughter

For Chesterton, the true Christian alternative to such inconceivable "pluck" is found in the moral necessity of holy war, and *Lepanto* (1911) is his most bellicose tribute to it. There is no need for a full exegesis of GKC's romping sanguinary celebration of the Christian victory over the Ottoman Turks in 1571, since Dale Ahlquist has identified most of the otherwise obscure historical allusions.[18] Yet it is necessary to answer Ahlquist's scorching complaint against the exclusion of *Lepanto* from the modern literary canon:

> [T]he problem with the poem is that it is a defense of the Catholic Church, of the Crusades, and of war: three things not generally looked kindly upon in today's English literature classes. Of course, neither are rhyme and meter. The only 20th century poetry that is permitted to be studied is that which clashes with everything: with the ear, with history, and with common sense.[19]

Ahlquist is right to protest the virtual banning of this fine paean to Christian combat; it should be taught alongside such classics of the antiwar tradition as Wilfred Owen's "Dulce et Decorum Est." As one who in fact teaches both poems, I believe it a worthwhile task to examine their respective theologies in some detail.

Chesterton celebrates Don John of Austria as a successor to the Crusaders and thus as the supreme chivalric defender of Christianity against the infidel Ottomans. For Chesterton, the Battle of Lepanto was the essential conflict that determined the fate of the Church, which he identified unabashedly with European civilization.[20] To the very end, he regarded Lepanto as the battle wherein Christendom fended off "the great Asiatic invasion."

> It must also be remembered that this last Moslem thrust was really a savage and incalculable thing, compared with the first thrust of Saladin and the Saracens. The high Arab culture of the Crusades had long perished; and the invaders were Tartars and Turks and rabble from really barbarous lands. . . . It was not Saladin against Richard or Averroes against Aquinas. . . .
>
> . . .
>
> When all is said, to the eyes of Mediterranean men especially, there passed across the shining sea merely the shadow of a great Destroyer. What they heard was the voice of Azrael rather than Allah. . . . The dry wind that drove before it a dust of broken idols was threatening the poised statues of Angelo and Donatello, where they shine on the high places around the central sea; and the sand of the high deserts descended, like moving mountains of dust and thirst and death, on the deep culture of the sacred vines; and the songs and the deep laughter of the vineyards. And above all, those clouds that were closing round them were like the curtains of the harem, from

whose corners look out the stony faces of the eunuchs; there spread like a vast shadow over shining courts and closing spaces the silence of the East, and its dumb compromises with the coarseness of man. These things, above all, were closing in upon that high and thwarted romance of the perfect Knight and Lady, which men of the Christian blood can never attain and never abandon.[21]

As the defender of all Christendom, Don John is much more than the brave twenty-six-year-old captain of the *Real* leading his fleet into battle.[22] For Chesterton, he is also the successor to Dante and the Provençal poets with their sweet new style, their *dolce stil nova*. Chesterton attempts nothing so lyrical or *soave* in his own poem, yet even pacifists with an ear for emotional fervor can be stirred by the four-beat palpitations of his rhyming couplets with their alliterative anapests and dactyls:

> Dim drums throbbing, in the hills half heard,
> Where only on a nameless throne a crownless prince has stirred,
> Where, risen from a doubtful seat and half-attainted stall,
> The last knight of Europe takes weapons from the wall,
> The last and lingering troubadour to whom the bird has sung,
> That once went singing southward when all the world was young,
> In that enormous silence, tiny and unafraid,
> Comes up a long and winding road the noise of the Crusade.
> Strong gongs groaning as the guns boom far,
> Don John of Austria is going to the war. . . .[23]

For Chesterton, the aim of a holy war such as the Battle of Lepanto was to strike terror not only in the Muslim enemy but also in Muhammad himself as he idly lounges in his decadent erotic paradise:

> Mahound is in his paradise above the evening star,[24]
> (*Don John of Austria is going to the war.*)
> He moves a mighty turban on the timeless houri's[25] knees,
> His turban that is woven of the sunset and the seas.

Chesterton depicts Muhammad as the Antichrist, finding nothing good in him except, as in Tolstoy, the consistency of a single idea: the sheer, naked monotheism that denies human freedom because everything exists under the all-determining and unknowable will of Allah called *kismet*. Mahound thus calls for his seamen to crush this successor to such early Crusaders as Richard the Lionheart, Raymond of Toulouse, and Godfrey of Lorraine. Christian martyrs are filled with joy, Mahound complains, in believing that their death shall gain them the contemptibly selfless glory of the Beatific Vision, whereas Muslim warriors die for a selfishly sensual paradise. Thus must the Muslim greeting of "Salaam" stamp out the Jewish "Shalom" no less than the Christian *Pax vobiscum*, "Peace be with you."

> "But a noise is in the mountains, in the mountains, and I know
> The voice that shook our palaces—four hundred years ago:
> It is he that saith not 'Kismet'; it is he that knows not Fate;
> It is Richard, it is Raymond, it is Godfrey in the gate!
> It is he whose loss is laughter when he counts the wager worth,
> Put down your feet upon him, that *our* peace be on the earth."
> For he heard drums groaning and he heard guns jar,
> (*Don John of Austria is going to the war.*)[26]

Since Muhammad's warriors are the chief foes of the Christian faith, they must be exterminated. Armageddon can wait. The Christian flag with its golden cross on a silver background must be soaked in gore if the Christian slaves rowing in the hulls of the Ottoman galleys are to be loosed and if all of Europe is to be liberated from the Muslim menace:

> Don John pounding from the slaughter-painted poop,
> Purpling all the ocean like a bloody pirate's sloop,[27]
> Scarlet running over on the silvers and the golds,
> Breaking of the hatches up and bursting of the holds,
> Thronging of the thousands up that labour under sea
> White for bliss and blind for sun and stunned for liberty.
> *Vivat Hispania!*
> *Domino Gloria!*
> Don John of Austria
> Has set his people free.[28]

For Chesterton, the victory at Lepanto was an immense Christian triumph, and he celebrated it with his most militaristic poem. It was for him a conquest achieved not only by the bravery of Don John but also by the intercessory prayers of Pope Pius V, together with the faithful throng who had gathered at the Basilica of Santa Maria Maggiore to recite the Rosary from dawn until dusk on October 7. Before appearing at his loggia looking onto St. Peter's Square, the Pope had prayed in his private chapel where the incense-engulfed Tabernacle containing the consecrated Host makes the Lord perennially present while also giving the globe its true scale and value in the divine order of things—tiny but precious, worthy even of the incarnate God's own death.

> The Pope was in his chapel before day or battle broke,
> (*Don John of Austria is hidden in the smoke.*)
> The hidden room in a man's house where God sits all the year,
> The secret window whence the world looks small and very dear.[29]

Don John in fact attributed the success of his fleet to the intercessions of the Rosary Queen. All sixty-five thousand of his Christian troops received the Eucharist on the morning of the battle, just as the ships were adorned with crucifixes, as the chaplains provided plenary absolution for all who might die, while many of the warriors continued to say the Rosary right up until the firing of the first shot.

At the dawn of the battle, the prevailing wind favored the Islamic forces, requiring the Christians to use all of their galley crews to row against it. Whether by divine action working through secondary causes or in straightforward miracle, the wind suddenly reversed itself, freeing the slaves below to fight rather than oar, considerably increasing the ranks of the still-outnumbered Christians. When news of the victory made its way back to Italy and Spain, it was indeed regarded as a miraculous deliverance. Huge crowds joined in singing the *Te Deum Laudamus*.[30] The Venetian Senate passed a resolution hailing Our Lady of the Most Holy Rosary for the defeat of the Ottomans. Pius V also established October 7 as the Feast of Our Lady of Victories,[31] although three centuries later a less bellicose pope, Leo XIII, changed the name to the Feast of Our Lady of the Most Holy Rosary.

It is necessary to challenge Chesterton's reading of both the human and superhuman powers at work in this celebrated victory of the Christians over the Muslims at Lepanto. Victor David Hanson, perhaps the most eminent war historian of our time, offers a searing counterverdict. Hanson argues that the intense religiosity of the Muslims worked to their *disadvantage*. Because there was no division between the Muslim state and the Islamic faith, their scholars were limited almost entirely to the teaching and interpretation of the Qur'an. "[N]o real research in [Muslim] universities," Hanson writes, could "lead to military innovation, technological progress, or an economic renaissance." While the Ottomans employed admirals who had all been born as European Christians, their galleys were grossly inferior to the galleasses of the Holy League.[32]

Hanson argues that the less devout Europeans made military advances that the Ottomans, in their superreligiosity, could not achieve. The comparative secularity of Western Christianity in the sixteenth century had been established because, as we have noticed, there was no subordination of political to religious authority. This war-enabling separation of statecraft from soulcraft enabled the Europeans to amass the necessary capital, to undertake the necessary technical innovations, and to develop the necessary strategies of warfare for victory during this new age of gunpowder. When skillfully combined, these tripartite forces won the greatest galley battle since Actium amidst the four-hour massacre of October 7, 1571. "More than 150 Muslims and Christians had been killed every minute of the fighting," Hanson writes, "ranking Lepanto's combined 40,000 dead—thousands more were wounded or missing—with Salamis, Cannae, and the Somme as one of the bloodiest single-day slaughters on land or sea in the history of warfare."[33]

Chesterton had no means for gathering such gruesome but illumining data, though it is not altogether certain that they would have altered his poem, since he affirmed Hanson's crucial claim: "Europe's citizens might have inherited a notion of personal freedom from classical antiquity and of spiritual brotherhood from Christ, but the survival of the West lay in how well they ignored the idea that killing was always sinful." Chesterton would have agreed that, under proper circumstances, military annihilation is not only unsinful but also quite salutary. Yet, knowing how vehemently Chesterton opposed the profit motive for subverting community and cooperation, as well as how angrily he abominated the rise of the English plutocracy, one can rightly imagine his disgust at Hanson's fundamental thesis—namely, that capitalism has given the West its unique capacity for carnage, far outdistancing all other cultures in war making:

Free capital is the key to war making on any large scale, what Cicero called "the sinews of war," without which an army cannot muster, be fed, or fight. Capital is the wellspring of technological innovation, which is inextricably tied to freedom, often the expression of individualism, and thus critical to military success throughout the ages. That capitalism was born in the West, expanded through Europe, survived the alternate Western-inspired paradigms of socialism and communism, and found itself inextricably tied with personal freedom and democracy in its latest global manifestation explains in no small part Western military dominance from the age of Salamis to the Gulf War. . . . The purpose of capitalism, even sixteenth-century Mediterranean capitalism, was not social justice or "intent" or the desire to be "legitimate," but, as it has always been, the acknowledgment of the eternal greed of man—critical in crafting a system that recognizes natural self-interest.[34]

Chesterton closes his fine poem with a vignette of the renowned Spanish writer Cervantes returning to Spain from Lepanto to take up his lifelong career as an ironist: "And he smiles, but not as Sultans smile, and settles back the blade. . . . / (*But Don John of Austria rides home from the Crusade.*)"[35] Though Cervantes boasted of his participation in the battle, where he lost the use of a hand, there is no braggadocio in Quixote's speech to Sancho Panza—even if the crazy couple has hardly fulfilled its Christian ideals:

"All these and many other great deeds [of military conquest by Cortés and similar military heroes] were, are and shall be works of fame, desired by mortals as the reward, the taste of immortality, that their exploits earn for them, even though we knights errant, Christian and Catholic, must be more concerned with the glory of the life to come, to be enjoyed throughout eternity in the ethereal and celestial regions, than with the vanity of the fame that can be achieved in this present transient life; for this fame, however long it lasts, will end when the world ends, at the time appointed. And so, O Sancho, our works must not stray beyond the limits imposed by the Christian religion that we profess. In slaying giants, we must slay pride; in our generosity and magnanimity, we must slay envy; in our tranquil demeanour and disposition, we must slay anger; in eating as little as we do, we must slay gluttony and somnolence; in our faithfulness to those whom we have made mistresses of our thoughts, we must slay lewdness and lust; in wandering all over the world in search of opportunities to become famous knights as well as good

Christians, we must slay sloth. Here, Sancho, you have the means by which
the high praise brought by fame can be achieved."[36]

Lest Cervantes' manifestly orthodox affirmation seem to be sardoni-
cally undercut by both its magniloquence and its supersincerity, the
felicitously named Fernando Cervantes makes an acute countercase:
"[T]he irony that modern readers of Cervantes often seem keen to
detect in the seemingly problematic coexistence of his admiration for
Rome's pagan past and his respect for Tridentine Catholic piety, tells
us more about modern preconceptions than about contemporary realities."[37] In Quixote's plangent summons to spiritual combat against six
of the seven mortal sins (avarice alone is excepted), Cervantes may
have been recalling his military exploits from a humbler posture than
Chesterton ascribes to him.[38]

Such oversight may account for a far deadlier failure. Even though
the Battle of Lepanto (like the Crusades) was sanctioned as a holy war,
it failed even to meet just war criteria—namely, as a morally justifiable
effort meant to stop the marauding Ottomans. Though such a claim
is surely debatable, there is little doubt that this alleged Christian triumph also marked the last gasp of Christendom. The conflation of the
interests of the Church with those of the state that began with Charlemagne would end with the state's virtual conscription of the Church
into the cause of its nationalist wars. Chesterton's celebration of the
Christian carnage at Lepanto may also explain his eagerness to justify
secular slaughter in his own time.

Chesterton as Apologist for the Deadliest of Wars

Chesterton's alarm over the decline of nineteenth-century Liberalism
with the concomitant rise of the twin evils of monopolistic capitalism and collectivist socialism did not deter his support for the military actions of the British nation. Indeed, his vindication of Britain's
role in World War I was uncritical from beginning to end. Concerning
his defense of this unprecedented bloodletting, Chesterton confessed
that he was "of one body with Englishmen from whom I differed on
the deepest vitals of the soul; one in that hour of death with atheists and pessimists and Manichean Puritans and even with Orangemen
from Belfast." What united such sundry souls, in Chesterton's mind,
were the supreme English virtues that his brother Cecil had exhibited

both in his living and his dying: "the two kinds of courage that have nourished the nation; the courage of the forum and of the field."[39] Chesterton failed to discern that modern totalistic war could not be comparable to the limited character of traditional battle, nor that the public square that had once been the arena for debate and argument would be dwarfed by the power considerations of the nation-state. The ragtag orators at Hyde Park Corner were rapidly becoming mere relics. In an essay significantly titled "A Nightmare of Nonsense," written only three years before the outbreak of war, Chesterton seems to have recognized this seismic shift:

> The terrible danger in the heart of our Society is that the tests are giving way. We are altering, not the evils, but the standards of good by which alone evils can be detected and defined. . . . [T]he moral scales that were meant to weigh our problems are themselves breaking under the weight of them. The philosophical instruments which were meant to dissect existence are bent and twisted against the toughness of the thing to be dissected. Because it is very hard work to apply principles of judgment to anything, people are everywhere abandoning the principles and practically deciding not to test life at all, but only let life test them.[40]

Perhaps because he failed to discern that such "standards of good" and their proper "application" must be maintained through ongoing communal traditions of sustained argument, rather than by solitary individuals alone, Chesterton himself remained unchecked by dissentient voices from within his own circle. Almost from the start, he envisioned the Great War as having but a single source: it was a barbarian Prussian attack on Christian civilization. Such monocausalism was the same evil that, as a newspaperman, Chesterton often condemned. He endlessly decried the failure of journalism to place things in context. Journalism takes up stories, he lamented, as if they had no beginning, no origins in distant prior sources. Yet this failure became Chesterton's own deadly error. He ignored the mutual and multiple grievances that led to the war, especially the bristling territorial and economic rivalries that had set Germany, France, Great Britain, Russia, and Austria-Hungary at each other's throats as nation-states preening with a new kind of potency—not only with the new power of machine guns and poison gas, of tanks and torpedoes and airplanes, but also with the new power of well-disciplined bureaucracy, well-funded scientific research, and well-managed techniques of control and manipulation. This potent complex of agencies and operations often produces what Christopher Dawson called a "denial of moral values and moral judgment," for the Leviathan state has the strength to shrink the "recalcitrant individual to the position of a criminal."[41]

Little did Chesterton know that he might have learned from his avowed enemy, Friedrich Nietzsche, how to name "the new idol" created by Bismarck and Kaiser Wilhelm. As Nietzsche saw, Prussia was but the epitome of the new omnicompetent politics that had emerged all across Europe and that would soon spread eastward.

> State is the name of the coldest of all cold monsters. Coldly it tells lies too; and this lie crawls out of its mouth: "I, the state, am the people."
>
> . . . It is annihilators who set traps for the many and call them "state": they hang a sword and a hundred appetites over them.
>
> . . . All-too-many are born: for the superfluous the state was invented. Behold, how it lures them, the all-too-many—and how it devours them, chews them, and ruminates!
>
> . . . Only where the state ends, there begins the human being who is not superfluous. . . .

Even those noble souls who, like Nietzsche, have broken through to unbelief and the autonomous will to power cannot escape this new all-devouring dragon: "Indeed, it detects you too, you vanquishers of the old god. . . . With heroes and honorable men it would surround itself, the new idol! It likes to bask in the sunshine of good consciences—the cold monster!"[42]

Less perceptive than Nietzsche if only in this one regard, Chesterton interpreted Prussia as nothing other than an atavistic embodiment of Teutonic tribalism and Protestant imperialism. England and France, by contrast, were supposedly preserved from such brutishness by the civilizing effects of Latinate Christianity.[43] Thus must the Huns from the pagan North be crushed. England's Christian character supposedly made it immune from the brutalities committed by the German aggressors.[44] Chesterton the inveterate Liberal also insisted that this war was being fought in order to defend small communities against gigantic impersonal forces, as if his adopted town itself were facing the German juggernaut: "[F]or me the War Memorial at Beaconsfield commemorates the rescue of Beaconsfield; not of an ideal Beaconsfield, but of the real Beaconsfield."[45] Margaret Canovan has noted the delusory quality of Chesterton's patriotic localism, since the war was not limited even to Germany and France, but stretched to Gallipoli and Jerusalem.[46]

Chesterton was not alone among English notables who served in the British Propaganda Office. In addition to Rudyard Kipling and John Buchan, there were other such prominent writers as John Galsworthy and Arnold Bennett working in tandem with Chesterton. What remains most remarkable is that even when the war stretched on interminably, with no good end in sight, and as the casualties mounted ever higher, including his own brother Cecil in 1918, Chesterton registered little if any misgiving against the horrors of this most incarnadine of wars.[47] Nowhere in his work do we find Chesterton reporting, for example, that the nine-month struggle at Verdun in 1915 ended with more than seven hundred thousand killed and injured but with the battle lines returned virtually to the same place as at the start. Nor does he mention such dreadful data (according to even the most restrained estimates) as the total of ten million dead and twenty million seriously wounded, leaving five million widows, nine million orphans, and ten million refugees.[48] As if completely oblivious to such nightmarish realities, Chesterton offers, in *The Ballad of St. Barbara*, a romping account of the Allied victory at the Battle of the Marne.[49] Unlike *Lepanto*'s rosaries said before battle, and far removed from Alfred's humbling vision of the Virgin in *The Ballad of the White Horse*, St. Barbara not only mystically watches the battle from her tower windows; she actually participates in the devastation herself, enabling the Allies to ravage both human and natural things for the sake of military triumph. Every hole blasted in the German palisades lets in more divine light:

> The touch and the tornado; all our guns give tongue together,
> St. Barbara for the gunnery and God defend the right,
> They are stopped and gapped and battered as we blast away the weather,
> Building window upon window to our lady of the light.
> For the light is come on Liberty, her foes are falling, falling,
> They are reeling, they are running, as the shameful years have run,
> She is risen for all the humble, she has heard the conquered calling,

St. Barbara of the Gunners, with her hand upon the gun.
They are burst asunder in the midst that eat of their own flatteries,
Whose lip is curled to order as its barbered hair is curled. . . .
Blast of the beauty of sudden death, St. Barbara of the batteries!
That blow the new white window in the wall of all the world.[50]

Chesterton's ballad meter is as flawed as his theology, the former clumsy and the latter bloody. "They are burst asunder in the midst that eat of their own flatteries" is especially inept. "Ruin is a builder of windows" and "the beauty of sudden death" are sentiments more befitting Nietzsche than Chesterton. There is also an abstractness about this celebration of slaughter that violates Chesterton's own loyalty to the specific and the concrete. Neither is there any numbering of the two million men who fought at the Marne, nor any mention of the more than five hundred thousand who were either wounded or killed there. Publishing his poem in 1914, the year of the battle, Chesterton could not have known that the only immediate effect of the Allied victory was to prevent a quick, war-ending German triumph. The long-term results of "the guns of September" were devastating, as both sides dug themselves in for four more years of trench warfare on the Western Front.

Yet Chesterton never seems to have had the slightest regret about the rightness of the Great War, even though it mainly entailed the killing of Christians by other Christians. Once again, he reverted to such hazy words as *something* and *ideal* to define the moral law that was meant to justify the war:

[W]e said that there is in Northern Europe a fountain of poison. . . . It is a thing of the spirit; it is not a nation; it is a heresy. It is an ideal outside the European ideal; outside what most of us would call the normal human ideal. It is something alien to Europe, which Europe cannot digest and Europe did not destroy. . . . The nearest definition I know is this. The civilised man, like the religious man, is one who recognises the strange and irritating fact that something exists besides himself. What Jefferson called, with his fine restraint, "a decent respect for the opinion of mankind"; what medieval people called Christendom or the judgment of all Christian princes; what any Christian will call the conscience of man as witness to the justice of God; that, in one form or another, does everywhere effect civilised people. . . . [I]n one way or other, that is the test; that the man does not think his dignity lowered by admitting a general law, though it may go against him.[51]

It is surprising that—unlike Yeats and Eliot, unlike Lawrence and Woolf and many other contemporary writers—Chesterton failed to recognize that the Victorian Age did not end nor did the twentieth century begin with the queen's death in 1901. August 1914 marks the cataclysmic change. Rather than ending all wars, the Great War inaugurated what Pope John Paul II would later call "the culture of death." A fundamental cleavage in Western culture occurred at Passchendaele and the Marne, at Ypres and the Somme. These battles were conducted no longer with swords and rifles alone but also with tanks and airplanes, with howitzers and poison gas. Such martial instruments were designed not to kill individual soldiers but to obliterate entire towns, to blast the countryside bare of forests and farms, annihilating almost every living thing.[52] This awful war caused a religious fault line to shear, the tectonic plates of Western tradition to shift, and the resulting strain produced an earthquake of monumental moral consequence. As Eliot's most celebrated metaphor made clear, modern men and women now occupied a spiritual Wasteland.[53]

Lest it seem anachronistic and unfair to measure Chesterton by later standards, we can consider the witness of his slightly older contemporary, the Congregationalist minister and theologian Peter Taylor Forsyth (1848–1921). Though no Christian pacifist or clamoring opponent of the war, Forsyth nonetheless offered trenchant theological judgments about it. Unlike Chesterton, who envisioned the war as a conflict between civilization and barbarism, Forsyth saw it as the product of a self-absorbed European civilization hideously wedded to a Christianity centered almost entirely on personal salvation in the world to come, and thus devoid of all concern for ethical and communal transformation. The result, already evident in the third year of the war, was inevitably nightmarish:

> War, with a national competition for God as ally, instead of a national obedience to Him as Sovereign, war with its eagerness to have Him on our side instead of having His side for ours, such a war is but the . . . fruit of the union of a civilisation which is fundamentally egoist, and a religion also egoist and propositional, sentimental, or what you will, only not holy. An egoist civilisation, an individualist salvation, and a non-moral theology in a world which belongs by right to the kingdom of conscience and God, and has that for its

great deep *nisus* [i.e., effort, endeavor]—such things do not make debacle strange or judgment wonderful. The shock would be if the combination did not so explode.[54]

It is not unfair, I believe, to ask why Chesterton found no religious grounds for protesting this slaughter that drew no distinctions between combatants and noncombatants, this bloodbath that mobilized every branch of public and private life for the sake of killing, this war that General Ludendorff would rightly name in the title of his book: *Der Totale Krieg*. We hear nothing from Chesterton akin to Eliot's doleful confession about "shoring fragments against our ruin." In a war poem titled "Blessed Are the Peacemakers," written in 1914, Chesterton offers an acidly ironic tribute to the Kaiser and the Prussians—not as fellow Christians who might still be called to account for their sin, but as gross barbarians having no conscience whatsoever. At last the Germans have ended their prewar recriminations against England, Chesterton jests, by finally launching military action:

> Therefore to you my thanks, O throne,
> O thousandfold and frozen folk;
> For whose cold frenzies all your own
> The Battle of the Rivers broke;
>
> Who have no faith a man could mourn,
> Nor freedom any man desires;
> But in a new clean light of scorn
> Close up my quarrel with my sires.
>
> Who bring my English heart to me,
> Who mend me like a broken toy;
> Till I can see you fight and flee,
> And laugh as if I were a boy.[55]

Well after the war was over, when there was no occasion to make callow jokes about the war, Chesterton remained steadfastly convinced that civilization had been saved from the savages: "What would the Kaiser, with his Mailed Fist and his boasts of being Attila and the leader of the Huns, even in time of peace, have been like if he had issued completely victorious out of [this] universal war?"[56] Even near the end of his life in 1936, Chesterton remained adamant: "For the truth is that what has really happened has completely justified the theory of Europe [i.e., as the bastion of Christendom] on which the Allies went to war."[57]

Did Chesterton ever read or mark, ever learn or inwardly digest, the dozens of antiwar poems, many of them penned from the Front, by such writers as Robert Graves and Siegfried Sassoon and Edmund Blunden?[58] There is no evidence that he did. The best of these war poets, Wilfred Owen, might have induced sleeplessness in even the most unrepentant advocates of the dubiously named Great War. "Nightmare" was Chesterton's recurrent metaphor for unspeakable horror; it also serves as the chief trope in the final stanza of Owen's most famous poem, "Dulce et Decorum Est":

> If in some smothering dreams, you too could pace
> Behind the wagon that we flung him in,
> And watch the white eyes writhing in his face,
> His hanging face, like a devil's sick of sin;
> If you could hear, at every jolt, the blood
> Come gargling from the froth-corrupted lungs,
> Obscene as cancer, bitter as the cud
> Of vile, incurable sores on innocent tongues,—
> My friend, you would not tell with such high zest
> To children ardent for some desperate glory,
> The old Lie: Dulce et decorum est
> Pro patria mori.[59]

Owen is haunted by memories of unspeakable misery, hoping that his readers might suffer such nightmares themselves, prompting them to demand that the killing be stopped, or at least that it not be glorified. The wounded soldier is treated as if he were already a corpse, so surely does death await him. He is thrown onto the wagon like a side of meat, a lump of animal flesh. He has no voice to speak his own protest, and so Owen speaks it for him, concentrating on the features of his face—his most human features. The soldier's eyes roll like those of a frightened animal, his face is hagridden by the ultrademonic things he has seen, and the jarring of the tumbrel brings up blood-flecked bubbles from his dying lungs. The foam is likened to the septic mucus that children spit from their abscessed mouths. Just as there is no innocent perfection in such a death as this, so does the irregular meter strain against the regular rhyme—artistic evidence that atrocity cannot be captured within strict poetic conventions.

Nor can Owen withhold his ironic address to the reader as his "friend," even though the typical Englishman's enthusiasm for the war surely makes him the enemy of both the poet and the dying man. Owen was a reluctant Christian at best, but he voices an implicitly Christian critique of the warfare that becomes the necessary mechanism of the almighty nation-state. If Christians are unable to persuade their earthly fatherland to order its virtues to love of the true Fatherland, then such pagan values become what Augustine called *splendida vitia*, "glittering vices." Defense of them is indefensible. It is neither sweet nor proper to defame this dying youth tossed onto a death cart by honoring him with a Horatian defilement.[60] Only a moral obtuseness of the worst kind can make such a horrid *mori* chime with glory.[61]

Chesterton as *Bonus Miles Christi Jesu*

It is legitimate, I believe, to ask whether the First World War might have elicited from Chesterton such a poem as Gerard Manley Hopkins' *The Wreck of the Deutschland*. Hopkins used the drowning of five Franciscan nuns—after they had been driven from Germany in 1875 as the consequence of Bismarck's anti-Catholic *Kulturkampf*—to offer a profound poetic meditation on the goodness of God amidst a nightmare world that seems to crush it. Chesterton might have done something similar with one of this war's most memorable and horrible images. The gilded statue of the Virgin and Child atop the ruined basilica at Albert in France, having been riddled with gunfire, dangled precariously from the church spire for almost two years. It was often pictured in newspapers, as if the Mother and her infant Son of God were the real victims of the fighting. Such a poet as Chesterton might have pondered the searing theological import of this truly barbarous sight. Yet at least in one single case, Chesterton did poetically register his outrage against the uselessness and needlessness of this war. He did so in "The Truce of Christmas," a poem written apparently in response to an actual event that occurred on Christmas Eve of 1914.[62]

Though the blood had been gushing in hand-to-hand battle for the previous three months, several field commanders on both sides arranged for a temporary cease-fire. Thus could the Germans and the

English gather in the no-man's-land that lay between their trenches, there jointly to celebrate the Feast of the Nativity.[63] Several of these unofficial "cessations of hostilities" involved soldiers from France, Belgium, Austria, and Russia—though the most celebrated instances occurred between German and British troops gathering along the Western Front to shake hands, exchange gifts, play games, and wish each other well. They also used the brief truce to bury the dead. This momentary respite from the brutality of war was organized by common soldiers and lower-command officers, since both German and British headquarters threatened severe punishment for "fraternization with the enemy," which was in fact a capital offense. British commanders even mounted attacks on the Germans in the hope of provoking a kindred aggression that would stave off any Christmas truce that might dampen the fires of soldierly sacrifice and ideological fervor. The results were often disastrous, especially at Ploegsteert Wood, which became ruefully known as "Plugstreet" to the soldiers. The British suffered "massive casualties, including many from poorly directed friendly artillery fire. Many of the dead remained unburied, some literally impaled on enemy barbed wire. . . ."[64]

The Germans seemed to have initiated the temporary peace, for at the time they were winning the war. Yet the British were hardly reluctant to accept the offer, as one of the British officers, Captain R. J. Armes, later recalled with an unaffected poignancy yet also an ominous foreboding:

> [My friend] and I walked across and held a conversation with the German officer in command. . . . I gave [him] permission to bury some German dead who were lying in between us, and we agreed to have no shooting until 12 midnight tomorrow [i.e., Christmas]. We talked together, 10 or more Germans gathered round. I was almost in their lines within a yard or so. We saluted each other, he thanked me for permission to bury his dead, and we fixed up how many men were to do it, and that otherwise both sides must remain in their trenches.
>
> Then we wished one another good night and a good night's rest, and a happy Xmas and parted with a salute. I got back to the trench. The Germans sang "*Die Wacht am Rhein*," it sounded well. Then our men sang quite well "Christians Awake," it sounded so well, and with a good night we all got back into

our trenches. It was a curious scene, a lovely moonlight night, the German trenches with small lights on them, and the men on both sides gathered in groups on the parapets. At times we heard the guns in the distance and an occasional rifle shot. I can hear them now, but about us is absolute quiet. I allowed one or two men to go out and meet a German or two halfway. They exchanged cigars, a smoke and talked. The officer I spoke to hopes we shall do the same on New Year's Day. I said "yes, if I am here."[65]

Because Chesterton's poem renders a powerful poetic verdict on the cruel irony of such an armistice, it is worth full quotation and detailed examination.

The Truce of Christmas

Passionate peace is in the sky—
And in the snow in silver sealed
The beasts are perfect in the field,[66]
And men seem men so suddenly—
    (But take ten swords and ten times ten,
    And blow the bugle in praising men;
    For we are for all men under the sun;
    And they are against us every one;
    And misers haggle and madmen clutch,
    And there is peril in praising much,
    And we have the terrible tongues uncurled
    That praise the world to the sons of the world.)

The idle humble hill and wood
Are bowed about the sacred birth,
And for one little hour the earth
Is lazy with the love of good—
    (But ready are you, and ready am I,
    If the battle blow and the guns go by;
    For we are for all men under the sun,
    And they are against us every one;
    And the men that hate herd all together
    To pride and gold and the great white feather,
    And the thing is graven in star and stone
    That the men that love are all alone.)

> Hunger is hard and time is tough,
> But bless the beggars and kiss the kings;
> For hope has broken the heart of things,
> And nothing was ever praised enough.
>> (But hold the shield for a sudden swing
>> And point the sword when you praise a thing,
>> For we are for all men under the sun,
>> And they are against us every one;
>> And mime and merchant, thane and thrall,
>> Hate us because we love them all;
>> Only till Christmastide goes by
>> Passionate peace is in the sky.)[67]

Each of the stanzas begins with a quiet iambic declaration of the true nature of Christmas as it has been recovered through this brief laying down of arms. The short armistice is not a mere "cease-fire," but a feat of passionate conviction about the divine peace accomplished in the Nativity. There are no personal pronouns in the three Petrarchan quatrains; instead, the momentary triumph of peace quietly conquers all merely private and selfish concerns. In this moment of ardent reverence, the beasts of the field are akin to the kneeling oxen in Hardy's Christmas poem. Yet we find none of Hardy's wistful and doubtful "hoping it might be so." These cattle are sealed in the timeless perfection of snow and moonlight. The frenzy of war is replaced with the stillness of the uplands and the copse, both of which seem to bow toward Bethlehem. For in the Christ child lies the real Hope for breaking the world's cruel cycle of killing and being killed, even if it is finally accomplished by the piercing of Christ's own heart.

The soldiers no longer behave as bestial killers but recover their full humanity, if only during this one small circling of the clock's hand. In one of Chesterton's most arresting phrases, the entire earth is declared to be "lazy with the love of good." This is not an easy alliteration. The word *lazy* is rooted in the Low German *lasich*, which means not only "languid" but also "idle," thus echoing the use of the word in line 13. Idle goodness is the perfect antonym to all the frenetic attempts to find militaristic surrogates for it. This moment of brotherhood is a deed of true virtue and honor that becomes metonymic for the reconciliation meant for the whole warring world. What is accomplished here is what is meant to prevail everywhere. With neither meanness as its motive nor luxury as its end, the truce remains transcendently, permanently good.

The eight-line insets offer stiffly rhymed couplets in drastic counterpoint to the looser quatrains that make both Christmas and Christian affirmations. These angry ripostes seem to come from an officer in high command, or else from a politician or munitions maker who wants to prolong the combat. Here the personal pronouns abound, as the speaker impatiently justifies this war that will require the soldiers to resume fighting as soon as the truce is ended. According to this hard-bitten speaker, the ordinary citizens back at home care nothing for the sacrifices made by the soldiers who protect them. Such doltish souls can do nothing other than live out their prescribed roles inherited from the Middle Ages. No one is to be trusted, the cynic insists. Like pinchpennies and lunatics, everyone is to be suspected of selfish motives, especially these so-called peaceable Germans.[68] Thus does the disparaging speechifier warn the British soldiers to be sparing of their praise and ready with their swords, lest this tribute to Germanic goodwill prove delusory. Only the British have the highest and noblest and purest aims. And because they fight allegedly for the sake of the whole world, they have uncoiled their snake-like tongues of fire to annihilate the Hunlike haters of the good.

In his second retort to the celebrants of the Christmas truce, the speaker's Nietzschean bravado becomes even shriller. He has nothing but scorn for the Germanic adversaries whose spiked and plumed helmets signal their arrogance and greed and insolence. The sooner the truce is over, therefore, the better. War may be hell, as William Tecumseh Sherman famously declared, but it is better than the false heaven of this temporary peace that will last only until Christmas is past. The motto of military potency is etched, according to this war-mongering voice, in the irresistible nature of things, whether it be written in astral constellations or on earthly monoliths. And this, in effect, is his cruel creed: "We realists of war abide in a lonely but glorious solitude, unlike the herdlike peacemongers who crowd together in the delusion of mutuality."

The sour and jaded voice of self-justifying bellicosity is given the final word, but his sentiments do not disclose the poem's ultimate import. The humble affirmations of the three quatrains make the truly indelible claims. The short peaceful interim of the truce both defines and refutes the violence of the war. Christmas breaks the world's sin-hardened heart so that its obstinate flint might be turned into compassionate flesh, fulfilling the promise of the prophet Ezekiel: "I will take away the stony heart of your flesh, and I will give you an heart of flesh" (Ezek 36:26). Thus do the Christmas-celebrating quatrains serve, in effect, to turn the motto of the warmonger upside down: "Those who live by love alone, are never alone." No matter how nightmarish the circumstances, Christmas marks the victory of divine love over all worldly segregations of the worthy from the unworthy, as kings become akin to beggars, each blessing and kissing the other.[69] Such goodness can never be overpraised, for the Feast of the Nativity may be the gladdest and deepest of all paradoxes, bringing its Peace by shattering the world's wars, whether by military truce or personal reconciliation.

Chesterton as the poetic soldier of the peacemaking Christ is a much more attractive figure than the militarist enthusiast for holy war, and "The Truce of Christmas" serves as a convincing counterpoint to Owen's "Dulce et Decorum Est." Wars we may always have with us, but the one permanent alternative to killing always remains—namely, the Way of the Cross, the path that leads to the saving rather than the slaying of enemies. The cause of the crucified God, Chesterton would declare with increasing emphasis, is the cause for which Christians are meant to become true warriors, in obedience to the injunction laid down in 2 Timothy 2:3: "Thou therefore endure hardness as a good soldier of Jesus Christ," as *bonus miles Christi Jesu*.

4

THE WANING OF THE WEST AND THE THREAT OF ISLAM
The New Jerusalem and *The Flying Inn*

Jesus Christ . . . made wine, not a medicine, but a sacrament.
But Omar [in Edward FitzGerald's rendering of *The Rubáiyát of Omar Khayyám*] makes it, not a sacrament, but a medicine. He feasts because life is not joyful; he revels because he is not glad. "Drink," he says, "for you know not whence you come nor why. Drink, for you know not when you go nor where. Drink, because the stars are cruel and the world as idle as a humming-top. Drink, because there is nothing worth trusting, nothing worth fighting for. Drink, because all things are lapsed in a base equality and an evil peace." So he stands offering us the cup in his hand. And at the high altar of Christianity stands another figure, in whose hand also is the cup of the vine. "Drink" he says "for the whole world is as red as this wine, with the crimson of the love and wrath of God. Drink, for the trumpets are blowing for battle and this is the stirrup-cup. Drink, for this my blood of the new testament that is shed for you. Drink, for I know of whence you come and why. Drink, for I know of when you go and where."
G. K. Chesterton, *Heretics* (1905)

In the face of late modern Islamist terrorism, it is a perilous thing to air Chesterton's complaints against Mohammedanism, as he called it. Chesterton could easily though wrongly be enlisted as a militant in "the clash of civilizations." Samuel Huntington famously invented this phrase to define his argument that, after the 1989 rending of the Iron

Curtain, the essential world-dividing line has become cultural rather than political and ideological. Nor is there any longer a real breach between East and West, even between North and South. The true conflict, Huntington maintains, lies *between civilizations*—together with the religions, languages, histories, and *mores* undergirding them. The great sundering chasm, the impassable crevasse, is the one separating those cultures that embrace secularization-*cum*-modernization over against those that do not.[1] Huntington regards the resurgence of both Islam and Christianity in the late twentieth century as largely a defensive reaction against the devastating effects of this hydra-headed beast of secular modernity—its individualism, its pluralism, its industrial capitalism, its emancipation of women, its elevation of the bureaucratic over the personal, its privatizing of religion, its democratizing of the social and political order.

Christianity and Islam grew markedly, Huntington asserts, as their new adherents sought refuge in community- and tradition-dependent claims to truth—claims that modernity and secularity cannot support.[2] Yet there are two essential differences, according to Huntington. Whereas Christianity is spread mainly by missionary effort, Islam grows by population no less than conversion. And with the advent of Islamist *jihad*, it also increases its power and presence by violence. In his book's single most controverted passage, Huntington asserts that "[i]n the early 1990s Muslims were engaged in more intriguing violence than were non-Muslims, and two-thirds to three-quarters of intercivilizational wars were between Muslims and non-Muslims. Islam's borders *are* bloody, and so are its innards."[3]

The aim of this chapter is not to deal with the rightness or wrongness of Huntington's thesis except as it bears on Chesterton's own treatment of Islam and *Der Untergang des Abendlandes*, as Oswald Spengler first named the Decline of the West in 1918 and again in 1923. We shall see that, at times, GKC joined those who have insisted that we face nothing less than a contest between "the West and the rest,"[4] as Huntington put it in yet another memorable phrase. Yet we shall also discover that Chesterton pulled back from such a wedding of Western culture and Christian faith, insisting that the Church stands as both the critic and transformer of all civilizations, including the increasingly alien cultures that it once birthed in Europe and America. In his latter years, Chesterton came to see that the Church, as the very Body of Christ, shall outlast the collapse of the West just as it once survived the decline and fall of Rome. We shall discern a similar set of alternatives in Chesterton's treatment of Islam. Whereas *The New Jerusalem* offers an almost entirely jaundiced estimate of Islam, *The Flying Inn* provides a far subtler and more convincing critique of the world's second largest religion. In this remarkable novel Chesterton accomplishes something infinitely more difficult than despising and dismissing an oppugnant religion. He gives convincing, if also hilarious fictional life to Christianity as a prophetic and sacramental Faith that celebrates God's reconciling presence in the world.

Medieval Christendom as the Wonder of the World

The crisis of the West has come to clearest focus, at least during our time, vis-à-vis Islam. With prophetic foresight, Chesterton foresaw the approaching cataclysm. He wasn't joking when he declared that the only justifiable wars are holy wars.[5] He believed that Christians had cause, as we have seen in *Lepanto*, to relish the bloody destruction of the Turks, lest the West be put under the thralldom of the discarnate Allah with his all-enveloping, all-confining Crescent. While Islam rescued monotheism from the various heresies of the East, Chesterton regarded it as a law-bound brand of theism devoted to the worship of a willful and lonely God. Christianity, by contrast, he saw as a sacramental, trinitarian, and nonlegalistic Faith. "If Christianity had never been anything but a simpler morality sweeping away polytheism," Chesterton observed, "there is no reason why Christendom should not have been swept into Islam. The truth is that Islam itself was a barbaric reaction against that very humane complexity that is really a Christian character. . . ."[6] Chesterton may well have acquired this estimate of Islam from Hilaire Belloc's critique of Muslim faith. Writing in 1938, two years after Chesterton's death, when the Islamic world was still mainly subject to the rule of European colonial powers, and when the prime threat to England lay in Fascism and Nazism, Belloc nonetheless prophesied the dangerous recrudescence of Islam as the chief menace to the West. Muslim culture, Belloc wrote, "happens to have fallen back in material applications; there is no reason whatever why it should not learn its new lesson and become our equal in all those temporal things which now *alone* give us our superiority over it—whereas in *Faith* we have fallen inferior to it."[7]

Chesterton's most extended treatment of Islam is found in *The New Jerusalem*. It is a crucial text if only because Chesterton there offers a rare extended argument, unlike his usual practice of gathering short and previously published essays into books. A set of revised notes taken while GKC was visiting Egypt and Palestine,[8] this work displays the various ways his tour prompted him to ponder the crisis already looming in the Middle East: how might Jews and Christians live amicably in a space occupied largely by Muslims? As he departs his own Buckinghamshire town under lowering late December skies, Chesterton notes that the plight of the Fertile Crescent is akin to the malaise of the West. Hence the melancholy significance of the four paths that meet in the marketplace of Beaconsfield: "As I looked for the last time at the pale roads under the load of cloud, I knew our civilisation had indeed come to the cross-roads. As the paths grew fainter, fading under the gathering shadow, I felt rather as if it had lost its way in a forest" (NJ, 11).[9]

The allusion to the opening lines of *The Divine Comedy*, where Dante the pilgrim finds himself "lost in a dark wood," hints at the remedy GKC will propose for the long-term health of the Middle East: he will call for the reclamation of medieval Jerusalem. This "old" Jerusalem is worthy of honor, according to Chesterton, because of the magnificent Christian civilization it produced. Like a twentieth-century Eusebius, he traces the rise of Europe as something akin to sacred history. He argues, as had Eusebius in the third century, that Roman culture constituted a virtual *preparatio evangelica*. For GKC, the Empire rather than the Republic had planted the divine seed that, with Christian cultivation, produced a plentiful harvest. It was not sufficient for the Gospel to have been embodied in the prophetic and sacramental life of the Church, Chesterton insists: a Christian civilization was also required.

> The Christian Church had from a very early date the idea of reconstructing a whole civilisation, and even a complex civilisation. It was the attempt to make a new balance, which differed from the old balance of the stoics of Rome; but which could not afford to lose its balance any more than they. It differed because the old system was one of many religions under one government, while the new was one of many governments under one religion. But

the idea of variety in unity remained though it was in a sense reversed. A historical instinct made the men of the new Europe try hard to find a place for everything in the system, however much might be denied to the individual. Christians might lose everything, but Christendom, if possible, must not lose anything. (NJ, 30)[10]

Chesterton does not regard the transition from paganism to Christianity as altogether seamless. The half millennium between the fall of Rome and the rise of Christendom heralded, among many other achievements, one feat that was virtually unthinkable—namely, the abolition of slavery, an institution without which Rome was hardly conceivable.[11] Yet he still maintains that the Christian civilization of the West took much that was virtuous in Roman culture and "crystallized it into Christendom" (NJ, 19). The medieval Christian Thing was made possible by one event above all others. Visiting the Church of the Nativity in Bethlehem, Chesterton beholds the marble columns allegedly erected on the command of Constantine, perhaps to commemorate his own conversion. GKC is almost brought to his knees by the recognition that, here as nowhere else, the dark wisdom and power of the pagan world bowed down before the single star shining above the bare stable now preserved as an even darker cavity:

> Never have I felt so vividly the great fact of our history; that the Christian religion is like a huge bridge across a boundless sea, which alone connects us with the men who made the world, and yet have utterly vanished from the world. . . . I can never recapture in words the waves of sympathy that went through me in that twilight of the tall pillars, like giants robed in purple, standing still and looking down into that dark hole in the ground. Here halted that imperial civilisation, when it had marched in triumph through the whole world; here in the evening of its days it came trailing all its panoply in the pathway of the three kings. For it came following not only a falling but a fallen star and one that dived before them into a birthplace darker than a grave. And the lord of the laurels [Constantine], clad in his sombre crimson, looked down into that darkness, and then looked up, and saw that all the stars in his own sky were dead. They were deities no longer but only a brilliant dust, scattered down the vain void of Lucretius. The stars were as stale as they were strong; they would never die for they had never lived; they were cursed with an incurable immortality that was but the extension of mortality; they were chained in the chains of causation and unchangeable as the dead. There

are not many men in the modern world who do not know that mood, though it was not discovered by the moderns; it was the final and seemingly fixed mood of nearly all the ancients. Only above the black hole of Bethlehem had they seen a star wandering like a lost spark; and it had done what the eternal suns and planets could not do. It had disappeared. (NJ, 143–44).[12]

This lengthy excerpt reveals Chesterton at his very best—eloquent, incisive, surprising, metaphorically brilliant, theologically discerning, and intellectually provocative in ways that few other modern writers are. These forgotten "men who made the world" are the converted Romans, he argues, and modern Christians of the West owe them an unpayable debt for planting the acorn that gradually grew into the sturdy oak of Christendom.[13]

Despite the rapid decline of medieval civilization that began in the fourteenth century, Christian Europe continued to make stellar accomplishments. It remained so strong, Chesterton insists, that nothing could halt it other than the wrong turnings taken two centuries later by the Renaissance and Reformation. In a remarkable essay titled "If Don John of Austria Had Married Mary Queen of Scots," Chesterton argues that, if these stellar Catholic figures had been matrimonially united, they could have engendered the full flowering of Christendom so as to have made Europe "entirely Christian." In the hero of Lepanto and in the true Catholic successor to the subversive Elizabeth, medieval chivalry and modern learning were splendidly embodied. Together, they could have engendered a "spirit that might have pervaded the whole world and the whole Church":

> There was a moment when religion could have digested Plato as it had once digested Aristotle. For that matter, it might have digested all that is sound in Rabelais and Montaigne and many others; it might have condemned some things in these thinkers; as it did in Aristotle. Only the shock of the new discoveries could have been absorbed (to a great extent it was absorbed) by the central Christian tradition.[14]

Christians as Citizens of the *Alteras Civitas*

There is a strong case to be made also against Chesterton's Eusebian reading of the triumphal ascent of European Christendom. The counterargument holds that, whenever Christianity becomes an instrument and ally of empire, it seriously compromises (and perhaps permanently surrenders) its character as the pilgrim people of God who dwell, even at best, in a tense and often conflicted relation with all other powers. According to this antithetical interpretation, ancient Rome and early Christianity were more alien than kindred. It was altogether natural that the democratic Republic of Rome should have been succeeded by the omnicompetent Empire and that the hegemonic *Pax Romana* should have persecuted Christians as a dire threat to its absolutist claims to divinity. So long as divine excellence is pursued by strictly human means, the cult of absolute power is sure to emerge, as Charles Cochrane once observed of antique Rome: "[T]he hopes and expectations of mankind are fixed upon the 'august' being to whom they have now placed themselves in tutelage. . . . [T]he deification of imperial virtue involves, as an inevitable corollary, the deification of imperial fortune."[15]

More recent critics speak of "the Constantinian fall of the Church," insisting that the alliance of throne and altar meant the loss of the Church's true vocation as the community that offers a prophetic and sacramental alternative to every other polity, no matter how apparently good.[16] The real damage was not done until the Carolingian period when, as we have seen, the Body of Christ was no longer identified with the Church but with the whole of society.[17] Because the early Christians refused any such dissolving of the walls between the City of God and the City of Man, the Romans were right to regard them as a revolutionary and even seditious people. Christianity was a movement consisting of converts who had transferred their ultimate public and political allegiance from the *civitas terrena* to the *civitas dei*. Theirs was an *altera civitas*, another city, one without walls in a radically new sense: Christians had no territory to defend. From among all nations and tribes, whosoever would come into the Body of Christ was welcome, even if the conditions for membership were stringent. With the arrival of God's messianic kingdom, a new aeon had dawned; the old had passed away. Far from wanting to isolate themselves as a holy sect living in contempt for their pagan neighbors, these early Christians sought to "redeem the time" by living according to "a more excellent way," the way of the Crucified:

> They dwell in their own fatherlands [wrote Mathetes to Diognetus in defense
> of his fellow Christians, late in the second century], but as if sojourners in
> them; they share all things as citizens, and suffer all things as strangers. Every
> foreign country is their fatherland, and every fatherland is a foreign country.
> They marry as men, they bear children, but they do not expose their off-
> spring. They offer free hospitality, but guard their purity. Their lot is cast "in
> the flesh," but they do not live "after the flesh."[18]

To take advantage of theological hindsight is not to make light of
Chesterton's uncritical estimate of medieval Christendom, so much as
it is to inquire about those aspects of his writing that may be appro-
priated for the *ecclesia militans* in our time. How might Chesterton
aid Christians who live not only in the twilight of Christendom but
amidst the collapse of Western civilization itself? How might we learn
to dwell within the earthly city as the people who constitute what, in
The City of God, St. Augustine called "the other city, the Heavenly City
on pilgrimage in this world"?

> She herself is the creation of the true God, and she herself is to be his
> true sacrifice. Nevertheless, both cities alike enjoy the good things, or are
> afflicted with the adversities of this temporal state, but with a different faith,
> a different expectation, a different love, until they are separated by the final
> judgement, and each receives her own end, of which there shall be no end.[19]

Islam as the Religion of Fate and the Ruin of Europe

For Chesterton, Islam is a religion whose most basic premises are
inherently inimical to the building of any such earthly version of the
civitas dei. It is always and only a religion of containment and exclusion.
He notices, for example, that while all Muslims are held to be equal, in
virtually democratic fashion, the narrowness of Islam also requires that
all non-Muslims be ostracized as *dhimmi*—as aliens to be carefully protected at best, arbitrarily persecuted and exiled at worst. In diagnosing
the collapse of Christendom, therefore, Chesterton detects no internal illnesses. He alleges, on the contrary, that the Middle Ages came
to a drastic halt because they were beset by an external plague: Islam.
It remained his permanent *bête noire*. While Dante places Muhammad
in the infernal circle of schismatics because he sundered the unity of
European Christianity, Chesterton goes much further. He blames the

rapid decline of medieval Europe on the loss of Jerusalem to the Muslims. The failure of the Crusades led, in his view, to the complete collapse of Christendom. It matters not that fourteenth-century Europe was swept by the Black Death, that the Roman Catholic Church was split by the Western Schism pitting pope against counterpope, that wars and peasant revolts wracked the entire continent, that newly discovered trade routes put the prosperity of newly founded nation-states in competition with waning ecclesial power, that the influx of classical texts and ideas threatened medieval Scholasticism, that the printing press and democratized learning helped prepare for the Protestant Reformation—none of these things count when compared to the sapping of the popular Christian spirit with the failure of the popular Christian attempt to reclaim the Holy City: "I believe the whole medieval society failed, because the heart went out of it with the loss of Jerusalem" (NJ, 172).[20]

Like Huntington, Chesterton treats Islam as a homogeneous and undifferentiated thing. On the contrary, there are as many competing versions of Islam as of Christianity. Even among Arab Muslims, there are numberless believers who reject the Talibanic version of their faith that regards America as the "Great Satan" and that employs jihadist terrorism as its fundamental instrument of operation. Vartan Gregorian points out, for instance, that "Muslims are as diverse as humanity itself," and that "only 15 percent of the world's 1.2 billion Muslims are Arab." Hence his summary refutation of all monolithic notions of Islam:

> The fact is that there is no unified "Muslim world" or unified Muslim ideology—just as there is no unified "Christian world" or unified Christian ideology, no unified "Buddhist world" or unified Buddhist ideology, no unified "Jewish world" or unified Jewish ideology. . . . [T]here is no single accepted Islamic theology, no single interpretation of Islamic law, no single issue around which all Muslim societies are willing to rally their people, futures, or fortunes.[21]

It is surprising that, as the severe critic of Islam, Chesterton seems never to have remarked the most drastic difference of all—the antithesis between Jesus and Muhammad regarding the sword. However much his actual participation in bloodshed may be disputed, there is no denying that Muhammad was a warrior prophet, serving as the

Islamic general at Medina for the last decade of his life (622–632).[22] To envision Jesus as a saber-wielding savior, by contrast, is virtually impossible. He drove the moneychangers from the Temple in an act of righteous ire, but this burst of wrath was an act of furious mercy, since the commercializers were desecrating the holy place where Jews found atonement for sin. Even so, the Church has never made Jesus' cleansing of the Temple serve as the defining act of his life and ministry; it has never venerated any icon of *Cristo Furioso*, as Chesterton himself wisely acknowledged:

> [T]here is something appalling, something that makes the blood run cold, in the idea of having a statue of Christ in wrath. There is something unsupportable even to the imagination in the idea of turning the corner of a street or coming out into the spaces of a marketplace, to meet the petrifying petrifaction of *that* figure as it turned upon a generation of vipers, or that face as it looked at the face of a hypocrite.[23]

Chesterton might well have employed this keen insight in making equally keen judgments against a militarist Christianity no less than a militarist Islam. As we have seen in *Lepanto*, he regarded the horned moon of Islam as the menacing enemy of everything Christian and civilized. In *The New Jerusalem*, he goes even further, describing Islam as the quintessential desert religion, a barren creed embraced by a nomadic people inhabiting the arid wastelands of the Middle East. Yet Chesterton also praises Islam as a religion of enormous strength, a faith whose power lies in its simplicity. There also lies, for Chesterton, its terrible limit. The central emphasis of Islam rests not in the subtlety of freedom but in the certainty of fate.[24] There is no room for the radical transformation of human life in Islam. It is and shall remain what it is, until everyone finally submits (the root meaning of the word *Islam*) to Allah, when at last there shall be *Salaam* on the earth.

Muhammad's followers were not inspired by a raw desire for territory, Chesterton argues, so much as by a strong sense of *inevitability* as they spread westward. Their inspiration was essentially theological, though their means were military, as Muslims rolled rapidly across northern Africa and all of Spain, northward to Tours before being defeated in 732, then eventually reaching the gates of Vienna in 1683, while in the following centuries still constituting a serious Ottoman threat in eastern Europe and Turkey.[25] Hence Chesterton's summary judgment: "It was exactly because it seemed self-evident, to Moslems as to Bolshevists, that their simple creed was suited to everybody, that they wished . . . to impose it on everybody. It was because Islam was broad that Moslems were narrow" (NJ, 179). That Islam began as a religion of military conquest thus makes it virtually incapable of becoming a religion of peace, except as it is radically recast—against the Qur'an's explicit insistence on a literal adherence to its jihadist demands.[26]

Jews, Christians, and the City of God

The issue here is not whether Chesterton is correct in his assessment of Islam. There are many points, in fact, about which he is egregiously wrong. He complains, for example, that the great citadel of Cairo was built by Saladin's stripping of the pyramids, as if Christians had not done something similar with the stones of the Roman Coliseum. As he approaches the great harbor of Alexandria, GKC remembers the Christian mob who there murdered the fourth-century neo-Platonic mathematician Hypatia, but then he adds, "I know the Christians tore Hypatia in pieces; but they did not tear Plato in pieces. The wild men that rode behind Omar the Arab would have thought nothing of tearing every page of Plato in pieces" (NJ, 19). Chesterton might have paused to recall that, under the Abbasid caliphate, the Islamic world became magnificently polyglot and absorptive:

> Translation centers were created. From the seventh to the ninth centuries, manuscripts were obtained from the far reaches of the empire and beyond and translated from their original languages (Sanskrit, Greek, Latin, Syriac, Coptic, and Persian) into Arabic. Thus, the best works of literature, philosophy, and the sciences from other cultures were made accessible: Aristotle, Plato, Galen, Hippocrates, Euclid, Ptolemy. The genesis of Islamic civilization was indeed a collaborative effort, incorporating the learning of many cultures and languages. As in government administration, Christians and Jews, who had been the intellectual and bureaucratic backbone of the Persian and Byzantine empires, participated in the process as well as Muslims.[27]

Chesterton might have also discerned that, despite such splendid achievements, Islam can only dubiously be called an Abrahamic religion. Though Muslims honor Abraham as a prophet, he is not the

Jewish Abraham who challenges and questions God. Islam, according to Chesterton, is incapable of radical self-critique, for its literalism lacks the Christian sense of life as a paradoxical and multifold affair of deeply layered levels of meaning, from the strictly literal to the profoundly spiritual. Christians can thus turn their Gospel against themselves whenever their faith becomes idolatrous, but there is no room for such drastic self-assessment in Islam. Its vision of paradise, for instance, is not only mundane and self-pleasuring but also threatening. "The fanatic of the desert is dangerous precisely because he does take his faith as a fact," Chesterton writes, "and not even as a truth in our more transcendental sense" (NJ, 27). Islam is a simple *datum*, a singular and stark revelation given by God, neither to be questioned nor to become the basis for self-questioning. There is nothing akin to the book of Job in Muslim tradition. Allah cannot be challenged. Least of all can it be said of Muhammad what Chesterton says of Christ at Gethsemane and Golgotha, where God is supremely present in his absence:

> When the world shook and the sun was wiped out of heaven, it was not at the crucifixion, but at the cry from the cross: the cry which confessed that God was forsaken of God. . . . Nay (the matter grows too difficult for human speech), but let the atheists themselves choose a god. They will find only one divinity who ever uttered their isolation; only one religion in which God seemed for an instant to be an atheist.[28]

Since Jesus' cry of abandonment is actually a quotation from Psalm 22, Chesterton might well have noted that Christians and Jews have much more in common with each other than with Islam. Instead, he offers an estimate of Jews that grossly misses this point. In a stunning turn of the argument, Chesterton accuses them of having failed to pass either of two requisite tests: the test of usury and the test of patriotism. He completely ignores the commonplace truth that, often confined to their ghettos, medieval Jews became wealthy moneylenders as much by necessity as by choice. He follows this slur against usurious Semites with the accusation that Jews cannot be trusted to be true patriots because their primary loyalties lie elsewhere than with their host nation. The sub-Christian quality of this allegation is altogether as egregious as its anti-Semitism. Chesterton seems to have forgotten that the Romans brought this same criticism of disloyalty against the early Christians, and that the British once arraigned Catholics on a similar charge. Because they "deliver themselves up to the protection and service of another prince," as we will hear John Locke lament, Catholics were not exempted from the religious penalties that the 1689 Act of Toleration lifted from Protestant Dissenters. Christians and Jews ought to be *joined*, Chesterton might have noted, in denying ultimate loyalty to any other principality than the Kingdom of God. Prime allegiance to the God of Abraham and Jesus not only ensures the prophetic freedom to bring unjust Caesar under divine judgment; it also guarantees that the People of Exile remain unsettled strangers and wayfarers within every earthly city, thereby offering it a single saving remnant. Not so for Chesterton, as he declares in this, perhaps his most disturbing, judgment:

> Patriotism is not merely dying for the nation. It is dying with the nation. It is regarding the fatherland not merely as a real resting-place like an inn, but as a final resting-place, like a house or even a grave. Even the most Jingo of the Jews do not feel like this about their adopted country; and I doubt that the most intelligent of the Jews would pretend that they did. . . . When the Jew in France or England says he is a good patriot he means only that he is a good citizen, and he would put it more truly if he said he was a good exile. (NJ, 197)[29]

Islamic Literalism and the Horror of Images

Our task is to determine where, within Chesterton's work, there may be found a distinctively Christian and nonreductive way of engaging Muslims. I believe that the answer lies, albeit ironically, in Chesterton's complaint against the literalistic character of Islam. Muslims have no real regard for the nuances of language, he argues, especially metaphor. The early twentieth-century Arabs of the Middle East were a People of the Tent, in his view, because their nomadism derived as much from nonfigural theology as from economic necessity. They were, in effect, the first nominalists. The biblical summons for God's people to remain perpetually on pilgrimage was treated in a literal way—namely, as a repudiation of all earthly analogies between home and heaven, between the settled life and paradise, between things human and divine. Such analogical opacity is not confined to itinerant Bedouins, according to

Chesterton. He is especially troubled that, after conquering Constantinople in 1453, the Ottoman Turks absorbed little or none of its long history and rich Christian culture. The Islamic repudiation of images keeps their religion insular and abstemious: "[T]he Moslem horror of idolatry, with the featureless austerity of its art and the whole of that somewhat inhuman simplicity . . . prevents them having local images and special shrines."[30] Hence the impossibility of any growth or development in Muslim theology, at least as Chesterton interprets it. It is built on what he calls

> . . . the secret of the obvious. But it will always be the same secret, for which thousands of these simple and serious and splendidly valiant men will die. The highest message of Mahomet is a piece of divine tautology. The very cry that God is God is a repetition of words. . . . The very phrase is like an everlasting echo, that can never cease to say the same sacred word. (NJ, 33)

Rémi Brague makes a case that resonates with Chesterton's. He maintains that, unlike Christian Scripture, the Qur'an promotes cultural arrogance and contempt. It lacks any sense of what Brague calls "secondarity"—that is, the fundamental sense of indebtedness to previous cultures and religions that leaves Christianity entwined with and dependent upon such preceding sources and their attendant languages. The Christian and Jewish revelations recorded in Scripture, according to the Qur'an, are either corrupted or fragmentary. Thus are they completely superseded. Arabic becomes the ultimate language, the very tongue of God, so that, while texts from other languages may be translated into Arabic, Brague argues that they need not be preserved in their own integrity. Neither is there any great need to cultivate the linguistic and historical skills necessary for learning the cultures that produced these now-surpassed texts and traditions of Judaism and Christianity. On the contrary, everything besides the Qur'an is not so much secondary as actually heretical. It teaches that the whole of humankind has pledged obedience to God, Brague points out, before the creation even occurs. What follows has immense consequence for both good and ill:

> Every son of Adam, i.e., each and every human being, has submitted to God from the outset. Islam (submission) is therefore the original and "natural" religion of mankind, whereas, according to a frequently quoted utterance of

Muhammad (hadith), the other religions are foisted upon children by their parents. . . . The lack of submission to God's will is not tough luck, or an error, nor a simple moral failure; it's a kind of treason. . . . Not only does Islam forbid apostasy, therefore, as an inexcusable offence; it has a tendency to regard the adherents of other faiths as already apostates, guilty of the primary sin against God.[31]

Brague's sharp critique of modern Islam—together with Chesterton's complaint that its tautologous literalism denies even the possibility of the Incarnation[32]—offers ironic promise for Christian–Muslim engagement in our time. Though there is still a clash of opposition, it is focused on the essential *theological* differences between Christianity and Islam rather than the "clash of civilizations" that they supposedly undergird. Chesterton's portrait of Islam in *The Flying Inn*, while frightening in its prophecy of the Islamicizing of Europe (sometimes now called "Eurabia"), does not attribute the Muslim threat to cultural conquest or mass migration, but to the West's own moral and intellectual flaccidity, especially the British propensity for embracing foggy philosophical and religious claims. In this remarkable novel, Chesterton does not locate the enemy as external, in Islam, but rather as internal, in the loss of sacramental Christianity. It is a sacramentalism, moreover, of which Islam is inherently incapable. For while Allah is inescapably near, closer than our own breath, the creation expresses nothing of his nature. God is not disclosed in a People or a Savior or in earthly analogies that follow from such personal self-identification, but in an impersonal text literally delivered, literally to be read, and literally to be obeyed.

The Nightmare Desire to Make the World Over Again

John Coates offers a compelling interpretation of *The Flying Inn* as Chesterton's fictional critique of the English propensity for "muddling through." This national disregard for hard argument makes the British public susceptible, Chesterton believed, to ideologies that should be natively alien to it—especially religious ideologies deriving from the East. The Eastern desire to absorb everything into a Higher Unity than the particular religions allow—into a grand Cosmic Whole—would seem utterly counter to the deep English love for the local and the particular and the individual. On the contrary, Chesterton's novel features a visiting Islamic "prophet" named Misysra Ammon, who has won a large following among the British elite. Coates demonstrates that Chesterton may well have modeled Ammon on Rabindranath Tagore, the Bengali poet who, in giving London lectures in 1912 and 1913, was hailed as a seer and sage journeying from the East like a new Magus. Tagore was lionized by such notables as the Irish nationalist-poet "A.E." (George Russell), the Oxford classicist Gilbert Murray, the expatriate poet-critic Ezra Pound, and above all William Butler Yeats, who hailed Tagore as one of the world's finest minds and greatest writers.[33]

Naïve British receptivity toward the airy mysticism of the East is not Chesterton's sole target in *The Flying Inn*. His satirical sword pierces several other bloated intellectual fashions of the time, including biblical Higher Criticism, political Progressivism, religious Spiritualism, artistic Futurism and, most especially, nihilistic Nietzscheanism.[34] Though Nietzsche is never named, Lord Philip Ivywood—a member of Parliament converted to Ammon's Islamist philosophy—has a decidedly Nietzschean cast of mind. Indeed, he regards himself as having been liberated from the conventional contraries of good and evil. "I see the breaking of the barriers," he declares in response to an exhibit of Futurist art; "beyond that I see nothing" (FI, 256).[35] Hence his self-declared ascent to the solitary self-sufficiency of the Nietzschean Superman:

> "I would walk where no man has walked; and find something beyond tears and laughter. My road shall be my road indeed. . . . And my adventures shall not be in the hedges and the gutters, but in the borders of the ever advancing human brain. I will think what was unthinkable until I thought it; I will love what was never loved until I loved it—I will be as lonely as the First Man." (FI, 255)[36]

Ivywood emerges, in fact, as an Enlightenment rationalist akin to the mental maniac we encounter in *Orthodoxy*. Supposedly standing outside all particular confessions and creeds, he selectively retrieves and unites what he regards as their most salutary beliefs into a new and compelling unity. Ivywood also believes that, among the world's various belief systems, as he might now call them, Islam has the greatest power to bring about perpetual peace. And since Islam has but a single defining dogma—that God is God—Ivywood regards it as an infinitely malleable tenet. Thus does he reconstrue Islam in totally inclusivist terms, as indeed the most progressive and open-ended of all religions:

"Not in vain, I think, is the symbol of that faith the Crescent, the growing thing. While other creeds carry emblems implying more or less of finality, for this great creed of hope its very imperfection is its pride, and men shall walk fearlessly in new and wonderful paths, following the increasing curve which contains and holds up before them the eternal promises of the orb." (FI, 79)

This reference to proud imperfection hints at the disclosure that will come toward the end, when Ivywood reveals his desire to risk what never has been tried. He wants to refashion, not English *mores* alone, but absolutely everything. Against the claim of the poet Dorian Wimpole that the "prime fact of identity is the limit set on all living things" (FI, 254), Ivywood denies all such boundaries. He dedicates himself to pure possibility, not only in personal but also in political terms. When asked by a chemist named Crooke whether Ivywood thinks he made the world and thus whether he "should make it over again so easily," this Faustian reformer offers a chilling reply: "The world was made badly," said Philip, with a terrible note in his voice, "and *I will make it over again*" (FI, 288, emphasis in original).[37]

Ivywood's aspiration to be a political Superman is a disturbing forecast of the century that would produce a whole horde of such limit-denying dictators, perhaps most notably the Cambodian genocidal killer Pol Pot. So fully did he desire "to make the world over again" that he redated the beginning of his regime to the Year Zero. In completely remaking his country, he destroyed a fifth of its population, roughly two million people. Thus does one of Chesterton's finest comic novels deal with horrors that would seem to have little or no connection with Islam. Lord Ivywood's complete recasting of the Muslim faith into such deadly religious and political categories certainly bears little if any resemblance to the historic religion itself. Yet it nonetheless raises a hard question: what might bring an end to such nightmarish delusions of omnicompetence, persuading inhabitants of the late modern world to embrace their proper limits and authentic possibilities?

The Presence That Is Silent and Yet Potent

At least one answer is to be found in the yet-untapped religious depths of *The Flying Inn*. Though the farcical plots and subplots are often difficult to follow, the novel's tenor is thoroughly, if also silently, sacramental. In fact, Chesterton almost fulfills T. S. Eliot's desire for a fully

Christian work of art that would contain not a single theological reference. Chesterton seamlessly weaves the novel's "theme," if it can be so called, into its fabric, its matter into its manner. He has repeated recourse to oxymorons, for instance, that set the sharp (*oxus*) alongside the dull (*moros*): "arctic magnanimity," "lyrical roar," "cold eagerness," "fussy self-effacement," "well-bred surprise," "worldly simplicity," "bursting silence," "fatalistic freedom," "sleepy explosion," "boisterous reverie," "hasty drawl," "sullen emotionalism." Taken in context, these oxymorons do not exhibit the flashy wordplay of Chestertonian wit; they provide, instead, a virtually Dostoevskian understanding of the contradictions inherent in most human acts and attitudes.

They may also suggest, however subtly, the supreme Oxymoron: the right-angled clash of human sin and divine redemption in the Cross. This prime collision is so catastrophic because human sinfulness is so disastrous. It was not meant to be. With his thoroughly Augustinian and Thomistic understanding of divine action, Chesterton knows that the realms of light and darkness, of the created and the Uncreated, are intended to overlap and intersect in a gracious complementarity. As N. T. Wright observes, Jews and Christians hold that heaven and earth are neither coterminous nor mutually exclusive spheres:

> The one true God made a world that was other than himself, because that is what love delights to do. And, having made such a world, he has remained in close, dynamic, and intimate relationship with it, without in any way being contained within it or having it contained within himself. To speak of God's action in the world, of heaven's action (if you like) on earth—and Christians speak of this every time they say the Lord's Prayer—is to speak not of an awkward metaphysical blunder, nor of a "miracle" in the sense of a random invasion by alien ("supernatural") forces but to speak of the loving Creator acting within the creation which has never lacked the signs of his presence.[38]

Accordingly, the novel's most religiously resonant passages are those wherein, without any overt allusion to Christian doctrine or practice, Chesterton enables readers to detect a mysterious if also unnamed Presence. Sunset and evening are natural occasions of such an interlocking of heaven and earth, and Chesterton's descriptions of them are more powerful and convincing than most conventional evocations of the Ultimate Other.[39] Here, for example, he employs repetition and alliteration and anagram, all within a single remarkable sentence: "The sun, in dropping finally, seemed to have broken as a blood orange might break; and lines of blood-red light were spilt along the split, low, level skies" (FI, 18).

Rudolf Otto taught us long ago that the numinous must always be understood as the *mysterium tremendum et fascinans*, the Sacred that alarms at the same time it allures. This is the lesson that Job learns in the whirlwind of the divine epiphany and that the author of Hebrews confirms: "It is a fearful thing to fall into the hands of the living God" (Heb 10:31). Chesterton thus depicts this silent and invisible Presence as no less frightening than enticing, especially in its twilight manifestation, when evening slips into darkness, and as King Lear's "monsters of the deep" are juxtaposed to the night sky that Luther famously declared God to have made for his own delight:

> The next moment they were in the wood itself, and winding in and out among the trees by a ribbon of paths. The emerald twilight between the stems, combined with the dragon-like contortions of the great grey roots of the beeches, had a suggestion of monsters and the deep sea; especially as a long litter of crimson and copper-coloured fungi, which might well have been the more gorgeous types of anemone or jelly-fish, reddened the ground like a sunset dropped from the sky. And yet, contradictorily enough, they had also a strong sense of being high up; and even near to heaven; and the brilliant summer stars that stared through the chinks of the leafy roof might almost have been white starry blossoms on the trees of the wood. (FI, 265)

The car "winding in and out among the trees" is occupied by Dorian Wimpole, a poet; Patrick Dalroy, a naval captain; and Humphrey Pump, an innkeeper of the Old Ship. This unlikely trio is in flight from police wanting to arrest them for the crime they have committed—namely, their violation of a recently promulgated law designed to shut down the public houses of England. This new statute has been devised by the aforementioned Lord Philip Ivywood, a government minister who has come under the influence of the Islamist guru named Misysra Ammon. Combining his prim desire to manage the moral hygiene of the nation with the Muslim condemnation of alcohol, Ivywood has persuaded his fellow parliamentarians to prohibit the public consumption of intoxicating beverages. No longer will the rabble stagger home from their neighborhood taverns, inebriated by what he calls the "sleepy poison" of liquorish drink (FI, 48). Instead, they will be blessed by the supposedly salubrious effects of Lord Ivywood's legislative act:

> "[T]he deleterious element of alcohol [will] be made illegal save in such few places as the Government may specially exempt for Parliamentary or other public reasons, and . . . the provocative and demoralising display on inn signs [will] be strictly forbidden except in the cases thus specially exempted: the absence of such temptations will, in our opinion, do much to improve the precarious financial conditions of the working class." (FI, 48)

Lord Ivywood's rigorous sumptuary law, allegedly intended to protect the poor against their own worst tendencies, includes a "grandfather" clause that provides an unintentional loophole. It decrees that, until all the inn signs advertising the nation's public houses can be taken down, alcohol may be served and drunk wherever such hoardings are still in place. So quickly have government agents removed these inn signs that only one remains in all of England. Ever so cleverly, the Irish naval captain Dalroy joins the English publican Pump in seizing this last banner of joy and delight to be found in friendly drinking: the sign of The Old Ship. Seizing also a large cask of rum and a huge round of Cheddar cheese, Dalroy and Pump take flight from the ethics police. These fleeing sign bearers thus create a flying inn wherever, albeit quite briefly, they plant their insignia and thus serve, albeit quite legally, their singular food and beverage.

Some of the most riotous scenes (both literally and figuratively) in all of Chesterton's work occur as this publican and captain create instant "locals" in the unlikeliest of places: in front of an inn slated for razing, on the property of a government-erected meeting hall meant to replace both inns and chapels, along the seashore, outside a pharmacy, even in Lord Ivywood's disused back garden. Along their merry and catastrophic way, Dalroy sings some of Chesterton's most memorable poems—verses to be voiced while clinking and then drinking glasses filled with spirituous concoctions. And since Lord Ivywood himself abstains from all cruelty to animals and thus from all eating of meat, Dalroy takes special delight in declaring that he too enjoys the various libations derived not from fauna but flora:

"You will find me drinking rum
Like a sailor in a slum,
  You will find me drinking beer like a Bavarian;
You will find me drinking gin
In the lowest kind of inn,
  Because I am a rigid Vegetarian." (FI, 138)

. . .

"No more the milk of cows
Shall pollute my private house,
Than the milk of the wild mares of the Barbarian;
I will stick to port and sherry,
For they are so very, very,
So very, very, very Vegetarian." (FI, 157)[40]

The Communal and Celebrative and Sacramental Life

Chesterton's ribald satire of Lord Ivywood and his pseudo-Islamic policies is subtler than it may seem. It is obvious that Chesterton joins Christopher Dawson and Georges Bernanos in protest against the pretense of the modern nation-state to manage the lives of their citizens[41]—in this case, not from a morally neutral viewpoint so much as from the modern assumption that the state precedes and thus presides over all of the basic institutions of society, chiefly the family and the schools. Yet the real gravamen of *The Flying Inn* lies primarily in the ban against public drinking. Chesterton is deeply concerned about the loss of an institution that, for him, stood as an essential corollary to home and Church; in fact, it served as the modern equivalent of the ancient public square:

> It is impossible to imagine a more splendid and sacred combination of words, a more august union of simplicity and glory, than this great phrase "a public house." It expresses in one word all that is oldest and soundest and most indestructible in the idea of human society: the house where every man is master; the house where every man is guest. As we have private ties, so should we have public ties. As we have private prayers, so should we have public prayers. As we have private houses, so we should have public houses. Even if we lament the license of their use, or regard them as having been

degraded into mere drugshops, we ought still to regard every public house as a temple, a temple that has been profaned.[42]

Chesterton was fond of citing Aristotle's claim that man is by nature a political animal. The Stagirite philosopher meant, of course, that we are social rather than solitary creatures, dwelling authentically not alone unto ourselves but always and only in relation to others. Living in mutuality, we constitute the human *polis*, the City of Man. Communal life is distinguished from solitude in a number of ways, mainly in its ritual habits and practices, not all of which have religious intent but almost all of which have religious implication. Chesterton found this to be supremely true in the ritualized consumption of alcohol, especially as it gladdens the hearts of the poor who are often ground down by the harshness of life.[43]

Here he is in thorough accord with Josef Pieper, who argues that festivals are surely the most central and vital of all human activities. They do more than deliver us from the harried strain and hurry of the daily round. *"To celebrate a festival means: to live out, for some special occasion and in an uncommon manner, the universal assent to the world as a whole."*[44] The uselessness of celebrations is their very essence. That they are extravagant and wasteful, that they serve always as an end and never as a means to something else, that they often spring up as an unbidden gift—these are the reasons that a life without the leisure of festivity is not worth living. Humphrey Pump and Patrick Dalroy seek joyfully, therefore, to overcome the joylessness that Pieper describes as characterizing much of modern life in the West: "There can be no festivity when man, imagining himself self-sufficient, refuses to recognize the Goodness of things which goes far beyond any conceivable utility; it is the Goodness of reality taken as a whole which validates all other particular goods and which man himself can never produce nor simply translate into social or individual 'welfare.'"[45] In the modern obsession with work, we have not only proven ourselves to be inheritors of our exiled Edenic parents who were punished with sweating labor, but also regressed to a virtually bestial state, as Chesterton himself notes:

All the human things are more dangerous than anything that affects the beasts—sex, poetry, property, religion. The real case against drunkenness is not that it calls up the beast, but that it calls up the Devil. . . . There is

nothing bestial about intoxication. . . . Man is always something worse or
something better than an animal. . . . Thus, in sex no animal is either chivalrous or obscene. And thus no animal ever invented anything so bad as drunkenness—or so good as drink.[46]

That consecrated wine serves as the sacrament of Christ's redeeming
blood—and thus of the ultimate Christian festival—makes the out-
lawed serving of rum function in a surprisingly sacramental fashion
in *The Flying Inn*. Though the liquorish drink provided by Dalroy and
Pump is hardly sanctified, their portable insignia of The Old Ship has
quasi-sacramental power. Wherever the sign is planted, rum is indeed
tapped and enjoyed, *there as nowhere else*. It proves to be nothing less
than an efficacious sign, conferring the rum-laden grace that it signifies. Indeed, it acts *ex opere operato*. The bibulations it proffers are made
possible not by the merits of the two scofflaws who tap the keg, but by
the work—the sign—itself!

Lord Ivywood cares nothing for the celebrative life or for the
emblems that point to it. He is opaque to such sacramental subtleties.
He regards the mark of The Old Ship as a mere notice board announcing the availability of alcohol to be consumed on the premises. "That
wooden sign," he declares, "can be cut up for firewood. It shall lead
decent citizens a devil's dance no more. Understand it once and for all,
before you learn it from policemen or prison warders. You are under
a new law. *That sign is the sign of nothing*" (FI, 286, emphasis added).
Ivywood's moral imagination, despite his immense gifts of verbal elo-
quence, is rarefied, discarnate, inhuman.

Rum, Romanism, and the Road Home

Ivywood has also fashioned his country estate after the pattern of
Islamic art so as to deny all finitude, as rooms open onto larger rooms
into virtual infinity. It makes Lady Joan Brett, the woman for whose
affections both Ivywood and Dalroy are contesting, feel as if she were
looking through a kaleidoscope, or as if she were dwelling in Keats'
"Ode to a Nightingale," amidst "perilous seas in fairy lands forlorn."
Yet this utter architectural artificiality, this complete disanalogy with
anything human, is precisely what Lord Ivywood desires:

"I want it to be like that," said Ivywood in a low and singularly moved into-
nation. "I want this to be the end of the house. I want this to be the end of
the world. Don't you feel that is the real beauty of all this eastern art; that it
is coloured like the edges of things, like the little clouds of morning and the
islands of the blest? Do you know," and he lowered his voice yet more, "it has
the power over me of making me feel as if I were myself absent and distant;
some oriental traveller who was lost and for whom men were looking. When
I see that greenish lemon yellow enamel there let into the white, I feel that I
am standing thousands of leagues from where I stand." (FI, 116–17)

To be thus abstracted from oneself is also to be prone to political no
less than aesthetic absoluteness—"to be the end of the world"—and
thus perhaps to be the means of the world's moral destruction.

Whether consciously or by osmosis, Ivywood has absorbed the
Islamic disregard for signs and symbols as proclaimed by Misysra
Ammon. The Muslim prophet boasts that Islam has no images of Allah
because none could ever satisfactorily convey the reality of God. While
this caveat against idolatry is patently true, it leads to the Islamic repudiation of *all* human analogues of God. Indeed, it is a bedrock principle of Islam that Allah could not become human. The fundamental
Christian claim, by contrast, is that in Jesus of Nazareth the fullness
of the invisible and uncreated Godhead has dwelt among us *bodily* (Col
2:9).[47] And because God has assumed human form and thus displayed
his own self-image, Christians are summoned to detect his creative
and redeeming likeness in other places as well.[48] Once the imagination has been sacramentally formed, Christians can discern analogies
between earthly and heavenly things almost everywhere. Indeed, the
poet Dorian Wimpole is converted from his temporary dalliance with
the ideas of Ivywood and Ammon by such a stirring of his analogical
imagination:

Cloudily there crowded into his mind ideas with which it was imperfectly
familiar, especially an idea he had heard called "The Image of God." It
seemed to him more and more that all these things, from the donkey to the
very docks and ferns by the roadside, were dignified and sanctified by their
partial resemblance to something else. It was as if they were baby drawings;
the wild, crude sketches of Nature in her first sketch-books of stone. (FI,
194)[49]

Given Chesterton's own sacramentally shaped imagination, we might rightly wonder why he did not make wine rather than rum serve as the forbidden alcoholic beverage at the center of his novel. Perhaps he feared that it would be too obviously Christian and perhaps also insufficiently *déclassé* to make it the preferred drink of the poor.[50] In any case, Chesterton chose to feature another libation—the drink of pirates and sailors and other common sorts: demon rum. Yet the substitution of a lesser drink for a greater hardly undermines its analogical validity. The poet Wimpole insists, on the contrary, that the intoxicating powers of rum may underlie the splendid stagger of English pathways. Hence the first and final stanzas of what has become one of Chesterton's most celebrated poems, "The Rolling English Road":

"Before the Romans came to Rye or out to Severn strode,
The rolling English drunkard made the rolling English road.
A reeling road, a rolling road, that rambles round the shire,
And after him the parson ran, the sexton and the squire.
A merry road, a mazy road, and such as we did tread
That night we went to Birmingham by way of Beachy Head."
. . .
"My friends, we will not go again or ape an ancient rage,
Or stretch the folly of our youth to be the shame of age.
But walk with clearer eyes and ears this path that wandereth,
And see undrugged in evening light the decent inn of death;
For there is good news yet to hear and fine things to be seen
Before we go to Paradise by way of Kensal Green." (FI, 270–71)

The lurching curves and twisting loops of English roads are clearly an analogue of life's own quality of wandering. The most important things are rarely found straightaway, Chesterton suggests, but usually by inadvertence, perhaps while seeking something else, almost always by surprise, rarely by intention, often by detours and bypaths. It is not a pragmatic way to live, of course, but therein lies its glory. "Pragmatism is a matter of human needs"; Chesterton observed, "and one of the first of human needs is to be something more than a pragmatist."[51] The most fundamental human requisite is the love of God, the reordering of life to it, and thus the multitudinous ways in which such redirected desires may be accomplished. To travel from London to the grim industrial city of Birmingham by way of the magnificent chalk cliffs at Beachy Head, the highest in England, is to take a circuitous route indeed. Yet precisely in encountering not only pleasant but perhaps unpleasant things as well, does the arrival become all the more wondrous. Better still to peregrinate one's way to Paradise, not easily and directly, but past both wonders and obstacles, arriving arduously and gradually at the Beatific Life via the "decent inn of death," as Chesterton called it, and then perhaps being laid to rest among the many eminent Victorians buried in Kensal Green, the famous London cemetery. Eight years earlier, in his excellent book on Dickens, Chesterton had foreseen such a divinely festive ending at the end of a winding path:

> The hour of absinthe is over. We shall not be much further troubled with the little artists who found Dickens too sane for their sorrows and too clean for their delights. But we have a long way to travel before we get back to what Dickens meant: and the passage is along a rambling English road, a twisting road such as Mr. Pickwick travelled. But this at least is part of what he meant; that comradeship and serious joy are not interludes in our travel; but that rather our travels are interludes in comradeship and joy, which through God shall endure for ever. The inn does not point to the road; the road points to the inn. And all roads point at last to an ultimate inn, where we shall meet Dickens and all his characters: and when we drink again it shall be from the great flagons in the tavern at the end of the world.[52]

From almost the beginning of his writing career, Chesterton was convinced that, for those whose joy is ordered to the joy of God, death is not an evil to be feared but a good to be embraced. For death gives life its focus, its direction, its end in the sense of the Greek word *telos*, which also means purpose. Throughout the novel, Lady Joan Brett has been facing her own life-and-death decision: whether she shall follow her original love and thus set her course on the narrow and circuitous path that marriage to the rambunctious Patrick Dalroy would entail, or whether she will adopt the plush life and follow the wide and smooth way that nuptials with Lord Philip Ivywood would provide. The master of Ivywood Hall regards her decision as a matter of *kismet*, for he believes that he is one of the world's eminent figures, a grand man fated to draw the perfect woman, magnetically and inexorably, to himself. Lady Joan is rescued from such a fate, quite literally, by Captain Dalroy's onrushing ragtag army of inns-men, who defeat Ivywood's Turkish defenders in a final battle. Thus does a supremely comic novel devoted to rollicking good fun and sacramental celebration end with one of the largest human analogies of divine love—the marriage of true minds and bodies.[53]

Yet the final scene is not devoted to the wedded love of Brett and Dalroy. No sooner has Lady Joan declared of her marriage that "we are so happy" than Lord Ivywood's caregiver contrasts their bliss with her master's: "Yes," said Enid, "but his happiness will last." That Enid weeps after making this dark confession reveals that nightmarish shadows belie the novel's radiant gaiety. The marriage of Patrick Dalroy and Joan Brett will no doubt be interrupted by the ordinary vicissitudes of marital life and thus be less than serenely happy.[54] Philip Ivywood's "happiness," by contrast, will be unbroken, for he has descended into the abyss of pure delusion, into the solipsistic arbitrariness of the final Übermensch talking to himself: "I have gone where God has never dared to go. I am above the silly supermen as they are above mere men. Where I walk in the Heavens, no man has walked before me; and I am alone in a garden. All this passing about me is like the lonely plucking of garden flowers. I will have this blossom, I will have that" (FI, 320). The novel's final words are devoted not to joyful celebration that victory has been won but to Joan's tears of pity and gratitude. She weeps in pity for the permanent madness of Ivywood, who believes he has become the solitary and brave new Adam when, instead, he is a pathetic old Lucifer repeating his mantra to himself forever: *non serviam.* Lady Joan also weeps in gratitude for having been awakened from the nightmare collapse of Western civilization that his insanity identifies. Marriage to such a wild and fanatic Christian as Dalroy, by contrast, gives her the hope of a true if also turbulent happiness. For Chesterton, it follows, this sacramental bond between a man and a woman is a microcosmic instance of the macrocosmic answer to both discarnational Islam and the nihilistic faith that, however unintentionally, it can spawn.

5

TYRANNICAL TOLERANCE AND FEROCIOUS HOSPITALITY
The Ball and the Cross

Bigotry may be roughly defined as the anger of men who have no
opinions. It is the resistance offered to definite ideas by that vague bulk
of people whose ideas are indefinite to excess. Bigotry may be called
the appalling frenzy of the indifferent. This frenzy of the indifferent is
in truth a terrible thing; it has made all monstrous and widely pervading persecutions. In this degree it was not the people who cared who
ever persecuted; the people who cared were not sufficiently numerous.
It was the people who did not care who filled the world with fire and
oppression. It was the hands of the indifferent that lit the faggots;
it was the hands of the indifferent that turned the rack. There have
come some persecutions out of the pain of a passionate certainty; but
these produced, not bigotry, but fanaticism—a very different and
a somewhat admirable thing. Bigotry in the main has always been
the pervading omnipotence of those who do not care crushing out
those who care in darkness and blood.

G. K. Chesterton, *Heretics* (1905)

"Modern toleration is really a tyranny," G. K. Chesterton asserts.
"It is a tyranny because it is a silence. To say that I must not
deny my opponent's faith is to say I must not discuss it."[1] In a similarly
barbed aphorism, Chesterton describes tolerance as "the virtue of a
man without convictions." The early Church, in its missional refusal to
regard the Faith as true only for Christians, rightly scandalized pagan

Rome. Christianity, says Chesterton, "was intolerable because it was intolerant."[2] Such angular convictions often lead to the dismissal of Chesterton as an antediluvian reactionary seeking an ark whereon he might survive the flood of modernity, a comic curmudgeon vainly hoping to reinstate an idealized version of the Middle Ages.

As we have noticed, Chesterton was no reactionary—on the contrary, he was an unrepentant enthusiast for modernity's defining event: the French Revolution and its democratic deliverance of the common man from his ancient bondage, elevating him to a social and political sufficiency heretofore unknown. We have thus heard GKC insisting that the events of 1789 helped the Church recover one of its own most severely neglected teachings: the equality in dignity and worth of every creature formed in the image and likeness of God. With democratic equality also comes an attendant pluralism in matters political and religious, since neither the Church nor the state can any longer exercise an externally imposed conformity to a single way of life. Instead, there are legitimate differences in both belief and behavior that the state must protect. The shorthand word for such a pluralistic political regime is *liberalism*, and we have seen that Chesterton styled himself as a Liberal from youth to age.[3] There are many kinds of Liberalism, of course, but Judith Sklar describes its most basic and generic conviction: "[E]very adult should be able to make as many effective decisions without fear or favor about as many aspects of her or his life as is compatible with the like freedom of every other adult."[4] As a man who made such an "effective decision" in becoming a Roman Catholic, Chesterton also embraced the religious pluralism that no longer called for an established state church. He crossed the Tiber, at least in part, because he sought a Faith that would provide both pith and heft for the making of his literary and theological witness in a pluralistic democracy.

That the religiously indifferent Chesterton first became a devout Anglican and then a Catholic convert indicates his early discernment that the Liberal project would not suffice unto itself. It had a canker at its core, and the worm eating at its heart was called "tolerance." For while Liberalism could offer protections against common evils, it would have increasing difficulty defining common goods. Chesterton was among the first to recognize that his own inherited Liberalism would issue in an unprecedented secularism, rapidly displacing religion from the center of human life. The movement that began with the aim of setting people free would threaten, in fact, to empty the public sphere of those virtues that alone might prevent a return to the brute and slavish state of nature that Thomas Hobbes envisioned: the "war of all against all." Hence the need briefly to survey the history of tolerance and to outline a Christian alternative to it before embarking on a reading of *The Ball and the Cross*.

The Triumph of an Intolerant Tolerance

Toleration is a subject that, almost more than any other, preoccupies modern mentality. Baruch Spinoza, John Milton, G. E. Lessing, Pierre Bayle, Roger Williams, and William Penn all devoted themselves to it. Yet it is John Locke's "Letter on Toleration" that still shapes the debate. Once the Protestant Reformation had finally exploded the already fissiparating unity of Europe, English life was soon riddled by repression and even civil war. Having been religiously exiled to the Dutch Republic, where a secular state had been founded in order to permit religious differences, Locke sought to bring a similar freedom from religious persecution to his own nation. As a deist perched high above the religious affray, he sought to judge it from an ostensibly neutral perspective that credited only those universal, tradition-free norms that all people of good will could discern.

The key to Locke's notion of toleration lies in his clear division between the civil and the religious realms: "He jumbles heaven and earth together, the things most remote and opposite, who mixes these two societies."[5] Our civil interests, as Locke defines them, are these: life, liberty, health, and property. Such public goods are construed as external and bodily, thus being properly governed by the magistrate or civil government. As such, they may and must be preserved by use of force, which is the government's chief legitimate power. Our religious interests, according to Locke, are internal and spiritual, for they chiefly concern salvation in the afterlife. The state has no authority, therefore, to rule in this private realm—neither to mandate the articles of faith, to dictate the forms of worship, nor to adjudicate religious disputes. In the Lockean scheme, religion is not to be understood as an outward, bodily, and public matter but as a private, individual, and spiritual matter. "The care . . . of every man's soul," Locke peremptorily declares, "belongs unto himself and is to be left unto himself."[6] Though he assumed that Anglicanism would remain the established state church, Locke urged that other expressions of Protestant Christianity should to be tolerated, so long as they themselves remained tolerant. Yet two groups, Locke insisted, are not to be tolerated at all: atheists and Roman Catholics. Atheists deny the God who is the basis for the natural law that allegedly undergirds both morality and the state.[7] Yet Catholics are also to be excluded, perhaps because they are even more subversive to the commonweal of such a religiously pluralistic state. Catholics "deliver themselves up," Locke memorably lamented, "to the protection and service of another prince."

The problem with Lockean tolerance lies not with the denial of state-induced religious belief. As Locke rightly observes, God himself refuses to coerce people against their will. There are religious requirements of both belief and practice that are rightly (though only) required by the churches.[8] Yet the state has no such mandatory power over Christians. Such governmental force would prompt empty conformity, not faithful obedience. Persuasion is the only legitimate means for promoting true faith. Thus far, thus good. The real trouble arises with Locke's Enlightenment distinction between morality as outward and public while religion remains private and inward. The Church has care of souls, Locke believed, while the state has care of bodies. This inward-outward dichotomy between religion and the state led to an even more pernicious split between the private and the public person. As a result, Christian discipline would become increasingly moralistic. Sins were condemned primarily as they harmed the so-called private self—for instance, the abuse of alcohol and the act of adultery—often to the utter disregard for the Church's teaching on such public vices as the neglect of the poor, the waging of unjust war, and (at least in the American South) the holding of slaves. Even such a devoutly tolerant believer as Roger Williams "subdivided every human being," writes Barry Harvey, "into an inner and an outer person.[9] By arranging the field in this manner Williams [like Locke] effectively cedes all claims to the bodies of Christians to the authority of secular institutions. . . ."[10]

It comes as no surprise that Locke should also exclude Catholics—with their refusal to contain Christianity within the private sphere —from religious tolerance. In warning against their allegiance to "another prince," Locke refers to the pope as a head of state allied with the various Catholic monarchs of Europe for political no less than religious purposes. Yet this was surely a religious canard. Despite the example of Guy Fawkes, there were few Catholics, even in the late seventeenth century, who would have regarded the papacy primarily as a political power unto whom they "delivered themselves up." Insofar as they were faithful sons and daughters of the Church, they should have sworn allegiance to the pope as the earthly representative of Another Prince. Indeed, *all* orthodox Christians are meant to put themselves under the primary "protection and service" of this same Sovereign who is neither monarch nor president of any worldly regime but Lord of his Body called Church. In the strict sense, therefore, Christians of all sorts and conditions should subvert *any* state that presumes to command the first and final loyalty of its citizens.[11] For Locke, however, there can be no hierarchy of loyalties between Church and state, no tournament of competing metanarratives,[12] since heaven and earth constitute two completely incommensurable societies: they must not be "mixed."

Among the many problems arising from the Lockean idea of tolerance, William Cavanaugh has identified the most acute complication. He argues that toleration, in claiming to halt the so-called "religious wars" of the seventeenth century, served as a political convenience even more than a political necessity. Protestants often slaughtered Protestants, and Catholics did the same to their own fellow believers—all in the service of their politically ambitious princes. According to Cavanaugh, these "wars of religion" mark the birth pangs of the sovereign nation-state, with its massive growth in size and its increasing alliance with national and international markets. Political power was centralized, Cavanaugh argues, so as to provide "a monopoly on violence within a defined territory." Public discourse was deliberately secularized during the Enlightenment, Cavanaugh maintains, in order to save the state from the threat posed by the churches: "Christianity produces divisions within the state body precisely because it pretends to be a body which transcends state boundaries." The Enlightenment ideal of toleration thus excludes the communal body called the Church, says Cavanaugh, "as a rival to the state body by redefining religion as a purely internal matter, an affair of the soul and not of the body."[13]

In the name of a benign inclusivity, therefore, a tyrannical exclusivity was promulgated. The state alone, not the Church, can set the terms of debate about the nature of the common good and the welfare of its citizens. It alone can establish a true commonwealth, for religion now pertains chiefly to the private sphere of mere personal opinion.

The Rise of Despotic Liberty

From such sentiments there emerges the modern individualism that values untrammeled liberty above all else—whether negatively defined as doing no harm to others, or else positively interpreted as constructing one's own life without let or hindrance. No longer is freedom understood as obedience to a *telos* radically transcending ourselves and thus wondrously delivering us from bondage to mere self-interest. Rather does liberty come to entail a life conducted entirely according to one's own private choices, with utter disregard for binding obligations to formative communities. Such freedom issues finally in solipsism, the right to exist as if nothing were real but one's own subjective construction of things. In *Planned Parenthood v. Casey*, the 1992 Supreme Court case upholding *Roe v. Wade*, a majority of the justices confirmed this notion of liberty by declaring that all Americans have the privilege of construing reality for themselves: "At the very heart of liberty is the right to define one's own concept of existence, of meaning, of the universe, of the mystery of life."[14]

At its extreme, such individualism holds that we can make up our identity entirely out of whole cloth, that we can strip away all bothersome particularities that locate us within concrete narrative traditions, and thus that we can find liberty only as we rid ourselves of any troublesome commitments or obligations that we have not chosen entirely for ourselves. In sum, we may and must become autarchic selves immunized from all moral and social obligations except those that we have independently elected.[15] The cataclysmic effects of such privatizing and individualizing of human existence have been obvious in both the moral and religious realms. The Church's moral practices cannot be introduced into courts of law, for example, despite being undergirded by two millennia of careful testing and development. In the matter of abortion, for instance, the Supreme Court's decision depended not on any teaching about the nature of the common good or the inviolability of the human person, but on a woman's right to privacy.[16]

This late modern notion of tolerance is usually advocated by those who have already attained such power that they can afford to tolerate their opponents—so long, it must be noted, as the "tolerated" abide by the rules laid down by their "tolerators," thus offering no real threat to established authority. Tolerance usually reveals that someone has already won and someone else has already lost. The American ideal of state neutrality in moral and religious matters often means that the governmental principalities and powers have already adopted a particular idea of the good, one built largely on Enlightenment assumptions about protecting the sovereign individual. Disputes are thus settled on the basis largely of procedural notions concerning utility and rights.[17]

How, then, are those who hold to radically opposing construals of reality to deal with each other, if not by an authoritarian tolerance that confines religion to the spiritual realm while the state devours bodies and souls alike? How might the morally vacant public square be reoccupied with open discussion of theological claims that bear not on Christians or Muslims or Jews alone, but on the entire *res publica*? Chesterton's *The Ball and the Cross* suggests that a certain kind of hospitality may be the answer. The word derives from *hostis*, a locution originally meaning not only "host" (as one who "welcomes and provides for"), but also "stranger" and even "enemy." Hospitality thus became an ancient Christian practice and discipline, a fundamental responsibility regarding those who are alien and perhaps even antagonistic. It requires, among other things, the willingness to welcome the gift that others represent—not the gifts that we expect or desire from them, but their often surprising and troubling gifts, especially when others have convictions that are fundamentally adverse to ours.

The word *tolerance*, by contrast, originally meant "to endure pain or hardship," and it eventually came to signify "allowing the opinions and practices of others." There is a decisive difference. Tolerance somewhat condescendingly declares that we will "put up with" others, even when their views and habits are noxious to us, by refusing seriously to engage them. Hospitality, by contrast, offers to "put them up" in the old-fashioned sense: we will make room even for enemies, both as guests whose fundamental convictions we gladly engage, but also as potential friends who may become comrades in belief and practice.[18] Hospitality thus becomes, for Christians, an earthly analogy of the Gospel itself. Just as we were once strangers and enemies whom God has patiently taken into his household (Rom 5:10), so must we offer hospitality to those who are alien and hostile to us.[19]

Hospitality must not be romanticized and idealized as a simple or easy practice. It does not entail a smiling kind of niceness, a prim-and-proper etiquette, not even a generosity in hosting gracious social affairs. Neither does it mean that we draw no distinctions among competing truth claims, as the proponents of tolerance often refuse to do. Such subtle inhospitality actually despairs of the truth. If all truth claims are true, then none is true, including this one. As we have repeatedly quoted Chesterton, "Morality is very much like art: it consists of drawing the line somewhere." Christian hospitality draws a clarifying line of distinction, but it does not raise an unbreachable barrier of opposition. On the contrary, Gospel hospitality is willing to hazard two radical risks. On the one hand, it must engage opponents so genuinely that they not only can recognize themselves in our representation of their most basic convictions, but also that we ourselves must be susceptible of conversion to their faith. On the other hand, we are also called to demonstrate the case for Christianity so persuasively, in both act and argument, that we help create the possibility of their conversion as well. In either case, we will not have merely tolerated each other; indeed, we will have rejected the modern separation of body and soul, of morality and religion, in order to embrace a hospitable—even if a sometimes ferocious—engagement.

The Horror of Honest Argument

The Ball and the Cross recounts the attempt of two vehement foes—one Christian, the other atheist—to undertake such an engagement. So important are their prime convictions that they have sworn not only to argue their ideas to conclusion but, failing to reach a satisfactory finish, then to fight each other to death in a sword duel.[20] They are convinced that no belief is worthy of our life unless it is also worthy of our death. That this philosophical dustup will take many surprising turns is indicated from the outset. Indeed, the central opposition is humorously set forth in the novel's opening scene. A professor named Dr. Lucifer has captured a Bulgarian monk named Father Michael from his mountain retreat and taken him aloft in his flying machine so as to demonstrate that space is a limitless void and that the welkin rings without sound of divinity: "This mere space, this mere quantity, terrifies a man more than tigers or the terrible plague. You know that since our science has spoken, the bottom has fallen out of the Universe. Now heaven is the hopeless thing, more hopeless than any hell" (BC, 2).[21] Rather stupidly mistaking the ball and cross atop St. Paul's Cathedral in London to be an actual planet, the professor almost crashes his airship into it. The monk takes the helm at the last minute and just barely avoids the collision, while Dr. Lucifer is recovering from his shock at seeing the cross for the first time, having experienced an almost successful exorcism!

Alison Milbank notes that Chesterton is seeking to destabilize the reader's imagination, turning the familiar London sight of St. Paul's into something no longer to be taken for granted but made arrestingly strange.[22] The mime-like and semiallegorical character of the novel is thus evident from the beginning. The monastic Michael possesses the faithfulness of the eponymous unfallen archangel, while the cleft-bearded Dr. Lucifer represents the mutinous archangel in modern form.[23] That the monk and the professor begin a philosophical argument while clinging to the dome of St. Paul's indicates that this is not realistic fiction so much as deliberate farce. Why would Chesterton resort to a patently unserious genre, with its virtually impossible situations, its extravagant occurrences, its frantic pace, and, above all, its wildly improbable conclusions? In a world becoming immune to the Gospel, Chesterton believed that only those art forms that have the disruptive power of mime and even melodrama can capture the Gospel's joyful outrageousness, its fantastic eccentricity, its scandalously glad claim that God himself has entered this human fray in Israel and Christ and the Church. "[O]f all the varied forms of the literature of joy," Chesterton claimed, "the form most truly worthy of moral reverence and artistic ambition is the form called 'farce'—or its wilder shape in pantomime."[24]

Farce and pantomime also enable the creation of outsized characters who body forth their representative beliefs in large and startling terms. Not the least of these figures is Father Michael. After he descends from atop the ball on St. Paul's Cathedral, he experiences a vision of the

entire universe as a grand rigmarole of both destruction and redemption. It is one of the most sublime moments in all of Chesterton:

> He felt suddenly happy and suddenly indescribably small. He fancied he had
> been changed into a child again; his eyes sought the pavement seriously as
> children's do, as if it were a thing with which something satisfactory could
> be done. He felt the full warmth of that pleasure from which the proud
> shut themselves out; the pleasure which not only goes with humiliation, but
> which almost is humiliation. Men who have escaped death by a hair have it,
> and men whose love is returned by a woman unexpectedly, and men whose
> sins are forgiven them. Everything his eye fell on it feasted on, not aestheti-
> cally, but with a plain, jolly appetite as of a boy eating buns. He relished the
> squareness of the houses; he liked their clean angles as if he had just cut them
> with a knife. The lit squares of the shop windows excited him as the young
> are excited by the lit stage of some promising pantomime. He happened
> to see in one shop which projected with a bulging bravery on to the pave-
> ment some square tins of potted meat, and it seemed like a hint of a hun-
> dred hilarious high teas in a hundred streets of the world. He was, perhaps,
> the happiest of all the children of men. For in that unendurable instant when
> he hung, half slipping, to the ball of St. Paul's, the whole universe had been
> destroyed and re-created. (BC, 11)

The yet unanswered question is whether *The Ball and the Cross* can give
persuasive fictional life to such a splendidly Beatific Vision.

The outcome depends on the essential antitheses that are embodied by an ardent English unbeliever named James Turnbull and an
equally devout Scots Catholic named Evan MacIan: an urban Low-
lander versus a rustic Highlander. They have come into conflict because
MacIan has smashed the window of the editorial office at *The Atheist*,
the journal that Turnbull edits. MacIan had been roused to wrath by
Turnbull's article offering an argument such as Sir James George Frazer
had made popular with *The Golden Bough* in 1890: the Virgin Mary is a
mere mythical figure typical of all primitive religions—a maiden who
had consorted with a divinity and given birth to a hero. For MacIan,
by contrast, she is the exemplary figure of Christian faith for having first professed belief in Jesus before he was even conceived. "Be
it done unto me according to thy word," Mary's faithful response to
the Annunciation given to her by the archangel Gabriel, is indeed the

acclamation that every Christian is called to make. She is the one about whom Christians make a staggeringly paradoxical claim—namely, that this teenaged Jewish virgin is in fact the very mother of God, the one who bore and parented the second person of the Trinity. Hence her magnetic centrality to Christian faith at least since the fourth century:

> Obediently standing at the side of the new Adam, Jesus Christ, the Virgin is the new Eve, the true mother of all the living, who with a mother's love cooperates in their birth and their formation in the order of grace. Virgin and Mother, Mary is the figure of the Church, its most perfect realization.[25]

In one of the novel's most comic but also most revealing scenes, MacIan the super-Catholic marks his first arrival in London by mistaking a giant sedentary statue of Queen Anne in front of St. Paul's as a figure of the Virgin Mary. Despite his cultural naïveté, MacIan's faith runs far deeper than the assurance of moribund Londoners that Queen Anne is permanently dead. Convinced, by contrast, that the Queen of Heaven is permanently alive, MacIan has been schooled to discern the natural via the supernatural. It is evident that Chesterton believes the Scots Catholic to have had the right kind of Christian formation, since he learned how to dwell amidst these intersecting and overlapping realms. Like Blake encountering the heavenly host in a hay field or as they filled a tree in Peckham Rye (their "bright angelic wings bespangling every bough like a star"), and like Frodo standing awestruck, "lost in wonder" at his first Edenic glimpse of Lórien,[26] Chesterton's narrator recounts the youthful MacIan's own supernaturalizing of the natural, as it led him ever deeper into the heart of the Mystery:

> On that fantastic fringe of the Gaelic land where he walked as a boy, the cliffs were as fantastic as the clouds. Heaven seemed to humble itself and come closer to the earth. The common paths of his little village began to climb quite suddenly and seemed resolved to go to heaven. The sky seemed to fall down towards the hills; the hills took hold upon the sky. In the sumptuous sunset of gold and purple and peacock green[,] cloudlets and islets were the same. Evan lived like a man walking on a borderland, the borderland between this world and another. Like so many men and nations who grow up with nature and the common things, he understood the supernatural before he understood the natural. He had looked at dim angels standing knee-deep in the grass before he had looked at the grass. He knew that Our Lady's

robes were blue before he knew the wild roses around her feet were red. The deeper his memory plunged into the dark house of childhood the nearer and nearer he came to the things that cannot be named.[27] All through his life he thought of the daylight world as a sort of divine débris, the broken remainder of his first vision. The skies and mountains were the splendid off-scourings of another place. The stars were lost jewels of the Queen. Our Lady had gone and left the stars by accident. (BC, 14–15)

Turnbull's blaspheming of the Blessed Lady, denying her uniqueness by reducing her to a mythic human confection is, for MacIan, a fighting matter indeed. Yet the ruling authorities of the realm regard this dispute as a bootless affair, even at best. Why does it matter whether one regards Mary as a figure produced by Mesopotamian myth or as the Virgin Mother of God? Surely this is a dispute of no great moral consequence. At most, it's one man's opinion against another's. Thus are the magistrates determined to prevent MacIan and Turnbull from having their argument. The alleged reason is that these men have pledged to conclude their theological debate with a sword duel unto death. The main forces arrayed against this physical and metaphysical joust are journalists and policemen and the judiciary. These three predominant shapers of modern life have been persuaded by "all the forward men of [the] age" (BC, 14) that dueling must be halted. Our tolerant and enlightened times have advanced far beyond such a benighted medieval practice.

It is not chiefly a battle with blades that the establishment forces want to stop. What these guardians of permissible thought regard as a contest belonging to the private and spiritual realm alone is, in fact, a dispute with huge moral and social import. Turnbull's conviction that Mary is a figure whom Christians have mythically divinized, for instance, is based on his physicalist philosophy that the only real things are empirically demonstrable facts. Since only a few if any moral virtues can be factually validated, one might well conclude that all ethical distinctions are but human inventions meant for human manipulation, as the powerful dominate the weak. MacIan's devotion to the Virgin Mary, by contrast, is premised on the conviction that the God who exists outside time and space has nonetheless dwelt bodily and temporally in our midst by way of his own Son and his Mother. And if the triune God is thus operating personally and sacramentally within

human life, it can be argued that such life is to be treasured and protected from the evils of war and pestilence, of murder and hunger and
rapine. Yet so long as the conflict between Turnbull and MacIan can be
confined to the private realm of personal and religious opinion, such
conclusions are rendered politically and socially nugatory. The atheist
Turnbull pierces to the core of the matter, albeit comically:

> "This man and I are alone in the modern world in that we think God essen-
> tially important. I think He does not exist; that is where the importance
> comes in for me. But this man [MacIan] thinks that He does exist, and think-
> ing that very properly thinks Him more important than anything else. Now
> we wish to make a great demonstration and assertion—something that will
> set the world on fire like the first Christian persecutions. If you like, we are
> attempting a mutual martyrdom." (BC, 49)

Though the Enlightenment prized the debate of ideas and their
consequences, Chesterton contends that the heirs of seventeenth-
century argumentation have shut down such a contest of ideas. They
have replaced philosophical dispute with a practicality and efficiency
that have no aim or purpose beyond their putatively neutral import.[28]
Broadmindedness has thus come to mean empty-mindedness, as our
culture remains blissfully opaque to Chesterton's tart aphorism: "The
object of opening the mind, as of opening the mouth, is to shut it
again on something solid."[29] Chesterton believed that well-founded
dogmas, whether theist or atheist, whether scientific of psychological,
are meant to nourish both soul and body in their utter inseparability:

> Man can be defined as an animal that makes dogmas. As he piles doctrine
> on doctrine and conclusion on conclusion in the formation of some tremen-
> dous scheme of philosophy and religion, he is, in the only legitimate sense of
> which the expression is capable, becoming more and more human. When he
> drops one doctrine after another in a refined skepticism, when he declines
> to tie himself to a system, when he says that he has outgrown definitions,
> when he says that he disbelieves in finality, when, in his own imagination,
> he sits as God, holding no form of creed but contemplating all, then he is by
> that very process sinking slowly backward into the vagueness of the vagrant
> animals and the unconsciousness of the grass. Trees have no dogmas. Turnips
> are singularly broad-minded.[30]

Yet the tolerant and "forward men of the age" amidst whom Turnbull and McIan are fated to dwell are unwilling to close their allegedly open minds on anything so solid as an argument. On the contrary, they are determined to prevent these philosophical antagonists from agitating the truly clamant questions concerning God and man and the world.[31] These argufiers must be restrained, therefore, not only from rapier thrusts but from intellectual debate as well—again, lest the moral and religious emptiness of the naked public square become evident.

MacIan's argument with Turnbull does not concern niggling niceties but the most fundamental of all matters: whether there is God, and thus whether there is man. The real issue, as MacIan discerns, is the relation of the ball and the cross atop the main dome of St. Paul's. Turnbull the atheist is committed to nothing other than the round earth and its inhabitants. At the same time, he claims to be a moral man willing to make huge personal sacrifices for the sake of "honour," "liberty," and "humanity" (BC, 24).[32] He believes, however, that such noble ideals can be maintained without faith in God or Christ or the Church. The globe does not need the rood riding it. His enemy MacIan salutes Turnbull for dedicating himself to such high virtues, but he insists that their metaphysical baselessness signals the death of man no less than the denial of God. Turnbull's humanistic values have no grounding or sustenance, MacIan argues. They are cut off from transcendent Reality, lacking all relation to any surpassing idea of the good or the true or the beautiful. Such an unsupported, free-floating humanism becomes tyrannically tolerant and thus religiously bigoted, argues MacIan. It also becomes politically bloody, as the end of the novel will demonstrate.

Whether directly or indirectly, MacIan has learned from the Platonists and St. Augustine that God is the root and aim, the source and end, of all true being. Without God, there is literally nonbeing: nothing. The corollary of the Augustinian doctrine that all good things pour forth from God is that evil is not truly real: it is a twisting and perversion of the good, an absence and a lack. MacIan will not attribute his abiding respect for Turnbull, therefore, to mere animal affection. On the contrary, the severe believer honors the arch-atheist because he is a creature formed *imago Dei*, a man whose capacity for both damnation and salvation—in this world no less than the next—derives from his existence as a creature made in the image of God:

"[U]nderstand this and understand it thoroughly, if I loved you my love might be divine. But in that I hate you, my hatred most surely is divine. No, it is not some trifle that we are fighting about. It is not some superstition or some symbol. When you wrote those words about Our Lady, you were in that act a wicked man doing a wicked thing. If I hate you it is because you have hated goodness. And if I like you . . . it is because you are good." (BC, 39, ellipsis in original)[33]

As this statement reveals, MacIan is a Thomist no less than an Augustinian. Turnbull's actions define his identity, just as God's character is revealed in his own acts of creation and redemption. Hence the Scotsman's confession to Turnbull that Christian faith regards the supernatural not as the absurd, but as the ultimately reasonable reality, when reason is understood as the mind's participation in the divine Logos, and not as a faculty for mere computation and quantification. Rather than reducing worldly things to insignificance, this high view of the mind and of the good creation itself—especially the wonder of nonmechanical things—renders both mind and heart indispensable. Both the eyes of the mind and the heart of faith—both the vision to discern and the will to obey—are required to embrace the divine kindliness hidden within the world's cruelties:

"To me this whole strange world is homely [i.e., cheerful, warm, homelike], because in the heart of it there is a home; to me this cruel world is kindly, because higher than the heavens there is something more human than humanity. If a man must not fight for this, may he fight for anything? I would fight for my friend, but if I lost my friend, I should still be there. I would fight for my country, but if I lost my country, I should still exist. But if what that devil [Turnbull] dreams were true, I should not be—I should burst like a bubble and be gone. I could not live in that imbecile universe. Shall I not fight for my own existence?" (BC, 19)

Tolstoy, Nietzsche, and the Contest of Metanarratives

What "that devil" named Turnbull "dreams" is the physicalism that we have encountered in *Orthodoxy*. Yet Turnbull is a better thinker than Darwin, if only because he sees the illusory optimism inherent in Darwin's idea of a supposedly primal reality that has been constantly developed by random selection alone. There is no such thing as "pure nature," argues Turnbull, to be interpreted as having progressively evolved. There is only the chaos that produces occasional order, which in turn produces more chaos. Nor can humanity be identified as having any origin or aim apart from the world's infinite loops of unoriginated and unending predation, the great chain of interference and domination. Turnbull subscribes to a radical physicalism that is compounded with a Humean skepticism:

> "I do not believe in nature, just as I do not believe in Odin. She is a myth. It is not merely that I do not believe that nature can guide us. It is that I do not believe that nature exists. I mean that nobody can discover what the original nature of things would have been if things had not interfered with it. The first blade of grass began to tear up the earth and eat it; it was interfering with nature, if there is any nature. The first wild ox began to tear up the grass and eat it; he was interfering with nature if there is any nature. In the same way," continued Turnbull, "the human when it asserts its dominance over nature is just as natural as the thing which it destroys." (BC, 57)

The Scotsman seeks to persuade the Englishman that his physicalism can account for neither scientific discovery nor religious belief. Like many other physicalists, Turnbull has too low an estimate of reason. Physical science and religious dogma are both rational enterprises, MacIan insists, because they are both tradition-dependent ways of knowing. As such, they are capable of real advance and development:

> "[T]here are only two things that really progress; and they both accept accumulations of authority. They may be progressing uphill or down; they may be growing steadily better or steadily worse; but they have . . . steadily advanced in a certain definable direction; they are the only two things, it seems, that ever *can* progress. The first is strictly physical science. The second is the Catholic Church." (BC, 64, emphasis in original)

The dogmas of the Church and the theories of science thrive only through engagement with the past, with antecedent experience, with doctrines and principles that require constant modification and enlargement. No matter how revolutionary these "paradigm shifts" may seem, they are still to be understood only in relation to their previous histories. Anticipating, albeit in different ways, the work of Thomas Kuhn and Stephen Toulmin, the Catholic protagonist claims that "if you want an example of anything which has progressed in the moral world by the same method as science in the material world, by continually adding to without unsettling what was there before, then I say that there is only one example. And that is Us" (BC, 65).

MacIan is clearly echoing John Henry Newman's idea of the development of doctrine. It is the notion that the original divine disclosure given to the Church by God in Christ through the Holy Spirit—the acorn of Christian revelation, so to speak—continues to ramify into the great oak tree of Christian doctrine, so that what is originally implicit is being made ever more explicit. Developments of Church doctrine serve to effloresce the seed of Faith often in surprisingly new ways, but they "unsettle" the past only as newly emerging scientific theories do so: by extending it. Neither Trinity nor Incarnation is anywhere made explicit in the New Testament, for example; yet the Church rightly developed them as what was already present *in nuce*. Even the Marian dogmas, those doctrines that seem furthest removed from biblical attestation and Christocentric focus, are the logical outworkings of the Church's tradition, Newman argues. He notes that, of all the major doctrines of the Church, only one was formulated not first of all from a theological quandary but from the long-attested witness of the laity and the clergy, mainly in the worship of the Eastern churches from early in the second century. This unique dogma was affirmed at the Synod of Ephesus in 431—namely, that the mother of Jesus is the *Theotokos*, the "Mother of God."[34]

In a letter addressed to the Anglican bishop Edward Pusey, Newman clarified the Church's early and vigorous devotion to the Blessed Lady: "when once we have mastered the idea, that Mary bore, suckled, and handled the Eternal in the form of a child, what limit is conceivable to the rush and flood of thoughts which such a doctrine involves? What awe and surprise must attend upon the knowledge, that a creature has been brought so close to the Divine Essence."[35] Pointing out that the indissoluble bond linking Virgin and Child is not a *novum*, since it is figured over and again in the catacombs, Newman adds, "Mary is there drawn with the Divine Infant in her lap, she with hands extended in prayer, He with His hand in the attitude of blessing. No representation can more forcibly convey the doctrine of the high dignity of the Mother, and, I will add, of her influence with the Son."[36] What may seem initially to be minimal references in the Scriptures thus become definitively maximal claims in the Tradition—yet, as Newman says, in full continuity with biblical teaching and proclamation.[37]

Henri de Lubac describes Tradition, understood very much in the fashion of Newman, as the Church's "constitutive thinking," while Dogma remains its "constituted thinking." The former is always elaborating and extending what is unchanging but implicit in the latter.[38] Odd though it seems to say, MacIan's implicit humanity is being made ever more explicit, a reality that he is acquiring no less than he has received. It flourishes only through its proper formation in the habits and practices of the Christian life as they, in turn, have been shaped by Christian dogma and tradition.[39] The real sticking point between Turnbull and MacIan, therefore, is not a breach between two untraditioned and noncommunal abstractions called atheism and theism, but rather between two different but complementary ways of knowing and living: physical science on the one hand, and Church doctrine on the other. What the latter reveals, as de Lubac says, is that the world was made for the sake of the Church, for in it alone does creation find its true end in the redemption of all things. That the gates of Hell shall not prevail against it (Matt 16:18) is no idle biblical boast but the deepest ontological claim concerning the ecclesial quality of Christian existence:

> "The Church is not a thing like the Athenæum Club," [MacIan] cried. "If the Athenæum Club lost all its members, the Athenæum Club would dissolve and cease to exist. But when we belong to the Church we belong to something which is outside all of us; which is outside everything you [Turnbull] talk about, outside [even] the Cardinals and the Pope. They belong to it, but it does not belong to them. If we all fell dead suddenly, the Church would still somehow exist in God. Confound it all, don't you see that I am more sure of its existence than I am of my own existence?" (BC, 38)[40]

Far from being a cozy coterie of the likeminded, the Church has taught MacIan to value strangers—even to honor enemies such as Turnbull—not with a condescending tolerance but with an engaging hospitality, if only by way of the oxymoronic hospitality of a sword fight! Hence the riotous irony of two would-be pugilists befriending each other as they are forced to flee—by ever more outrageous escapes—from the forces of the law and the press.

> "I must kill you now," said the fanatic [MacIan], "because—"
>
> "Well, because," said Turnbull, patiently.
>
> "Because I have begun to like you," [answers MacIan]. . . .
>
> "Your affection expresses itself in an abrupt form," [Turnbull] began. . . .
>
> "You know what I mean," [MacIan continues]. "You mean the same yourself. We must fight now or else—"
>
> "Or else?" repeated Turnbull, staring at him with an almost blinding gravity.
>
> "Or else we may not want to fight at all," answered Evan, and the end of his speech was like a despairing cry. (BC, 37)

These hilariously failed enemies soon encounter two real adversaries. Though initially eager to engage MacIan and Turnbull, each finally refuses them hospitality. The first of these unwelcoming souls is a Tolstoyan espousing a philosophy of universal peace based on an undiscriminating love of life. All sentient creatures have equal importance, he argues—so that cats and dogs and children are on a level plane, none to be exalted over the other. Physical suffering thus becomes the ultimate evil, since everything must be kept alive at all costs. To differentiate animals from humans is, in the ugly argot of this present age, to be guilty of speciesism. It is noteworthy that Turnbull the hardheaded humanist is appalled by such a flattening of important distinctions. MacIan the much less tough-minded believer is almost persuaded by the Tolstoyan's benign philosophy of "caring," so closely does it seem to approximate the Christian mission to relieve misery. In his hospitable desire to "take in" other viewpoints, MacIan is himself almost "taken in." But then he recognizes that this Tolstoyan angel of light is, like Dr. Lucifer, a demon of darkness meant to shock MacIan out of his sentimentality. Love, MacIan learns from this benign-seeming devil, becomes wickedly saccharine if it is not rooted in the redemption that, because it is wrought by Christ's own Cross, requires its recipients to embrace a life of conflict with the world:

> "But then [the Tolstoyan] came," broke out MacIan, "and my soul said to me: 'Give up fighting, and you will become like That [i.e., the Tolstoyan]. Give up vows and dogmas, and fixed things, and you may grow like That. . . . You

> may grow fond of that mire of crawling, cowardly morals, and you may come
> to think a blow bad, because it hurts, and not because it humiliates. You
> may come to think murder wrong, because it is violent, and not because it is
> unjust.'" (BC, 44)[41]

The fleeing and frustrated contestants soon encounter a more significant ideological devil than the Tolstoyan pacifist—namely, a Nietzschean worshipper of brute resolve and relentless drive. Like his nihilist philosophical hero, Wimpey is enamored of the will to power. Again in imitation of Nietzsche, he despises the slavish advocates of humanitarianism—those moral weaklings who, instead of honoring the power relations that underwrite all human exchanges, emphasize such limp-wristed virtues as pity. Wimpey worships "Force"—the god who "loves blood" (BC, 52). Convinced that the universe is ruled by amoral might alone, Wimpey hails what he calls "that naked and awful arbitration which is the only thing that balances the stars—a still, continuous violence. *Væ Victis!* [*Woe to the vanquished! The conquered have no rights!*] Down, down, with the defeated! Victory is the only ultimate fact" (BC, 53).

Just as MacIan was made to discern the limits of Tolstoyan compassion, so does Turnbull begin to undergo a philosophical (if not yet a theological) conversion upon seeing that his physicalism has little means of answering Wimpey's Nietzschean nihilism. Absent a vision of nature as ordered to the good of both humanity and divinity—mysterious and paradoxical though this order surely is[42]—the Nietzschean shall always reduce scientific discovery to his own maleficent purposes. It is altogether appropriate, therefore, that (like the nameless Tolstoyan) Wimpey should extend no hospitality to MacIan and Turnbull. In a totally perspectival world, hospitality can have no more moral registry than hostility. Arbitrary will to power, or else personal aesthetic preference, is the only adjudicator of values amidst the welter of unlimited perspectives. As in *Orthodoxy*, so in *The Ball and the Cross*: Chesterton foresaw that a softheaded tenderness and a coldhearted cruelty would become the chief modern enemies of science and theology alike.

Yet Chesterton does not allow MacIan and Turnbull either to flatten their opponents or to demonize each other, as if their own standpoints were without flaws. "Idolatry is committed, not merely by setting up false gods," Chesterton wisely observed, "but also by setting up false devils."[43] The erstwhile combatants learn their limits after their last and most frantic escape leads them into the garden of an insane asylum. There MacIan and Turnbull experience nightmare visions of what the world would be like if their *own* philosophies were allowed to triumph unchecked. MacIan discovers that, if Christianity could be imposed on others by force rather than converting them by persuasion and example, it would produce a cruel theocracy. Turnbull is shown something similar at work in a tyrannous version of his physicalism. His allegedly humanist regime, as he learns from his ghostly incubus, would rid itself of "a hopeless slave population" (BC, 141). As Stephen Clark has noticed, it is primarily the poor who are "despised and murdered" under the hard boot of all utopias.[44] Turnbull's ghoulish double teaches him what could easily become his own chilling premise: "No man should be unemployed. Employ the employables. Destroy the unemployables" (BC, 141). In a statement that would become the virtual motto for the twentieth-century culture of death, Turnbull's tormenting *doppelgänger* proudly declares that "Life is sacred—but lives are not sacred. We are improving Life by removing lives" (BC, 141–42).

That Turnbull is horrified by such a euthanasian perversion of his own physicalist humanism is not altogether surprising. He has been caught in a similar inconsistency earlier in the novel. After he has ridiculed the Mass that his future bride makes the center of her life, she brings him up short by reminding him of the instinctive reverence that he displayed toward the Eucharist:

> "You think it is only a bit of bread," said the girl, and her lips tightened ever so little.
>
> "I know it is only a bit of bread," said Turnbull, with violence.
>
> She flung back her open face and smiled. "Then why did you refuse to eat it?" she said.
>
> James Turnbull made a little step backward, and for the first time in his life there seemed to break out and blaze in his head thoughts that were not his own. (BC, 100)

The upshot of this long attempt to have a decent duel unto death is that MacIan learns that Christianity must never entail coercion, while Turnbull finds that physicalism can lead to the manipulation of human life to antihuman ends. MacIan and Turnbull have both been radically humbled by their respective nightmares. They have discovered the truth of Chesterton's crisp dictum: "It is not bigotry to be certain we are right; but it is bigotry to be unable to imagine how we might possibly have gone wrong."[45] Having been shown how dreadfully they might have gone wrong, MacIan and Turnbull are no longer bent on rivalistic conquest—either by swords or arguments. On the contrary, they have become the most hospitable of friends.

Antiseptic Health and the Sanity of the Spike

Their blossoming friendship is not confined to themselves alone. They are made to care for others when they discover the character of the mental institution where they have been locked away. The asylum is a physically sanitary but a morally monstrous place. While its incarcerated souls have been provided the food and space necessary for living, they have been deprived of the freedom that makes life worth living. Chesterton thus prophesies the coming dehumanization of modern life by way of an ostensible liberty that is, in fact, a disguised form of slavery:

> For these great scientific organizers insisted that a man should be healthy even if he was miserable. . . . It seemed never to have occurred to them that the benefit of exercise belongs partly to the benefit of liberty. They had not entertained the suggestion that the open air is only one of the advantages of the open sky. They administered air in secret, but in sufficient doses, as if it were a medicine. They suggested walking, as if no man had ever felt inclined to walk. Above all, the asylum authorities insisted on their own extraordinary cleanliness. (BC, 146–47)

This asylum has been established via a mandate issued by the House of Commons. Though the novel was published in 1909, this order goes well beyond Winston Churchill's "Feeble-Minded Bill" of 1914. It requires the actual imprisonment of everyone who cannot be medically certified as *compos mentis*. This vast prison house of the allegedly mad contains, in fact, all of the truly sane people whom Turnbull and MacIan have encountered during their flight, perhaps all of the remaining sane souls in England. The chief executive officer is, of course, Dr. Lucifer. Neither Turnbull nor MacIan nor anyone else hopes to escape this sanitary madhouse, for they would soon be arrested by the medical police and returned to the sanitarium. "In the first village you entered," they are told, "the village constable would notice that you were not wearing on the left lapel of your coat the small pewter **S** which is now necessary for any one who walks about beyond asylum bounds or outside asylum hours" (BC, 157).

This entire scene is stunningly prophetic. Chesterton foresaw, a quarter century in advance, that even democratic nations are capable of branding their citizens with stigmata of either inclusion or exclusion. In *The Ball and the Cross* those declared certifiably normal and balanced are "rewarded" with an **S**, whereas, under Hitler, Jews would soon be identified with white armbands featuring the blue Star of David. The first exclusion brings spiritual death, while the latter often meant literal death as well. The hygienic totalitarianism forecast in *The Ball and the Cross* may be even more nightmarish, in fact, than the squalid tyrannies established by Hitler and Stalin and Mao—if only because its antiseptic health seems so benign. Dr. Lucifer's giant rehabilitation scheme does not at first seem malign. The creation of a public not riven by bloody disputes over questions too large for ready solution might seem salutary. Yet to empty the public arena of substantial moral and religious debate, Chesterton prophesied, is to produce a populace consisting of those whom Nietzsche called "the last men"—those wan and apathetic creatures who lack all conviction, who make no promises, who venture no risks because they have ceased to struggle with the most fundamental of all quandaries: human nature and ultimate destiny.

The question of sanity lies at the core Chesterton's work. In his treatise on Distributism titled *The Outline of Sanity* as well as in *Orthodoxy*, he argues that the fundamental modern condition is not sinfulness and rebellion against God, but rather mental madness: either a deranged rationalism or else an equally insane irrationalism. Nor was lunacy a mere theoretical concern for Chesterton. He was himself almost reduced to insanity while a student at the Slade School of Fine Art. In a chapter of his *Autobiography* titled "How To Be a Lunatic," he confesses his own nightmarish descent into a mental hell:

> At this time I did not very clearly distinguish between dreaming and waking; not only as a mood, but as a metaphysical doubt, I felt as if everything might

be a dream. It was as if I had myself projected the universe from within, with its trees and stars; and that is so near to the notion of being God that it is manifestly even nearer to going mad.[46]

We can hardly expect a slender and farcical novel to provide a definitive remedy for tyrannical tolerance. But at least it offers two crucial hints. The first comes by way of an outright miracle performed by Father Michael. Chesterton almost lets us forget the priest-monk; in fact, he disappears from the novel's action after he is immediately imprisoned as a madman for claiming that he had landed in London via a flying ship. At the sanitarium where MacIan and Turnbull have been remanded, the Bulgarian religious has also been held captive. His tormentors have sought to break his resistance by confining him to a lightless room having neither windows nor doors, by forming his chamber with irregular dimensions, and by giving prominence to a stake-like protrusion from one of its walls. This absurdly asymmetrical cell with its mindless projection is meant to drive the monk, if not into cooperative submission, then into raving mania.

Yet Michael has kept himself sane by constantly touching this seemingly meaningless spike.[47] Against the logic of the sanitizers, he recognizes that it sticks out from his prison wall precisely as the cross juts from the orb atop St. Paul's, not in absurd uselessness but in a clear summons to a divine ordering of human life—indeed, to the cruciform wisdom that the world regards as spike-like foolishness (1 Cor 1:18-39). Father Michael had come to this central discernment in his first confrontation with his erstwhile pilot as they were circling above St. Paul's.

> "The cross is arbitrary [complains Professor Lucifer]. Above all the globe is at unity with itself; the cross is primarily and above all things at enmity with itself. The cross is a conflict between two hostile lines, of irreconcilable direction. That silent thing up there is a collision, a crash, a struggle in stone. . . . Away with the thing! . . . The ball should be on top of the cross. The cross is a mere barbaric prop; the ball is perfection. The cross at its best is but the bitter tree of man's history; the ball is rounded, the ripe and final fruit. And the fruit should be at the top of the tree, not at the bottom of it."
> (BC, 5)

Not at all daunted by such a seemingly benign and humane argument, the aged monk sets forth the hope that will sustain him during his dark ordeal. It is especially noteworthy that the Bulgarian ascetic makes his case not in strictly theological terms but in Christian humanist language:

> "What you say [about the cross] is perfectly true," said Michael, with seren-
> ity. "But we like contradictions in terms. Man is a contradiction in terms; he
> is a beast whose superiority to other beasts consists in having fallen. That
> cross is, as you say, an eternal collision; so am I. That is a struggle in stone.
> Every form of life is a struggle in flesh. . . . You say the cross is a quadruped
> with one limb longer than the rest. I say man is a quadruped who only uses
> two of his legs." (BC, 5)

While the monk's body has been confined to this prison-house containing those who have been declared mad, his spirit has not been deadened. He possesses the inner resources to keep himself spiritually sane amidst the total lunacy of the so-called sanitarium. In fact, his eternal soul has been transforming his mortal body so as to make it immortal and thus immune even to physical agony. As the asylum is being consumed by fires that threaten to incinerate them all, Father Michael thus "walks through that white-hot hell . . . singing like a bird" (BC, 175). Approaching the holocaust with unearthly gaiety, he creates a path of deliverance for all the sane inhabitants of this sanitized hell, much as Moses parted the waters for the Israelites to be rescued from bondage. We may require an apocalyptic miracle performed by a latter-day St. Benedict or St. Michael, Chesterton suggests, in order for our death-and-hell-bent world to be rescued from its demoniac madness.[48]

Chesterton's second clue for a cure to our bigoted tolerance is even more theologically convincing. The monk's miraculous passage through the flames must be rightly perceived and truly embraced for it to have proper effect. It is not an idle display of divine might. As with Jesus' own miracles, it does not astound so much as it delivers those who are enslaved, whether physically or spiritually. Turnbull so receives and so embraces it, despite his miracle-denying physicalism. His willingness to honor empirical evidence will not permit him to deny a manifest miracle. With one hand on the shoulder of Madeleine Durand, the Christian woman he hopes to marry, and the other on the shoulder of Evan McIan, his believing friend, the atheist abandons what he had called the "certainties of materialism" (BC, 177) for the risks of faith. However reluctantly, therefore, Turnbull joins the others in falling to his knees in an act of implicit conversion.

The Ball and the Cross offers no suggestion that, because Turnbull and MacIan have learned to depend on each other in mutual hospitality, their religious beliefs are also complementary, much less necessary to each other.[49] Chesterton never splits differences. As we have seen, there is considerable truth in physicalism. Many of the world's operations can be indeed explained according to the logic of cause and effect. Yet physicalism gives only a partial rather than a full account of the natural order. We have noticed, for example, that a full-orbed metaphysics is necessary to describe the evolutionary processes. Christianity offers such a teleological understanding of the universe. It centers the cosmic operations on the creative and redemptive purposes of the triune God, and it envisions miracles akin to the one that Monk Michael enacts as the fulfillment rather than the breach or overthrow of secondary causes.

While physicalism is incapable of embracing Christianity, the reverse is not true. MacIan will learn to incorporate the limited truth of physicalism within his own doctrinal faith. The converted Turnbull, in becoming a Christian, will come to espouse a teleology that will presumably modify rather than obliterate his physicalism. Chesterton reveals the Gospel's capacity to complete and perfect all partial truths by describing it as not only the largest thing *in* the world, but as actually larger *than* the world. The Christian metanarrative accounts for the world's entire existence from beginning to end. Yet Chesterton also makes it evident that this metanarrative is no eagle-eyrie worldview that can be abstractly adopted from the outside. On the contrary, Christianity is an embodied tradition, a way of living no less than thinking. *Fiunt, non nascuntur christiani*, declared Tertullian. Jean Daniélou translates this motto to drive home its point: "Pagans are born, but Christians are made."[50] They are made in one of two ways: either through MacIan's formation within the Church, or else through Turnbull's conversion to it. And in both cases, lifelong transformation must be the result.

MacIan sometimes acts as a Catholic who, though he embraces sacramental Christianity from within, treats his faith as something akin to a worldview. He thus seeks to overcome Turnbull's atheism by way of an intellectual argument that the thought police seek to prevent. At his best, however, he knows that behavior usually determines belief, as he explains to the allegedly all-loving Tolstoyan. It is better to comprehend the Gospel and honestly reject it than to embrace it as an idea without being transformed by its Reality.

> MacIan turned upon him with a white face and bitter lip. "Sir," he said, "talk about the principle of love as much as you like. You seem to me colder than a lump of stone. . . . Talk about love, then, till the world is sick of the word. But don't you talk about Christianity. Don't you dare to say one word, white or black, about it. Christianity is, as far as you are concerned, a horrible mystery. Keep clear of it, keep silent upon it, as you would upon an abomination. It is a thing that has made men slay and torture each other; and you will never know why. It is a thing that has made men do evil that good might come; and you will never understand the evil, let alone the good. Christianity is a thing that could only make you vomit, *till you are other than you are. I would not justify it to you even if I could.* . . . It is a monstrous thing, for which men die. And if you will stand here and talk about love for another ten minutes it is very probable that you will see a man die for it." (BC, 43, emphasis added)[51]

MacIan never subjects Turnbull to such a wittily violent threat as he directs against this Tolstoyan advocate of nonviolence. In fact, his effort to convert the atheist succeeds, at least in the negative sense, by helping Turnbull discern that his physicalism is incapable of sustaining his humanism.[52] Apologetics, Chesterton thus implies, may have its chief Christian use in pointing up the limits and contradictions inherent in other metanarratives, thus clearing the ground for potential conversion. Turnbull is prepared to receive Father Michael's miracle, therefore, because he has become "other than you are"—or at least other than he was. He has been transformed by witnessing an exemplary kind of Christianity exhibited not only in the woman for whom the Eucharist is the center of life but also in MacIan, the man who was once his worst enemy but who has become his most hospitable friend.

Chesterton does not give MacIan an easy or one-sided victory. As a humanist no less than an atheist, Turnbull has repeatedly befriended (and even rescued) MacIan. Unless the atheist had engaged the Christian, moreover, the Scots Catholic might have become a complacent propagandist, convinced that abstract and disembodied argument would suffice to convert unbelievers. MacIan also makes clear, in an earlier confession, that he is also Turnbull's companion in wickedness, even if the Englishman is not yet his brother in Faith. In one of the novel's most remarkable passages, MacIan confesses not only his own sinful devices and desires, but also the evils committed by his Church:

> "[A]ll England has gone into captivity in order to take us captive. All England has turned into a lunatic asylum in order to prove us lunatics. . . . When I saw that, I saw everything; I saw the Church and the world. The Church in its earthly action has really touched morbid things—tortures and bleeding visions and blasts of extermination. The Church has had her madnesses, and I am one of them. I am the massacre of St. Bartholomew. I am the Inquisition of Spain. I do not say that we have never gone mad, but I say that we are fit to act as keepers to our enemies." (BC, 167)[53]

"To act as fit keepers to our enemies" is not to vanquish them. It is not to seek a triumphalist kind of victory at all. In perhaps the novel's single most lapidary statement, MacIan declares that "[t]he cross cannot be defeated because it is Defeat" (BC, 90).[54] This divine Defeat constitutes the only lasting Victory, the Foolishness that is the one permanent Sanity, by way of the bloody Victim who overcomes the vengeful shedding of blood. MacIan and Turnbull were indeed mad in wanting to gore each other. They are saved not by a tyrannical tolerance that prohibits the engagement of ideas, but by the hospitality that creates friendship. "A few days ago," MacIan again confesses, "you and I were the maddest people in England. Now, by God! I believe we are the sanest. That is the only real question—whether the Church is really madder than the world" (BC, 168).

The Ball and the Cross offers a powerful fictional demonstration that the mad earth requires the even madder Cross, the instrument of suffering and shame that the incarnate God has transformed into the shape of Hospitality by mounting it himself, inviting all to bow before the ultimate act of divine humility. Such a Company of redemption and reconciliation does not require any state-established Church, as Chesterton repeatedly made clear.[55] Indeed, he came at the end to surrender his nostalgic hope for a restored Christendom. Thus did he also anticipate Pope Benedict's confession of its permanent demise.

Hence the pontiff's call for a revitalized Christian minority that might yet serve as ecclesial leaven for the yeastless lump of modern European and American life:

> Maybe we are facing a new and different kind of epoch in the Church's history, where Christianity will again be characterized more by the mustard seed, where it will exist in small, seemingly insignificant groups that nonetheless live in an intensive struggle against evil and [that] bring good into the world—that let God in. . . . [T]he Church will, in the foreseeable future, no longer simply be the form of life for the whole society, . . . there won't be another Middle Ages, at least not in the near future. It will always be what you could call a complementary movement, if not a countermovement, with respect to the prevailing world view. At the same time, however, it will prove its necessity and its human legitimacy. . . . She will be less identified with the great societies, [she will be] more a minority Church; she will live in small, vital circles of really convinced believers who live their faith. But precisely in this way she will, biblically speaking, become the salt of the earth again. In this upheaval, constancy—keeping what is essential to man from being destroyed—is once again more important, and the powers of preservation that can sustain [man] in his humanity are even more necessary.[56]

The Ball and the Cross offers a convincing literary commendation for the means of "sustaining man in his humanity." As MacIan declares near the novel's conclusion, "Turnbull, we cannot trust the ball to be always a ball; we cannot trust reason to be reasonable. In the end the great terrestrial globe will go quite lop-sided, and only the cross will stand upright" (BC, 168). Bigoted notions of tolerance, Chesterton has fictionally demonstrated, often make the world wobble wildly on its axis, especially when they evacuate the public forum of substantial moral and religious argument. In the name of a sanitary inclusivity, they produce a tyrannous exclusion. Only in the properly humbled and thoroughly ecclesial sense does the all-welcoming rood rightly crown the circling orb. It is not a knife thrust into the heart of the world, seeking to subdue and control it. It is, instead, a handle of hospitality set atop this bobbling buoy called earth, so that all its floundering inhabitants might grab hold and be saved.

6

THE BANE AND BLESSING OF CIVILIZATION
Torture, Democracy, and *The Ballad of the White Horse*

> Torture is not a relic of barbarism at all. In actuality it is simply
> a relic of sin; but in comparative history it may well be called a relic
> of civilisation. It has always been most artistic and elaborate when
> everything else was most artistic and elaborate. . . . This is, first and last,
> the frightful thing we must remember. In so far as we grow instructed
> and refined we are not (in any sense whatever) naturally moving away
> from torture. We may be moving towards torture. We must know what
> we are doing, if we are to avoid the enormous secret cruelty which has
> crowned every historic civilisation.
> G. K. Chesterton, *Tremendous Trifles* (1909)

Despite the patriotic militancy of his great hymns, Chesterton came to have doubts about English nationalism. He discerned that his democratic vision of social and political life was possible only in small city-states such as the Greeks inhabited. He regretted that England had come to be called "a nation of shopkeepers," and he despised the "industrialized individualism" that William Cobbett had both feared and prophesied. In fact, Chesterton increasingly identified himself with Cobbett's inward-turning gloom, as if he were describing himself in this account of Cobbett: "He began by having the ordinary optimistic patriotism that looks outwards, and it changed into a pessimistic patriotism that looked inwards."[1]

Chesterton's Conflict over Democracy and Civilization

Chesterton was neither pessimistic nor inward-turning in his faith. Yet patriotism occupied a smaller place in his later work. He came to care more about the condition of the Church than the Matter of Britain. This change becomes evident only by tracing Chesterton's lifelong concern with the fate of European civilization. In his early years, as we have seen, he regarded it as having a symbiotic relation to Christianity. For him, Christendom was both exceptional and superior to other cultures, as in this typical passage from *Orthodoxy*, first published in 1908:

> The highest gratitude and respect are due to the great human civilizations such as the old Egyptian or the existing Chinese. Nevertheless it is no injustice for them to say that only modern Europe has exhibited incessantly a power of self-renewal recurring often at the shortest intervals and descending to the smallest facts of building or costume. All other societies die finally and with dignity. We die daily. We are always being born again with almost indecent obstetrics. It is hardly an exaggeration to say that there is in historic Christendom a sort of unnatural life: it could be explained as a supernatural life. It could be explained as an awful galvanic life working in what would have been a corpse. For our civilization *ought* to have died, by all parallels, by all sociological probability, in the Ragnorak [*sic*] of the end of Rome. That is the weird inspiration of our estate: you and I have no business to be here at all. We are all *revenants*; all living Christians are dead pagans walking about. Just as Europe was about to be gathered in silence to Assyria and Babylon, something entered into its body. And Europe has had a strange life—it is not too much to say that it has had the *jumps*—ever since.[2]

It is crucial to note that Chesterton never went so far in his conflation of the Church and its culture as did his friend Hilaire Belloc, who famously declared that "Europe is the Faith, the Faith is Europe." Yet even Belloc came to doubt this equation, as in this remarkably prophetic disclaimer recorded in a letter from 1936:

> I have never said that the Church was necessarily European. The Church will last forever, and, on this earth, until the end of the world; and our remote descendants may find its chief membership to have passed to Africans or Asiatics in some civilisation yet unborn. What I have said is that the European thing is essentially a Catholic thing, and that European values would disappear with the disappearance of Catholicism.[3]

Chesterton would certainly have assented to this far-seeing claim that, though the Church may well cease to be European and American, it will find ever-new expressions in other places and at other times. "The Church must be divine," Belloc famously declared; "no merely human institution run with such knavish imbecility could have lasted a fortnight." Chesterton embraced this thorny kind of Bellocian Catholicism in other ways as well—for example, in Belloc's challenge to a largely Protestant audience when he was standing for Parliament in 1906. Though his Salford constituency numbered only eight hundred Catholics among eight thousand non-Catholic voters, Belloc the Liberal refused to tergiversate:

> "Gentlemen, I am a Catholic. As far as possible I go to Mass every day. This [taking a rosary out of his jacket pocket] is a rosary. As far as possible I kneel down and tell these beads every day. If you reject me on account of my religion, I shall thank God that He has spared me the indignity of being your representative."[4]

The Chesterbelloc, as H. G. Wells called these fast friends, also held to the conviction that Christianity reached its highest peak in the Middle Ages, when it could be unconsciously assumed no less than consciously professed. In place of the *ecclesia militans* always struggling to remain faithful even amidst sympathetic cultures, Belloc extols the Church that dwells in least tension with the world. Hence this celebrated account from his 1901 walking tour of Europe when, at dusk, Belloc happened upon a vesper service at a medieval Swiss church set beside a brook in Undervelier:

> As I was watching that stream against those old stones, my cigar now being half smoked, a bell began tolling, and it seemed as if the whole village were pouring into the church. At this I was very much surprised, not having been used at any time of my life to the unanimous devotion of an entire population, but having always thought of the Faith as something fighting odds, and having seen unanimity only in places where some sham religion or other glozed over our tragedies and excused our sins. Certainly to see all the men, women, and children of a place taking Catholicism for granted was a new sight, and so I put my cigar carefully down under a stone on the top of the wall and went in with them.[5]

For the later Chesterton and Belloc alike, such congruence of religion and culture is no longer possible. Christianity in the modern world must remain a fighting rather than a contented faith. "Whatever we do," Chesterton declared in 1920, "we shall not return to that insular innocence and comfortable unconsciousness of Christendom. . . ."[6] The Church must put the glad tidings of the Gospel in combat with the sad evils of the world. The *ecclesia militans* emerges as the *ecclesia triumphans* only at the end of time. During the interim, Christians refuse to let the world go to smash, isolating themselves in cozy immunity from its problems.

This refusal to retreat into a Christian ghetto gave Chesterton a deeply conflicted attitude toward both democracy and civilization. He expressed his contempt, for example, for the ever more commercial and industrial quality of Western culture, while still hoping that the creative energy of the *demos* would suffice to resist it. Like many other critics of modernity, Chesterton lamented "the huge modern heresy of altering the human soul to fit its conditions [i.e., those created by 'commercial despotism'], instead of altering human conditions to fit the human soul. . . . If civilization really cannot get on with democracy," he warned, "so much the worse for civilization, not for democracy."[7] In this paean to the hope that human beings will always overthrow even those benevolent tyrants who would reduce them to a subhuman state, whether political or commercial, Chesterton was echoing his early faith in "the artist Man."

As the only creatures who artistically fashion their own milieu, rather than creating merely functional habitats in animal fashion, human beings threaten all attempts at domestication. The "creative violence" of our species, as Chesterton names it, "is as reckless as playing on the fiddle; as dogmatic as drawing a picture; as brutal as building a house. In short, it is what all human action is; it is an interference with [natural] life and growth."[8] The untrammeled power of human creativity presents such a challenge that civilizations atrophy and die when they suppress it. "Once flinch from this creative authority of man, and the whole courageous raid which we call civilization wavers and falls to pieces."[9] Yet Chesterton feared that the mechanical and bureaucratic cultures of the modern West had responded to human innovation in ways that do not produce inevitable self-correction; instead, they destroy men's souls while preserving their bodies.

Chesterton died in 1936, just as Europe and Asia and America stood at the brink of unprecedented atrocities. These nightmare horrors would not have surprised him. Nor would he have been shocked by Richard Rubenstein's argument that terror is inherent within all civilizations. As himself a Jew, Rubenstein is careful to observe that the Nazis acted in the name of justice. All of the anti-Jewish decrees instituted by Hitler's regime between 1933 and 1945 were technically legal, Rubenstein observes, having been duly ratified and promulgated by the Reichstag. Hence his dire judgment against all attempts to baptize civilization as an inherent and unambiguous good:

> *It is an error to imagine that civilization and savage cruelty are antitheses.* . . . Mankind never emerged out of savagery into civilization. Mankind moved from one type of civilization involving its distinctive modes of sanctity and inhumanity to another. In our times the cruelties, like most other aspects of our world, have become far more effectively administered than ever before. They have not and they will not cease to exist. Both creation and destruction are inseparable parts of what we call civilization.[10]

Equally stark is George Steiner's claim that Hitler's triumph occurred, not in spite of German artistic and intellectual achievements, but in direct relation to them. Nazi officers could enjoy opera and sing Christmas carols in the evenings after managing the death camps during the day. Steiner maintains that this was actually not an anomaly. Scientific research and aesthetic high culture may produce a deadly distancing and objectifying effect, prompting a moral torpor that sanctions the most macabre evils: "Where sensibility and understanding are schooled to respond most intensely to the cry in the poem, to the agony in the painting or to the absolute in the philosophic proposition or scientific axiom, the cry in the street may go unheard."[11]

Chesterton himself offered a remarkably incisive forecast of what would become the bloodiest of all human centuries. Considered within "comparative history," torture is a relic—not of barbarism, he wrote in 1909, but of *civilization*. He cites major instances: late Rome, sixteenth-century France, modern China. Then he concludes with claims so remarkably prophetic that they would have served him well a few years later, when he mistakenly pitched the battle against Germany as a fight on behalf of Christian civilization against Prussian heathenism. Here, by contrast, he names torture as the legacy of *all* who descend from the founder of the first civilization, Cain the killer of his brother Abel:

> This is, first and last, the frightful thing we must remember. In so far as we grow instructed and refined we are not (in any sense whatever) naturally moving away from torture. We may be moving towards torture. We must know what we are doing, if we are to avoid the enormous secret cruelty which has crowned every historic civilisation.[12]

Chesterton would never fully abandon this piercing insight. Civilization, he wrote in 1930, contains "all the hideous corruptions of culture, the pride, the perversions, the intellectual cruelties, the horrors of emotional exhaustion."[13] He was especially impatient with humanists such as Thomas Henry Huxley, who equated civilization with refinement and decency, denying that any cultured person would ever swear fealty to evil, as Milton's Satan does. "Nothing is more certain," replied Chesterton, "than that certain highly lucid, cultivated, and deliberate men have said, 'Evil, be thou my good'; men like Gilles de Rais and the Marquis de Sade."[14]

With uncanny prescience, Chesterton prophesied in 1905 that our "highly lucid" and "cultivated" world would produce monsters far worse than such necrophiliacs as de Rais and de Sade. He predicted, in fact, that ours would be the most savage of ages: "The earnest Freethinkers need not worry themselves so much about the persecutions of the past. Before the Liberal idea is dead or triumphant, we shall see wars and persecutions the like of which the world has never seen."[15] What Chesterton foresaw in dread is precisely what Nietzsche celebrated in delight: "We now confront a succession of a few warlike centuries that have no parallel in history; in short, . . . we have entered *the classical age of war*, of scientific and at the same time popular war on the largest scale (in weapons, talents, and discipline). All coming centuries will look back on it with envy and awe for its perfection."[16] Unlike Chesterton, Nietzsche regarded war as the elixir and tonic for moribund cultures:

> *War as remedy.* — To nations growing wretched and feeble war may be recommended as a remedy, assuming they want to continue on living at all; for national consumption is also susceptible to a brutal cure. The desire to live

forever and inability to die is, however, itself already a sign of senility of the faculties—the more fully and ably one lives, the readier one is to relinquish one's life for a single good sensation. A nation that lives and feels in this way has no need of wars.[17]

"Naught for Your Comfort": The Dark Character of Christian Joy

Chesterton's most important poem, *The Ballad of the White Horse*, offers his most convincing response, not only to Nietzsche and the nihilists, but also to those who, like himself, confess the awful duality of civilization as both a constructive and destructive force. His epic work shares none of the triumphalism of *Lepanto* or *The New Jerusalem*. On the contrary, there is a darkness at the heart of this poem, an unvarnished candor about the uphill struggle of faith within a nightmare world of ethical nihilism and the perennially collapsing character of civilization. From the outset, Chesterton makes clear his worry that the essential human things can disappear and that our humanity can thus be lost. It is first of all the problem of transience, the rise and the eventual collapse, of all human accomplishment. He confesses that the permanent drag of impermanence plagues believers and pagans alike. Both Christian monasteries and pagan hill carvings are akin to the flowers that wilt and wither.[18] King Alfred, disguised as a wandering minstrel, confesses this hard truth to the gathered Danish army, who know not that a Christian voice speaks to them:

"Nor monkish order only
    Slides down, as field to fen,
All things achieved and chosen pass,
As the White Horse fades in the grass,
    No work of Christian men." (BWH, III, 357–61)[19]

In the opening lines of the poem, Chesterton has already pondered the temporal obliteration of things that "shall not return." These initial stanzas are dedicated to his wife Frances as the woman who prompted Chesterton's gradual conversion to the things that do indeed return—not in eternal repetition but in Eternal Life. Her disciplined Christian practice no less than her orthodox Christian belief made her the person, Chesterton confesses, "[w]ho brought the cross to me." Marriage to Frances Blogg was itself a perilous quest, a joint call to arms such as Chesterton articulated in some of his most celebrated witticisms: "Marriage is a duel to the death, which no man of honour should decline." "Variability is one of the virtues of a woman. It avoids the crude requirement of polygamy. So long as you have one good wife you are sure to have a spiritual harem."[20] Here in the *Ballad* Chesterton declares the conjugal life to be a summons to faithfulness of the deepest kind—to what Eugene Peterson calls "a long obedience in the same direction."[21] These dedicatory lines to his true muse reveal the solemn tone that, though with exceptions, prevails throughout the poem:

> And I thought, "I will go with you,
> > As man with God has gone,
> And wander with a wandering star,
> The wandering heart of things that are,
> The fiery cross of love and war
> > That like yourself, goes on." (BWH, "Dedication," 65–70)

Chesterton is recalling a trip that he and Frances had made to the Vale of the White Horse in Berkshire, when he was first inspired to write an epic poem devoted to Alfred the Great, the only English monarch so designated.[22] Yet it seemed vain, Chesterton admits, even metaphorically to dig in the dirt of Ethandune, the site of the famous battle, in the hope of finding permanent light amidst the enveloping historical gloom. Might the whole effort be worse than pointless, in fact, with the mystery being even more fully obscured by stirring the ancient dust so as to becloud the truthful legend? Chesterton's complex answer is as intricate as the structure of the poem itself, for the dread of a Final Night of nothingness suffuses the entire work.

> Of great limbs gone to chaos,
> > A great face turned to night—
> Why bend above a shapeless shroud
> Seeking in such archaic cloud
> > Sight of strong lords and light?
>
> Where seven sunken Englands[23]
> > Lie buried one by one,
> Why should one idle spade, I wonder,

> Shake up the dust of thanes like thunder
>> To smoke and choke the sun? (BWH, "Dedication," 1–10)[24]

Already pagan notes are sounded, as if to warn that the poem's Christian affirmations will be made only in the face of nightmarish negations.[25] Alfred's Danish foes believe that all things both come from and return to the dark, as even the gods themselves shall be reduced to chaos and unmeaning at Ragnarøk at the end of all things.

Having been captured by the Danes but mistaken as a wandering minstrel, Alfred confronts their King Guthrum encamped with his chief officers, Harold and Elf and Ogier. They enter a contest of set speeches that reveal the essential contraries of the poem. The brazen Viking lords accuse Alfred and his Christian thanes of being effeminate and cowardly in bowing to their Cross of suffering and in shaving their beards of manliness. This is Nietzsche's charge, of course. He accused Christians of *ressentiment*, a fundamental feeling of hostility and inferiority in facing the hardness that characterizes the rough rule of the strong over the weak, the jubilant pride in destruction that ancient pagans vigorously embraced. Christianity is, for Nietzsche, a womanish weakness, an ascetic religion fit for slaves and cowards, an unacknowledged nihilism whose only use lies in its creation of such false virtues as pity and self-abnegation and self-sacrifice. Yet these effete "values" serve an ironically positive end. They induce a sense of guilt in the manly and the brave who would otherwise wield their will to power without constraint. Thus do civilization and culture emerge, ironically, from such artificial and arbitrary limits:

> Assuming that what is at any rate believed as "truth" were indeed true, that it is the *meaning of all culture* to breed a tame and civilized animal, a *household pet*, out of the beast of prey "man," then would one undoubtedly have to view all instinctive reaction and instinctive *ressentiment*, by means of which the noble races and their ideals were finally wrecked and overpowered, as the actual *instruments of all culture*. . . . These bearers of oppressive, vindictive instincts, the descendants of all European and non-European slavery, in particular of all pre-Aryan population—represent the decline of mankind! These "instruments of culture" are a disgrace to man, more a grounds for suspicion of, or argument against, "culture," in general![26]

For Chesterton, the Danes are Nietzscheans *avant la lettre*.[27] They are scornful of Christian self-abnegation, enchanted by the mysticism of death, and thus eager to find their final ecstasy in dying, whether by hanging or drowning, whether in battle among men or among the gods at Ragnarøk—the last orgy of chaos and mayhem that echoes nature's seeming delight in destruction for its own sake. Hence Earl Ogier's paean to killing and being killed, in the sheer *frisson* of the orgasmic death-moment:

"There lives one moment for a man
  When the door at his shoulder shakes,
When the taut rope parts under the pull,
And the barest branch is beautiful
  One moment, while it breaks.[28]

"So rides my soul upon the sea
  That drinks the howling ships,
Though in black jest it bows and nods
Under the moons with silver rods,
I know it is roaring at the gods,
  Waiting the last eclipse.

"And in the last eclipse the sea
  Shall stand up like a tower,
Above all moons made dark and riven,
Hold up its foaming head in heaven,
  And laugh, knowing its hour." (BWH, III, 205–20)

When Guthrum ends this colloquy with a final speech on behalf of the Danes, he betrays his own secret fear of death, confessing that, since there is nothing beyond the world but the black void, killing becomes a pagan kind of *ressentiment*, a momentary means of fending off the nihilistic truth, a strange nuptial gift brought for a marriage to nothingness:

"Wherefore I am a great king,
  And waste the world in vain,
Because man hath not other power,
Save that in dealing death for dower,

He may forget it for an hour

To remember it again." (BWH, III, 288–93)

Alfred seizes upon this confessed fear of Nothingness by claiming that those who are baptized make braver warriors than even the fiercest Danes. Viking banquets are a desperate recompense for life's emptiness, while Christian sacrifice is given in sheer gladness. Hence Alfred's boast that it is "better to fast for joy / Than feast for misery" (BWH, III, 355–56). Against the "Christless chivalry" of the pagans, as Alfred calls it, the Blessed Mother voices a similar conviction: those who have been marked by the incarnate God's own death have no cause to fear either their earthly end or the judgment that lies beyond it, except insofar as they are disgraced by their own insufficient service to the Crucified:

"But the men signed of the cross of Christ

Go gaily in the dark.

. . .

"But the men that drink the blood of God

Go singing to their shame." (BWH, I, 233–34, 237–38)

Alfred himself gives voice to such holy jocularity as he assembles his warriors before the first battle of Ethandune. There he outdoes Nietzsche, laughing not at his foes but at himself. Indeed, he bursts with joy over the one Event that reorders all customs and calendars by way of a divine revaluation of all values:

The giant laughter of Christian men

That roars through a thousand tales,

Where greed is an ape and pride is an ass,

And Jack's away with his master's lass,

And the miser is banged with all his brass,

The farmer with all his flails;

Tales that tumble and tales that trick

Yet end not all in scorning—

Of kings and clowns in a merry plight,

And the clock gone wrong and the world gone right,

That the mummers sing upon Christmas night

And Christmas Day in the morning. (BWH, IV, 236–47)

Alfred's carefree mirth would be no real answer to pagan nihilism if it were not undergirded by substantial faith and hope. These are what the king acquires in his early encounter with the Virgin Mary. Having failed to receive help from Charlemagne and other Christian lords of Europe, the English monarch assumes that he must fight the Danes alone, and thus that his effort must surely be doomed. The Mother of God then miraculously appears to him, not with tidings of easy joy but in an apparition most notable for its somber realism. She begins by refusing to guarantee an English victory. In so doing, she announces the hard fact that we can never know in advance whether our lives will end well or ill: "But if he fail or if he win / To no good man is told." Instead, the Marian voice announces the real cause for true strength even in the face of seeming defeat. Christians do not put their hope in the brawn and bravery of the powerful so much as in the "little people" who enter the Kingdom through the door of suffering, as the Virgin Mother sings most poignantly:

"The gates of heaven are lightly locked,
    We do not guard our gain,
The heaviest hind* may easily   *farm laborer
Come silently and suddenly
    Upon me in a lane,

"And any little maid that walks
    In good thoughts apart,
May break the guard of the Three Kings*   *the Magi?
And see the dear and dreadful things
    I hid within my heart." (BWH, I, 209–18)

What peasant lass and lad alike discover is that they can bear their own afflictions by giving them over to the Mater Dolorosa, the Maid who has pondered the weight of suffering. Their griefs may be healed by participation in hers. The poem's central paradox lies precisely here, in the sorrowful joy that enables Christians not to despair when confronting the nightmare terrors of human existence. Indeed, the ballad's *leitmotif* lies in the unblinkered wisdom contained in the poem's most famous lines. They are twice spoken by the Queen of Heaven to the King of the Anglo-Saxons:

"I tell you naught for your comfort,
    Yea, naught for your desire,
Save that the sky grows darker yet
    And the sea rises higher."

"Night shall be thrice night over you,
    And heaven an iron cope.
Do you have joy without a cause,
    Yea, faith without a hope?" (BWH, I, 254–61)

Maisie Ward reports that many British soldiers carried a copy of the *Ballad* into the trenches of the First War. And after the stunning British loss at the Battle of Crete in May of 1941—almost eighteen thousand casualties for the Commonwealth, with fewer than seven thousand for the Germans—the *Times* published the briefest editorial in its history under the simple heading *Sursum Corda*. Hoping that the nation would indeed lift up its heart despite the disaster, the editor then quoted the Blessed Lady's speech.[29] It contains nothing of the unquivering stoic chin or the British stiff upper lip, no Camusian injunction to keep rolling the Sisyphean rock up the mountain, and least of all any promise of comfort if the human effort be sufficiently courageous. On the contrary, Chesterton has the Mother of God declare the precise quality of Christian faith and joy—namely, by answering the terror of nothingness with a pitiless *naught* that becomes, ever so strangely, a most gracious *ought*.

The faith and the joy that have no earthly source are based not on the promise, much less the assurance of victory. As Aidan Nichols explains, "Joy . . . lies deeper than happiness or unhappiness, pleasure or pain. All of these are reactions to particular conditions or events within existence, whereas joy is the reaction to the fact that there should be such a thing as existence at all."[30] So it is with Christian hope. It is identified in St. Paul's praise of Abraham as the founder of God's people, the patriarch who "against hope believed in hope" (Rom 4:18). This is the supernal hope that begins where all human hope ends, enabling the faithful to fare forward joyfully, without worried regard for a victorious outcome. Even when the welkin rings hollow and the darkness descends, Marian faith and joy and hope hold fast.

Why Christians Guard Even Heathen Things

In his crucial colloquy with King Guthrum and the Danish captains, Alfred foretells something hugely more important than the defeat of the valiant Vikings by the undermanned English. It is not only military mastery that he prophesies so much as it is the redemptive attitude of Christians toward their conquered enemies:

> "Therefore your end is on you,
>   Is on you and your kings,
> Not for a fire in Ely fen,[31]
> Not that your gods are nine or ten,
> But because it is only Christian men
>   Guard even heathen things.
>
> "For our God hath blessed creation,
>   Calling it good. I know
> What spirit with whom you blindly band
> Hath blessed destruction with his hand;
> Yet by God's death the stars shall stand
>   And the small apples grow." (BWH, III, 367–78)

In claiming that "only Christian men / Guard even heathen things," Alfred underscores Chesterton's central conviction—one that suffuses the whole of his work—that Christians differ from pagans, among many other ways, in this most remarkable dissimilarity: they praise and preserve the virtues of the very same foes whom they vanquish.[32] Alfred thus predicts that the Danish army will be defeated because the Christians are stirred to valor as they behold the most important pagan emblem that his fellow believers have preserved: the White Horse of Uffington. Rather than destroying the prehistoric equine figure carved into the Berkshire hillside, the early English Christians protected and maintained it. Whether wittingly or not, they were heeding the following instructions written by Pope Gregory in 601 and later recorded by the Venerable Bede, as Abbot Mellitus was departing for Britain:

> We wish you to inform him [Bishop Augustine of Canterbury] that we have been giving careful thought to the affairs of the English, and have come to the conclusion that the temples of the idols among that people should on no account be destroyed. The idols are to be destroyed, but the temples

themselves are to be aspersed with holy water, altars set up within them, and relics deposited there. For if these temples are well-built, they must be purified from the worship of demons and dedicated to the service of the true God. In this way, we hope that the people, seeing that their temples are not destroyed, may abandon their error and, flocking more readily to their accustomed resorts, may come to know and adore the true God.[33]

The Anglo-Saxon preservers of the White Horse were also heeding the counsel of St. Augustine, who had famously urged Christians to follow the practice of the fleeing Israelites by taking "the spoils of the Egyptians," possessing and converting heathen truth to Christian use.[34] This was not an act of plunder, the Bishop of Hippo explains, but a deed of justice, since the Egyptians had treated the Israelites tyrannously. Such seizing of pagan virtues is also an act of restoration since, in assuming the fullness of human nature, Christ has healed the whole of human creativity across the entirety of time. The good things that were present only partially and potentially within the pagan world can now be made full and actual in Christ. The ancient Berkshire churchmen were realizing the most central Christian claim—not only that Christ reveals himself to man, but also that "Christ reveals man to himself."[35]

This Christian humanist conviction is voiced most clearly in the battle cry shouted by Alfred's captain named Mark. He regards all genuine works of imagination as a far-off reflection of the divine making, the work of the Poet who pronounced his artistically wrought world to be "very good."[36] As a Roman Christian convert, Mark thus urges his troops to preserve the life of ordinary created things by striking down the Danish fatalists (doom lovers) and racialists (blood tribes) who worship death and thus the destruction of all human manufacture:

"Spears at the charge!" yelled Mark amain,
    "Death on the gods of death!
Over the thrones of doom and blood
Goeth God that is a craftsman good
And gold and iron, earth and wood,
    Loveth and laboureth.

"The fruits leap up in all your farms,
    The lamps in each abode;
God of all good things done on earth,

All wheels or webs of any worth,
The God that makes the roof, Gurth,*   *one of Mark's warriors
   The God that makes the road." (BWH, VI, 155–66)

Rémi Brague, the French cultural analyst, helps clarify Alfred's claim that Christians are unique in hallowing all well-made things, even heathen things. Brague rejects the popular notion—made into a virtual shibboleth by Tertullian in the third century—that Jerusalem and Athens, Orient and Occident, revelation and reason, stand in polar opposition. Brague argues that there is a third and unifying phenomenon that he calls "Romanity." This is the term he applies to European civilization as gladly owning its debt to Israel and Greece—indeed, as recognizing them to be superior cultures in their own drastically different ways:

> To say that we are Roman is entirely the contrary of identifying ourselves with a prestigious ancestor. It is rather a divestiture, not a claim. It is to recognize that fundamentally we have invented nothing, but simply that we learned how to transmit a current come from higher up, without interrupting it, and all the while placing ourselves back into it.[37]

Such "cultural secondarity" has enabled appropriately modest Christians—though Brague does not draw this conclusion—to discern and to adopt what is divinely good in cultures other than Israel and Greece. Such appropriation does not entail any wholesale hybridizing of Christianity for the sake of mere inclusiveness. As we have seen, there are pagan values that must be vehemently foresworn. But with Christ and his Church and Kingdom as the criteria—since in them Jewish law is fulfilled and Greek reason completed and perfected, albeit as they are also transformed—Christians have at once the basis and the cause to "guard even heathen things."

The Courage of Partially Converted Christians

This desire to honor and incorporate non-Christian virtues becomes evident in Alfred's choosing of his three Christian commanders and their respective soldiers. Mark the Roman may be the most significant of these representative chieftains because he retains a good deal of the Stoic in him. He cares not where he will be buried since, as a cosmopolitan Christian humanist, the entire world is his city:

"Lift not my head from bloody ground
> Bear not my body home,
For all the earth is Roman earth
> And I shall die in Rome." (BWH, V, 148–51)

More remarkable still is the nature of Mark's faith. He is a Christian whose "secondarity" makes him strong. The bright Roman light that illumines both integers and syllogisms, determining both the veracity and fallacy of arguments, has forced Mark to agonize over the perennial religious quandaries. He found them answered not in Roman religious syncretism based on an amalgam of all beliefs as reflected in the practice of erecting an altar even "TO THE UNKNOWN GOD" (Acts 17:23). Instead, Mark has discovered permanent Truth in the odd rationality of Christian revelation, the faith-imbued reason that engages the most difficult doubts. Here is the one belief that answers all questions because it is built on the interrogatives of the catechism, though culminating in the stunning skepticism of the Crucified himself:[38]

But Mark was come of the glittering towns
> Where hot white details show,
Where men can number and expound,
And his faith grew in a hard ground
Of doubt and reason and falsehood found,
> Where no faith else could grow.

Belief that grew of all beliefs
> One moment back was blown
And belief that stood on unbelief
> Stood up iron and alone. (BWH, VI, 130–39)

Eldred is the stolid Saxon farmer and herder who is not at all eager to follow the notoriously unsuccessful Alfred to war,[39] leaving behind his fattening swine and his ripening plums. Yet when this ruddy and unimaginative franklin (a landowner, but not of noble birth) finally answers Alfred's call, his loyalty becomes as large as his girth and appetite:

A mighty man was Eldred,
> A bulk for casks to fill,

His face a dreaming furnace,

    His body a walking hill. (BWH, II, 42–45)

After their defeat in the first battle with the Danes, each of the commanders grieves in his own ethnic manner, sorrowing "as he stood / In the fashion of his blood." Thinking all hope to be finished, the impervious Eldred does not despair. He worries, instead, about the thieves who have stolen his apples and drunk his wine. Deferring uncritically to the powers that be, he is like many other soldiers in remaining unclear about the nature and purpose of the battle; he fights because Alfred the King has enlisted him in the royal cause. All that Eldred wants, in the end, is to be mourned and buried by his own kith and kin:

"O, drunkards in my cellar,

    Boys in my apple tree,

The world grows stern and strange and new,

And wise men shall govern you,

    And you shall weep for me.

"But yoke me my own oxen,

    Down to my own farm;

My own dog will whine for me,

My own friends will bend the knee,

And the foes I slew openly,

    Have never wished me harm." (BWH, V, 97–107)

Colan, the poetic and mystical Welshman who remains half pagan in his Druidic reverence for serpents and trees, might seem to be an unreliable warrior no less than a half-converted Christian. Far from being focused on the war, he is ashamed that the original invading Danes had driven his fellow Gaels back into Ireland, leaving the remaining British Celts a diminished race. Colan thus reverses the customary order of things, being joyful when fighting and mournful when singing, as the narrator memorably observes:

His harp was carved and cunning,

    As the Celtic craftsman makes,

Graven all over with twisting shapes

    Like many heedless snakes.

His harp was carved and cunning,[40]
> His sword prompt and sharp,
And he was gay when he held the sword,
> Sad when he held the harp.

For the great Gaels of Ireland
> Are the men that God made mad,
For all their wars are merry,
> And all their songs are sad. (BWH, II, 212–23)

Yet Colan is no dreamer when it comes to fighting; indeed, he is the last and fiercest of Alfred's warriors to die. And when he ponders death, he remains as much Druid as Christian. A minimally converted pagan, he hopes that he will still be listening to the trees when he meets his end, even as the sign of his Savior will lie atop his corpse:

"Yet I could lie and listen
> With a cross upon my clay,
And hear unhurt for ever
> What the trees of Britain say." (BWH, V, 136–39)

That Alfred's representative chieftains are but imperfect Christians constitutes Chesterton's confession that the Church is only partially successful in making converts. It is also a confession that the Faith is almost always compromised. Except in the rare case of truly sainted lives, the congregation of the faithful remains decidedly mixed. The pilgrim people of God are an emblem, not a copy, of the Eternal City. Saint Augustine thus refuses to equate the earthly Church with the heavenly kingdom:

[W]hile the City of God is on pilgrimage in this world, she has in her midst some who are united with her in participation in the sacraments, but who will not join her in the eternal destiny of the saints. Some of these are hidden; some are well known, for they do not hesitate to murmur against God, whose sacramental sign they bear, even in the company of his acknowledged enemies. At one time they join his enemies in filling the theatres, at another they join us in filling the churches. . . . In truth, those two cities are interwoven and intermixed in this era, and await separation at the last judgment.[41]

Marian Faithfulness amidst Darkening Skies and Rising Floods

Since the English warriors remain a motley and semifaithful flock, how can Alfred be regarded as Chesterton's exemplary Christian king? How, more specifically, does his faith serve as an answer to the *Liebestod* of the Danes, the love of death whose nihilistic character Chesterton regarded as the nightmare quality of our time? As we have noticed, Chesterton follows Augustine and almost all other Christian thinkers in regarding evil as *privatio boni*, the unnatural perversion and twisting of the good. Because evil is always parasitic and derivative, there can be no dualistic competition between good and evil. In every case the real defines the unreal, as light defines darkness and substance creates shadows. The malignant discloses itself only in relation to the benignant, since evil has no independent existence of its own.

> I say you cannot really understand any myths till you have found that one of them is not a myth. Turnip ghosts mean nothing if there are no real ghosts. Forged bank-notes mean nothing if there are no real bank-notes. Heathen gods mean nothing, and must always mean nothing, to those . . . that deny the Christian God. When once a god is admitted, even a false god, the Cosmos begins to know its place: which is the second place. When once it is the real God the Cosmos falls down before Him, offering flowers in spring as flames in winter.[42]

In the last battle at Ethandune, this distinction concerning evil as the perversion of good may not seem to hold, since the astonishing fierceness of the Christian warriors appears to be as deliriously bloodthirsty as the death-loving resistance of their Danish counterparts. The Christians seem indeed to return evil for evil, relishing carnage lest they be macerated themselves. Thus do we hear that these combatants of the Crucified came "roaring down to die," a sanguinary thrill seething within them as they "sang the slaughter." Yet, as also in *Lepanto*, they fight not for their self-preservation alone but, at least from the narrator's perspective, for the whole of Christian Europe. The verbs shift to the present tense as readers are invited to participate in the phantasmagoric mayhem:

Then bursting all and blasting
    Came Christendom like death,
Kicked of such catapults of will,
The staves shiver, the barrels spill,
The waggons waver and crash and kill
    The waggoners beneath.

Barriers go backwards, banners rend,
    Great shields groan like a gong
Horses like horns of nightmare
    Neigh horribly and long. (BWH, VII, 225–34)

Yet the pitilessness of the pitifully small band of English warriors, with their "hopeless lance" and "hopeless horn," would not have sufficed against the mighty Danes unless they had possessed the "faith without hope" first proffered by the Queen of Heaven. Our Lady reappears, in fact, during the heat of the final fray, not blazing with righteous wrath, but with eyes full of uncontrived woe: "Her dress was soft as western sky / And she was a queen most womanly— / But she was a queen of men" (BWH, VII, 197–99). Because her own heart has been pierced with the sorrows prophesied long before her Son and Savior's death (Luke 2:35), she can herself bear a sword. Yet the Blessed Virgin wields it not in bloodshed but in encouragement, as she is borne aloft on "dreadful cherubs." Apparently visible to all, she stuns the Danes and inspires the English. Alfred thus summons his troops to Marian boldness amidst darkening skies and rising waters. Human nature takes on Supernature, and manly courage becomes Christian valor, as the Saxons reverse the rushing current of seeming defeat:

"The high tide!" King Alfred cried,
    "The high tide and the turn!
As a tide turns on the tall grey seas,
See how they waver in the trees,
How stray their spears, how knock their knees,
    How wild their watchfires burn!

"The Mother of God hovers over them,
    Walking on wind and flame,

And the storm-cloud drifts from city and dale,
And the White Horse stamps in the White Horse Vale,
And we all shall yet drink Christian ale,
    In the village of our name." (BWH, VII, 241–52)

The English triumph proves to be Christian rather than pagan, at least in the manner of the Middle Ages: the defeated King Guthrum is offered peace terms that include his conversion. Once a mocker of all things Christian, a Viking who vainly regarded the world as his pleasure cup, filling its seeming vacancy with his own brutish libations, Guthrum will now drink from a different vessel. He will imbibe the sacramental wine, for he has been incorporated into the Body of Christ and allowed peacefully to return to Denmark.[43] Even so, the scene of final victory remains as much ghoulish as joyful:

There rose to the birds flying
A roar of dead and dying;
In deafness and strong crying
    We signed him with the cross.

Far out to the winding river
    The blood ran down for days,
When we put the cross on Guthrum
    In the parting of the ways. (BWH, VII, 361–70)

The Coming of the New Heathen and the Perennial Christian Task

"The Scouring of the White Horse," the poem's final section, contains Chesterton's profoundest judgment on the responsibility of Christians to seek the welfare of whatever earthly city they inhabit. Though *The Ballad of the White Horse* can be read as Chesterton's paean to Anglophone civilization as it was almost slain at the start by the invading Vikings, it does not end in triumphalist fashion. There are brief allusions, of course, to Alfred's sterling accomplishments in literature and charity and legal reform, but Chesterton does not dwell on the achievements for which Alfred eventually became known as "the Great." Far more important is the description of Alfred walking in his orchard with "the little book in his bosom" (BWH, VIII, 31). This may be a reference to Alfred's *Handboc* or *Enchiridion*, a collection (now lost) of proverbs and quotations that he had gathered for his own edification, perhaps from the four works that he himself translated from Latin to Old English: the *Dialogues* of Gregory the Great, Boethius' *Consolation of Philosophy*, St. Augustine's *Soliloquies*, and the first fifty hymns of the Psalter. Alfred seems, in fact, to be drawing from this small volume pressed against his chest when he is arraigned by his military advisers for failing to extend his victory at Ethandune still further north in order to defeat the Danes who rule there. Alfred answers with a proverb whose modesty and humility permeate the final section of the poem:

"When all philosophies shall fail,
　　This word alone shall fit;
That a sage feels too small for life,
　　And a fool too large for it." (BWH, VIII, 94–97)

Alfred tells his liege men that he has no desire to rule over all of England but that he wishes, instead, to remain at his fortress hideout on the little island of Athelney amidst the marshy swamps of Somerset. Ensconced there where he had received his Marian apparition before undertaking the battle against Guthrum and the Danes, Alfred is now an elderly king living in reflective retirement. When news comes that the Danes have struck yet again—perhaps a historical reference to their final onslaught in 892–893, five years after Ethandune—Alfred's thanes accuse him of weakness of will and abdication of duty. Aroused by this false charge, he leads his army to the defeat and permanent rout of the Vikings in the battle of London Town. But while the poem concludes on a note of triumph, its somber gravamen lies in Alfred's visionary prophecy of the "undying heathen" that shall besiege England in the future.

As when Dante has characters foresee events that have already occurred, so does Chesterton use this occasion to prophesy the small-mindedness of our own culture of comfort and convenience, our commercial success and religious emptiness. These forthcoming barbarians will have clean fingernails and hygienic bodies, Alfred prophesies, but they will also be "trousered apes" and "men without chests," as C. S. Lewis called them—creatures who will have no moral center or substance, living and dying by bloated abstractions, reducing their ideas to

brain synapses ("By thought a crawling ruin"), their souls to long lita-
nies of confessed psychological "complexes" ("By detail of the sinning, /
And denial of the sin"), their wondrous sun reduced to a dwarf star, and
their lovely earth shrunk to tiny pea now lost "[i]n high heaven's tower-
ing forestry" (BWH, VIII, 295, 293–94, 264–65).

Chesterton here joins his voice to a litany of literary complaints
against the shrinkage of human souls when they flee from life in God's
own Company. It stretches from Dante's contempt for the vacuous
neutrals who dwell in the vestibule of Hell, unworthy even of damnation; to Dostoevsky's Grand Inquisitor in his taunting prophecy that
men will slavishly surrender their risk-laden freedom in exchange for
easy security; on to Kierkegaard's complaint that this present "talk-
ative age" consists of pusillanimous creatures who resemble geese
more than men.

Alfred himself serves as the most succinct and terrifying of such
Cassandras, for the king offers a plangent Augustinian lament that the
coming of these new heathen shall mark "the end of the world's desire."
"Desire" names all human longings, whether physical or metaphysical,
whether sexual or spiritual. The Scots Catholic novelist Bruce Marshall
has his priest-protagonist put the Chestertonian case succinctly: "[T]he
young man who rings the bell at the brothel is unconsciously looking
for God."[44] Walker Percy, another Catholic convert-novelist, is equally
plaintive, as he speaks in the voice of his narrator Dr. Thomas More:

> The first thing a man remembers is longing and the last thing he is con-
> scious of before death is exactly the same longing. I have never seen a man
> who did not die in longing. When I was ten years old I woke one sum-
> mer morning to a sensation of longing. Besides the longing I was in love
> with a girl named Louise. . . . At the breakfast table, I took a look at my
> father with his round head, his iron-colored hair, his chipper red cheeks,
> and I wondered to myself: at what age does a man get over this longing?
> The answer is, he doesn't.[45]

Chesterton's fear is not that men will become sex-driven subhu-
mans so much as demonic superhumans devoid of all *eros*, all desire
that takes them out of themselves in search of the manifold fulfill-
ments that they are meant to enjoy, the chief of them being participation in God's own triune life. The death of the world's desire, the

end of all yearning, means that human beings will no longer be shaped by divine aims and ends. Alfred thus prophesies that, deprived of all means for rightly ordering their loves, bereft of both the upward ascent to paradise and the downward plunge to perdition, such creatures will become pismire shufflers of paper.

Such denunciations of modern calamity often lead to *Schadenfreude*, to a perverse shiver of delight at the calamitous collapse of the Enlightenment project, despite ample warning. More often these jeremiads are followed by high-minded calls for moral excellence by reinstating Christian virtue against the barbarians who have long been within the gates. Chesterton is often enlisted in the ranks of such culture warriors who are determined to "take back" Western civilization from the marauders. Remarkably, *The Ballad of the White Horse* relishes no such reactionary sentiments. Instead, Chesterton has Alfred summon all of his people—princes and thanes and peasants—to the lowly and humble task of pulling back the turf which, if not thus plucked clean to expose the limestone beneath, will soon obliterate the White Horse and the noble paganism for which it stands. Hence the king's final speech as he rides off to his last clash with the Danes:

"And I go riding against the raid,
      And ye know not where I am;
But ye shall know in a day or year,
When one green star of grass grows here;
Chaos has charged you, charger and spear,
      Battle-axe and battering ram.

"And though skies alter and empires melt,
      This word shall still be true:
If we would have the horse of old,
      Scour ye the horse anew.

"One time I followed a dancing star
      That seemed to sing and nod,
And ring upon earth all evil's knell;
But now I wot if ye scour not well
Red rust shall grow on God's great bell
      And grass in the streets of God." (BTW, VIII, 198–213)

It is noteworthy that Alfred does not call his people to wield the saber of Christian righteousness against the pagans, whether old or new. Only when the sword is held at the hilt and pointed downward does it form a cross. The king confesses, in fact, his mistaken early belief that, by following the swaying star that stood over Bethlehem, he might become the English Charlemagne, a mighty monarch putting a halt to the spread of barbarism—perhaps by collapsing the distinction between Church and society as Charles the Great had done. Slowly Alfred has learned that such totalizing triumphs are delusory; indeed, they are not Christian at all. The Kingdom comes neither by cultural accommodation nor by cultural domination, even if Christians must occasionally wield arms to protect the innocent. "The only defensible war," Chesterton wrote near the end of his life, "is a war of defence."[46] Alfred's expulsion of the Danes has been such a just war, at least in its aims if not its methods, and now that the ninth-century pagans from Denmark have been routed, the king is concerned about the distant future even more than the immediate return of the "undying heathen."

What is most remarkable about Alfred's final speech is that he calls for the preservation of non-Christian no less than Christian virtues. Hence his summons to the diligent cleansing of the *pagan* emblem of the Snowy Steed sculpted into the sod of the Berkshire hillside. "The horse of old" represents not only the past in general but, quite specifically, the highest virtues of the pre-Christian world, especially the virtue of courage in the face of seeming (perhaps even sure) defeat. It must be scoured ever afresh, lest the ever-returning weeds choke off the ancient emblem. The implication is clear. Despite his critique of the Vikings' nihilistic love of death, Alfred regards heathen beauty and dignity as indispensable for Christian existence. Yet he also knows that such prehistoric virtues will not suffice unto themselves. They must be adapted and transformed and ordered to the love of God. Hence his reference also to the peal that rings from the belfry, summoning Christians to the worship that gives life, even as it also tolls the death from which they shall be raised. Christian tradition is by no means self-sustaining; it must be deliberately cultivated if it is to be kept vital. When left unrung and unburnished, the bell will corrode and thus clang with an uncertain sound. The paths that lead from the Church to the world and back again will also return to a brute state of nature unless they too are kept clear, in order that sacramental and prophetic Christianity might be maintained in the house of God. There is nothing grandiose about this perennial task of nurturing pagan and Christian virtues alike. This most basic endeavor does not often require deeds of daring, Alfred concludes, so much as the humble and repetitive daily round of moral and religious faithfulness.

The Manner of Christian Men Devoted to the Lord of the Lance

Chesterton observed that the only hope to be found in nightmares is that we awaken from them. Even so, hard questions remain. Who awakens us? Are we aroused to dawn or to further darkness? And to what kind of life are we quickened, to real newness or to old repetitiveness? Despite his celebrated optimism, Chesterton came to doubt the validity of the term. Optimism expects the best of outcomes by relying on hopeful patterns found within the walls of the world. "Faith without worldly hope" furnishes an altogether different kind of freedom:

> It is idle to talk to a Catholic about optimism or pessimism; for he himself shall decide whether the universe shall be, for him, the best or the worst of all possible worlds. It is useless to tell him that he might be more at one with the universal life as a Buddhist or a pantheist. . . . It is his whole hope and glory that he is not at one with universal life; but stands out from it, an exception and even a miracle.[47]

In three underestimated episodes from *The Ballad of the White Horse*, Chesterton accounts for this miraculous and otherwise unaccountable freedom—one of them belonging to folk legend but not the other two. Before the first onset of battle, Alfred visits the mythic old "woman of the forest" who is baking yeast cakes as she has done for the whole of her dreary life. The king laments the failure of the Kingdom to come on earth and thus to deliver such souls from their long and dreary labors:

> "But even though such days endure,
>   How shall it profit her?
> Who shall go groaning to the grave,
> With many a meek and mighty slave,

Field-breaker and fisher on the wave,

And woodman and waggoner." (BWH, IV, 145–50)

Concentrating his mind on such hard questions, Alfred neglects to monitor the yeast cakes, thus letting them fall into the ashes and be ruined. The baker woman, angered by the king's inattention, flings one of the burnt scones into Alfred's face, humbling him and "[l]eaving a scarlet star." Even kings can abuse their freedom, Alfred discovers, thus making their realm into the "worst of all possible worlds" if they proudly neglect the little things that matter to the little people whom they are meant to serve. Such meekness is not a pagan virtue, and so Alfred the Christian king is permanently marked with a reminder to ground himself in "the firm feet of humility" (BWH, IV, 258), perhaps remembering that the word derives from *humus*, the soil.

Book VII, "Ethandune: The Last Charge," opens with a mysterious meditation devoted to a child playing on the distant upland of the White Horse hill, pulling at the turf and piling the stones into make-believe castles and towns, only to have the little edifices repeatedly collapse. Nothing daunted by these failures, the child continues to divert himself in a timeless and tireless activity that Chesterton likens to larger efforts. Just as the child sings at his play, so does Alfred approach the final struggle with a similar insouciance, ready to smite the Danes with a nonchalance rooted in a faithfulness that counts infinitely more than success. There is something divinely wondrous about the child's carefreeness:

For he dwelleth in high divisions

Too simple to understand,

Seeing on what morn of mystery

The Uncreated rent the sea

With roarings, from the land. (BWH, VII, 11–15)

The child's unwearied acts of re-creation become a metaphor of the Creation itself. Just as the heedlessly caroling child pulls apart stones from grass, God accomplishes the primal separations—the heavens from the waters, the earth from the oceans, the day from the night—as narrated in Genesis 1.

Chesterton's metaphysical conceit would seem finally to founder, since the divine surety in Making cannot be compared to the childlike attempt to erect an ephemeral castle of chalk pebbles that always falls into shambles. Yet this may be precisely the point at which the analogy holds. In his fiction and essays Chesterton repeatedly likens God to a Child, as both the Master of the Universe and the most easygoing gamine enjoy a transcendent freedom from mere earthly cares.[48] Here he finds similarity between a child's game-playing patience and the unwearied forbearance of God—even though, as always, there is a condition upon which such Joy depends:

> And crimson kings on battle-towers,
>   And saints on Gothic spires,
> And hermits on their peaks of snow,
>   And heroes on their pyres,
>
> And patriots riding royally,
>   That rush the rocking town,
> Stretch hands, and hunger and aspire,
> Seeking to mount where high and higher,
> The child whom Time can never tire,
>   Sings over White Horse Down. (BWH, VII, 21–30)

Chesterton suggests that the noblest of efforts, whether political or religious, is inevitably frustrated by human finitude and fallenness. Weariness and even despair would seem equally inevitable. Yet the endless moral and spiritual equivalents of scouring the White Horse can be endlessly and joyfully undertaken if—and this is Chesterton's repeated condition—*if* there is reason to sing.[49]

The poem's most notable episode meets this final test. It concerns the highest of the virtues as it is miraculously infused with divine grace to constitute the greatest of miracles. Charity is found in the inexplicable freedom to surrender one's most precious possession for the sake of the one final Kingdom and the one ultimate Love. After Colan the Welsh bard has flung away his broadsword in slaying the Danish prince Harold, Alfred summons his English earls to offer their own swords to the weaponless Colan. Finally, the king relinquishes his own blade:

> And the King said, "Do thou take my sword
>   Who have done this deed of fire,
> For this is the manner of Christian men,

Whether of steel or priestly pen,

That they cast their hearts out of their ken*   *range of foresight

    To get their hearts' desire.

"And whether ye swear a hive of monks,

    Or one fair wife to friend,

This is the manner of Christian men,

    That their oath endures the end." (BWH, V, 270–79)

Christians keep their promises, Alfred concludes, not from their own unflinching will, as with the pagans, but from the faithfulness of their arrow-wielding Savior. His own heart having been both literally pierced and figuratively rent by sin, Christ has absorbed all broken vows into himself in order to restore them. As God's own brazen Knight in Arms, he flings his arrow at the hearts of men, spearing their sin and winning their love. Thus does Christ charge hard upon human lives, in a constant apocalypse of the Divine Eros:[50]

"For Love, our Lord, at the end of the world,

    Sits a red horse like a throne,

With a brazen helm and an iron bow,

    But one arrow alone.

"Love with the shield of the Broken Heart

    Ever his bow doth bend,

With a single shaft for a single prize,

And the ultimate bolt that parts and flies

Comes with a thunder of split skies,

    And a sound of souls that rend." (BWH, V, 280–89)

Divine love is a lance. It wounds in order that it may heal, as Pope Benedict XVI claims:

God is the absolute and ultimate source of all being; but this universal principle of creation—the Logos, primordial reason—is at the same time a lover with all the passion of a true love. Eros is thus supremely ennobled, yet at the same time so purified as to become one with agape. . . . Thus the Song of Songs became, both in Christian and Jewish literature, a source of mystical knowledge and experience, an expression of the essence of biblical faith: that man can indeed enter into union with God—his primordial aspiration. But this union is no mere fusion, a sinking into the nameless ocean of the Divine; it is a unity which creates love, a unity in which both God and man remain themselves and yet become fully one.[51]

The divine rending remains, paradoxically, a lance thrust that we crave even as we dread, for there is no other means of healing human desire than by what Chesterton, in one of his finest poems, called "The Sword of Surprise":

Sunder me from my bones, O sword of God,
Till they stand stark and strange as do the trees;
That I whose heart goes up with the soaring woods
May marvel as much at these.

Sunder me from my blood that in the dark
I hear that red ancestral river run,
Like branching buried floods that find the sea
But never see the sun.

Give me miraculous eyes to see my eyes,
Those rolling mirrors made alive in me,
Terrible crystal more incredible
Than all the things they see.

Sunder me from my soul, that I may see
The sins like streaming wounds, the life's brave beat;
Till I shall save myself as I would save
A stranger in the street.[52]

This, then, is the supernal hope to which Chesterton gives remarkable poetic life in *The Ballad of the White Horse*. It is the key for living faithfully amidst the nightmare of a collapsing civilization.

7

THE NIGHTMARE MYSTERY OF DIVINE ACTION
The Man Who Was Thursday

Chesterton's most famous novel has almost as many interpretations as it has readers. I confess, in fact, to having reached different conclusions about the novel's central mystery on each of the several times I have read it. That there is nothing approaching a consensus about the meaning of *The Man Who Was Thursday* may be a sure sign of its artistic richness. All great works of art are subject to diverse and even contradictory interpretations. William Empson's *Seven Types of Ambiguity* remains the magisterial example of multiple meanings to be found within the same text. Readers who ignore such imaginative fecundity are tempted to reduce art, Flannery O'Connor worried, to a disembodied formulation of its significance, as if they were solving a quadratic equation: find x. Not only does such an approach reduce fiction to algebra but, she added, "when [readers] do find or think they find this abstraction, x, then they go off with an elaborate sense of satisfaction . . . that they have 'understood' the story."[1] There is no such x to be found in *Thursday*, and there is thus no danger of reducing it to a formula that we can neatly file away in some forgotten drawer.

Yet there is another explanation for the enigmatic character of *Thursday*. The novel may yield various and antithetical interpretations, not because it strikes unfathomable depths, but because it is a muddled work. Chesterton's intention and performance may have been hopelessly at odds. He was a notoriously rapid writer, often dictating hurriedly rather than composing carefully. To admit that Chesterton

makes one argument here and a quite different one elsewhere is but
to remind ourselves that, as Emerson said, "a foolish consistency is the
hobgoblin of small minds." Chesterton was neither foolish nor small-
minded. Better instead to liken him to of one of his early heroes, Walt
Whitman. At the very outset of his signature poem, the bard who sings
of himself offers this blithe boast:

> "Do I contradict myself?
> Very well, then, I contradict myself.
> (I am large, I contain multitudes)."[2]

While I reject the notion that Chesterton's most highly regarded work
of fiction is a literary mishmash, neither will I seek to demonstrate its
faultless unity. The novel's subtitle, "A Nightmare," effectively ensures
that it is likely to be disjointed, that it may violate conventional canons
of time and space, indeed, that it will have a phantasmagoric and hal-
lucinatory quality.

As we have seen, the word *nightmare* originally connoted something
far more sinister than a bad dream. It signaled something demonic: the
visitation of succubi, those female spirits that virtually throttle and
suffocate their victims, leaving them with an oppressive sense of fear
and dread. "Nightmare properly so-called"—thus ran a sentence from
a 1909 issue of London's *Daily Chronicle*—"is . . . the further insanity
of dreamland." In the novel's dedicatory poem addressed to his friend
E. C. Bentley, Chesterton recalls the moral madness that befell both
of them—indeed, the spiritual strangulation that seemed to grip their
entire world—before they made their shivering escape from it:

> This is a tale of those old fears, even of those emptied hells,
> And none but you shall understand the true thing that it tells—
> Of what colossal gods of shame could cow men and yet crash,
> Of what huge devils hid the stars, yet fell at a pistol flash.
> The doubts that were so plain to chase, so dreadful to withstand—
> Oh, who shall understand but you; yea, who shall understand? (MT, 28)[3]

Dreams, especially when nightmarish, are notably revealing, no
matter how much they may also conceal. From ancient Greece and
Egypt and Israel, on through the medieval Christian and Islamic
worlds, down to Freud and Jung in our own age, dreams have been

regarded as revelatory. Joseph advances in stature under the pharaohs because he can interpret dreams. Daniel does much the same in Babylon, instructing King Nebuchadnezzar rightly how to construe the mysterious "handwriting on the wall." Unlike those biblical texts, Chesterton provides no Daniel- or Joseph-like deliverance from our nihilistic nightmare, no Theseus-like escape from the Minotaur's maze of late modern life. Yet there is at least one thread that, if not exactly the single figure uniting a perfectly patterned carpet, may serve as a slender string leading beyond the labyrinth. I refer, of course, to the novel's chief mystery: the identity of Sunday, the mystifying head of the Central European Council of Seven Anarchs. "What did it all mean?" asks the narrator near the novel's end; "what was Sunday?" (MT, 220). I maintain that he is a strange amalgam of darkness and light, of distance and nearness, of the hidden and the revealed—a figure who, in sum, throws everything off balance by not being easily identifiable. His paradoxical presence makes *Thursday* a novel that, like the book of Job, is altogether as discomfiting as it is assuring.

The Complex Contest between Anarchy and Order

On an initial reading of *Thursday*, one is tempted to conclude that Chesterton is engaged in a neat polemical game in which the forces of anarchy and mayhem will be defeated and put to rout by the paragons of virtue and truth. It seems to be a battle unto "honour and death" (MT, 72) between Lucian Gregory the anarchist and Gabriel Syme the poet— the former an advocate of unbridled license, the latter a devotee of order and form.[4] Gregory often appears, in fact, to be a stick figure meant to be knocked flat, a God-bothering atheist who repeatedly hoists himself with his own petard. Gregory is a stern advocate of anarchic terror, for example, and yet he demands that he and Syme both promise not to reveal the truth about themselves—namely, that Gregory is an authentic terrorist, while Syme is a faux anarchist and double agent. Yet how can Gregory, a Nietzschean denier of morality—one who allegedly dwells "beyond good and evil"—insist on promise making and pledge keeping? His self-contradiction reveals, from the start, that at least a minimal regard for natural law is inescapable, that the most fundamental axioms are grounded in transcendent truthfulness, and thus that there must be honor among anarchists even if not among thieves.

Not only does Gregory live by the divinely instilled moral law that he denies; he is also revealed to be a fool in many other ways, as when he boasts of abolishing not only Government but God as well:

"We do not only want to upset a few despotisms and police regulations. . . . We dig deeper and we blow you higher. We wish to deny all those arbitrary distinctions of vice and virtue, honour and treachery, upon which mere rebels base themselves. The silly sentimentalists of the French Revolution talked of the Rights of Man! We hate Rights as we hate Wrongs. We have abolished Right and Wrong." (MT, 54)

To this ringing anarchist affirmation, Syme adds his own japing hope that right and left as ordinary directions might also be eliminated: "They are much more troublesome to me," he wittily confesses (MT, 52). For Chesterton, it would seem, good and evil are as clear and determinate as fore and aft, as the larboard and starboard sides of a ship—indeed, as objectively real as the sun and the stars themselves. Gregory, by contrast, appears to be the sappiest of sentimentalists, an anarchist whose mind is as gelatinous as his will is calcified. Hence Comrade Buttons' repeated jibes at Gregory, especially when he praises a fellow anarchist for hating pain so much that he had "died through his faith in a hygienic mixture of chalk and water as a substitute for milk, which beverage he regarded as barbaric, and as involving cruelty to the cow" (MT, 63).

It would appear that Chesterton is determined to put paid to the personal crisis he suffered as a result of his disturbing experience as a student at the Slade School of Fine Art in London. The fashionable aestheticism he encountered there almost reduced him to madness. Chesterton gave various names to this sickness that brought him almost unto suicide. He called it "pessimism," "impressionism," "nihilism," even "solipsism."[5] Though he was not yet acquainted with the history of modern philosophy, the young Chesterton was concerned about the subversion of external reality entailed by Kant's epistemological "turn to the subject." Very roughly speaking, Kantian epistemology holds that everyone sees the world in more or less the same way, not because the world exists in the way we all see it, but because the human mind structures the world according to its own categories of space, time, causation, and the like. We cannot know things as they really *are*, it follows, but only as they *appear* to us—not as noumenal *realities*, that is, but only as phenomenal *semblances*.

Chesterton feared that, once the mind takes flight from the world of the senses into epistemic abstractions, it yanks the created world inside out like a sock turned backward. This was his chief complaint against the Impressionists. Their attempt to "impress their own personalities" onto the world struck him as the triumph of Kant's transcendental ego with its mere "apperceptions." As Aidan Nichols notes, Chesterton feared that Impressionism led to "an increasing inability to believe one lives outside an all-consuming dream of self."[6] For GKC, the Impressionist paintings of even the relatively "realistic" Whistler had taken Kantian skepticism to its nihilistic conclusion: "[T]hings only exist as we perceive them, or . . . things do not exist at all. . . . At a very early age I had thought my way back to thought itself. It is a very dreadful thing to do; for it may lead to thinking that there is nothing but thought."[7]

Many readers have interpreted *Thursday* as answering such omni-illusionism just as Chesterton claims to have answered it in his own life—namely, by bestriding the succubus who would otherwise have mounted and sucked the life out of him, as in the conclusion to his satirical essay titled "The Nightmare":

> Therefore I see no wrong in riding with the Nightmare to-night; she whinnies to me from the rocking tree-tops and the roaring wind; I will catch her and ride her through the awful air. Woods and weeds are alike tugging at the roots in the rising tempest, as if all wished to fly with us over the moon, like that wild amorous cow whose child was the Moon-Calf.[8] We will rise to that mad infinite where there is neither up nor down, the high topsy-turveydom of the heavens. I will answer the call of chaos and old night. I will ride on the Nightmare; but she shall not ride on me.[9]

In his novel as not in his essay, Chesterton is far more modest about riding down the various succubi and incubi who were his terror-striking night visitors. Also in his late-composed *Autobiography*, GKC confesses what was boastful in his youthful triumph over despair. There he admits that the prevailing pessimism of the time tempted him with "a strong inward impulse to revolt." He sought to throw off his metaphysical nightmare by inventing "a rudimentary and makeshift mystical theory of my own." Chesterton's fabled optimism, as he developed it by way of Whitman and Browning and Stevenson, lay in "a sort of mystical minimum of gratitude": "At the back of our brains, so to speak, there was a forgotten blaze or burst of astonishment at our own existence. The object of the artistic and spiritual life was to dig for this submerged sunrise of wonder."[10] Yet Chesterton came gradually to discern that his uncritical Blakean celebration of everything that has life, though it won him a considerable following, risked turning him into a heresiarch. "Heresy is not a lie," he explained to W. R. Titterton; "it is a truth isolated from all the other truths. And I discovered that my praise of Anything taken alone was a good excuse for the tyrant, the oppressor of the poor, and other damnable Things-as-they-are." Not all living things are worthy of praise, Chesterton learned; many of them are outright evil. They are not only to be avoided but also abjured. "This is God's universe all right," Chesterton continued. "But there is the enemy."[11]

The Man Who Was Thursday poses an exceedingly difficult question: how to detect the enemy, how to combat maleficence? Given Syme's own status as a double agent—a standing that, as we gradually learn, he shares with all the other faux anarchists except one—how is evil even to be identified? Is it altogether as subtle and unobvious as goodness? Could they, in fact, be the countersides of a single coin? The apparent answer is no. Just as Syme and Gregory are patent opposites, surely good and evil are also perfect contraries. The yea-saying Chesterton was persuaded by this simple dichotomy. As if in homage to his recovery from his metaphysical nightmare, he gives fictional life to his youthful optimism in *Thursday*. Hence Syme's ebullient affirmation that order almost always prevails over chaos, just as things more often go well than ill:

> "The rare, strange thing is to hit the mark; the gross, obvious thing is to miss it. We feel it is epical when man with one wild arrow strikes a distant bird. Is it not also epical when man with one wild engine strikes a distant [train] station? Chaos is dull; because in chaos the train might indeed go anywhere, to Baker Street or to Bagdad. But man is a magician, and his whole magic is in this, that he does say Victoria, and lo! it is Victoria. . . .
>
> "I tell you," went on Syme with passion, "that every time a train comes in I feel that it has broken past batteries of besiegers, and that man has won a

battle against chaos. . . . And when I hear the guard shout out the word 'Victoria,' it is not an unmeaning word. It is to me the cry of a herald announcing conquest. It is to me indeed 'Victoria'; it is the victory of Adam." (MT, 40–41)

Chesterton's schoolboy knowledge of Greek and Latin would have reminded him that *hamartia*, the Greek word for "sin," literally means "missing the mark," just as the Latin *evangelium* refers to the glad tidings that ancient runners shouted upon returning from the battlefield to announce the good news of victory. Syme thus reminds Gregory that we should be provoked to a staggering wonder at the sheer existence of stable things, at the massive network of interlocking successful operations, both great and small, that constitute our quotidian existence. This myriad of unacknowledged ways whereby life "hits the mark" should indeed be an occasion for evangelical joy, an earthly sign and echo of the Gospel itself.[12] Syme experiences a similar restoration of grateful astonishment at the sheer aliveness of things after his harrowing first encounter with the anarchists. Fearing that he is himself soon to be outed and thus executed as a double agent, he is rescued from his fright by a common turn-of-the-century London street noise, the playing of a hurdy-gurdy that will be sounded again in the novel.

Upon hearing such simple and joyful music, Syme experiences an overwhelming sense of metaphysical assurance. It convinces him that ordinary people making their way through the workaday world, with no fear that they are whistling past the Abyss, are the truly admirable ones:

A barrel-organ in the street suddenly sprang with a jerk into a jovial tune. Syme stood up taut, as if it had been a bugle before the battle. He found himself filled with a supernatural courage that came from nowhere. That jingling music seemed full of the vivacity, the vulgarity, and the irrational valour of the poor, who in all those unclean streets were all clinging to the decencies and the charities of Christendom. . . . [He felt] himself as the ambassador of all these common and kindly people in the street, who every day marched into battle to the music of the barrel-organ. And this high pride in being human had lifted him unaccountably to an infinite height above the monstrous men around him. For an instant, at least, he looked down upon all their sprawling eccentricities from the starry pinnacle of the commonplace. . . . There clanged in his mind the unanswerable and terrible truism in the song of Roland:

"Païens ont tort et Chrétiens ont droit,"

which in the old nasal French has the clang and groan of great iron. (MT, 107–10)

These unpretentious and unreflective folk, assured unquestioningly that the pagans are wrong and the Christians are right, go about their daily round as if Christendom had not collapsed. Syme takes courage from their humble faith as he faces what seems to be his imminent death. Unlike the anarchists whom he believes will soon kill him, Syme has found something true and worthy to die for: these simple people and their simple faith. He will embrace death by refusing to deny his double agency as a pretended dynamiter of the innocent. Even if it costs him his life, he will maintain his persona as a false insurgent, keeping his word with his fellow anarchists, "miscreants" though they be.[13]

Like the early Chesterton, Gabriel Syme derives inspiration from lampposts and policemen and trains arriving at their stations, even from "our digestions . . . going sacredly and silently right" (MT, 43). Yet again, readers are pressed to ask about the things that go horribly and noisily wrong, as in the novel they often do. What solace is there to be found when Christians are much *worse* than pagans at producing indigestible poetry and distasteful culture, when they underwrite a static notion of law and order, often in a reactionary defense of the status quo? Is Syme's brave but uncomplicated faith a sufficient answer to Gregory's skeptical conviction that the world has no firm foundation beneath our subjective perceptions of it? Lacking philosophical and theological underpinnings, Syme's shining optimism is little more than a mirror reflection of the dark pessimism Chesterton had encountered at the Slade. As with Chesterton's early summons to an astonished gratitude before the gratuity of the universe, these assurances may prove to be but a temporary means for staving off the fear that the *only* real things are those endlessly rescripted narratives that we invent in a vain effort to impose order on a completely chaotic world, there being no objective Reality at all.

When Reality Becomes Illusion

The immense difficulty of discerning the real from the unreal, the true from the false, is made evident from the beginning of the novel. Gabriel Syme is attending a garden party in Saffron Park, talking amiably with a red-haired beauty named Rosamund. But when Syme rises from his chair, he finds that the entire garden is empty and that his head feels as if it were filled with champagne. Then his poetic antagonist Julian Gregory suddenly reappears, inviting him to an evening's entertainment at a distant drinking house. There, as they begin to lift their champagne glasses, the floor opens beneath them and the table at which they are sitting makes a sudden, swirling descent to an underground steel vault full of bombs. Is this macabre subterranean world real or feigned?[14] Is the novel's entire action a disguised dream—rather like Bunyan's in the *Pilgrim's Progress*, one of Chesterton's favorite books? Has Syme been transported into a counterrealm, much as the child Diamond is wafted into an alternate world in George MacDonald's *At the Back of the North Wind*, another work much loved by Chesterton?

Chesterton does not make the answer easy when he has the narrator subvert the most ostensibly sane character in the novel, Gabriel Syme. On the contrary, Syme's eagerness to serve as a double agent—as a philosophical policeman spying on anarchists by masquerading as one of their own—reveals the ambiguity of his own character. We learn, for example, that this poet of moral and artistic order had been reared by "a family of cranks" who embraced faddish and extremist causes. In fact, his parents had never given the child any drink "between the extremes of absinth and cocoa" (MT, 74). As the inheritor of such ethical and dietary foolishness, young Syme seems to lack the ballast that would enable him to deal responsibly with the "dynamite outrage" he had once happened upon. The narrator declares, in fact, that Syme is something of a deranged reactionary, the virtual mirror image of Julian Gregory as well as the other nihilistic terrorists whom he seeks to defeat:

> Being surrounded with every conceivable kind of revolt from infancy, Gabriel had to revolt into something, so he revolted into the only thing left—sanity. But there was just enough in him of the blood of these fanatics to make even his protest for common-sense a little too fierce to be sensible. . . . *[T]here was a spot on his mind that was not sane.* He did not regard anarchists, as most of us do, as a handful of morbid men, combining ignorance with intellectualism. He regarded them as a huge and pitiless peril, like a Chinese invasion. (MT, 75, emphasis added)[15]

The literary critic Wayne Booth taught us to question the reliability of narrators in much of modern fiction. Especially in the work of such writers as Henry James, the reader is often made to discover the ambiguous truth only by discovering the narrator's own delusions, which are themselves the result of the implied author's moral ambivalence.[16] Is Chesterton engaged in such an enterprise? Is the narrator speaking truly or falsely by taking us into his confidence with the friendly and assuring phrase, "as most of us do"? Is Syme wrong, therefore, to look upon anarchists as "a huge and pitiless peril"? Or does the narrator himself err in belittling the insane fierceness of Syme's protest against anarchism? Though London had been beset with bomb-throwing terrorists only twenty years earlier,[17] are we meant to regard them as little more than the work of ignorant intellectuals, and thus as the hypertrophied nihilism of a few "morbid men"? Worse still, is Chesterton subjecting his readers, whether consciously or not, to Nietzsche's philosophical perspectivism: the idea that our perception of the world is entirely determined by the emotional states or conceptual schemes through which we view it? Is there no singular truth about the nature of things, instead only a kaleidoscope of perspectives, truth being but an aesthetic choice among a welter of competing and often contradictory viewpoints, so that reality is little else than what we create or dream it to be? These were Chesterton's own life-and-death questions, and insofar as the novel is itself a nightmare, as its subtitle indicates, perhaps he means to leave us stranded in their midst without relief.

There is plenty of evidence to indicate that this is not so. *The Man Who Was Thursday* is Chesterton's fictional rendering of his own philosophical nightmare, a literary exorcism of the incubus that virtually sucked the moral and mental life out of him. Chesterton wants his readers to assent, I believe, to the narrator's judgment of Syme as a kind of fanatic, an overzealous scourge of "modern lawlessness," a superrighteous denouncer of what he regards as this "deluge of barbaric denial" (MT, 75).[18]

> As he paced the Thames Embankment, bitterly biting a cheap cigar and brooding on the advance of Anarchy, there was no anarchist with a bomb in his pocket so savage or so solitary as he. Indeed, he always felt that Government stood alone and desperate, with its back to the wall. He was too quixotic to have cared for it otherwise. (MT, 75, 77)

Syme's "quixotic" philosophical rage beclouds his vision, as he now sees everything through the lens of his fury.

As the critic of impressionism, Syme has become an impressionist himself, filtering everything through his own spectacles. He is afflicted with a deadly delusion, a sickness of the soul that causes him to impose his hellish internal fears on the oft-benign external world, as the decisive adverb indicates:

> [Syme] walked on the Embankment . . . under a dark red sunset. The red river reflected the red sky, and they both reflected his anger. The sky, indeed, was so swarthy, and the light on the river *relatively* so lurid, that the water almost seemed of fiercer flame than the sunset it mirrored. It looked like a stream of literal fire winding under the vast caverns of a subterranean country. (MT, 77, emphasis added)[19]

In a similar fashion, "the great dripping stones" of the Embankment make Syme feel as if he were a newly knighted paladin embarked on a "deadly errand" (MT, 91), "landing on the colossal steps of some Egyptian palace; . . . for he was, *in his own mind*, mounting to attack the solid thrones of horrible and heathen kings" (MT, 89, emphasis added).

Syme remains a sympathetic character despite his delusions of moral and philosophical grandeur. We are made to share his fear of being exposed when, at his first meeting with the Anarchist Council, the President announces portentously that there may "be one actually among us who is not of us, who knows our grave purpose, but does not share it . . ." (MT, 112). To Syme's great shock, the President instead outs Gogol as supposedly the sole spy in their midst. This act serves as no conventional detective-novel "red herring." It is not a false but an authentic clue to the circular character of the conspiracy. That Gogol is an ordinary Brit naively attempting to impersonate a Pole makes him a comic figure, so much so that the Chief Anarch asks him to leave behind his beard along with his police identity card—Gogol's Polish accent being as wildly unconvincing as his artificial whiskers. That Gogol's blue card establishing his constabulary credentials resembles Syme's own antianarchist certificate should have made him (and us) suspect that everyone present is an impostor.[20] All six of them should have caught the real import of Sunday's suggestion that Gogol may not have been the *only* traitor present.

Impatiently overruling Secretary Monday's demand that the Council freely discuss their anarchist plans, President Sunday all but discloses the truth about their fraudulent conspiracy: "'Why, you dancing donkey,' he roared, rising, 'you didn't want to be overheard by a spy [such as Gogol], didn't you? How do you know that you aren't overheard now?'" (MT, 116). Perhaps each of the other five joins Syme in assuming that Sunday refers to him, and thus that he alone stands in great peril of being outed and executed. Even so, Syme almost comes to his senses. Having lunch at a Soho restaurant just after the scandalous scene at the first Council of Anarchs, Syme suddenly abandons his xenophobic fear that all foreigners are spies. He sees, instead, that the comradely insouciance of these international diners is akin to a good dream come true. If so, then why wasn't the Council nightmarishly false? Even more truthfully, why cannot Syme assure himself that he has bolted *from* illusory unreality *into* the surety of quotidian life?

> He remembered that in old days he had imagined that all these harmless and kindly aliens were anarchists. He shuddered, remembering the real thing [i.e., the Council]. But even the shudder had the delightful shame of escape. The wine, the common food, the familiar place, the faces of natural and talkative men, made him almost feel as if the Council of the Seven Days had been a bad dream; and although he knew it was nevertheless an objective reality, it was at least a distant one. Tall houses and populous streets lay between him and his last sight of the shameful seven; he was free in free London, and drinking wine among the free. (MT, 119)

Nihilism and Its Fabrications

In *Chesterton and Evil* Mark Knight acutely analyzes the nature of Chesterton's long struggle with nihilism.[21] For GKC, nihilism is the distinctively modern fright that the universe has no final floor, the fear that we are floating over an Abyss, and thus the dread that there is only Nothing rather than Something. Chesterton was extraordinarily prescient in naming Nietzsche as the chief voice of our modern terror, even though the great German thinker had but recently been translated into English. As we have noticed, Nietzsche was the first to teach that all virtues—indeed, the very distinction between good and evil—are but the products of slaves and weaklings who once revolted against the rule of the mighty and masterful, those Übermenschen who love strength for its own sake. Charity and hope and faith thus became the devices of the resentful masses to overwhelm the strong elites by making them feel guilty about their brazen will to power. Even so, argues Nietzsche, the human race is ennobled by the victory of such falsifying slave institutions as marriage. Such utterly artificial constraints help the willfully amoral masters to become self-restrained rather than self-abandoned beasts:

> Think of institutions and customs [such as marriage] which have created out of fiery abandonment of the moment perpetual fidelity, out of the enjoyment of anger perpetual vengeance, out of despair perpetual mourning, out of a single and unpremeditated word a perpetual obligation. The transformation has each time introduced a very great deal of hypocrisy and lying into the world: but each time too, and at this cost, it has introduced a new *suprahuman* concept which elevates mankind.[22]

Once we discern this human-all-too-human genealogy of our morals—so Nietzsche teaches—then all such "values" can be transvalued into those of the Overman, the one who lives without such illusory consolations of morality. Instead, he exalts capricious willfulness over charity and justice and other "artificial" virtues. This leonine creature brazenly bares his claws in the presence of cowardly Christian sheep in order to humiliate them with the reminder that he *could* indeed devour them, though he does not.

The critique of Nietzsche that we have seen Chesterton elaborating in *Orthodoxy* (1908) began two years earlier in *The Man Who Was Thursday* by way of Dr. Bull, the anarchist designated as Saturday. He observes a basic contradiction at work in Secretary Buttons' nihilistic desire to devastate and destroy. "'[I]f the only end of the [dynamiting] is nothing,' said Dr. Bull with his sphinx-like smile, 'it hardly seems worth doing. . . . Every man knows in his heart,' he said, 'that nothing is worth doing'" (MT, 106–7). Bull has exposed the exquisite contradiction entrapping the nihilist: the alleged worthlessness of life calls either for a sullen refusal of all action, or else for an ostentatious activism that displays the universal uselessness. In either case, the nihilist does something rather than nothing, since even the choice not to act is still an act. Melville's Bartleby the Scrivener chooses the former, while

Oscar Wilde and his fellow Decadents elected the latter, cultivating a fey deliquescence during the final Mauve Decade of the nineteenth century. In *The Devils*, Dostoevsky's Kirilov makes the second decision more honestly. He determines not passively to *observe* nothingness but passionately to *perform* it. And so he kills himself as the final proof of his ostensible freedom. In either case, nothingness finally amounts to nothing, however destructive it may prove.

Chesterton remained convinced that nihilism is the most serious challenge to modern life in general and to Christianity in particular. If there be no triune and creator God, no authentic Israel or Christ or the Church, if the universe is fundamentally unsponsored and undirected, then life is indeed a house of mirrors, a world of continuous but meaningless flux, a phantasmagoria of masks and ghosts and nightmares. Indeed, the world is but a brutal arena where the strong slaughter the weak, whether physically or spiritually. As Ivan Karamazov declares, "If God is dead, all things are permitted," there being no transcendent measure by which anything can be called either good *or* evil. Gabriel Syme is right, therefore, in his urgent desire to flush out dangerous ideas that have dangerous consequences. He knows that there are philosophers who, like Nietzsche, have proposed schemes of thought that can be hideously enacted by killers no less than calmly debated by thinkers.

To combat the anarchist nihilism inspired by such deadly theorizing, a remarkably astute constable has recruited Gabriel Syme to become a "philosophical policeman." This unnamed lawman believes that the police should leave off their ignominious "harrying of the poor," together with their oppressive "spying upon the unfortunate," in order to perform their properly majestic work: "the punishment of powerful traitors in the State and powerful heresiarchs in the Church. The moderns say we must not punish heretics. My only doubt is whether we have a right to punish anybody else" (MT, 82). This drastic claim is not meant merely to shock Chesterton's readers. It is a statement of his basic conviction that intellectual nihilists are more dangerous than common criminals. "We deny the snobbish English assumption," the constable confesses, "that the uneducated are the dangerous criminals. . . . We say that the dangerous criminal is the educated criminal.

We say that the most dangerous criminal now is the entirely lawless modern philosopher" (MT, 81).

The ordinary felon is far from being a creature of incarnate evil. Instead, he is "a conditional good man," says the constable. This fellow has surely gone wrong, yet his will is not utterly wicked; instead, his loves are seriously disordered. He might yet learn to "go right" by observing the elflandish conditions we have observed in *Orthodoxy*: obedience, gratitude, wonder, joy. Then would we no longer regard him sadly as a botched job, a pathetic might-have-been; instead, we would gladly hail him as "a Great Might-Not-Have-Been."[23] The garden-variety burglar is no monster, therefore; instead, he privileges his private good over the common good. In biblical terms, he worships the creation rather than the Creator. Thieves are great respecters of property, the witty constable observes, so long as they can respect the property of others by claiming it as their own![24] Pernicious thinkers, by contrast, are akin to Dostoevsky's Grand Inquisitor and Nietzsche's Overman: they seek to escape the categories of good and evil altogether. They reject the basic axioms of ethical existence—not the moral law alone, but also the givenness of life itself. These utopian anarchists, argues the anonymous constable, despise the vitality of the common man because they love only death:

> "They . . . speak to applauding crowds of the happiness of the future, and of mankind freed at last. But in their mouths . . . these happy phrases have a horrible meaning. They are under no illusions; they are too intellectual to think that man upon this earth can ever be quite free of original sin and the struggle. And they mean death. When they say mankind shall be free at last, they mean that mankind shall commit suicide. When they talk of a paradise without right or wrong, they mean the grave. They have but two objects, to destroy first humanity and then themselves. That is why they throw bombs instead of firing pistols. The innocent rank and file [of anarchists] are disappointed because the bomb has not killed the king; but the high-priesthood [of the terrorists] are happy because it has killed somebody." (MT, 84)[25]

Chesterton's constable could hardly have offered a more farsighted judgment of the new era that was then dawning. The eight-year-old century would soon produce the culture of death and the age of ashes, an epoch dominated by men who were "under no illusions" and who thus sought to "save" humanity by leading it to the grave. The wielding of brute power, chiefly by superstates slaughtering millions by means of bombs and death camps, by forced starvation and repatriation, would become the hallmark of the century that Chesterton so clearly foresaw in 1908. It is altogether appropriate, therefore, that the anarchists are dynamiters. The word "dynamite" comes from *dunamis*, the Greek name for power, as Buttons, the Secretary of the anarchists, clearly understands:

> "The knife was merely the expression of the old personal quarrel with a personal tyrant. Dynamite is not only our best tool, but our best symbol. It is as perfect a symbol of us as is incense of the prayers of the Christians. It expands; it only destroys because it broadens; even so, thought only destroys because it broadens. A man's brain is a bomb," he cried out, loosening suddenly his strange passion and striking his own skull with violence. "My brain feels like a bomb, night and day. It must expand! It must expand! A man's brain must expand, if it breaks up the universe." (MT, 106)[26]

Here we have no original rectitude gone wrong but something far more sinister. This is diabolism, the willful embrace of malevolence, the confession made by Milton's Satan: "Evil, be thou my good."[27]

If evil were always a comprehensible perversion of the good, then it could be dealt with reasonably if not readily: the precise motives of malefactors could be discovered and appropriate remedies could be devised. Wickedness would not be a nightmare so much as a gruesomely unpleasant dream. The macabre quality of evil in *The Man Who Was Thursday* often derives, by contrast, from our not knowing who is good and who is evil, or even how we might distinguish between them. That six of the anarchists are double agents creates a further perplexity: Does Secretary Buttons' eventual outing as a faux anarchist serve to nullify his nihilistic arguments? Since he is making the case for nihilism in order to obscure his identity, is his case to be taken seriously? Such perplexities serve as a reminder that the serpent is the craftiest beast of the field, and that Satan is the Father of Lies. Such deceptions lay at the core of Chesterton's own nightmare encounter with inexplicable evil: "Whether it is produced by some subconscious but still human force, or by some powers, good, bad, or indifferent, which are external to humanity, I would not myself attempt to decide. The only thing I will say with complete confidence, about that mystic and invisible power, is that it tells lies."[28]

When Illusion Itself Becomes Illusory

Nietzsche would also seem to be Chesterton's target in the scholar-anarchist with an unappetizing Germanic name: Professor de Worms. Like Julian Gregory, de Worms is caught in the contradiction entailed in his confessed belief in Nothing. "Perjury or treason is the only crime I haven't committed. If I did that I shouldn't know the difference between right and wrong" (MT, 163). De Worms appears to be a paralytic old man who has perhaps suffered a stroke and whose limping walk makes him seem on the verge of lurching right into the grave, succumbing to "the last imbecility of the body" (MT, 122). Yet instead of pursuing his proper anarchical work, the decrepit professor rapidly pursues the swiftly escaping Syme, even keeping astride with the omnibus that Gabriel boards. Clearly suspecting that Syme too is a detective rather than an anarchist, de Worms finally catches his prey in "a foul tavern." Soon the professor confesses that he is indeed a policeman, and gradually he extracts a similar confession from Syme. De Worms is, in fact, an actor named Wilks who has been impersonating a moribund German philosopher. He is not really Nietzsche *après la lettre*. The German nihilist certainly exalted the will to power, but not annihilation for its own sake. De Worms' name reflects, instead, his verminous vitalism[29]—his conviction "that the destructive principle in the universe was God; hence he insisted on the need for a furious and incessant energy, rending all things in pieces. Energy, he said, was the All" (MT, 140).

Wilks had originally been recruited as philosophical double agent because of his enormous thespian powers. He can impersonate almost anyone because he is perpetually enacting a rôle. So perfectly has Wilks imitated the German thinker that he has become indistinguishable from him, completely disappearing behind his professorial mask, becoming Germanic even in his beer drinking! In fact, Wilks is now assumed to be the *real* de Worms—whereas the actual professor is "received everywhere in Europe as a delightful impostor" (MT, 143). Wilks is such a compleat actor that he is addressed as "the Professor" throughout the rest of the novel, even after his unmasking. Though Wilks/de Worms is a comic figure, Chesterton makes the nightmarish suggestion that one can assume a mask so fully that nothing is left behind it, as if the parasite had totally overtaken its host, leaving no real person, only an empty simulacrum. There may also be something demonic about de Worms' loss of identity. Chesterton observes, in fact, that "popular tales about bad magic are specially full of the idea that evil destroys the personality. . . . In all such distinctive literature the denial of identity is the very signature of Satan."[30]

That the novel grapples with the difficult question of illusion and reality seems obvious, even if its answers seem obscure, not only elusive but also illusive. What remains clear is that the remaining fictitious anarchists embark upon the intricate enterprise of discovering what has been suggested by Sunday already—namely, that all six of them are double agents seeking to stop a dynamite conspiracy that does not exist. Yet their venture proves to be an adventure in the romantic sense: a chivalric pursuit of an illusory goal that, in the very undertaking of it, enables them to locate the ostensibly real. Indeed, they all end by allegorically disclosing their essential character in relation to Sunday himself. They may thus be said to represent six ways of comprehending the world's vexing, seemingly contradictory, perhaps even meaningless complexity. As Dr. Bull will declare at the end, "Each man of you finds Sunday quite different, yet each man of you can only find one thing to compare him to—the universe itself" (MT, 245).

A careful examination of the novel's entire plot—with the gradual disclosure that all six of the secret anarchists are apes of the real thing—would entail the tracing of the many hilarious undeceptions of these would-be deceivers. Mime and slapstick are piled atop the farcical and the grotesque—in a veritable farrago of incidents whose nonsensical implausibility is their essence. The entire chase scene, for instance, has the quality of a mock epic, as each of the secret anarchs proves to be a law officer of ideas. When Syme first meets the anarchist Marquis de Saint Eustache, for example, he proposes a duel with the French nobleman—complete with attendants—only to discover that his deadly sword thrusts draw no blood. The Marquis' seemingly preternatural powers make Syme fear that he is doing battle with Satan himself. Yet Syme remains undaunted. Demonstrating the truth of Dr.

Johnson's claim that the sentence of hanging wonderfully clarifies the mind, the poet ratchets up the courage to die as a martyr for everything excellent and true:

> When Syme had that thought [of the Marquis as Satan] he drew himself up, and all that was good in him sang high up in the air as a high wind sings in the trees. He thought of all the human things in his story—of the Chinese lanterns in Saffron Park, of the girl's red hair in the garden, of the honest, beer-swilling sailors down by the dock, of his loyal companions standing by. Perhaps he had been chosen as a champion of all these fresh and kindly things to cross swords with the enemy of all creation. "After all," he said to himself, "I am more than a devil; I am a man. I can do the one thing which Satan himself cannot do—I can die." (MT, 177)

Despite the rodomontade of his blustering piety, Syme actually speaks the truth. Being immortal and discarnate, the demonic angels do not naturally perish, though of course they can be destroyed. Neither can they make jokes. The pseudo-anarchists, by contrast, are expert jesters—as when the Marquis *demands* that Syme pull his nose, the better to reveal that he is wearing a false face, a "pasteboard proboscis," as well as clothes stuffed like a scarecrow. No wonder that the bloodless French duelist proves to be none other than Inspector Ratcliffe.

None of Syme's previous battles with existential fear and trembling can compare with his final and worst encounter with deception and despair. It occurs as Syme and three of his fellow policemen disguised as anarchists have fled to France in order to escape the pursuit of Sunday and Buttons, while these two in turn are joined by what seems to be a horde of true though still disguised anarchists. Since Syme and his faithful comrades have all adopted masks, he is made to wonder whether *everything* might be an affair of veils and shadows, mirages and chimeras:

> Was [the ex-marquis] wearing a mask? Was any one wearing a mask? Was any one anything? This wood of witchery, in which men's faces turned black and white by turns, in which their figures first swelled into sunlight and then faded into formless night, this mere chaos of chiaroscuro (after the clear daylight outside), seemed to Syme a perfect symbol of the world in which he had been moving for three days. . . . He felt almost inclined to ask after all these bewilderments what was a friend and what an enemy. Was there anything

that was apart from what it seemed? . . . Was not everything, after all, like this bewildering woodland, this dance of dark and light? Everything only a glimpse, the glimpse always unforeseen, and always forgotten. For Gabriel Syme had found in the heart of that sun-splashed wood . . . that final scepticism which can find no floor to the universe. (MT, 189–90)

The shock of total unreason causes Syme to abandon the swaggering grandiosity of the would-be knight errant eager to slay the enemies of poetic and political order. He comes humbly to agree with his anti-anarchist companion Ducroix that their real hope lies in the masses who will not join the dynamiters, since they have a stake in maintaining a stable and decent polity as the wealthy do not: "The poor have sometimes objected to being governed badly," he observes; "the rich have always objected to being governed at all" (MT, 191).[31] Syme is also learning not to fear Sunday, monstrously powerful though he seems. The poet declares, for instance, that the almighty Sunday would be unable to frighten ordinary citizens into joining the anarchist cause, since their dull placidity makes them impervious to radicalism. In the midst of his headlong flight to France in escape from his supposed pursuers, Syme encounters one of these stolid swains, a latter-day Cincinnatus at his plow. The man restores Syme's "common sense" by means of his "almost awful actuality":

> Burnt by the sun and stained with perspiration, and grave with the bottomless gravity of small necessary toils, a heavy French peasant was cutting wood with a hatchet. His cart stood a few yards off, already half full of timber; and the horse that cropped the grass was, like his master, valorous but not desperate; like his master, he was even prosperous, but yet was almost sad. The man was a Norman . . . ; and his swarthy figure stood dark against a square of sunlight, almost like some allegoric figure of labour frescoed on a ground of gold. (MT, 192)

This sentimental romanticizing of rustics marks no real advance in Syme's pilgrimage from the nightmare of nihilism toward the daylight of sanity. He has returned exactly where he began when he first raised his hand in an involuntary salute at the sight of the cross atop the orb of St. Paul's Cathedral and when he first glorified the sound of a barrel organ as if it were celestial music. The poet's progress is in fact frenziedly circular, as Syme has become yet again the complacent advocate of things as they are, even further deceived by what he takes to be bedrock truth. The novel seems to be spiraling downward into the vortex of *humour noir*, a very black comedy indeed.

The Enigma of Sunday's Mask and Face

One of the chief pleasures to be found in repeated perusals of *Thursday* is to relish the many ways in which Syme (like everyone else except perhaps Gregory) was deluded from the start. We thus experience the delights of undeception alongside Thursday himself as well as the novel's other double-agent anarchists. Most rereadings of detective stories are usually concentrated, by contrast, upon the clues we had missed the first time through, and thus upon our discovery of the motives of the actual murderer(s), as we ask whether the author provided sufficient signs for us to identify the killer(s), before the heroic investigator finally unravels the skein. Not so with *Thursday*. The nerve-wracking venture that keeps us turning pages on an initial reading requires a notably different kind of second response. Expecting the worst, we had encountered the best. We now know that, in fact, there were no real terrorists to expose. It was all moonshine, and all that ends well seems well indeed.[32] "Nothing is so delightful as a nightmare," Chesterton declared three years after *Thursday* was first published, "—when you know it is a nightmare."[33]

Yet there remains a terrible mystery that repeated readings of *Thursday* require us to resolve, an enigma that casts an otherwise impenetrable darkness over the whole book: who is Sunday, and what does he represent? Like Syme, we gradually come to discern that Sunday the Chief Anarch is also Sunday the Prime Detective. Instead of being the master plotter about to rain fiery ruin on London and Europe, Sunday is the master officer of his six "philosophical policemen" who, in the guise of anarchists, were to infiltrate and thus to stanch the incendiary mischief of a London terrorist cell. Yet there is no such insurrectionist cabal: it is all a huge hoax. Here, then, lies the novel's central conundrum. Do we awake from the novel's nihilistic nightmare only to find that it was but a harmless dream, a macabre prank without consequence? Exactly to the contrary, Chesterton confessed his extreme impatience with writers who revel in such antic frivolity, delightfully depicting the cosmos as an absurdity that mocks us:

In the whole world of things conceivable there is nothing so unmercifully hopeless as an infinity of mere facetiousness, a tyrannical nightmare of jesting. All the really popular humorists such as Sterne and Dickens have really owed their place by the fireside, not to the fact that they were humorous, but to the fact that they were serious, that all their jokes were bubbles upon a great sea of sympathy. . . . [T]he world of pure levity is a world by itself; its bloodless and godless inhabitants have never had any serious moments, and to a man with any capacity for joy their faces are all as strange and cruel as those of invaders from some other planet. To dream of such a world of unremitting and inevitable jest . . . would be an atheistic nightmare from which a man might with a good deal of relief awake to be hanged.[34]

There is little doubt that Chesterton is again remembering the Slade School crisis that caused him almost to lose his mind. Yet in *Thursday*, written six years after this poignant confession, he has worked his way to a profounder answer than simply to say that he had suffered a temporary delusion, that the universe had quickly righted itself after turning topsy-turvy, and thus that he was never to be troubled again by such cosmic doubts. The apparent senselessness and futility of the novel's action constitute, in my view, the heart of the mystery surrounding Sunday. Almost all readers have assumed, quite rightly, that he is a figure of the Divine, if only because, at the end, Sunday identifies himself as "the peace of God" and because the book of Genesis records Yahweh as having "rested" on the Sabbath following his creation of the universe. Sunday's code names for his six policemen of ideas are also taken from the days of the week—surely an echo of the biblical creation story as well the gods of pagan Europe. But in what particular sense, if at all, can the blithe Sunday be said to represent the somber Lord who was hanged from a gibbet?

In an important interview from 1926, Chesterton seems to suggest that there is none, for he identifies Sunday only as "the mask of Nature." Nature is his term for all the secondary causes at work in the world's chance-laden and probabilistic processes. Speaking imaginatively rather than straightjacketing himself in strictly conceptual categories, Chesterton has recourse to metaphors that aptly describe the tumble and scramble of nature's "wild exuberance," replete with "all its strange pranks, all its seeming indifference to the wants and feelings of men." Like Sunday, "the mask of Nature" is "[h]uge, boisterous, full of vitality, dancing with a hundred legs, bright with the glare of the sun, and at first sight, somewhat regardless of us and our desires."[35]

Such a description, like the main tendencies of *Thursday* itself, would seem to be decidedly sub-Christian. Indeed, it appears to confirm the implicit pantheism that troubled Chesterton's friends about the novel. Such a divinity might just as well describe the dancing Indian deity named Shiva, who is both beneficent and destructive, at once malignant and benign, no less terrible than honorable. The Chief Anarch who stands for this naturalistic aspect of the Deity thus confesses that "it would annoy me for just about two and a half minutes if I heard that you [Gogol] had died in torments. . . . On your discomfort I will not dwell. Good day. Mind the step." Such apparent disregard for human suffering causes Sunday not to grieve but to yawn oxymoronically "like an unobtrusive earthquake" (MT, 115–16).

Taking his cue from such passages, Martin Gardner insists that there is no relation between the Sunday of the novel and the Christ of the Cross. The huge and shapeless Sunday is an unfeeling monstrosity, Gardner declares, a nature deity who gives not a fig for human well-being.

> Sunday is God's immanence. He is Nature, the Universe, with its unalterable God-given, God-upheld laws that seem so obviously indifferent to our welfare. . . . Nature lavishes on us a thousand gifts that make us happy and grateful to be alive, yet the same Nature can destroy entire cities with seemingly random earthquakes. It can drown us with floods, kill us with tornadoes and diseases. Ultimately it will execute us. . . . Nature cares not a rap whether you or I live or die, or even whether the human race will survive.[36]

This claim is unsatisfactory on several accounts, not the least of which is Gardner's serious theological error in assuming that divine immanence can be known apart from divine transcendence. There are no "God-given, God-upheld laws" of nature unless divine purpose and intent undergird them. Aidan Nichols clarifies the basic point that Gardner misses: "Divine transcendence makes possible divine immanence, since it is only inasmuch as God differs from the world can he be present to it and in it without transgression of the world's inherent character as creation."[37]

Even so, the question remains: how can Sunday represent anything akin to a Christian understanding of the God who seems pitilessly immanent in the Creation but also lovingly transcendent in the Redemption?[38] Perhaps it is best to hear Sunday himself address the question of his identity. Like Yahweh allowing Moses to behold him only from the rear, and then identifying himself simply as the "I AM THAT I AM" (Exod 3:14), Sunday warns against the human presumption of claiming to know the Unknowable:

> "I? What am I?" roared the President, and he rose slowly to an incredible height, like some enormous wave about to arch above them and break. "You want to know what I am, do you? Bull, you are a man of science. Grub in the roots of trees and find out the truth about them. Syme, you are a poet. Stare at those morning clouds, and tell me or any one the truth about morning clouds. But I tell you this, that you will have found out the truth of the last tree and the topmost cloud before the truth about me. You will understand the sea, and I shall still be a riddle; you shall know what the stars are, and not know what I am. Since the beginning of the world all men have hunted me like a wolf—kings and sages, and poets and law-givers, all the churches, and all the philosophies. But I have never been caught yet, and the skies will fall in the time I turn to bay." (MT, 224–25)[39]

For Sunday never to have been "caught" and "bayed" is not to say that he has not been identified, much less that he has not identified himself. Hence Chesterton's own claim "that when the mask of Nature is lifted you find God behind."[40] What he means, it seems, is that God is not to be equated with Nature but to be understood, at least partially, as the Creator who is not unfeelingly *absent* but terrifyingly *present* within its roughshod actions. These operations are likely to be off-putting at best, appalling at worst, as Chesterton confirms: "Men do not . . . love beetles or cats or crocodiles with a wholly personal love; they salute them as expressions of that abstract and anonymous energy in nature which to any one is awful, and to an atheist might be frightful."[41]

"Frightful" to an atheist but only "awful" to believers? Why? For atheists to be confronted with the divine presence at work within the seemingly godless operations of the natural order would threaten their basic faith that there is no God and thus no transcendent Reality with whom they must reckon. Christians, on the other hand, are "awe-filled" by the revelation that, as both Creator and Redeemer, God is working out his loving purposes in and through the apparent cruelties of natural causation. As Job learns, these brutalities do not entail God's deliberate infliction of misery on his creatures. Such suffering is the result, instead, of some other good that God is accomplishing, as Alfred Freddoso explains:

> God's causality is universal and thus extends to everything. . . . St. Thomas holds that chance or randomness is a relative notion, and that what is chance with respect to one order of causes might not be a chance effect with respect to some other order. More specifically, nothing is a chance effect with respect to the order of divine governance. Every created effect is included in God's eternal plan for the world. . . . He knows things because He knows what He wills to effect both by Himself alone [i.e., miraculously] and by Himself in conjunction with secondary causes. So He knows, for any moment of time *t*, which causes are operating to effect at *t* whatever is effected at *t*. Furthermore, He knows evils because He knows the good that created things ought to have. . . . While particular agents strive for effects that are free of defects, a universal agent might well allow certain defects or evils to occur in order to promote the good of the whole. . . . In the world of nature, many things that are bad for particular things are good for other particular things. So such goods would be absent if no defects or evils were permitted. The same holds for the moral sphere.[42]

Though without the aid of such judicious Thomistic theology, Syme comes to a similar conclusion in his initial discernment of Sunday's identity. As the novel's only professed Christian, and thus as one schooled in analogical similitudes and differences, Syme is able to distinguish between mask and face. Sunday's *mask* is revealed in his role as the Supreme Anarch, the terrorist who would reduce everything to chaos and lawlessness. He presides over the openly clandestine meetings of the Council because, like nature itself, he has nothing to hide. In the final scenes of the chase, therefore, he becomes a frivolous and unfeeling prankster, akin to a cat playing with the mouse it is soon to devour. He is often seen, usually surrounded by light. He thus represents "the peace of God," for he is the undisturbed Creator who is past all change, the immortal and impassible One, the unknowable and inaccessible Lord whose tranquility is not disrupted by tsunamis and hurricanes and tornadoes. They are the by-products of his divine will-for-the-world without which there would be no cosmos at all. This is the God before whom Job, having learned that Yahweh intended nothing evil in his servant's suffering, repents in sackcloth and ashes (Job 42:6).

Sunday's *face*, by contrast, is made manifest in the President of the Philosophical Policemen. He remains hidden in darkness, except when he is glimpsed briefly from the rear. As with Moses, so with Gabriel Syme. He is given a glimpse of the President's very visage. Like Jeremiah and Isaiah, Syme discovers that Sunday hides himself lest we be blinded by the Beatific Vision:

> "His face frightened me, as it did everyone; but not because it was brutal, not because it was evil. On the contrary, it frightened me because it was so beautiful, because it was so good. . . . It was like the face of some ancient archangel, judging justly after heroic wars. There was laughter in the eyes, and in the mouth honour and sorrow. . . . Then, and again and always, . . . that has been for me the mystery of Sunday, and it is also the mystery of the world. When I see the horrible back, I am sure the noble face is but a *mask*. When I see the *face* but for an instant, I know the back is only a jest. Bad is so bad, that we cannot but think good an accident; good is so good, that we feel certain that evil could be explained. . . . I was suddenly possessed with the idea that the blind, blank back of his head really was his face—an awful eyeless face staring at me! And I fancied that the figure running in front of me was really a figure running backwards, and dancing as he ran. . . . It was exactly the worst instant of my life. And yet ten minutes afterwards, when he put his head out of the cab and made a grimace like a gargoyle, I knew that he was only like a father playing hide-and-seek with his children. . . . Listen to me!" cried Syme with extraordinary emphasis. "Shall I tell you the secret of the whole world? It is that we have only known the back of the world. We see everything from behind, and it looks brutal. That is not a tree, but the back of a tree. That is not a cloud, but the back of a cloud. Cannot you see that everything is stooping and hiding a face? If we could only get round in front—?" (MT, 245–47, emphasis added)

The Beautiful, the Ugly, and the Holy

The only way to discern the front of things is by way of indirection, by means of what Hopkins names as the "counter, original, spare, strange"—in short, the grotesque. It is the main mark of Chesterton's theological and artistic liberty. "This freedom is most obviously present," Alison Milbank maintains, "in the grotesque, which recombines the forms of nature and art to make something new and surprising."[43] "Exaggeration," Chesterton himself announced in his study of Dickens, "is the definition of art. . . . Art is, in its inmost nature, fantastic."[44] We have largely lost our liberty to relish the world's mystery, Milbank affirms with Chesterton, not because we perceive and thus desire too much, but because we envision and thus create too little.[45] Our pathetic purblindness shuts us off from both the perception and the creation of the fantastic. It blinkers us from the mysterious transformation of one thing into another, especially the making of sinners into saints. This drastic *metanoia* occurs because everything natural has its own entelechy, its inherent aim and goal that pushes it toward its completion and fulfillment within a larger, indeed within a final *telos*. Because all "things [tend] to a greater end," Chesterton declares in his splendid little book on St. Thomas subtitled *The Dumb Ox*, "they are even more real than we think them. If they seem to have a relative unreality (so to speak) it is because they are potential and not actual; they are unfulfilled, like packets of seeds or boxes of fireworks. They have it in them to be more real than they are."[46]

Our finite and fallen imaginations cannot behold this surplus of transforming life that pervades the entirety of created being. Chesterton, by contrast, discerned it almost from the beginning. His analogical mind thus espied things both wonderful and terrible: "The tree above my head is flapping like some gigantic bird standing on one leg; the moon is like the eye of a cyclops."[47] Chesterton has repeated recourse to farce and mime, to melodrama and slapstick, Milbank insists, in the hope of breaking the shackles that imprison our imagination. She cites perhaps the greatest of the apophatic theologians to explain the deliberately destabilizing character of Chesterton's work. "[S]imilitudes drawn from things farthest away from God form within us," declared

Pseudo-Dionysius the Areopagite, "a truer estimate that God is above whatsoever we may say or think of Him."[48]

God is not so abstract and far removed as to be truant, much less nonexistent. On the contrary, he is so near and actual that he cannot be defined. He is always bearing down on or pushing up through the world's life. The result is that every created thing, both natural and human—from toadstools to pillar-boxes and political revolutions—offers occasion for sacramental discernment, as the Incarnation becomes the lens for detecting what is evil and what is good, what reflects the glory of God and what obscures it. The world is full of such similitudes, if only we had eyes to see and ears to hear, hands to feel and nostrils to scent, and perhaps most especially tongues to taste (Ps 34:8). Hence Chesterton's effort in *The Man Who Was Thursday* to embrace the world's divine asymmetry, its holy otherness descried in hornbills and pelicans, and to do so through fantasy. Chesterton's fiction gives imaginative life to human worlds altogether as astonishing in their unlikeness to our dull acts of de-creation as are the elephantine and hippopotamic products of nature itself.

Chesterton is also drawing on the counterintuitive tradition that links the Holy with the ugly. He explained this strange connection in an essay written in 1908, a year prior to the publication of *Thursday*. There he argued that Dickens always depicts Christmas in freakish terms, celebrating the happiest of events by means of goblins and ghosts, the bulb nosed and the miserly. Dickens' figures are forbidding because their transformation is meant to be at once remarkable and real. Visited by nightmare remembrances of his many failures in charity, Scrooge is gradually made capable of conversion. His late won happiness is all the more credible for being so dramatic a reversal of his lifelong misery. He is saved in the most fundamental sense: his everlasting worth is salvaged from the worthless wreck that was once his life. From having been grotesquely sad and evil, Scrooge becomes grotesquely gay and good.[49] "We have a feeling somehow," writes Chesterton, "that Scrooge looked even uglier when he was kind than he had looked when he was cruel. The turkey that Scrooge bought was so fat, says Dickens, that it could never have stood upright. That top-heavy and monstrous bird is a good symbol of the top-heavy happiness of [Dickens' Christmas] stories."[50]

Beauty, by contrast, is often allied with sadness and even revolt. Graham Greene's whiskey priest astutely observes that the mutinous angels cast from heaven were not the unlovely seraphim and cherubim: "I'm a bad priest," he confesses. "I know—from experience—how much beauty Satan carried down with him when he fell. Nobody ever said that the fallen angels were the ugly ones. Oh no, they were just as quick and light and. . . ."[51] Even when unfallen, beauty often remains an outward and fleeting thing. The lovely mien, like the gorgeous autumn scene, cannot last. Nor do the ideal balances and symmetries of conventional beauty leave room for refinement and enhancement, but only for static perfection, if not decay and decline. The repugnant, by contrast, is often open to blissful transformation in ways that beauty is not. The ugly can end in rancor and resentment, of course, especially if their unsightliness is not their own doing. But at least they are not likely to be stuffed with self-importance.[52] Insofar as grotesque deformity frees Chesterton's characters from a top-heavy seriousness about themselves, it offers them a joyful avenue to the Holy. Satan, we have heard Chesterton wonderfully pun, fell by the force of his gravity. Utopias are grim and heavy places because they leave no room for the frolicsome, the foolish, the incongruous. These latter folk, like the unfallen angels, can still fly because they take themselves so lightly.[53]

Chesterton's early intuition that everything is bursting with a hidden wonder and glory seems at last made manifest in the huge gala that occurs near the end of *Thursday*. "About the whole cosmos," he had written in *The Defendant* (1901), "there is a tense and secret festivity. . . . Eternity is the eve of something. I never look up at the stars without feeling that they are the fires of a schoolboy's rocket, fixed in their everlasting fall."[54] So it comes to pass in the dreamlike enthronement of the six philosophical policemen attired in costumes befitting the days for which they have been named. Their elaborate disguises serve to reveal rather than to hide. Even the sympathetic Syme "seemed to be for the first time himself and no one else" (MT, 254). This wondrous paradisal perichoresis constitutes a veritable "revel of masquerade," as Syme calls it, "a vast carnival of people . . . dancing in motley dress" (MT, 255). Unlike the gigantic Leviathan and Behemoth, the frightening beasts whom Yahweh commands Job to behold in terror, these costumed figures celebrate the goodness of the entire human and animal creation, both the commonplace and the fantastic. In this "huge masquerade of mankind" (MT, 257), it seems that the grand panoply of costumed characters is celebrating their existence on the brink of Paradise. Only in masks are faces revealed:

> There was a man dressed as a windmill with enormous sails, a man dressed as an elephant, a man dressed as a balloon. . . . Syme even saw, with a queer thrill, one dancer dressed like an enormous hornbill, with a beak twice as big as himself. . . . There was a dancing lamp-post, a dancing apple-tree, a dancing ship. One would have thought that the untamable tune of some mad musician had set all the common objects of field and street dancing an eternal jig. (MT, 255)

The Nightmare Goodness of God

This final festive scene—a reverie within a reverie—is succeeded by a return to the primary world, where Gabriel Syme is reunited (eventually in marriage) with Rosamund Gregory. If *The Man Who Was Thursday* had ended on this triumphant note, Chesterton's nightmare would have been turned into a pipe dream. The novel's confrontation with the most difficult questions about good and evil, illusion and reality, immanence and transcendence, would simply have been funked. Instead, Chesterton grants a final and awful liberty to the narrative's most skeptical and mistrustful character, Julian Gregory—much as Dostoevsky refused to thwart the devastating doubts of Ivan Karamazov. Gregory is the one figure who never took a code name, since he is an authentic and not a spurious terrorist. He looks upon the masquerade ball with contempt, convinced that the faux anarchists have too easily embraced the irony that they were working against themselves, too quickly welcomed the discovery that they were preventing evils that never existed. Gregory boasts that he alone understands that the universe contains no mind- and soul-twisting paradoxes, no enigmas concerning the fearful nearness of good and evil. For him, governmental authority, like all other expressions of oppressive lawfulness, is an unmitigated evil and thus should be dynamited. The six bogus incendiaries can blithely abandon their former duplicity, he charges, because they never suffered his own agony as the solitary terrorist willing to annihilate the world's despotic order:

"You!" he cried. "You never hated because you never lived. . . . I do not curse you for being cruel. I do not curse you (though I might) for being kind. I curse you for being safe! You sit in your chairs of stone, and have never come down from them. You are the seven angels from heaven, and you have had no troubles. Oh, I could forgive you everything, you that rule all mankind, if I could feel for once that you had suffered for one hour a real agony such as I—." (MT, 262)

Furious at Gregory's assault on the alleged complacency of the double-agents, Syme interrupts with a statement that takes us to the core of Chesterton's theology.[55] Syme candidly admits that the apparently heartless operations of nature find their parallel in the human realm. Evil often produces unintended good, he openly confesses, just as good often becomes the occasion for inadvertent evil. Such contradictions inhere in creation, Syme shouts, not in lament but praise. The world's endemic suffering is not the mark of its godlessness, Syme contends; such affliction is indeed the will of God. Only "by tears and torture," only in being "broken upon the wheel," only in "descend[ing] into hell," Syme affirms, can we both discern and embrace the deepest and truest things—bravery and goodness and glory.[56] Hence Chesterton's praise for the mysterious divine visitation that Job receives in place of a plain theological explanation. For God, as he notes, comes in the end

. . . not to answer riddles, but to propound them. . . . Verbally speaking the enigmas of Jehovah seem darker and more desolate than the enigmas of Job; yet Job was comfortless before the speech of Jehovah and is comforted after it. He has been told nothing, but he feels the terrible and tingling atmosphere of something which is too good to be told. The refusal of God to explain His design is itself a burning hint of His design. The riddles of God are more satisfying than the solutions of man.[57]

The late Pope John Paul II made a similar case in *Salvifici Doloris* (1984). There he affirms that not all suffering is due to human sinfulness, much less is it all deserved. Immense agony and grief spring from the catastrophes of nature itself, but especially from the evils that malefactors inflict on others. The former Karol Wojtyla was nonetheless adamant in his claim that suffering is

. . . essential to the nature of man. It is as deep as man himself, precisely because it manifests in its own way that depth which is proper to man, and in its own way surpasses it. Suffering seems to belong to man's transcendence: it is one of those points at which man is in a certain sense "destined" to go beyond himself, and he is called to this [destiny] in a mysterious way. . . . We could say that man suffers *because of a good* in which he does not share, from which in a certain sense he is cut off, or of which he has deprived himself. He particularly suffers when he "ought"—in the normal order of things—to have a share in this good and does not have it.[58]

When we reject this vocation to suffering, we often begin to regard prosperity as the sign of righteousness, like Job's "comforters":

For when once people have begun to believe that prosperity is the reward of virtue their next calamity is obvious. If prosperity is regarded as the reward of virtue it will be regarded as the symptom of virtue. Men will leave off the heavy task of making good men successful. They will adopt the easier task of making successful men good.[59]

Worse still, we begin to pluck the tares from the wheat, to winnow evil from good according to our own measure. Seeking perfection, we wreak destruction. For in ripping out the tares, we uproot the wheat as well, mangling everything. Yet this is precisely the charge that the novel's nihilist welcomes when Dr. Bull likens Gregory to the Satan who appears among the sons of God in the opening chapter of Job: "You are right, . . . I am a destroyer. I would destroy the world if I could" (MT, 261).

Gregory proposes to shatter life's nightmarish paradoxes by means of demonic annihilation. The only alternative to his nihilism—found both in Jesus' Matthean parable as well as in Chesterton's novel—lies in the constant uphill effort to do good and to restrain evil, yet without returning the latter in kind. Lest the whole be ruined, the two must often be allowed to grow up together until the final time of harvest. Hence Sunday's commendation of his six faithful philosophical policemen for enduring rather than refusing this frightful contrariety. Chesterton thus declines to turn his dark narrative into a bright and shining lie. Sunday's penultimate declaration, given from his central chair among the enthroned Days of the Week, is a somber benediction indeed. He speaks as if he were presiding over a Final Supper:

"Let us remain together a little, we who have loved each other so sadly, and have fought so long. . . . I sent you out to war. I sat in the darkness, where there is not any created thing, and to you I was only a voice commanding valour and an unnatural virtue. You heard the voice in the dark, and you never heard it again. The sun in heaven denied it, the earth and sky denied it, all human wisdom denied it. . . . But you were men. You did not forget your secret honour, though the whole cosmos turned an engine of torture to tear it out of you. I knew how near you were to hell." (MT, 259)

Sunday reveals, in a last and awful interrogative, why he can assure his six policemen that their suffering is salutary. It turns out that he has visited Hell himself. He has not been cast there like Satan, as Chesterton elsewhere observes; he has descended there voluntarily. It is not surprising that Chesterton read the book of Job in precisely such christological terms: "I need not say that in the freest and most philosophical sense there is one Old Testament figure who is truly a type; or say what is prefigured in the wounds of Job."⁶⁰ Sunday thus asks his own Christ-like question in response to the angry cry of Julian Gregory, who has been outraged by Sunday's strange smile after he had pronounced his final blessing on his six policemen. Gregory alleges that Sunday has allowed his speciously appointed detectives to suffer while the President himself has remained immune from their misery and distress. "'Have you,' [this true anarch] cried in a dreadful voice, 'have you ever suffered?'" Demanding a theodicy from Sunday, Gregory is given something at once far better and far worse—a Job-like epiphany:

> As [Gregory] gazed, the great face [of Sunday] grew to an awful size, grew larger than the colossal mask of Memnon,⁶¹ which had made him scream as a child. It grew larger and larger, filling the whole sky; then everything went black. Only in the blackness before it entirely destroyed his brain [Julian] seemed to hear a distant voice saying a commonplace text that he had heard somewhere, "Can ye drink of the cup that I drink of?" (MT, 263)

Unlike Job, who encounters Yahweh in a fearsome whirlwind, Gregory has heard but not seen Sunday, lest he be blasted into permanent blindness. Gregory is made to listen amidst sheer darkness⁶² after Sunday has suddenly disappeared into an all-answering invisibility. Neither the mask nor the face of Sunday could have thus queried Gregory. The divine presence within the moral and natural order does not suffer and it does not speak. This cosmic silence is, alas, the source of the world's nightmare, making the soundlessness of the starry spaces frighten even so devout a believer as Pascal.[63] Yet redemptive awakening from the metaphysical horror is not to be found within the muteness of nature. It is to be located nowhere else than in the speech voiced by the invisible Sunday at the end of the novel, as he repeats the question asked by the incarnate Second Person of the Trinity on his way to Golgotha.[64] Can we, in sum, find a strange nourishment in the chalice of Christ's own suffering that is infinitely—indeed, immeasurably—greater in every regard than our own?

Without this literally devastating interrogation of Gregory, Sunday's earlier injunctions to gain wisdom from affliction would make the novel's outlook essentially Socratic and Stoic. The Greco-Roman ideal of "education through suffering" is widespread in Eastern cultures as well. In the Christian world, this perennial moral lesson is radically recast. The One who asked that the cup of rejection might be removed from his lips does not summon his disciples to a life of moral rigor alone. He is not appealing for them courageously to transform their torment into understanding. Nor does he speak out of dread for his own imminent and supremely unjust death. He is pleading that his Kingdom might come by some other means than the cruciform suffering that his disciples will surely encounter because of their faithfulness to him and his gospel. As with the silent but firm answer that Jesus receives in Gethsemane, so with the equally clear though implied answer to Sunday's hard query: There is no other way to redemption than the Cross.

Such suffering does not belong wholly or even primarily to humanity, as in the wisdom afforded by both the Socratic and Stoic traditions. It belongs pre-eminently to God. The divine grief has twin sources.[65] God works in the natural realm through secondary causes so that his chance- and probability-driven cosmos might be free rather than fixed, even though these natural processes sometimes produce unspeakable misery for men and animals alike. Yet God is not passive before the horror of such suffering. In both creating and redeeming the cosmos from beyond it, God experiences transcendent sadness over such human suffering, even while knowing that it will finally redound to the glory and redemption of everything. Even more grievous to God are the devastating evils deriving from sinfully disordered human freedom.

Alienation and unbelief reach their awful apogee in the Crucifixion. There the Son of God himself drains the grail of totally undeserved anguish. There is no other way for humankind to be reclaimed and restored than by life in his Kingdom of sorrowful joy.[66]

That all six of the novel's main characters—Gregory excepted—find peace and reconciliation together in the presence of Sunday indicates that, for Chesterton, redemption is not primarily an inward and solitary but an outward and communal affair. It is the great glad News that the slain and risen God has created the Community that can both command and enable the way of suffering as the way of happiness. The People of God can suffer and redeem the abominations of both moral and natural evil, Chesterton makes clear, because God himself has both suffered and redeemed them. This is the staggering paradox that animates Chesterton's entire work. It is also animates his most disturbing and cheering novel, *The Man Who Was Thursday*. Despite his reputation as a merry prankster and punster, Chesterton is the poet of nightmare. His work is gay and lighthearted because he discerns the darkest and deepest of all truths. Whether its source be natural or human or even divine, our nightmarish affliction can be healed only by what appears to be an even greater nightmare—the nightmare goodness of God.

Appendix to Chapter 1
Chesterton as the Daylight Scourge to the Ghoulish Dream of Eugenics

In 1883 Francis Galton, a cousin to Charles Darwin, invented the term *eugenics* (from the Greek for "well born") to describe the science that, by eliminating the weak and the diseased and the degenerate, could improve civilization mightily. He urged that the same Mendelian principles used for increasing the productivity of animals and plants should be applied to human beings in order to create a genetically superior species of men and women: "[I]t is easy," declared Galton, "to obtain by careful selection a permanent breed of dogs or horses gifted with peculiar powers of running, or of doing anything else, so it would be quite practicable to produce a highly gifted race of men by judicious marriages during several consecutive generations."[1] Far from being considered heretical and antihuman, Galton's idea was embraced by, among other notable British figures, G. B. Shaw, H. G. Wells, Virginia Woolf, Bertrand Russell, Beatrice and Sidney Webb, as well as William Inge, who was the Dean of St. Paul's. American enthusiasts for eugenics included Theodore Roosevelt, Alexander Graham Bell, Margaret Sanger, and, most notoriously, Oliver Wendell Holmes,[2] with his famous claim that "Three generations of imbeciles are enough."[3]

Though he died just as the Nazis came to power, Chesterton all too accurately prophesied that the German dictatorship would install a massive eugenics regime. Yet it was the future opponent of the eugenicist Adolf Hitler—namely, Winston Churchill—who put the case for eugenics before the House of Commons:

> The unnatural and increasingly rapid growth of the feeble-minded and
> insane classes, coupled as it is with a steady restriction among all the thrifty,
> energetic and superior stocks, constitutes a national and race danger which
> it is impossible to exaggerate. . . . I feel that the source from which all the
> streams of madness is fed should be cut off and sealed up before the year has
> passed. . . . [A] simple surgical operation would allow these individuals to live
> in the world without causing much inconvenience to others.[4]

In 1913 Churchill introduced the Mental Deficiency Act. It followed the Lunacy Act of 1890, which had given physicians virtual *carte
blanche* in confining the allegedly mad to asylums.[5] Churchill proposed,
among other restrictions, that those lacking "sufficient" intelligence
should be denied the right to marry and thus to propagate themselves.[6]
Yet the real animus was directed against the so-called "unproductive"
poor. Chesterton was one of the few to recognize this scheme for
ostensible social improvement as a satanic form of Darwinism. It was
also a savage combination of capitalism and socialism. Having forced
the destitute and the pauperized to find their chief earthly delights
in drink and sex, high-minded socialists joined plutocratic philanthropists to curb even these ordinary consolations of the poor. Chesterton protested not only such attacks on the personal freedoms of the
impoverished, he also inveighed against something far more wicked:
the attempt of the state to establish its own priority to and hegemony
over everything else, even marriage and the family. Such an omnicompetent government could presume even to define sanity itself:

> It is not only openly said, it is eagerly urged, that the aim of the [Churchillian]
> measure is to prevent any person whom these propagandists do not happen
> to think intelligent from having any wife or children. Every tramp who is
> sulky, every labourer who is shy, every rustic who is eccentric, can quite easily
> be brought under such conditions as were designed for homicidal maniacs.[7]

Don Shipley specifies the primary reasons behind this desperate
desire to improve the species, especially in Britain. Many advocates of
eugenics, writes Shipley, "believed that the genetically superior classes
in England were not reproducing themselves as bountifully as were the
genetically inferior working class and poor of England." The matrix in
which eugenics flourished, Shipley explains, was a seedbed of fears—
the fear of increased poverty among the underclasses, the fear also

of their uncontrollable criminality, the fear of overpopulation among such "undesirables," and the consequent fear of race suicide among Anglo-Saxon elites.[8] As usual, Chesterton penetrated both the rhetoric and the ethics of the eugenicists, demonstrating Orwell's case that big words oft bless evil deeds:

> Most Eugenists are Euphemists. I mean merely that short words startle them, while long words soothe them. And they are utterly incapable of translating the one into the other, however obviously they mean the same thing. Say to them "The persuasive and even coercive powers of the citizen should enable him to make sure that the burden of longevity in the previous generation does not become disproportionate and intolerable, especially to the females"; say this to them and they sway slightly to and fro like babies sent to sleep in cradles. Say to them "Murder your mother," and they sit up quite suddenly. Yet the two sentences, in cold logic, are exactly the same.[9]

Chesterton discerned what was demonic in the eugenics movement from its first entrance onto the British literary and journalistic scene at the turn of the twentieth century. He saw that to conceive of humanity as a malleable animal, a commodity to be manipulated (and eliminated), is to transgress the most fundamental moral limit: "When once one begins to think of man as a shifting and alterable thing, it is always easy for the strong and crafty to twist him into new shapes for all kinds of unnatural purposes."[10] The eugenicist desire to sterilize the "unfit"—or at least to keep them from marrying and "breeding"— was for Chesterton a nightmarish abomination because it was a literal defacing of the divine image. "Christ from the very first moment of his existence," writes Henri de Lubac, "virtually bears all men within himself. . . . For the Word did not merely take a human body. . . . He incorporated himself into our humanity, and incorporated it in himself. *Universitatis nostrae caro est factus.* [He became the flesh of our universal humanity.]"[11] Chesterton the Christian humanist saw that to "improve the human race" by means of eugenics was to crucify Christ afresh. It was and remains an attempt to sterilize the incarnate Son of the Father, rendering him "unfit to have children." Against our demonic dream of remaking humanity in our own sinful image, Chesterton warned that, like Milton's Satan whispering into the ear of sleeping Eve, the Tempter transforms this macabre urge into a seemingly benign enticement.

APPENDIX TO CHAPTER 4
Chesterton, Dawson, and Bernanos
on the Setting Sun of the West

Concerning the crisis of the West, it is instructive to compare Chesterton with two other Catholic thinkers who dealt with the collapse of Christendom a generation later: Christopher Dawson (1889–1970) and Georges Bernanos (1888–1948). The first was a distinguished Catholic historian, the latter a distinguished Catholic novelist, and they both wrestled with the crisis of Western culture. Because they also shared many of Chesterton's basic tenets, and because they often quoted him, the three are sometimes regarded as virtual trio of identical voices in their prophecies against the decline and fall of European civilization.[1] On the contrary, there is a crucial division within their common Catholic house.

Like both Chesterton and Bernanos, Dawson lamented the creeping terror of what Jacques Ellul called "the technological society." "The whole tendency of modern life," Dawson wrote, "is toward scientific planning and organization, central control and specialization." The industrialism and commercialism that Chesterton so thoroughly contemned have found their horrible fulfillment in a moral no less than a political totalitarianism. Above all else, it remains the chief menace to human existence in our time. Remarkably, Dawson does not confine his critique of totalistic governments to the obvious cases of Germany and Russia and China. He excoriates democratic states as well:

In fact all modern states are totalitarian in so far as they seek to embrace the spheres of economics and culture, as well as politics in the strict sense of the word. They are concerned not merely with the maintenance of public order and the defense of the people against its external enemies. They have taken on responsibility for all the different forms of communal activity which were formerly left to the individual or to independent social organizations such as the churches, and they watch over the welfare of their citizens from the cradle to the grave.[2]

Such omnicompetent governments exercise a moral guardianship over their citizens, Dawson argues, in ways that would have been unimaginable to "the absolute monarchies of the past."[3] More sinister still, these seemingly benign tyrannies work on the assumption that the nation-state exists prior to and thus defines such crucial institutions as the family. Most dreadful of all, they seek to manage the ethical lives of their subjects from a putatively "neutral" stance. In their refusal to order public life to any transcendent conception of truth and justice and goodness—nor to acknowledge the dignity and independence of nongovernmental institutions—our democratic regimes rule by means of a presumed impartiality and tolerance that have proven to be inhumane at best, nihilistic at worst. Reversing Chesterton's celebrated claim that America is a nation "with the soul of a church," Dawson declares that the bourgeois liberal state has become a Church without a soul:

Religion gradually retreated into man's inner life and left social and economic life to a civilization which grew steadily more secularized. A man's debt to religion was paid by an hour or two in church on Sundays, and the rest of the week was devoted to the real business of life—above all, the making of money.

Such a division of life into two compartments—and very unequal ones at that—was not the Christian solution, nor could it be permanently successful. If religion loses its hold on social life, it eventually loses its hold on life altogether. And this is what has happened in the case of modern Europe. The new secularized civilization is not content to dominate the outer world and to leave man's inner life to religion; it claims the whole man. Once more Christianity is faced, as it was at the beginning, with the challenge of a world which will accept no appeal from its judgment and which recognizes no higher power than its own will.[4]

There is much in these claims that Chesterton would affirm, especially Dawson's protest against the privatizing of religion in the modern West. To confine religious life largely to the personal sphere of individual conduct, to reduce religious activity to a single day of the week rather than making it an entire way of life, to allow society and politics to go their own unchecked way—this is surely to produce the decay and eventual death of Church and culture alike. Yet about the most fundamental matter—the witness of the Church within the twilight of European civilization—Dawson and Chesterton disagreed in ways previously undiscerned. Dawson argues, for example, that there is a symbiotic relation between all religions and civilizations that gives them a basic kinship. On the one hand, religious beliefs and practices serve to unite cultures and to give them their transcendent basis; on the other hand, these same religious beliefs and practices are focused on an otherworldly Reality that enables them to offer a moral critique of their host cultures when they become oppressive and unjust.

Accordingly, Dawson develops an anthropology that provides him a lens for reading all of the "great" civilizations as dwelling amidst a life-giving tension with their founding religions.[5] He embraces a religious humanism that defines humanity as *Homo religiosus*. All people have a hunger for the Holy that, according to his argument, produces religious rites and ceremonies, and these, in turn, become the basis for their respective civilizations. For Dawson, therefore, the eminent civilizations and religions differ mainly in degree, not in kind. "[T]he life of humanity," he writes, "is being leavened and permeated by a transcendent principle, and every culture or human way of life is capable of being influenced and remoulded by this divine influence." In a similar vein, Dawson avers that "we have lost that spiritual vision man formerly possessed—the sense of an eternal world on which the transitory temporal world of human affairs was dependent. *This vision is not only a Christian insight: for it is intrinsic to the great civilizations of the ancient East and to the pagan world. . . .*" The crisis of the modern West, according to Dawson, is not so much that we have squandered our uniquely Christian patrimony as that we have forsaken the funded wisdom of our species:

> [A]ll the great civilizations of the ancient world believed in a transcendent
> divine order which manifested itself alike in the cosmic order—the law of

heaven; in the moral order—the law of justice; and in religious ritual; and it was only in so far as society was co-ordinated with the divine order by the sacred religious order of ritual and sacrifice that it had the right to exist and to be considered a civilized way of life.[6]

This means, among other things, that Dawson values Christianity as an instance—albeit the highest and noblest—of the allegedly universal phenomenon called "religion." Adam Schwartz, one of Dawson's finest defenders, observes that Dawson "considers the sacred not just as a force within history, but also the source of its significance. Dawson in particular found 'a natural affinity and concordance between the spirit of Catholicism and the spirit of history' in his day."[7] Chesterton, by contrast, regards humanity's natural longing for God as reaching its only true completion and perfection and transformation in Christ and his Church. For him, therefore, there are drastic differences—of kind no less than degree—among religions and cultures.[8] Unlike Dawson, he never sets Christian culture alongside Chinese, Indian, and Islamic cultures as essentially alike.[9] Despite their apparent similarities, they are fundamentally incommensurable, indeed contradictory, as we have seen in GKC's harsh critique of Islam and in his loathing of the mandala as the basic Eastern image of life's circular and repetitive character. To read Chesterton's later works—*Where All Roads Lead*, *The Catholic Church and Conversion*, *The Thing: Why I Am a Catholic*—is to encounter an ethos far removed from Dawson's wan appeals to spiritual unity and religious experience in the name of a rather vague Christendom.

A second point of disjuncture with Chesterton is that Dawson seems to envision no alternatives for the modern West than either a fully Christian or else a fully secular culture. Societies operate as "a single unit," Dawson maintains. "Either it may be a Christian unit which is governed by spiritual standards and directed toward spiritual ends, or it is wholly secular—a power machine for the production of wealth or population." Hence his call for Christians to provide liberal democracies with "a unifying spiritual vision" that "will restore the lost balance between the outer world of mechanized activity and the inner world of spiritual experience." Only then, Dawson maintains, will citizens of such democratic states embrace "higher moral values . . . not merely as rules imposed by society for its own welfare but as a sacred law which finds its tribunal in the human heart and the individual conscience."[10] Yet he never explains how Christians might supply this "unifying spiritual vision" and such "sacred law"—whether by seeking election to office, by obtaining major government posts, or else by quietly imbuing the cultural ethos with something called "the spirit of Christianity." Dawson is quite clear, however, in claiming that the collapse of the West will bring down the rest with it: "[T]he survival or restoration of Christian culture involves not only the fate of our own people and our civilization but the fate of humanity and the future of the world." We have reached the unbridgeable abyss of opposition between Christianity and nihilism:

> For a secular civilization that has no end beyond its own satisfaction is a monstrosity—a cancerous growth which will ultimately destroy itself. The only power that can liberate man from this kingdom of darkness is the Christian faith. For in the modern Western world there are no alternative solutions, no choice of possible other religions. It is a choice between Christianity or nothing.[11]

Even if we accept Dawson's assessment of Western secularism as ethically (if unconsciously) nihilistic, this does not entail an approval of his antidote. Chesterton certainly did not hope for the revival of a cultural Christendom—an inherited "spirit" as much as a confessed and practiced Faith—to cure the moral malaise of the West, as if such a ghostly thing could still guarantee the religious unity of Europe and America. Dawson's recourse to spiritualizing and inwardizing language stands at a far remove from the robustly outward and ecclesial character of Chesterton's late work. There he is chiefly concerned with the Church as God's agency for the formation of Christian character in a public and visible way, so that the Christians might make their decisive and angular witness to secular culture rather than undergirding its vaguely religious assumptions.

As we have seen, Chesterton called for the *conversion* of pagan modernity, not for installing a humanistic latter-day version of Christendom. As we have also seen, he did not retain any great confidence in civilization itself. He did not live to witness the savagery that would soon outrank all others by way of Hitler and Stalin and Mao and Pol Pot (together with Hiroshima and Dresden, with Auschwitz and the Gulag, with Babi Yar and the Chinese forced "reeducation through labor" programs). Even so, he prophesied that an acculturated kind of Christianity could not serve as the curative for a fractured though still democratic Europe. An attenuated Gospel would not suffice even against the vagaries of republican freedom, since democracy also entails the liberty to elect tyrants, as the pluralities that Hitler achieved in July and November of 1932 had already demonstrated.[12]

The French novelist and essayist Georges Bernanos is much closer to Chesterton in his analysis of collapsing Western culture, though his critique is much more drastic. In four searing essays prepared for publication shortly before his death in 1948, Bernanos offers a severe critique of modern Europe and America as constituting nothing less than antihuman places. He confesses that all civilizations are exceedingly fragile constructions, and that they are meant to serve as protections and refuges from human savagery. An authentic homeland, a true *patrie*, therefore, "is a moral being that has right and duties, that can demand much of us but cannot claim anything in the name of the law that governs animals, that sacrifices the bee to the hive and the individual to the species."[13] Unlike any previous culture, the modern West devours and destroys its citizens by subjecting them to totalitarian means of management and control. It does so, Bernanos maintains, through the triumph of machines. By no means a Luddite and technophobe, he affirms that we belong to the genus *Homo faber* and that, as such, we are meant to make machines. Yet all prior civilizations have created these mechanisms for human use. Ours is the first ever to reverse this order: to regard technics not as a means but as an end, so that human life itself might be used for their sake.

Whereas the grasping greed of our fallen race was once held in check by the duties and disciplines nurtured via Church and state alike, human avarice was prodigiously unleashed in the cotton mills of nineteenth-century Manchester. These factories were fueled not only by the profit motive of the owners but also by the theoretical undergirding of Malthus and Mill, of Adam Smith and David Ricardo. As a result, we have created what Bernanos names—in a metaphor especially apropos of Chesterton—as "this nightmare of hands." He sees the black market as but the mirror image of capitalism, since they both are centered upon things that can be snatched and held for oneself alone. The upshot of such unrestrained plutocracy is that the traditional culture of the West found itself completely overwhelmed, utterly unable to resist the onslaught of what Bernanos unabashedly calls *"totalitarian capitalism"* (LE, 203, emphasis in original). He combines these allegedly oxymoronic terms because he sees Marxism and Liberalism as the twin nineteenth-century inventions, even though they have evolved into separate but deeply related forms of economic dictatorship:

> Doesn't it conform to the logic of things that the thousands and thousands of capitalistic enterprises that are started are gradually reduced in number as they increase in power and efficiency? Large corporations are born this way, and themselves become less and less numerous, until the day when the state substitutes itself for the last among them and becomes the corporation of corporations, the only corporation, one and indivisible. (LE, 82)

Just as the Church once subsumed the whole of society during the Carolingian era, so does the centralized nation-state control the lives of its citizens from birth to death. It operates by means of an ever-increasing plethora of state regulations, many of them contradictory,[14] in order to rob its subjects of the religious and ethical power to adjudicate the most important matters for themselves. A supposed moral neutrality enables Western nations to rule by the tyranny of opinion and propaganda, by a tolerance and openness that leave people prey to what Bernanos calls the most hateful violence of all—namely, a deeply destructive indifference to verity and falsity alike:

> Of course, this indifference hides a weariness, something like a disgust with the faculty of judgment. But the faculty of judgment cannot be exercised without a certain interior pledge. Anyone who judges, pledges himself. Modern man does not pledge himself any more, because he no longer has anything to pledge. Called upon to decide with truth or falsehood, good or evil, Christian man pledged his soul at the same time, that is to say he risked its salvation. Metaphysical faith was in him an inexhaustible source of energy. Modern man is still capable of judging, since he is still capable of reasoning. But his judgment doesn't function any more than a motor functions without fuel: no part of the motor is missing, but there is no gas in the tank. (LE, 116–17).

For Bernanos, the deadliest of these moral deprivations concerns war. Unlike Chesterton, he does not regard the Great War as a battle to save civilization from the Prussians, nor does he hail the Second World War as the necessary evil required to halt Nazism. He remains deeply vexed by the cynical appeasement ensconced in the Munich Pact of 1938, as well as by the spineless support of the Vichy regime by his own countrymen. Yet he is horrified by something far more worrying: by the pathological and hysterical self-hatred that makes modern combat "more like epidemics than like wars" (LE, 164). Modern wars are virtually without beginning and end, he maintains, because they do not concern actual political conflict.[15] These wars are also totalistic because they are fought in the name and for the sake of machines. The darkest irony of all is that the work of machines is more spiritual than physical. They annihilate matter, Bernanos argues, in a furious victory of Hegelian *Geist*, as technics enable us to evade the burden of bodily freedom and suffering for the ease of an illusory existence. We have not mastered nature, as Descartes desired, nor has it mastered us, as C. S. Lewis feared. The material and natural world has been obliterated:

> As wine, milk, meat, bread, all the necessities of life, disappear in the journey from middleman to middleman, that is, from hand to hand, so matter itself goes up in smoke, the last leap of the devil bursting through the circus tent. By grace of the new sacrament, the sacrament of Bikini,[16] man really becomes spirit—but in another way than he dreamed. . . . In the name of the Thumb and the Index Finger and the Middle Finger and the Ring Finger and the Little Finger, five personages in only one god, Amen! (LE, 178)

The publisher of Bernanos' last essays wisely included "Our Friends the Saints." For there this most prophetic of modern French writers argues that saints are the antithesis of totalitarian man.[17] They live by the interior freedom that enables them to reverence rather than incinerate the exterior world. The Church lives off their sanctity because they demonstrate the way to avoid such damnation—which Bernanos defines as the life-denying rejection of the freedom that inheres in all faculties of the soul. The saints participate in the rhythm of the universe itself, and thus in the life of the triune God who creates and redeems it. By refusing the false comfort found in "the self-assurance of mediocre Christians," the saints ensure that the Church remains no mere human institution but a revolutionary agency, "a moving spirit, a force on the march" (LE, 223). Bernanos thus shares Chesterton's commitment to the Church's own distinctive witness in the face not only of the western but also of the world crisis.

"When I am dead," Bernanos wrote near the end of his life, "please tell the sweet kingdom of this Earth that I loved it more than I ever dared to say." The final confession of this often abrasive and wounding writer is best illuminated by his best interpreter, the Swiss Catholic theologian Hans Urs von Balthasar:

> A good proof of this love is the way Bernanos totally renounces the usual methods of apologetics intended to convince the unbeliever of the truth of Christianity. At bottom, Bernanos builds no bridges; what he does is tear down all the sham linkages between the world and the Church in order to make these face one another, each as its clean self. This is indeed the Johannine way: to move from alleged dialogue—which becomes more and more fraught with impossibility and misunderstanding—back to the pure confrontation of light and darkness. In this confrontation, the light must suffer, and the hour of darkness appears to win the day. But, once one has despaired of all possibility of mutual understanding on an earthly basis, grace breaks through with its final synthesis.[18]

The subtitle of von Balthasar's treatise on Bernanos—*An Ecclesial Existence*—reveals that Chesterton was fundamentally agreed with him, at least concerning the singular Christian alternative to what Oswald Spengler famously described as *der Untergang des Abendlandes*. It is fair to say, in fact, that Chesterton reversed his earlier course in this regard. Unlike his initial unqualified reverence for "tradition" as the "the democracy of the dead," Chesterton came to recognize that, from a Christian angle of vision, many traditions must be regarded as morally and spiritually malign. Still more discerning is his late insight that "[t]he mark of the Faith is not tradition; it is conversion." And because the Faith is a stumbling block and an offense against even the noblest of customs and *mores*, conversion comes through "the miracle by which men find truth in spite of tradition and often with the rending of all the roots of humanity."[19]

Nor will it suffice to describe Christianity as a religion belonging to "a class of human religions," just as the Catholic Church "does not merely belong to a class of Christian churches."[20] On the contrary,

Christianity and Catholicism are coterminous and *sui generis*. "There is only one species," Chesterton claims, "and there is only one example." This singular and scandalous Thing finds no variants in the world religions. Lying at the core of Chesterton's later work, and offering his most radical answer to the descent of modern European culture into the abyss of chaos and destruction, is a remarkable claim. In it GKC makes no appeal to "traditional Western values," or to the restoration of Christendom in modified form, but to the living Body of Christ: "Christianity is not a religion; it is a Church. There may be a Moslem religion; but it would not come natural to anybody to talk about the Moslem church.[21] There may be a Buddhist religion; but nobody would call it the Buddhist Church."[22]

That the Church is not only a human institution akin to all others but also an extension of the Incarnation is an offensive claim, and Chesterton makes no attempt to finesse it. He unapologetically confesses, instead, that the Church demands either radical service or radical scorn: "The Church really is like Antichrist in the sense that it is as unique as Christ. Indeed, if it be not Christ it probably is Antichrist; but certainly it is not Moses or Mahomet or Buddha or Plato or Pythagoras."[23] Rather than constricting human freedom, Chesterton remains convinced that that the Church constitutes its ultimate enlargement, since nothing within space or time—indeed, nothing *beyond* space and time—lies outside its compass: "I would say chiefly of the Catholic Church that is catholic . . . that it is not only larger than me, but larger than anything in the world; that it is indeed larger than the world."[24]

APPENDIX TO CHAPTER 6
Tolkien and Chesterton on Northernness and Nihilism

J. R. R. Tolkien objected vehemently to Chesterton's account of ancient pagan Northernness in *The Ballad of the White Horse* as having a nihilistic character: "The brilliant smash and glitter of words and phrases (when they come off, and are not mere loud colours) cannot disguise the fact that GKC knew nothing whatever about the 'North,' heathen or Christian."[1] Far from believing in nothing, the pagans of the antique North lived by a high code of virtue built on loyalty and courage. In his celebrated essay on *Beowulf*, Tolkien argues that this seventh-century (perhaps ninth-century?) Anglo-Saxon poem was composed by a Christian, probably a monk, who poetically recounted the pagan legend of Beowulf's long battle with Grendel—a struggle wherein, while the dragon is killed, so is Beowulf. This nameless Christian author sought faithfully to preserve the brutality and sternness of the pagan life-world figured in the ancient Danish legend. Thus does the anonymous writer describe bloody battles and extol fierce loyalties, even as he shows that both men and events are overruled by the inexorable power of Fate, whose lowering clouds overshadow everything. At the final battle of Ragnarök, the entire cosmos will be destroyed, and even the gods will die, as everything returns to "Chaos and Unreason." Even so, the cosmology of the ancient North is more linear than circular, and thus surprisingly analogous to Christian mythography. Chesterton had misgivings about the circle as a theological metaphor, since almost all of the pagan religions envision the motions of time repeating themselves endlessly. The cosmology of the Nordic and Teutonic peoples, by contrast, understands time as having an inexorable end, even if (in contrast to Christian linearity) the end is annihilating.[2]

For Tolkien, this was yet further reason for admiring the heroes of the mythic Northern narratives. Indeed, he extols their "doomed resistance" against inevitable defeat and death. The dragons of the deep were made all the more ghastly because the manly Nordic warriors believed that the demonic powers could assume actual form, and thus that "the evil spirits entered into the monsters and took visible shape in the hideous bodies." The heathen heroism of the Anglo-Saxons thus remains pertinent, Tolkien insists, not only to Darwinians haunted by the seeming unguided randomness of the universe but also to Christians convinced of its ultimately providential order. Their "creed of unyielding will," their "absolute resistance is [made] perfect because [it was] without hope," their belief "that man, each and all men, and all their works shall die"—such bravery and valor among the Northmen were, for Tolkien, "a theme no Christian need despise."[3]

That Chesterton possessed no careful historical knowledge of the primeval world of the North does not undermine the poem's immense moral and spiritual strength. In his Prefatory Note to *The Ballad of the White Horse*, Chesterton deliberately disclaims any pretense to historical accuracy:

> All of [the poem] that is not frankly fictitious, as in any prose romance about the past, is meant to emphasize tradition rather than history. King Alfred is not a legend in the sense that King Arthur may be a legend; that is, in the sense that he may possibly be a lie. But King Alfred is a legend in this broader and more human sense, that the legends are the most important things about him.
>
> The cult of Alfred was a popular cult, from the darkness of the ninth century to the deepening twilight of the twentieth. It is wholly as a popular legend that I deal with him here. . . .
>
> Alfred has come down to us in the best way (that is by national legends) solely for the same reason as Arthur and Roland and the other giants of that darkness, because he fought for the Christian civilization against the heathen nihilism. (BWH, Prefatory Note, xxxiii, xxxv)

This is no small point. A great deal of modern agonizing over von Ranke's insistence that historians must render "what really happened" might have been avoided by heeding Chesterton's insistence that it is not only impossible but also unnecessary to make a strict separation of legend and history. The two often meet and fuse in ways that enrich both. In laying out the manner of Christian doctrinal development, John Henry Newman was one of the first to offer an alternative to modern historicism, even if with a *soupçon* of irony:

> If the alleged facts did not occur, they ought to have occurred (if I may so speak); they are such as might have occurred, and would have occurred, under circumstances; and they belong to the parties to whom they are attributed, potentially, if not actually; or the like of them did occur; or occurred to others similarly circumstanced, though not to those very persons.[4]

As a matter of historical fact, the Vikings who invaded England in the ninth century worshipped many deities and thus were pagans rather than nihilists. They believed in and obeyed their gods. They did not regard their virtues as human inventions devised for survival in a random and pointless universe. In this sense, Tolkien was right to protest against Chesterton's characterization of the Danes as nihilists.[5] Yet Chesterton was not entirely wrong to insist that their morality and religion had nihilistic *implications*. Insofar as the twilight battle of the Nordic gods at the cosmos-closing event of Ragnarøk leaves the universe as void of significance in the end as it was in the beginning— all things coming from and returning to nothing—the Northmen dwelt within nihilistic confines. They denied that their virtues were grounded in anything eternally transcendent, anything having absolute authority to create and command, to judge and forgive.[6]

NOTES

Preface

1   All biblical quotations will be taken from the King James Version since, in both memory and imagination, Chesterton was decisively shaped by it.

Introduction

1   G. K. Chesterton, *Autobiography* (New York: Sheed & Ward, 1936), 97–98. The word "nightmare" appears fifteen times in this late summing up of his life.

2   "Nightmare," in *The Compact Edition of the Oxford English Dictionary,* vol. 1 (New York: Oxford University Press, 1971), 146.

3   Thomas Carlyle, *Sartor Resartus* (New York: Oxford World's Classics, 1987), 89, emphasis added. It's altogether typical of Chesterton that, even though he regards Carlyle's work as issuing in a pernicious Nietzschean exaltation of undisciplined Will, he also praises the great Victorian for his service to English literature. As "the founder of modern irrationalism," Carlyle understood, like Chesterton, that all reasoning proceeds from unquestioned axioms and unproven assumptions. This "mystical" conviction enabled Carlyle to deny "every one of the postulates on which the age of reason had based itself. He denied the theory of progress which assumed that we must be better off than the people of the twelfth century. Whether we were [morally] better than the people of the twelfth century according to him depended on whether we chose or deserved to be." G. K. Chesterton, *Twelve Types* (1902; repr., Norfolk, Va.: IHS Press, 2003), 58.

4   G. K. Chesterton, *Charles Dickens* (1906; repr., New York: Schocken, 1965), 23. Maisie Ward records similar sentiments that the young Chesterton expressed in his early Notebooks: "Are we all dust? What a beautiful thing dust is though. This round earth may be a soap-bubble, but it must be admitted that there are some pretty colours on it. What is the good of life, it is fleeting; what is the good of a cup of coffee, it is fleeting. Ha Ha Ha." *Gilbert Keith Chesterton* (London: Sheed & Ward, 1944), 57.

5   Evelyn Waugh, "Chesterton," in *The Essays, Articles and Reviews of Evelyn Waugh*, ed. Donat Gallagher (Boston: Little, Brown, 1984), 558.

6   C. S. Lewis tells of a letter he received from a friend who, in having become Catholic, feared that her friendship with Lewis the Ulster Protestant was in jeopardy. Lewis replied, with great discernment, that in such a late time as ours, Christians who stand at the center of their own particular traditions will be drawn ever more deeply to each other, even as they will find themselves made distant from those who occupy the extremes within their own denominations.

7   G. K. Chesterton, *The Everlasting Man*, in *Collected Works of G. K. Chesterton*, vol. 2 (San Francisco: Ignatius, 1986), 143.

8   G. K. Chesterton, *Saint Francis of Assisi* (1924; repr., New York: Doubleday, 1957), 12.

9   G. K. Chesterton, *Orthodoxy* (1908; repr., San Francisco: Ignatius, 1995), 128. All citations from this edition are identified within the text as O.

Chapter 1

1   Sayers was put off by the rather prim faith of her schoolmasters, and she objected strongly to being confirmed at age fourteen without her consent. She confessed, much later in life, that she might well have abandoned Christianity altogether had it not been for the vigorous example of G. K. Chesterton, especially as displayed in *Orthodoxy*. She found in him what she would come eventually to articulate herself: the conviction that belief in God should engender the supreme excitement and interest, never becoming an exercise in dullness and boredom. Hence her praise of Chesterton for demonstrating that the Christian faith is "one whirling adventure [. . . in which] the heavenly chariot flies thundering through the ages, the dull heresies sprawling and prostrate, the wild truth reeling but erect." Qtd. in James Brabazon, *Dorothy L. Sayers: A Biography* (New York: Scribners, 1981), 35.

2   Such praise of *Orthodoxy* has not been universal. After having been mandated for many years as a required text in freshman English at Marquette University, it was finally dropped only in the 1980s. The students are

reported to have then mounted a huge holocaust on the school's main quadrangle, with but a single immolated victim for their gleeful burning: Chesterton's *Orthodoxy*.

3 Qtd. in S. T. Joshi, *God's Defenders* (Amherst, N.Y.: Prometheus, 2003), 86. Mencken goes on to dismiss Chesterton as the purveyor of false comfort in such totally discredited illusions as "the influence of mind over matter." "Not even Chesterton," he concludes, "with all his skill at writing, and with his general cleverness—and he is the cleverest man, I believe, in the world today—can turn that truth [i.e., that ours is a closed physicalist cosmos] into anything else" (87).

4 Anselm extended Augustine's catchphrase with one of his own: *Neque enim quaero intelligere ut credam, sed credo ut intelligam. Nam et hoc credo, quia, nisi credidero, non intelligam* ("Nor do I seek to understand that I may believe, but I believe that I may understand. For this, too, I believe, that, unless I first believe, I shall not understand").

5 "Man had bliss in Paradise," writes Aquinas, "but not that perfect bliss into which he was to have been translated, and which consists in beholding the divine essence" (S.T. Ia, 94, 1). *St Thomas Aquinas: Summa Theologiae*, vol. 13, *Man Made to God's Image*, trans. Edmund Hill, O.P. (London: Blackfriars, 1964), 91.

6 This is a metaphor borrowed from Flannery O'Connor. "Man is so free that with his last breath he can say No." *Mystery and Manners*, sel. and ed. Robert and Sally Fitzgerald (New York: Farrar, Straus & Giroux, 1970), 182.

7 Nowhere in Scripture is the Christian humanist vision set forth more fully than in St. Paul's celebrated sermon on Mars Hill in Athens. To demonstrate that the Athenians have an ingrained knowledge of the Holy, Paul quotes the Stoic poet Aratus, who described God as the one in whom "we live, and move, and have our being." Paul demonstrates to his hearers that, in their many shrines to multiple deities, they are akin to a blind man touching his hands along a wall in order to feel his way forward. Like all other people, the Athenians have a true longing and desire for God, but they cannot discern him because they have treated natural and human goods as if they were God, regarding the beneficent things of earth as ends in themselves rather than as means for the love of God and neighbor. The Areopagites cannot locate the true God by their own effort, Paul makes clear, but only as He has identified himself in Jesus Christ as his one true Son: "he hath made of one blood all nations of men for to dwell on all the face of the earth, . . . that they should seek the LORD, if haply they might feel after him, and find him, though he be not far from every one of us" (Acts 17:26-27).

The human hunger for God, soured as it is by sin, cannot be satisfied of its own accord. Frederick Buechner put the matter memorably in defining lust, for example, as "a craving for salt of a man dying of thirst." Thus do most of the Athenians turn away from the offense of the Gospel, scoffing at Paul's declaration that God has raised Jesus from death and that he "commandeth all men every where to repent: [b]ecause he hath appointed a day, in which he will judge the world in righteousness by [that] man whom he hath ordained" (Acts 17:29-32). Christian humanism does not remove the scandal of the Gospel, as the Mars Hill episode reveals. It does not envision nature and grace as complements perfectly joined to each other. The Gospel always remains an offense even amidst the best of cultures and the noblest of persons, though the scandal lies less in its condemnations than its affirmations. "God threatens terrible things," said Jeremy Taylor, the seventeenth-century Anglican divine, "if we will not be happy."

8   Though Chesterton's debate with the "new theology" of Robert Blatchford was the immediate occasion for his writing of *Orthodoxy*, we diminish the greatness of GKC's work if we confine it to such a small context. Most theological readers of Chesterton have much more wisely compared him to two more contemporaneous Catholics, Jacques Maritain and Etienne Gilson. This is altogether appropriate, since Gilson made the astonishing confession that, after a lifetime of studying the Angelic Doctor, he could not have produced such a succinct and compelling synopsis of Aquinas' teaching as Chesterton's splendid primer on St. Thomas' theology, *The Dumb Ox*. Chesterton turned it out in a bare six weeks, and with only glancing attention to the *Summa* itself. Yet I remain convinced that Chesterton's work is more fully illuminated by linking it to the *nouvelle* theologians, for he shares much of their deeply ecclesial understanding of salvation, as well as their estimate of the natural order as always and already graced, rather than as having its own quasi-independent purposes. This leaves Chesterton free to speak of Christianity indirectly and analogously, and thus to win many converts who would be put off by more overt Christian claims that seem to require the adoption of an entirely new vocabulary and grammar before they could even entertain the possibility of taking the Faith seriously.

9   Hans Boersma, "A Sacramental Journey to the Beatific Vision: The Intellectualism of Pierre Rousselot," *Heythrop Journal* 49, no. 6 (2008): 1015.

10 Consider, for instance, Chesterton's remarkable poem about a man so crazed with loathing for another man, perhaps a neighbor, that he decides

to kill him. Seizing a knife to strike the man dead, the narrator hears a
voice calling to him in biblical admonition:

"This is a common man: knowest thou, O soul,
What this thing is? Somewhere where seasons roll
There is some living thing for whom this man
Is as seven heavens girt into a span,
For some one soul you take the world away—
Now know you well your deed and purpose. Slay!"
Then I cast down the knife upon the ground
And saw that mean man for one moment crowned.
I turned and laughed: for there was no one by—
The man that I had sought to slay was I.

"Thou Shalt Not Kill," in *Collected Works of G. K. Chesterton*, vol. 10, *Collected Poetry, Part 1* (San Francisco: Ignatious, 1994), 255–56. Suicide, for
Chesterton, is not a private choice but, as St. Thomas taught, an evil *contra naturam*. It goes against the grain of the universe, the very nature of
things as they are imbued with a divinely graced order, indeed with God's
own image. "The man who kills himself, kills all men" (*Orthodoxy*, 78).

11   Henri de Lubac, *Catholicism: Christ and the Common Destiny of Man* (1938;
      repr., San Francisco: Ignatius, 1988), 29.

12   That these are claims made about every human being, not about Christians alone, gives them immense moral import. They impinge most obviously on the two chief forms of physical death in the modern world:
      abortion and war.

13   De Lubac, *Catholicism*, 35, 39.

14   Qtd. in de Lubac, *Catholicism*, 33.

15   Qtd. in de Lubac, *Catholicism*, 34.

16   Such stress on human freedom does much to resolve the problem of evil,
      though of course it admits of no completely satisfactory solution. I owe
      this crucial point to my former student Bryan Hollon: "Because sin has
      harmed nature and rendered inaccessible a natural beatitude in proportion to human nature, humankind will remain frustrated, incomplete,
      and unfulfilled without the satisfaction brought by supernatural beatitude. . . . In this way, de Lubac is right to say that only (saving) grace
      completes and perfects nature. This also means that de Lubac is correct
      when he suggests that 'the "desire to see God" cannot be permanently
      frustrated without an essential suffering.'" Bryan C. Hollon, *Everything Is
      Sacred: Spiritual Exegesis in the Political Theology of Henri de Lubac* (Eugene,
      Ore.: Cascade, 2009), 91n55.

17 Aquinas himself insists that man was created in grace, so that even his natural powers derive from God and not from nature: "This rightness [of man's original state] was a matter of the reason being submissive to God, the lower powers to the reason, the body to the soul. . . . Now it is plain that submission of body to soul and lower powers to reason was not by nature; otherwise it would have persisted after sin. . . . From this it is plain that that primary submissiveness in which the reason put itself under God was not something merely natural either, but was by a gift of supernatural grace. For an effect cannot be more potent than its cause" (S.T. Ia, 95, 1). *St Thomas Aquinas: Summa Theologiae*, vol. 13, 109.

18 It is well known that these exponents of *la nouvelle théologie* exercised considerable influence on the work of the Second Vatican Council, especially on two of its most central "constitutions": *Dei verbum* (on divine revelation) and *Gaudium et spes* (on the Church in the modern world). It is less well known that what began as a single theological effort eventually split into antithetical camps: those theologians who, centered on the work of Karl Rahner, founded the journal *Concilium*; and their opponents who, focused largely on the theology of Henri de Lubac, sponsored a counterperiodical named *Communio*. This rift was complicated. Suffice it to say that the Rahner cohort argued that de Lubac and his friends, by making the supernatural inherent in human existence as such, denied the real gratuity of God's self-offering. The de Lubac group accused Rahner and his colleagues, by contrast, of "naturalizing the supernatural"—i.e., joining nature and grace in such a seamless and commonplace fashion so as to deny the horror of radical evil, even the necessity of the crucifixion. De Lubac and von Balthasar speak, on the contrary, of "supernaturalizing the natural"—i.e., envisioning nature as completed and perfected only as it is radically transformed through the prophetic and sacramental life of the Church. It is also significant that Pope Benedict XVI, as the former Cardinal Ratzinger, was an originating sponsor of *Communio*.

19 *Collected Works of G. K. Chesterton*, vol. 34, *Illustrated London News 1926–28* (San Francisco: Ignatius, 1986), 518.

20 Though cast in the sawdust-tasting language of formal theology, the relation of desire and gift has been succinctly phrased by Stephen J. Duffy in what remains perhaps the best guide to the enormously vexed subject specified in his subtitle: "Nature and Grace in Modern Catholic Thought." "[T]he desire for God is the most absolute of desires. Although human beings cannot of themselves and without grace bring this desire to fulfillment and possess as their own the gratuitous divine Self-gift, it is not for all that a conditional desire. To desire a gift as a gift is surely not

to postulate an exigency or a right. The desire in question is essentially humble. The human spirit finds itself in a waiting posture. For it aspires to God's grace; it does not demand it. The natural desire of the finite spirit is hobbled by a radical inability to elicit its term. It is, therefore, inefficacious. It can only be hopeful expectancy of a gift. God, however, will not renege on completing a tendency freely willed by Godself. The desire is also, therefore, absolute, unconditioned and unfrustrable on God's part. . . . There is the paradox. Humanity hungers for God; but for God as God can only be, i.e., as Love, freely giving Godself." *The Graced Horizon* (Collegeville, Minn.: Liturgical Press, 1992), 68.

21   Samuel Taylor Coleridge, for instance, regarded the imagination as "the living Power and prime Agent of all human Perception, and as a repetition in the finite mind of the eternal act of creation in the infinite I AM." By means of such exalted speech, Coleridge sought to convey his grand conviction that truly poetic acts are analogous to God's own creativity: the imagination breaks down the sense impressions received from the natural realm into newly perceived unities that amount to new worlds of meaning and significance.

        This was the battleground for the "Great War" between Owen Barfield and C. S. Lewis, their two-year debate (1925–1927) on the nature of the imagination. Lewis held out for a primarily passive view of imagination as a receptive agent for perceiving the sacred reality already ensconced in things, whereas Barfield argued for the active involvement of imagination in a cooperative Divine-human shaping of reality. Hence the power of poetry to prompt in the reader a similar creative engagement with the world, a "felt change of consciousness," as he called it. See especially *Poetic Diction: A Study in Meaning* (1928; repr., Middletown, Conn.: Wesleyan University Press, 1973).

22   *The Man Who Was Orthodox: A Selection from the Uncollected Writings of G.K. Chesterton*, ed. A. L. Maycock (London: Dennis Dobson, 1963), 147. The Dominican theologian Gerald Vann captured Chesterton's central conviction in a concise Thomistic statement of what it means for human beings to be cocreators with God: "To man's ontological status as a midpoint between the worlds of matter and spirit there corresponds a mediating function: to incarnate—to give material expression to—spiritual reality and to spiritualize or humanize material reality. . . . *Ars perficit naturam.*" Gerald Vann, O.P., "Modern Culture and Christian Renewal," excerpted in *Image* 52 (2007), http://imagejournal.org/page/journal/editorial-statements/modern-culture-and-christian-renewal.

23 G. K. Chesterton, *Saint Thomas Aquinas* (1933; repr., Garden City, N.Y.: Doubleday, 1956), 184, emphasis in original.

24 De Lubac's *The Drama of Atheist Humanism* (San Francisco: Ignatius, 1995) is a good example of his desire to engage not only such German masters of suspicion as Marx and Nietzsche and Feuerbach but also the atheist prince of the French Enlightenment, Auguste Comte.

25 Qtd. in de Lubac, *Catholicism*, 309. De Régis could have added that the same mistake prompted certain neo-scholastic Thomists to become eager supporters of Marshal Pétain and Generalissimo Franco. Their integralist theology led them, for example, to oppose the Third Republic and to seek a reconstitution of the monarchy as the only way for the Church to restore its divine right of "indirect power" within French society. "Grace seizes nature from the inside," de Lubac argued against the integralists, "and, far from lowering it, lifts it up to have it serve its ends. It is from the interior that faith transforms reason, that the Church influences the State. The Church is the messenger of Christ, not the guardian of the State. The Church ennobles the State. . . ." Qtd. in Hollon, *Everything Is Sacred*, 44–45. For the more recent effects of integralism in the political sphere, see Douglas R. Holmes, *Integral Europe: Fast-Capitalism, Multiculturalism, Neofascism* (Princeton, N.J.: Princeton University Press, 2000).

26 G. K. Chesterton, *A Miscellany of Men* (1912; repr., Philadelphia: Dufour, 1969), 156–57.

27 It was not in Chesterton's nature to hold forth solemnly about even the most solemn things. "It is the test of a good religion," he declared, "whether you can make a joke about it."

28 "The Secret of Father Brown," in *The Penguin Complete Father Brown* (1927; repr., New York: Penguin, 1981), 465–66. Hence GKC's story about attending a funeral held for a cultured heathen. One of Chesterton's friends commented on the handsome attire of the corpse: "All dressed up and nowhere to go." "I'll bet he wishes it were so," replied the candid Christian of Beaconsfield.

29 Chesterton, *A Miscellany of Men*, 155–56. There is a deep congruence between this affirmation of God's "merciless mercy" and Hans Urs von Balthasar's powerful treatise on the question of universal salvation in *Dare We Hope That All Men Be Saved? With a Short Discourse on Hell*, trans. David Kipp and Lothar Krauth (San Francisco: Ignatius, 1988).

30 G. K. Chesterton, *The Defendant* (1901; repr., Letchworth, UK: Temple, 1940), 103.

31 G. K. Chesterton, *Lunacy and Letters*, ed. Dorothy Collins (New York: Sheed & Ward, 1958), 192.

32 G. K. Chesterton, *Alarms and Discursions* (New York: Dodd, Mead, 1911), 12.

33 G. K. Chesterton, *Orthodoxy* (1908; repr., San Francisco: Ignatius, 1995).

34 Given the extraordinary power of Chesterton's rhetoric, coupled with his jovial and genial demeanor, there is little wonder that GKC bested the dour Clarence Darrow in a debate on the opening chapters of Genesis held in 1931 at Mecca Temple in New York. Chesterton won almost all of his debates, if only by making fun of himself rather than his opponent. One of his lectures at the University of Notre Dame was given after GKC had become too large to stand for long stretches, and so he sat at a desk with a microphone before him. "Ladies and gentlemen," he began, "I am *not* as large as I seem. This machine has *amplified* me." No wonder that he made hash of the dour Darrow. This is an excerpt from Henry Hazlitt's report on the debate, published in the left-leaning *Nation*: "Ostensibly the defender of science against Mr. Chesterton, [Mr. Darrow] obviously knew much less about science than Mr. Chesterton did; when he essayed to answer his opponent on the views of Eddington and Jeans, it was patent that he did not have the remotest conception of what the new physics was all about. [Darrow's] victory over Mr. Bryan at Dayton had been too cheap and easy; he remembered it not wisely but too well. His arguments are still the arguments of the village atheist of the Ingersoll period; at Mecca Temple he still seemed to be trying to shock and convince yokels.

"Mr. Chesterton's deportment was irreproachable, but I am sure that he was secretly unhappy. He had been on the platform many times against George Bernard Shaw. This opponent could not extend his powers. He was not getting his exercise." Qtd. in Timothy S. Goeglein, "A Note on the Vote," *Catholic Heritage*, January-February (1996): 28.

35 *Collected Works of G. K. Chesterton*, vol. 32, *Illustrated London News 1920–1922* (San Francisco: Ignatius, 1989), 57–58.

36 In opposing Darwin, Chesterton was never the advocate of anything so crude as creationism, which mistakes scriptural revelation for scientific information, turning the Bible into a dated book of facts rather than the Church's own canonized and perennially engaging story of God's unique people first named Israel and finally identified as the Body of Christ.

37 Qtd. in Keith Ward, *God, Chance & Necessity* (Oxford, UK: Oneworld, 1996), 62. Though an evolutionist himself, Ward criticizes Darwin's attempt to explain the most complex of all things—human life—by making this single naturalist law absolute. "The Darwinian worldview is the view of evolutionary naturalism. It is old-style materialism writ large" (13). "[I]t seems a rather drastic procedure," Ward adds, "to pretend that all distinctive human characteristics (especially the development of

consciousness, morality, rationality, science and art) can be adequately explained by showing that they were conducive to more efficient domination or reproduction" (71).

38 Chesterton, *The Everlasting Man*, 167, 170, emphasis in original. As we shall see, God does indeed create the soul "outside time," since all direct divine action is eternal and not temporal. Yet this claim does not deny that human beings develop temporally so as to prepare them to receive this miraculously nontemporal act.

39 Chesterton, *The Everlasting Man*, 165–66, 168–69, emphasis added. Quite apart from its intrinsic merits, Chesterton's argument makes a dubious anthropological claim, since the drawings at Lascaux are not the only artworks fashioned by prehistoric humans. Nor do all other aboriginal figurations deal with animals in ways that suggest reverence for creatures unlike themselves. There are equally primordial depictions of vulvas and phalluses, indicating that Paleolithic man had become sexually no less than artistically self-conscious, concerned as much with his own pleasure in procreating as in contemplating the otherness of fellow creatures.

40 G. K. Chesterton, *The Ball and the Cross* (1910; repr., Mineola, N.Y.: Dover, 1995), 1.

41 The resolution of this question is all-important. As Ward confesses, Darwin's partially (if not largely) erroneous theory of natural selection "has possibly changed our view of human existence more than any other theory in the history of human thought" (Ward, *God, Chance*, 62).

42 Chesterton was making similar claims in his journalistic work: "We should always endeavor to wonder at the permanent thing, not at the mere exception. We should be startled by the sun, and not by the eclipse. We should wonder less at the earthquake, and wonder more at the earth." *Illustrated London News*, October 21, 1905 (U.S. edition).

43 Chesterton, "On Darwinism and Mystery," in *Collected Works of G. K. Chesterton*, vol. 32, *Illustrated London News 1920–1922* (San Francisco: Ignatius, 1989), 76. Austin Farrer provides a fine (if unintentional) rejoinder to GKC: "Most of us have little insight into the singularity of sparrows [or bats]. We can do better with the human case. For you to be what you are involves a universe; and if your being what you are is the work of God, then an infinity of events was under his hand. It was his skill to draw you out of the genetic pattern of your ancestry, the culture of your time, and the complex of relationships surrounding you." Austin Farrer, *Saving Belief: A Discussion of Essentials* (London: Hodder and Stoughton, 1964), 54.

44 G. K. Chesterton, "Doubts about Darwinism," in *Collected Works of G. K.*

Chesterton, vol. 30, *Illustrated London News 1920–1922* (San Francisco: Ignatius, 1989), 57.

45 At one point Chesterton almost concedes that God's presence vis-à-vis the evolutionary process is surely immanent no less than transcendent. "What remains is mystery—an unfathomed and perhaps unfathomable mystery. What remains after Darwin is exactly what existed before Darwin—a darkness which I, for quite other reasons, believe to be divine. But whether or no it is divine, it is certainly dark. What is the real truth, what really happened in the variations of creatures, must have been something which has not yet suggested itself to the imagination of man. I for one should be very much surprised if that truth, when discovered, did not contain at least a large element of evolution." "On Darwinism and Mystery," 76.

46 Ward has numerous theological and scientific compatriots who join him in interpreting evolution teleologically, even if they differ in certain particulars—for example, E. L. Mascall, Arthur Peacocke, John Polkinghorne, Richard Swinburne, Francis Collins.

47 David J. Bartholomew, *God, Chance and Purpose* (Cambridge: Cambridge University Press, 2008), x, 37, 40, 42. I am grateful to Alasdair MacIntyre for recommending this remarkable study.

48 De Lubac offers a similar embrace of evolution in the historical no less than in the natural realm: "Spiritual life, like all life, takes shape in a suitable organism only after much hesitation. Outbursts of sudden energy are followed by long barren periods, and not every promise of progress is followed by fulfillment. For every concentration of fruitful effort there is a whole heap of material which seems wasted. One success comes after hundreds of more or less abortive efforts and involves a certain number of miscarriages. . . . [N]ature had to produce an unbelievably extravagant profusion of living species so that in the end the human body could appear. . . ." *Catholicism*, 232.

49 "Truth Cannot Contradict Truth," address of Pope John Paul II to the Pontifical Academy of Sciences (October 22, 1996), par. 5, http://www.newadvent.org/library/docs_jp02tc.htm, emphasis in original. The late pope adds this further illumining observation: "The moment of transition to the spiritual cannot be the object of this [scientific] kind of observation, which nevertheless can discover at the experimental level a series of very valuable signs indicating what is specific to the human being. But the experience of metaphysical knowledge, of self-awareness and self-reflection, of moral conscience, freedom, or again of aesthetic and religious experience, falls within the competence of philosophical analysis

and reflection, while theology brings out its ultimate meaning according to the Creator's plans." "Truth Cannot Contradict Truth," par. 5.

50   This means, among many other things, that big bang cosmology does not lend credence to the biblical account nor to the theological doctrine of creation. The original explosion of the universe into existence involved a change from an antecedent state containing the potential for such a cosmic outburst. The doctrine of *creatio ex nihilo* holds that God creates the universe from no *preexisting state whatsoever*. It is thus a metaphysical and theological, not a scientific, claim.

51   Michael W. Tkacz, "Aquinas vs. Intelligent Design," *This Rock* 19, no. 9 (2008), 26–27. The Anglican theologian Austin Farrer puts the matter crisply: "When we contemplate the physical creation, we see an unimaginable complex, organized on many planes one above another; atomic, molecular, cellular; vegetable, animal, social. And the marvel of it is that at every level the constituent elements run themselves, and, by their mutual interaction, run the world. *God not only makes the world, he makes it make itself; or rather he causes its innumerable constituents to make it.*" Farrer, *Saving Belief*, 51, emphasis added.

52   Barr points out that this traditional argument that the "power and working" of natural phenomena reflect the power and wisdom of God is actually undermined by the advocates of "intelligent design." In fact, they hold theology "hostage to every advance in biological science. Science must fail for ID to succeed. In the famous 'explanatory filter' of William A. Dembski, one finds 'design' by eliminating 'law' and 'chance' as explanations. This, in effect, makes it a zero-sum game between God and nature. What nature does and science can explain is crossed off the list, and what remains is the evidence for God. This conception of design plays right into the hands of atheists, whose caricature of religion has always been that it is a substitute for the scientific understanding of nature." Stephen M. Barr, "The End of Intelligent Design?" http://www.firstthings.com/onthesquare/2010/02/the-end-of-intelligent-design.

53   In claiming that "[p]hysical nature must not be made the direct object of obedience" (O, 82), Chesterton seems to eliminate mediating analogies for the ethical life as they can be discerned in the created order. In this regard at least, he is much closer to Tennyson than the psalmists. For if nature is *only* "red in tooth and claw"—*nothing else* than predation—then it should not indeed be morally imitated. Yet this is hardly the estimate of nature found in Psalm 19, where humanity is envisioned as doing its daily work for the glory of God, much as do all other creatures, including the ravenous lion.

54 Alasdair MacIntyre, *Dependent Rational Animals: Why Human Beings Need the Virtues* (Chicago: Open Court, 1999), 49. My favorite example of this claim comes from a former colleague at Samford University, Karen Joines. When one of his horses died, Joines buried it with the aid of a backhoe, digging the grave deep enough to block any foul odors emanating from the carcass. For several days the other horses in Joines' herd stood over the freshly turned ground, mourning the loss of their dead companion.

55 Chesterton acknowledges this point, seeing that the enemies of materialism pose a much greater danger: "Materialists . . . are at least near enough to heaven to accept the earth and not imagine that they made it." "The dreadful doubts," Gabriel Gale prophetically observes, "are not the doubts of the materialist. The dreadful doubts, the deadly and damnable doubts, are the doubts of the idealist." G. K. Chesterton, *The Poets and the Lunatics: Episodes in the Life of Gabriel Gale* (New York: Dodd, Mead, 1929), 124.

56 Hugh Kenner points out that Chesterton employed the word mysticism until he came to understand St. Thomas' metaphysical conception of being.

57 In fact, H. L. Mencken published *The Philosophy of Nietzsche* in 1908 (Boston: Luce).

58 Qtd. in *The Man Who Was Orthodox*, 86–87.

59 Though Chesterton acknowledges that Nietzsche had a gift for high sarcasm, he fails to mention his utter lack of self-derisory humor.

60 Perhaps Chesterton was thinking of this distinction in penning the following aphorism: "When it comes to life the critical thing is whether you take things for granted or take them with gratitude."

61 Chesterton regards such decisions also as the cure to hyper-rationalism: "A man cannot think himself out of mental evil; for it is actually the organ of thought that has become diseased, ungovernable, and, as it were, independent. He can only be saved by will or faith. . . . Decision is the whole business here; a door must be shut for ever. Every remedy is a desperate remedy. Every cure is a miraculous cure. Curing a madman is not arguing with a philosopher; it is casting out a devil. . . . [The madman] must stop thinking, if he is to go on living. [The wisest] counsel is one of intellectual amputation. If thy *head* offend thee, cut it off; for it is better, not merely to enter the Kingdom of Heaven as a child, but to enter it as an imbecile, rather than with your whole intellect to be cast into hell—or into Hanwell" (O, 26, emphasis in original). Hanwell is an insane asylum located in northwest London.

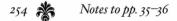

62 Evelyn Waugh regards joylessness as the fundamental modern complaint because it is the monstrous progeny of *acedia*: "Man is made for joy in the love of God, a love which he expresses in service. If he deliberately turns away from that joy, he is denying the purpose of his existence. The malice of Sloth lies not merely in the neglect of duty (though that can be a symptom of it) but in the refusal of joy. It is allied to despair." "Sloth," in *The Essays, Articles and Reviews of Evelyn Waugh*, ed. Donat Gallagher (Boston: Little, Brown, 1984), 573.

63 G. K. Chesterton, *George Bernard Shaw* (1908; repr., New York: Hill & Wang, 1956), 151.

64 Chesterton specifies some of the most salutary moral truths to be learned from fairy tales: "There is the chivalrous lesson of 'Jack the Giant Killer'; that giants should be killed because they are gigantic. It is a manly mutiny against pride as such. For the rebel is older than all the kingdoms. . . . There is the lesson of 'Cinderella,' which is the same as that of the Magnificat—*exaltavit humiles*. There is the great lesson of 'Beauty and the Beast'; that a thing must be loved *before* it is loveable. There is the terrible allegory of 'Sleeping Beauty,' which tells how the human creature was blessed with all birthday gifts, yet cursed with death; and how death also may be softened to a sleep" (O, 55).

65 The incomprehensible does not mean the arbitrary and the capricious, much less the insane and the irrational. Though it may at first seem unintelligible, upon further exploration the incomprehensible reveals its own strange rationality and order. The aboriginal human pair denies this distinction between the arbitrary and the incomprehensible. Why enjoy the bounty of all other plants in the garden, they ask, yet capriciously be denied the delights of only this one? Rather than seeking to fathom the deep logic of the forbidden tree, they open themselves to the deceits of the tempter, "and the hope of God is gone."

66 G. K. Chesterton, *A Short History of England,* in *Collected Works of G. K. Chesterton*, vol. 20 (San Francisco: Ignatius, 2001), 463.

67 Hence one of Chesterton's sparkling early poems:
You say grace before meals.
All right.
But I say grace before the play and the opera,
And grace before the concert and pantomime,
And grace before I open a book,
And grace before sketching, painting,

Swimming, fencing, boxing, walking, playing, dancing;

And grace before I dip the pen in the ink. (*Collected Poetry*, Part 1, 43)
Hence also one of his latest and darkest caveats: "Rossetti makes the remark
somewhere, bitterly but with great truth, that the worst moment for the
atheist is when he is really thankful and has nobody to thank." Chesterton,
Saint Francis of Assisi (1924; repr., New York: Doubleday, 1957), 78.

68 I owe this important distinction to my friend and colleague, Barry Harvey.

69 Chesterton may recall Aquinas' insistence that the natural virtues must
be theologically "infused" in order for them to be made Christian. Thus is
the Greek and Roman regard for the virtue of courage completely transformed by the Church. For the noble ancients, the highest expression of
fortitude is found in death on the battlefield, either in killing or being
killed. For Christians, by contrast, the most faithful form of courage lies
in a willingness to accept persecution and martyrdom, being slain rather
than forsaking the Faith.

70 "Nearly all the fundamental facts of mankind are to be found in its fables.
And there is a singularly sane truth in all the old stories of the monsters—
such as centaurs, mermaids, sphinxes, and the rest. It will be noted that
in each of these the humanity, though imperfect in extent, is perfect in
its quality. The mermaid is half a lady and half a fish; but there is nothing fishy about the lady. The centaur is half a gentleman and half a horse.
But there is nothing horsey about the gentleman. The centaur is a manly
sort of man—up to a certain point. The mermaid is a womanly woman—
so far as she goes. The human parts of these monsters are handsome,
like heroes, or lovely, like nymphs; their bestial appendages do not affect
the full perfection of their humanity—what there is of it. There is nothing humanly wrong with the centaur, except that he rides a horse without a head. There is nothing humanly wrong with the mermaid; Hood
put a good comic motto to his picture of a mermaid: 'All's well that ends
well.' It is, perhaps, quite true, it all depends which end. Those old wild
images included a crucial truth. *Man is a monster. And he is all the more a
monster because one part of him is perfect.* It is not true, as the evolutionists
say, that man moves perpetually up a slope from imperfection to perfection, changing ceaselessly, so as to be suitable. The immortal part of a
man and the deadly part are jarringly distinct, and have always been."
G. K. Chesterton, *The Uses of Diversity* (1920; repr., London: Methuen,
1937), 179, emphasis added.

Chapter 2

1 Maisie Ward, *Gilbert Keith Chesterton* (London: Sheed & Ward, 1944), 245.

2   Julia Stapleton, *Christianity, Patriotism, and Nationhood: The England of G. K. Chesterton* (Lanham, Md.: Lexington Books, 2009), 8.

3   G. K. Chesterton, *Charles Dickens* (1906; repr., New York: Schocken, 1965), 155. It is noteworthy that GKC omitted industrialism as a native English product.

4   See especially William Oddie's fine account of GKC's early years in *Chesterton and the Romance of Orthodoxy: The Making of GKC 1874–1908* (New York: Oxford University Press, 2008).

5   Chesterton, *Charles Dickens*, 161.

6   G. K. Chesterton, *George Bernard Shaw,* 15. This is hardly to say that Chesterton did not lament what was missing in Shaw: "For the truth is that Mr. Shaw has never seen things as they really are. If he had he would have fallen on his knees before them. When we really see men as they are, we don't criticize, but worship and very rightly. For a monster with mysterious eyes and miraculous thumbs, with strange dreams in his skull, and a queer tenderness for this place or that baby, is truly a wonderful and unnerving matter. And Mr. Shaw, on the practical side perhaps the most humane man alive, is in this sense inhumane. He has even been infected to some extent with the primary intellectual weakness of his new master, Nietzsche, the strange notion that the greater and stronger a man was the more he would despise other things. The greater and stronger a man is the more he would be inclined to prostrate himself before a periwinkle." G. K. Chesterton, *Heretics* (1905; repr., London: Bodley Head, 1960), 64.

7   *The Man Who Was Orthodox: A Selection from the Uncollected Writings of G. K. Chesterton*, ed. A. L. Maycock (London: Dennis Dobson, 1963), 35.

8   Max Weber, "Politics as a Vocation," in *From Max Weber: Essays in Sociology*, ed. H. H. Gerth and C. Wright Mills (New York: Oxford University Press, 1958), 96.

9   G. K. Chesterton, *William Cobbett* (1925; repr., London: House of Stratus, 2000), 48.

10 Chesterton, *The Man Who Was Orthodox*, 14–15.

11 G. K. Chesterton, *Robert Browning* (London: Macmillan, 1903), 175–76.

12 Chesterton, *Robert Browning*, 86–87.

13 Chesterton, *Robert Browning*, 52.

14 Chesterton, *Robert Browning*, 89.

15 Qtd. in J. B. Priestley, *The Edwardians* (New York: Harper & Row, 1970), 26. Chesterton had little use for England's grand country houses built by the aristocracy in the seventeenth and eighteenth centuries and made famous by their literary occupants and advocates—Jane Austen's Mansfield Park, Churchill's Blenheim, D. H. Lawrence's Garsington Manor,

Evelyn Waugh's Brideshead, Virginia Woolf's Knole House, and so on. They were neither authentic castles nor Tudor manors, Chesterton complained, but products of "the revolution of the rich," as he called the seizure of both the monasteries and public lands that began with Henry VIII. He commends Cobbett for seeing that a palatial residence of this kind was not ancient but modern in design, looking "more like a General Post Office than a feudal fortress. Such ornament as it has is a curious cold exuberance of heathen nymphs and hollow temples. Because it stands for the age of the sceptics, its gods are not only dead but have never been alive. Its gardens are full of shrines without idols or idols without idolaters." Chesterton, *William Cobbett*, 54.

16 Chesterton, *Charles Dickens*, 10.

17 G. K. Chesterton, *Tremendous Trifles* (New York: Dodd, Mead, 1909), 255–56.

18 "The Englishman's house is most sacred, not merely when the King cannot enter it, but when the Englishman cannot get out of it. . . . The English poor shut all their doors and windows until their rooms reek like the Black Hole. They are suffering for an idea . . . 'cosiness,' a word not translatable. One, at least, of the essentials of it is smallness, smallness in preference to largeness, smallness for smallness' sake. The merry-maker wants a pleasant parlour, he would not give twopence for a continent." Chesterton, *Charles Dickens*, 165.

19 Stapleton, *Christianity, Patriotism, and Nationhood*, 7.

20 Chesterton, *Collected Works*, vol. 10, *Collected Poetry, Part 1*, 408–9.

21 The poem's most memorable lines are found not in the swagger but the invective, as Chesterton prophesies the triumph of T. S. Eliot's "hollow men":

> They have given us into the hand of new unhappy lords,
> Lords without anger or honour, who dare not carry their swords.
> They fight by shuffling papers; they have bright dead alien eyes;
> They look at our labour and laughter as a tired man looks at flies.
> And the load of their loveless pity is worse than the ancient wrongs,
> Their doors are shut in the evening; and they know no songs.
>
> (*Collected Poetry, Part 1*, 410–11)

22 "A Plea for Political Unreason," *London Daily News*, June 24, 1905, qtd. in Stapleton, *Christianity, Patriotism, and Nationhood*, 88. Stephen R. L. Clark wisely observes that Chesterton "may, like others of the time (including Orwell and John Buchan), have romanticized the working masses . . . but he was not wrong to think that those masses were (and are) oppressed, nor wrong to think that fashionable remedies would make things worse."

"How Chesterton Read History," *Inquiry: An Interdisciplinary Journal of Philosophy* 39, nos. 3–4 (1996): 347.

23 Stapleton, *Christianity, Patriotism, and Nationhood*, 89.

24 The Muslim refusal to separate religion and politics is the very basis for strong Islamic states. Chesterton's negative regard for Jews was unfortunately rooted in the bitter experience of the Marconi affair, but he still might have found hope in the Jewish refusal to assimilate to their host and/or captor countries since, as the unique people of God, they would thus forsake their mission of perpetual refusal of all final loyalties other than to Yahweh. As we shall discover, Chesterton will offer a similar call to Christians vis-à-vis their own relation to the nation-state.

25 G. K. Chesterton, *G. K. C. as M. C.: Being a Collection of Thirty-Seven Introductions by G. K. Chesterton*, ed. J. de Fonseka (London: Methuen, 1929), 193.

26 Qtd. in Stephen R. L. Clark, "How Chesterton Read History." Adam Wayne makes a similar claim: "Notting Hill is a nation. Why should it condescend to become a mere Empire?" G. K. Chesterton, *The Napoleon of Notting Hill* (1904; repr., New York: Paulist, 1978), 179.

27 Qtd. in Stapleton, *Christianity, Patriotism, and Nationhood*, 64.

28 G. K. Chesterton, *Orthodoxy* (1908; repr., San Francisco: Ignatius, 1995), 53. Jaroslav Pelikan smartly revised Chesterton's aperçu by declaring that "tradition is the living faith of the dead," while "traditionalism is the dead faith of the living." *The Vindication of Tradition* (New Haven, Conn.: Yale University Press, 1984), 65.

29 Daniel Jenkins, *The British: Their Identity and Their Religion* (London: SCM Press, 1975), 18.

30 Jenkins, *The British*, 19–20.

31 Jenkins, *The British*, 20.

32 This arrangement was meant to avoid the conflation of the earthly and heavenly cities, so that the Church would not be usurped by the Empire. But it led to grave abuses, as Dante famously protested by consigning Pope Boniface VIII to Hell well before his actual death. There in the circle of simonists who used the papal office to enlarge their own power and wealth, Boniface suffers an infernal and eternal reversal of baptism. The simonists are placed, ignominiously, with their heads down into dark and narrow pits, not into the open and regenerating holy water of baptismal fonts. Far from cleansing and purifying them, the fire burns their feet as well as their souls, for these same feet have figuratively traversed unholy and unpapal places.

33 Oliver O'Donovan, *The Desire of the Nations: Rediscovering the Roots of Political Theology* (New York: Cambridge University Press, 1996), 204, 212. I am

indebted to my colleague and friend Barry Harvey not only for offering this conspectus of O'Donovan's thesis but also for instructing me in many other key theological distinctions.

34 Ernst H. Kantorowicz, *The King's Two Bodies: A Study in Mediaeval Political Theology* (Princeton, N.J.: Princeton University Press, 1957), 232–34. We shall discover that Wilfred Owen's satiric attack on the Horatian tag *dulce et decorum est pro patria mori* constitutes a profound (if implicit) Christian critique of what would become the earliest manifestation of the culture of death: the grossly misnamed "Great War."

35 Kantorowicz, *King's Two Bodies*, 235.

36 Kantorowicz, *King's Two Bodies*, 242. I owe this recension of Kantoro-wicz' argument to the excellent work of my graduate assistant, David Wilmington.

37 Stephen Toulmin, *Cosmopolis: The Hidden Agenda of Modernity* (Chicago: University of Chicago, 1990), 7. Ross Douthat argues that this tension continues to tear at the body politic of the United States: "There's an America where it doesn't matter what language you speak, what god you worship, or how deep your New World roots run. An America where allegiance to the Constitution trumps ethnic differences, language barriers and religious divides. An America where the newest arrival to our shores is no less American than the ever-so-great granddaughter of the Pilgrims.

"But there's another America as well, one that understands itself as a distinctive culture, rather than just a set of political propositions. This America speaks English, not Spanish or Chinese or Arabic. It looks back to a particular religious heritage: Protestantism originally, and then a Judeo-Christian consensus that accommodated Jews and Catholics as well. It draws its social norms from the *mores* of the Anglo-Saxon diaspora—and it expects new arrivals to assimilate themselves to these norms, and quickly." "Islam in Two Americas," *The New York Times*, August 15, 2010, A19.

38 Simon Oliver, "What Is Radical Orthodoxy?" in *The Radical Orthodoxy Reader*, ed. John Milbank and Simon Oliver (New York: Routledge, 2009), 9–10.

39 G. K. Chesterton, *The New Jerusalem* (1920; repr., Champaign, Ill.: Book Jungle, 2007), 27–28.

40 This view was shared by Abraham Lincoln: "Labor is prior to, and independent of, capital. Capital is only the fruit of labor, and could never have existed if labor had not first existed. Labor is the superior of capital, and deserves much the higher consideration." First annual message to Congress, December 3, 1861. *The Language of Liberty: The Political Speeches and*

Writings of Abraham Lincoln, 2nd ed., ed. Joseph R. Fornieri (Washington, D.C.: Regnery, 2009), 619.

41 Chesterton, *William Cobbett*, 11.

42 "The mere privation of indulgences," Mill coldly confessed in 1834, "and the sacrifice of so much liberty as is given up by submitting to the discipline of a well-regulated workhouse, are quite sufficient, if properly enforced, to make every able-bodied pauper to extricate himself from pauperism; and whenever this has been tried, all, or nearly all, the able-bodied paupers have speedily found employment, not only without a fall, but with an actual rise, of wages throughout the parish." *Newspaper Writings*, in *The Collected Works of John Stuart Mill*, ed. Ann Robson and John Robson (Toronto: University of Toronto Press, 1986), 687.

43 Chesterton, *William Cobbett*, 14–15. In yet another reprise of his recurrent trope, Chesterton declared that Cobbett "did not draw precise diagrams of things as they were. He only had frantic and fantastic nightmares of things as they are" (22).

44 G. K. Chesterton, *The Victorian Age in Literature* (1913; repr., London: Oxford University Press, 1966), 33. Though Chesterton was critical of Victorian vices—"religious doubt, intellectual unrest, a hungry credulity about new things, a complete lack of equilibrium"—he also hailed its merits, especially those virtues that Oscar Wilde, Lytton Strachey, and the other Decadents mocked: "a rich sense of romance, a passionate desire to make the love of man and woman once more what it was in Eden, a strong sense of the absolute necessity of some significance in human life." G. K. Chesterton, *Autobiography*, 142.

45 Chesterton, *William Cobbett*, 85–86. The Luddites were not opposed to mechanical looms as such but to the massive loss of work and the heartless destruction of traditional ways of life produced by such machines.

46 W. R. Titterton, *G. K. Chesterton: A Portrait* (London: Douglas Organ, 1936), 59.

47 Chesterton rightly linked their imperialism to a perverse use of Darwin. If nature is an unsponsored and undirected force, a juggernaut of the strong crushing the weak, then history must constitute a similarly deterministic process, an ineluctable empowering of the worthy over the allegedly unworthy. Those whom Kipling infamously described as "lesser breeds without the law" should submit to the inevitability of "progress" and "civilized" British rule.

48 Unlike the pacifists, Chesterton defended the right of the Boer Republics to defend themselves against British imperialism. As a Liberal in the Radical tradition, Chesterton often kept strange company, even as he kept

himself apart from many of their causes. For example, he never joined other Radicals in supporting anti-vivisectionism, vegetarianism, women's suffrage, or total abstinence from alcohol.

49 G. K. Chesterton, *Saint Francis of Assisi* (1924; repr., New York: Doubleday, 1957), 15.

50 "The things the poor hate are the modern things, the rationalist things—doctors, inspectors, poor law guardians, professional philanthropy. They never showed any reluctance to be helped by the old and corrupt monasteries. They will often die rather than be helped by the modern and efficient workhouse." Chesterton, *Charles Dickens*, 174.

51 Chesterton, *Charles Dickens*, 175.

52 Couching his case in individualist terms that he would later qualify, Chesterton was in search of a Christian idea of cultural transformation from the beginning, as in this letter written in 1896 to his future wife, Frances Blogg: "The modern socialist regards his theory of regeneration as a duty which society owes to him, the early Christian regarded it as a duty he owed to society; the modern socialist is busy framing schemes for its fulfillment, the early Christian was busy considering whether he would himself fulfill it there and then; the ideal of modern socialism is an elaborate Utopia to which he hopes the world may be tending, the ideal of the early Christian was an actual nucleus 'living the new life' to whom he might join himself if he liked." Qtd. in Race Mathews, *Jobs of Our Own: Building a Stake-Holder Society* (London: Pluto, 1999), 93–94.

53 Although *The Brothers Karamazov* had only recently been translated into English, Chesterton and Belloc seem intuitively to have absorbed the fearful truth of the Grand Inquisitor's demonic vision—the prophecy that the masses will finally demand the womb-like security of the omni-competent state in place of the difficult liberty won through self-sacrifice and self-determination.

54 Hilaire Belloc, *The Servile State* (1913; repr., Indianapolis: Liberty Fund, 1977), 134–35. Chesterton was thoroughly agreed: "It is almost the definition of a slave that he does receive unemployment pay. That is, he receives board and lodging, whether his master wants him to work at that moment or no. The whole point of the servile relation is that the master does undertake the whole support of the slave, idle or busy, but receives in turn the right to decide when he shall be busy and when idle. Expressed in modern terms, the slave-owner agree[s] to give unemployment pay, on condition of getting rid of strikes. To a very large proportion of perfectly humane and intelligent businessmen to-day, it would seem a very workable compromise. It would be a very workable compromise. It would

also be slavery—or the Servile State." "What Mr. Belloc's Servile State Means," in *Collected Works of G. K. Chesterton*, vol. 32, *Illustrated London News, 1920–1922* (San Francisco: Ignatius, 1986), 237.

55 Though an anti-Christian, H. G. Wells gladly acknowledged that he and Shaw were Chesterton's kinsmen rather than his enemies: "We all three hate equally and sympathetically the spectacle of human beings blown up with windy wealth and irresponsible power as cruelly and absurdly as boys blow up frogs; we all three detest the complex causes that dwarf and cripple lives from the moment of birth and starve and debase great masses of mankind. We want as much as possible the jolly life, men and women warm-blooded and well-aired, acting freely and joyously, gathering life as a child gathers corn-cockles in corn. We all three want people to have property of a real and personal sort, to have the son, as Chesterton puts it, bringing up the port his father laid down, and pride in the pears one has grown in one's own garden. And I agree with Chesterton that giving—giving oneself out of love and fellowship—is the salt of life." Qtd. in Mathews, *Jobs of Our Own*, 105–6, from 177 of Wells' *An Englishman Looks at the World*.

56 Chesterton, *Orthodoxy*, 125. Chesterton's diatribes against wealth are unrelenting, even though he died as a wealthy man. "There are two ways to get enough: one is to continue to accumulate more and more. The other is to desire less." "The poor man really has a stake in the country. The rich man hasn't; he can go away to New Guinea in a yacht." (G. K. Chesterton, *The Annotated Thursday: G. K. Chesterton's Masterpiece "The Man Who Was Thursday,"* annotated by Martin Gardner [1907; repr., San Francisco: Ignatius, 1999], 190–91). "That which is large enough for the rich to covet is large enough for the poor to defend" (G. K. Chesterton, *The Napoleon of Notting Hill*, in *Collected Works of G. K. Chesterton*, vol. 6 [San Francisco: Ignatius, 1991], 274). "[A]mong the very rich you will never find a really generous man even by accident. They may give their money away, but they will never give themselves away; they are egotistic, secretive, dry as old bones. To be smart enough to get all that money you must be dull enough to want it" (G. K. Chesterton, *A Miscellany of Men* [New York: Dodd, Mead, 1912], 172).

57 Josef Pieper, *The Four Cardinal Virtues: Prudence, Justice, Fortitude, Temperance* (Notre Dame, Ind.: University of Notre Dame Press, 1965), 98–99.

58 Qtd. in Mathews, *Jobs of Our Own*, 100.

59 G. K. Chesterton, *What's Wrong with the World* (1910; repr., San Francisco: Ignatius, 1994), 42.

60 Qtd. in Ward, *Gilbert Keith Chesterton*, headnote to chap. 26.

61 Ian Boyd, C.S.B., "The Fiction of Chesterton," http://distributist .blogspot.com/2007/03/fiction-of-chesterton.html.

62 Qtd. in Boyd, "Fiction of Chesterton," from "Prohibition and Property," *New Witness*, October 7, 1921, 198.

63 G. K. Chesterton, *The Outline of Sanity* (1926; repr., Norfolk, Va.: IHS, 2001), 98. The opposite of folly and damnation, for Chesterton, is sanity in the full sense of the word—*sanus*, health, wholeness, salvation.

64 Chesterton, *The Outline of Sanity*, 128. Chesterton did not blench at the attendant difficulties such a system would entail, stressing instead the moral and religious qualities necessary for its fulfillment: "If I am asked what I should immediately do with a machine, I have no doubt about the sort of practical programme that could be a preliminary to a possible spiritual revolution of a much wider sort. In so far as the machine cannot be shared, I would have the ownership of it shared; that is, the direction of it shared and the profits of it shared. But when I say 'shared' I mean it in the modern mercantile sense of the word 'shares.' That is, I mean something divided and not merely something pooled. Our business friends bustle forward to tell us that all this is impossible; completely unconscious, apparently, that all this part of the business exists already. You cannot distribute a steam-engine, in the sense of giving one wheel to each shareholder to take home with him, clasped in his arms. But you not only can, but you already do distribute the ownership and profit of the steam-engine; and you distribute it in the form of private property. Only you do not distribute it enough, or to the right people, or to the people who really require it or could really do work for it. . . . My own preference, on the whole, would be that any such necessary machine should be owned by a small local guild, on principles of profit-sharing, or rather profit-dividing: but of real profit-sharing and real profit-dividing, not to be confounded with capitalist patronage" (125–26).

65 Herbert McCabe, O.P., *On Aquinas*, ed. Brian Davies, O.P. (London: Continuum, 2008), 155. Pope Benedict XVI seems to have refreshed himself at the Distributist font, as he revealed in his very first encyclical *Caritas in Veritate* from 2009. There he argues that the market does not exist in a neutral or value-free state but is always freighted with moral assumptions and consequences. Hence his call for economic decisions to be determined by a transcendent order based on the assumption that "the *primary capital to be safeguarded and valued is man, the human person in his or her integrity.*" This means, among other things, that "in *commercial relationships* the *principle of gratuitousness* and the logic of gift as an expression of fraternity can and must *find their place within normal economic activity. . . . Economic life*

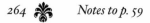

undoubtedly requires *contracts*, in order to regulate relations of exchange between goods of equivalent value. But it also needs *just laws* and *forms of redistribution* governed by politics, and what is more, it needs works redolent of the *spirit of gift*." While such a *"civilizing [of] the economy"* cannot be left entirely to government, the pope admits that, amidst a global financial system in serious crisis, "the State's role seems destined to grow." *CarVer*, sec. 25 par. 2, sec. 36 par. 4, sec. 37 par. 2, sec. 38 par. 1, sec. 41 par. 2, emphasis in original. http://www.vatican.va/holy_father/benedict_xvi/encyclicals/documents/hf_ben-xvi_enc_20090629_caritas-in-veritate_en.html.

66 Clark, "How Chesterton Read History," 351.

67 Chesterton, *Charles Dickens*, 152.

68 G. K. Chesterton, *Chaucer* (New York: Farrar, Rinehart, 1932), 182. The American equivalent might be something akin to dying for Walmart, as Adam K. Webb suggests: "Once one probes below the glitter of high living standards, I think liberal culture is intrinsically unsatisfying. That would be true even if [especially if?] it delivered an iPod in every pocket and a Lexus beside every olive tree a century or two from now." Webb, "10 questions for Adam K. Webb," *Gene Expression*, http://www.gnxp.com/blog/2006/06/10-questions-for-adam-k-webb.php.

Yet even so humane a writer as Orwell could only sneer at Chesterton as a troglodyte who wanted to laugh out of existence all those things he despised. "I don't myself feel at all certain that this civilisation will survive," Orwell wrote in 1946, "but if it does survive I think it is quite obvious that it will not revert again towards economic chaos and individualism [his totally uncomprehending view of Distributism]. Whether we like it or not, the trend is toward centralism and planning and it is more useful to try to humanise the collectivist society that is certainly coming than to pretend . . . that we could revert to a past phase." Orwell, *Collected Essays, Journalism and Letters of George Orwell*, vol. 4, *In Front of Your Nose: 1945–1950*, ed. Sonia Orwell and Ian Angus (New York: Harcourt Brace, 1968), 103. H. V. Routh makes the similarly wrong-headed judgment that Chesterton and Belloc "became a centre and an example for those who loved England but hated what England was trying to become, and still believed that most evil things could be proved to be silly." Qtd. in Robert Speaight, *The Life of Hilaire Belloc* (New York: Farrar, Straus & Cudahy, 1957), 149.

69 Chesterton foresaw the nightmarish link between unbridled greed and economic collapse: "Anybody who can think in theories, those highly practical things, will see that sooner or later this paralysis in the system is inevitable. . . . Capitalism is a contradiction; it is even a contradiction in terms. . . . Capitalism is contradictory as soon as it is complete; because

it is dealing with the mass of men in two opposite ways at once. When most men are wage-earners, it is more and more difficult for most men to be customers. For, the capitalist is always trying to cut down what his servant demands, and in doing so is cutting down what his customer can spend. As soon as his business is in any difficulties, as at present in the coal business, he tries to reduce what he has to spend on wages, and in doing so reduces what others have to spend on coal. He is wanting the same man to be rich and poor at the same time. This contradiction in capitalism does not appear in the earlier stages, because there are still populations not reduced to the common proletarian condition. But as soon as the wealthy as a whole are employing the wage-earners as a whole, this contradiction stares them in the face like an ironic doom and judgment" (Chesterton, *Outline of Sanity*, 43).

70 John Médaille, "Who Owns Our Jobs?" *Front Porch Republic*, August 10, 2009, http://www.frontporchrepublic.com/?p=5215. Adam Webb and Lew Daly are both seeking to address the global culture wars by way of something akin to Distributism. They both refuse to endorse capitalistic "development" of rural China, for instance, as the only means of bringing peasants out of their bondage to stoop-shouldered labor—as if real freedom could be found only in leaving their farms for wage-earning jobs in cities. Instead, Daly and Webb advocate state redistribution of land and improved agricultural methods as better means of ensuring a traditional and rural and self-sufficient way of life. See Adam K. Webb, *Beyond the Global Culture War* (New York: Routledge, 2006) and Lew Daly, *God's Economy: Faith-Based Initiatives and the Caring State* (Chicago: University of Chicago Press, 2009). A wholesale rejection of Distributism can be found in Marcus Epstein, Walter Block, and Thomas E. Woods Jr., "Chesterton and Belloc: A Critique," *Independent Review* 11, no. 4 (2007): 579–94.

71 Jay Corrin, *G. K. Chesterton & Hilaire Belloc: The Battle against Modernity* (Athens: Ohio University Press, 1981), 209. Whittaker Chambers made much the same judgment about the nature of conservatism in a letter to his friend William F. Buckley Jr. written on Christmas Eve of 1958. Chambers explained that he was not himself a conservative but a capitalist and that their essential conflict lay in Buckley's Christian conviction over against his own unbelief: "I claim that capitalism is not, and by its essential nature cannot conceivably be, conservative. This is particularly true of capitalism in the United States, which knew no Middle Age; which was born, in so far as it was ideological, in the Enlightenment. . . . America was the first capitalist power that started from scratch in a raw continent. We are something new under the sun. . . . Moreover, as the

contending capitalism of Europe (and Japan) destroyed themselves in war, American capitalism grew massive as the unassailed arsenal. At the same time, with the favorable trade balance, it freed itself from Europe's financial grip and became itself the guardian of the hoard whose symbol is Fort Knox. . . . *Conservatism is alien to the very nature of capitalism* whose love of life and growth is perpetual change. We are living in one of its periods of breathless acceleration of change. . . . I am saying that conservatism and capitalism are mutually exclusive manifestations, and antipathetic at root." Whittaker Chambers, *Odyssey of a Friend: Whittaker Chambers' Letters to William F. Buckley Jr., 1954–1961* (New York: Putnam, 1969), 228–29, emphasis added.

Louis Simpson offers a similar judgment about the American South, the nation's only region with an ostensibly conservative culture. Industrial and commercial cultures inevitably turn avarice and consumption into the ultimate goods, Simpson claims, destroying all organic communities "of kinship and custom, of tradition and myth." *The Brazen Face of History: Studies of Literary Consciousness in America* (Athens: University of Georgia Press, 1980), 76.

72 G. K. Chesterton, *Varied Types* (New York: Dodd, Mead, 1903), 252. Chesterton did not believe that it is always necessary to shout a cry of alarm, as in this Christmas meditation from 1910: "It is true that in certain acute and painful crises of oppression or disgrace, discontent is a duty, and shame should call us like a trumpet. But it is not true that man should look at life with an eye of discontent, however high-minded. It is not true that in his primary, naked relation to the world, in his relation to sex, to pain, to comradeship, to the grave or to the weather, man ought to make discontent his ideal; it is black lunacy. Half his poor little hopes of happiness hang on his thinking a small house pretty, a plain wife charming, a lame foot not unbearable, and bad cards not so bad. The voice of the special rebels and prophets, recommending discontent, should, as I have said, sound now and then suddenly, like a trumpet. But the voices of the saints and sages, recommending contentment, should sound unceasingly, like the sea." *The Man Who Was Orthodox*, 126.

Chesterton also learned from Dickens that contentment does not entail complacency: "People produce changes by being contented. The man who said that 'revolutions are not made with rose-water' was obviously inexperienced in practical human affairs. Men like Rousseau and Shelley do make revolutions, and they do make them with rose-water; that is, with a too rosy and sentimental view of human goodness. Figures that come before and create convulsion and change (e.g., the central figure of the New Testament) always have the air of walking in an unnatural

sweetness and calm." Chesterton, *Charles Dickens*, 272.

73 Qtd. in Adam Schwartz, *The Third Spring: G. K. Chesterton, Graham Greene, Christopher Dawson, and David Jones* (Washington, D.C.: Catholic University of America Press, 2005), 383, emphasis in original. Jay Corrin concurs with Eliot. He provides a fine conspectus of the widespread (and often contradictory) effects of the Distributists. Perhaps their chief accomplishment was to help usher in the twentieth-century Catholic cultural revival, as they encouraged their coreligionists to speak openly on social and economic issues as they had not done before. "[T]here can be little doubt that Chesterton, Belloc, and the Distributist circle shattered the intellectual inferiority complex of British Catholics. The Chesterbelloc did not bring Distributism into the flesh, but Catholicism in Britain certainly gained a new confidence in its mission to return the modern world to 'Christian sanity.'" Corrin, *G. K. Chesterton & Hilaire Belloc*, 171.

74 A Congregationalist pastor's careful but uncritical interpretation of the hymn can be found at http://www.fccoshkosh.org/GodofEarthandAltar .html.

75 Concluded in May 1902, this three-year-long conflict was the last British imperial war. It was also the most expensive (over £200 million) and disastrous of all British wars between 1815 and 1914. Aidan Mackey lists the hymn as being composed in 1906, but he confesses that he has had to rely largely on undated manuscripts, differences in GKC's penmanship, and other such historical intangibles.

76 Chesterton, *Collected Poetry, Part 1*, 141.

77 Since Chesterton had as little use for the Liberals' David Lloyd-George as for the Tories' Joseph Chamberlain, he may be making a generic rather than a specific confession here, though he does again employ the word *falter* in "The Church Militant."

78 Stephen R. L. Clark argues that this is the only occurrence of the familiar medieval trope in Chesterton's work, but he also confesses that GKC "was seriously misled about the virtues of the sword—which is to say, in practice, of the machine-gun and the bomb (since that is how, outside Notting Hill, even the wars of local patriotism are fought . . .)." Clark, "How Chesterton Read History," 345. Many readers have noted the immense influence of Hilaire Belloc on Chesterton's idealization of the high Middle Ages. Belloc's description of the "living tether" that secured the unity of Europe from the eleventh through the fourteenth centuries is virtually identical to Chesterton's final vision in "A Hymn": "The king ruled, the knight fought, the peasant dug in his own ground, and the priest believed." Qtd. in Corrin, *G. K. Chesterton & Hilaire Belloc*, 19.

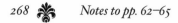

79 On September 10, 1939, a week after England declared war on Germany, C. S. Lewis wrote to his brother Warren in Shanghai to declare his keen displeasure with the following petition that the vicar had inserted into the litany at their home parish of Holy Trinity, Headington Quarry: "Prosper, oh Lord, our righteous cause." "I ventured to protest [to the vicar on the church porch]," Lewis wrote, "against the audacity of informing God that our cause was righteous—a point on which He may have His own view." Lewis, *Collected Letters of C. S. Lewis*, vol. 2, ed. Walter Hooper (San Francisco: Harper, 2004), 272.

80 Chesterton, *Collected Poetry, Part 1*, 141–42.

81 For Chesterton, true humility is the source of true creativity: "[I]f a man would make his world large, he must be always making himself small. Even the haughty visions, the tall cities, and the toppling pinnacles are creations of humility. Giants that tread down forests like grass are the creations of humility. . . . For towers are not tall unless we look up at them; and giants are not giants unless they are larger than we. . . . It is impossible without humility to enjoy anything—even pride." Chesterton, *Orthodoxy*, 36.

82 If this poem were written as early as 1905, Chesterton may be offering a swift answer to the swagger not only of Kipling's "Recessional" (1897) but also "The White Man's Burden" (1899):

> Take up the White Man's burden—
> Send forth the best ye breed—
> Go, bind your sons to exile
> To serve your captives' need;
> To wait, in heavy harness,
> On fluttered folk and wild—
> Your new-caught sullen peoples,
> Half devil and half child.

83 Chesterton, *Saint Francis of Assisi*, 80. Chesterton envisions St. Francis not only as the merry tumbler of the Lord but also as the agonized stigmatist of Mt. Alverno: "Through all his plunging and restless days ran the refrain: I have not suffered enough; I have not sacrificed enough; I am not yet worthy even of the shadow of the crown of thorns. He wandered about the valleys of the world looking for the hill that has the outline of a skull" (124).

84 Chesterton was hardly an anticredalist: "Nothing else than dogma could have resisted the riot of imaginative invention with which the [Gnostics] were waging their war on nature; with their Aeons and Demiurge, their strange Logos and their sinister Sophia. If the Church had not insisted on theology, it would have melted into a mad mythology of the mystics, yet

further removed from reason and even from rationalism; and, above all, yet further removed from life and from the love of life." G. K. Chesterton, *The Everlasting Man* (1925; repr., New York: Doubleday, 1955), 229.

85 G. K. Chesterton, *Christendom in Dublin*, in *Collected Works of G. K. Chesterton*, vol. 20 (San Francisco: Ignatius, 1986), 44. Legend holds that St. Dominic made a pilgrimage to Rome where Pope Innocent III is said to have taken him on a personal tour of the Church of St. John Lateran. Of this opulent basilica, the pope is supposed to have boasted to St. Dominic: "No longer need we say 'silver and gold have I none,'" alluding to the reply of Peter to the poor man in the book of Acts. Yet the humble St. Dominic is suppose to have answered: "Yes, but neither can the church any longer say: 'Rise up and walk.'"

86 Chesterton, *Orthodoxy*, 152.

87 As one deeply devoted to the Virgin Mother of God, Chesterton may have also chosen this prayer because it echoes a phrase from the Rosary: *Maria regnans in Patria, Ora pro nobis in via* ("Mary, reigning in the Fatherland, pray for us who are on the way").

Chapter 3

1 Charles Williams, *Poetry at Present* (1930; repr., Oxford, UK: Clarendon, 1931), 98–99.

2 G. K. Chesterton, *Saint Francis of Assisi* (1924; repr., New York: Doubleday, 1957), 117, 120, 125. This view of Francis' mission is largely mythical. Virtually nothing is known about what happened at this fabled meeting, as John Victor Toland has recently shown in *Saint Francis and the Sultan: The Curious History of a Christian–Muslim Encounter* (New York: Oxford University Press, 2009). In any case, Chesterton was surely wrong to claim that "Francis, as much as St. Dominic, would ultimately have defended the defence of Christian unity by arms" (*Saint Francis of Assisi*, 125). Yet the far-reaching consequences of Francis' visit to Egypt have in fact been documented. When the Muslims ended the Crusader Kingdom of Jerusalem at the Battle of Acre in 1291, seventy years after Francis' trip to Egypt, they allowed only the Franciscans, among all other Catholics, to remain as Christian "Custodians of the Holy Land."

3 Chesterton, *The Everlasting Man*, (1925; repr., New York: Doubleday, 1955) 323. On the contrary, there is one occasion when Jesus does indeed mention war: "And when ye shall hear of wars and rumors of wars, be ye not troubled: for such things must needs be; but the end shall not be yet" (Mark 13:7). That wars "must needs be" in no way indicates that Christians are instrumental in either fomenting or fighting them. Exactly to

the contrary, Jesus calls for his disciples *not* to regard the world's war-fare—nation rising up against nation—as signs, much less proofs, that the Kingdom of Heaven has come on earth.

4 Larry Rasmussen, ed., *Reinhold Niebuhr: Theologian of Public Life* (Minneapolis, Minn.: Fortress, 1991), 127. Niebuhr's chief antagonist has been the Mennonite theologian John Howard Yoder. Yoder acknowledges that God uses the power of pagan and secular states to accomplish his will in the world, mainly by *ordering* them, "sovereignly [telling] them where they belong, what is their place." Yet through his people called the Body of Christ, God radically *reorders* the world by means of the Church when it exists as God's new humanity: "[I]t is *par excellence* with reference to enmity between peoples, the extension of neighbor-love to the enemy, and the renunciation of violence even [for] the most righteous cause, that [God's] promise takes on flesh in the most original, the most authentic, the most frightening and scandalous, and therefore in the most evangelical way. It is the Good News that my enemy and I are united, through no merit or work of our own, in a new humanity that forbids henceforth my ever taking his life in my hands." Here alone does powerlessness become power, the Victim become the Victor—in a cross-bearing that brings "the inevitable suffering of those whose only goal is to be faithful to that love which puts one at the mercy of one's neighbor, which abandons claims to justice for oneself and for one's own in an overriding concern for the reconciling of the adversary and the estranged." John Howard Yoder, *The Politics of Jesus* (Grand Rapids: Eerdmans, 1972), 203, 231–32, 243.

5 It is doubtful that Chesterton carried a swordstick as an actual Christian weapon against potential attackers, so much as a wry reminder that men once held convictions so strongly that they would duel over them unto death.

6 "In classical Islam *jihad* was a technical term referring to wars undertaken to convert infidels, specifically the Jewish and Christian population of a territory, and to enforce land and poll taxes on the non-Islamic population." Ben C. Ollenburger, "Introduction" to Gerhard von Rad, *Holy War in Ancient Israel* (1958; repr., Grand Rapids: Eerdmans, 1991), 6.

7 "On the oracle was based the utterly unshakeable certainty of victory, which was the characteristic defining holy war." Ollenburger, "Introduction," 42.

8 The most notorious but also the least characteristic call to carnage concerns the treatment of the remaining Midianites after all the adult males have been slain: "Now therefore kill every male among the little ones, and kill every woman that hath known man by lying with him. But all the

women children, that have not known a man by lying with him, keep alive for yourselves" (Num 31:17-18).

9   Ollenburger, "Introduction," 31, 32.

10 In a similarly metaphoric warning, the Lord threatens saber-wielding wrath against unrepentant individuals no less than nations: "If he turn not, [God] will whet his sword; he hath bent his bow, and made it ready" (Ps 7:12).

11 The violent sword images used to describe the returning Christ in the book of Revelation are manifestly symbolic features of apocalyptic vision. This is not to say that there will be no cataclysmic end to the world, no final Armageddon of woeful destruction, but that it will redound to the credit of God rather than man: "And out of his mouth goeth a sharp sword, that with it he should smite the nations: and he shall rule them with a rod of iron: and he treadeth the winepress of the fierceness and the wrath of Almighty God. And he hath on [his] vesture and on his thigh a name written, KING OF KINGS, AND LORD OF LORDS" (Rev 19:15-16).

12 "Blessed are the peacemakers: for they shall be called the children of God" (Matt 5:9). "But I say unto you, Love your enemies, bless them that curse you, do good to them that hate you, and pray for them which despitefully use you, and persecute you. . . . For if ye love them which love you, what reward have ye?" (Matt 5:44, 46). "If it be possible, as much as lieth in you, live peaceably with all men. Dearly beloved, avenge not yourselves, but rather give place unto wrath: for it is written, Vengeance is mine; I will repay, saith the LORD" (Rom 12:18-19). "See that none render evil for evil unto any man; but ever follow that which is good, both among yourselves, and to all men" (1 Thess 5:15). "Follow peace with all men, and holiness, without which no man shall see the LORD" (Heb 12:14).

13 Qtd. from John Cadoux, *The Early Christian Attitude to War* (London: Headley Brothers, 1919) in Laurence M. Vance, "The Early Christian Attitude to War," http://www.lewrockwell.com/vance/vance60.html.

14 G. K. Chesterton, "Christianity and War," in *Chesterton on War and Peace*, ed. Michael W. Perry (Seattle: Inkling Books, 2008), 356. Chesterton would have received no help from Aristotle regarding the innate dignity even of such enemies as the Persians. Aristotle was not slow, Peter Green observes, "to find intellectual argument in support of Alexander's passionate longing to win glory at the expense of the Barbarian. . . . He believed slavery to be a natural institution, and equally that all 'barbarians' (i.e., non-Greeks) were slaves by nature. It was therefore right and fitting for Greeks to rule over barbarians, but not for barbarians to rule

over Greeks. . . . In one celebrated fragment he counsels Alexander to be 'a hegemon' [leader] to the Greeks and a despot to the barbarians, to look after the former as after friends and relatives, and to deal with the latter as beasts or plants." Peter Green, *Alexander of Macedon, 336–323 B.C.: A Historical Biography* (Berkeley: University of California, 1992), 58.

15   G. K. Chesterton, *Twelve Types* (1902; repr., Norfolk, Va.: IHS Press, 2003), 67. Chesterton fails to observe that St. George slew not a human but a bestial enemy of God and man. One also wonders what Chesterton might have made of the seven Trappist monks in Algeria who refused to flee their monastery at Tibhirine despite the rampant Muslim violence directed especially against foreigners and Catholic religious. They elected to remain with the local people whom they loved in order to offer their Christian witness to nonviolence and reconciliation. In 1996 they were all brutally murdered and beheaded by terrorists linked to al-Qaeda. It was later discovered that Brother Christian, the prior of the community who had studied Islamics in Rome and who had cultivated interreligious understanding with Muslims, had written a letter to be opened only after his death. Among other caveats, it urged that Algerian Muslims not be stereotyped as savage anti-Christians. Then, with stunning Christian charity, Brother Christian offered this farewell to his killer: "Yes, for you, too, I wish this thank-you, this 'A Dieu' whose image is in you also, that we may meet in heaven, like good thieves, if it pleases God, our common Father. Amen! Insha'Allah!" Qtd. in Lawrence S. Cunningham, *A Brief History of Saints* (Malden, Mass.: Blackwell, 2005), 146.

16   Thomas Aquinas specifies the three conditions for just war in the *Summa Theologica* 2.2.40. Church teaching later elaborated these constraints under the rubrics of *jus ad bellum*, *jus in bello*, and *jus post bellum*. Almost all advocates of just war adhere to seven common criteria: (1) the cause must be for the correction of a grave public evil; (2) the injustice suffered by those who have been wronged must significantly outweigh the suffering entailed in righting the wrong; (3) the war can be waged only by a legitimate public authority; (4) the military response must not be for the sake of economic or political gain but only with the intention of establishing justice; (5) the overall destruction caused by the martial corrective must be outweighed by the good it achieves; (6) the war can be waged only after all peaceful alternatives have been exhausted; (7) the militants must target only the unjust combatants, with no direct attack on enemy civilians.

Dorothy Day, among others, has argued that modern weaponry is so promiscuously destructive that there can never again be a just war, much less a holy war.

17 Chesterton, *Twelve Types*, 66.

18 *Lepanto by G. K. Chesterton*, with explanatory notes and commentary by Dale Ahlquist (Minneapolis, Minn.: American Chesterton Society, 2003).

19 *Lepanto*, 75.

20 "Christendom," Chesterton declared, "is the only philosophical name of Europe." "Christendom and Pride," in G. K. Chesterton, *The End of the Armistice* (London: Sheed & Ward, 1940), 217.

21 G. K. Chesterton, *The Common Man* (New York: Sheed & Ward, 1950), 269–70. Islamic theology regards Azrael as the Angel of Death, though always subordinate to the will of God. In *The New Jerusalem*, Chesterton envisions Islam itself as the demonic Destroyer, so that the Crusaders rightly sought to slay it. G. K. Chesterton, *The New Jerusalem* (1920; repr., Champaign, Ill.: Book Jungle, 2007).

22 His harangue to his own fighters is one of the most famous calls to arms in military history: "Gentlemen, this is not a time to discuss but to fight" (Victor Davis Hanson, "Don John of Austria Is Riding to the Sea," *First Things* 175 [August–September 2007]: 55). "My children," added the Austrian naval commander, "we are here to conquer or die as Heaven may determine." "The Christians," Hanson notes, "not the supposed 'fanatical' Muslims, would fight like men possessed." "All contemporary sources remark that once Christian infantrymen boarded the Turkish galleys, they fought with an almost inhuman savagery." "[M]ost of the Turkish dead at Lepanto were probably killed in cold blood as they begged for mercy on deck or floated helplessly among the debris on the water." Victor Davis Hanson, *Culture and Carnage: Landmark Battles in the Rise of Western Power* (New York: Doubleday, 2001), 235, 254, 237.

23 G. K. Chesterton, *Collected Poetry, Part 1*, 549.

24 *The Universal Oxford Dictionary* (rev. and ed. C. T. Onions, 3rd ed. [Oxford: Clarendon, 1955], 1188) lists several unsavory meanings for this unsavory word: a false god, an idol, a name for the devil. Rachel Biale argues that Muhammad is the most maligned of all major religious leaders: "Attacked in the past as a heretic, an imposter, or a sensualist, it is still possible to find him referred to as 'the false prophet.' A modern German writer accuses Muhammad of sensuality, surrounding himself with young women. This man was not married until he was twenty-five years of age, then he and his wife lived in happiness and fidelity for twenty-four years, until her death when he was forty-nine. Only between the age of fifty and his death at sixty-two did Muhammad take other wives [a polygynous practice that also characterized both biblical and post-biblical Judaism], only one of whom was a virgin, and most of them were taken for dynastic

and political reasons. Certainly the Prophet's record was better than that
head of the Church of England, Henry VIII." Qtd. in John L. Esposito,
Islam: The Straight Path, expanded ed. (New York: Oxford University Press,
1991), 18.

25 Chesterton, *Collected Poetry, Part 1*, 549. This name for the beautiful virgin
companions of the faithful men in the Muslim paradise derives from the
plural of the Arabic *ahwar*: "having eyes with a marked contrast of black
and white."

26 Chesterton, *Collected Poetry, Part 1*, 550, emphasis added.

27 This is no exaggeration, since the contemporary Italian historian Con-
tarini described the battle waters as *tutto il mare sanguinoso*—"the completely bloody sea." Hanson, *Culture and Carnage*, 241.

28 Chesterton, *Collected Poetry, Part 1*, 552. Charles Williams, in a sympathetic
treatment of Chesterton's war poetry, cannot refrain from noting that,
in addition to the estimated 12,000 or 15,000 Christian slaves freed by
the triumph of the Holy League, "at least 7,200 Turkish slaves were dis-
tributed among the Christian princes (Don John himself receiving 174
as a present from the Pope)." "G. K. Chesterton," in Williams, *Poetry at
Present*, 105. It is also noteworthy that the shout of victory first hails the
Spanish nation and then, in second place, the glory of the Lord. With the
Carolingian revolution, as we have seen, the triumphant empire is no longer separable from the Kingdom of God.

29 Chesterton, *Collected Poetry, Part 1*, 551.

30 Hanson, *Culture and Carnage*, 252.

31 Chesterton's close friend and biographer, Maisie Ward, refused to regard
the Rosary Queen as the patroness of World War II: "We often hear today
people who indignantly reject our duty to love our national enemies. Let
them repent, we are told. Until they do, hatred and destruction are our
duty—for they are evil incarnate. No man can, of course be evil incarnate: while any man lives, there is hope for repentance—but Our Lady did
not wait for repentance. She accepted, she loved the whole human race,
not excluding her Son's executioners. At the foot of the Cross she asked
for mercy for the merciless race of men." Maisie Ward, *The Splendour of
the Rosary*, with prayers by Caryll Houselander and with pictures by Fra
Angelico (New York: Sheed & Ward, 1945), 159.

32 Hanson, *Culture and Carnage*, 266. The lightweight Turkish and North
African ships were designed to raid coastal waters and to protect mer-
chant vessels, whereas the Christians had devised heavier sea craft bearing cannons that could launch a six-ounce ball for more than a mile's
distance. The Spaniards also employed harquebusier (heavy matchlock

guns) that could fire a two-pound ball four or five hundred yards, leaving the Ottoman warriors virtually helpless with their scimitars and arrows. "In addition to the six galleasses [large ships propelled by sails no less than oars], themselves originating from the abstract study of ship design dating back to Hellenistic Greece, and greater number of cannon and firearms, the Christians had rigged up steel boarding nets designed to protect their own galleys, as gunners targeted the enemy. Don Juan later claimed that thanks to his nets not a single Christian ship was boarded by the Ottomans" (Hanson, *Culture and Carnage*, 249).

33 Hanson, *Culture and Carnage*, 239.

34 Hanson, *Culture and Carnage*, 256, 270–71.

35 Chesterton, *Collected Poetry, Part 1*, 552, ellipsis in original.

36 Miguel de Cervantes Saavedra, *The Ingenious Hidalgo Don Quixote de la Mancha*, trans. John Rutherford (New York: Penguin, 2003), 536.

37 Fernando Cervantes, "Cervantes in Italy: Christian Humanism and the Visual Impact of Renaissance Rome," *Journal of the History of Ideas* 66, no. 3 (2005): 330.

38 Chesterton hailed St. Thomas More's diamond-like mind as having the power to cut glass, slicing "through things that seemed equally transparent, but were at once less solid and less many-sided." More had his own head severed because he cut through the lucid but idolatrous claim of Henry VIII that the state was not only the equal of the Church but actually took precedence over it. Chesterton also cites More's witty confidence in God as he requested help in ascending the gallows, while promising to shift for himself coming down. *The Well and the Shallows,* in *Collected Works of G. K. Chesterton*, vol. 3 (San Francisco: Ignatius, 1990), 506, 508.

Chesterton might have been less bloody-minded in writing *Lepanto* if he had recalled More's final instructions before his beheading: "If one would say that we may with good conscience wish an evil man harm lest he should do harm to other folk who are innocent and good, I will not now dispute upon that point, for that root has more branches to be well weighed and considered than I can now conveniently write (having no other pen than a coal). But truly will I give counsel to every good friend of mine that unless he be put in such a position as to punish an evil man in his charge by reason of his office, he should leave the desire of punishing to God and to such other folk who are so grounded in charity and so fast cleaved to God that no secretly malicious or cruel affection can creep in and undermine them under the cloak of a just and a virtuous zeal. But let us that are no better than men of a mean sort ever pray for such merciful amendment in other folk as our own conscience shows us that we have need of in ourselves." Saint Thomas More, "How to Treat Those Who Wrong Us," in *The Sadness of Christ, and Final Prayers and Instructions* (New York: Scepter, 1993), 142–43.

39 G. K. Chesterton, *Autobiography* (New York: Sheed & Ward, 1936), 257, 264.

40 *Collected Works of G. K. Chesterton*, vol. 29, *Illustrated London News 1911–1913* (San Francisco: Ignatius, 1988), 60.

41 Qtd. in John D. Coates, *G. K. Chesterton as Controversialist, Essayist, Novelist, and Critic* (Lewiston, Maine: Edwin Mellen, 2002), 9–10.

42 Nietzsche, *Thus Spake Zarathustra*, in *The Portable Nietzsche*, comp. and trans. Walter Kaufmann (New York: Viking, 1954), 160, 161, 163.

43 W. H. Auden noted the dubiety of Chesterton's reading of the European scene: "On the subject of international politics, Chesterton was, to put it mildly, unreliable. He seems to have believed that, in political life, there is a direct correlation between Faith and Morals: a Catholic State, holding the true faith, will behave better politically than a Protestant State. France, Austria, Poland were to be trusted: Prussia was not. . . . After [Prussia's] defeat in 1918, he continued to cling to his old belief so that, when Hitler came to power in 1933, he misread this as a Prussian phenomenon. In fact, aside from the economic conditions which enabled it to succeed, the National Socialist Movement was essentially the revenge of Catholic Bavaria and Austria for their previous subordination to Protestant Bismarckian Prussia. It was not an accident that Hitler was a lapsed Catholic. . . . Hitler himself hated the Prussian Junkers and was planning, if he won the war, to liquidate them all." W. H. Auden, "Chesterton's Non-Fictional Prose," in *Forewords and Afterwords*, comp. Edward Mendelson (New York: Random House, 1973), 402.

44 Thomas Mann made precisely the same argument about Germany, except in reverse. German *Kultur* represented, for him, the virile and adventurous heroism of the European future, while France typified the exhausted civilization created by the liberalism of the past. "Civilization he defined by the words *Vernunft, Aufklärung, Sanftheit, Geist* (reason, enlightenment, gentleness, spirit). *Kultur* he defined as 'a sublimation of the daemonic . . . a spiritual organization of the world . . . above morality, above reason, above science.' In a short poem of his own composition, Mann proclaimed that men deteriorate in peace, that law is a leveling force that only benefits the weak, and that war brings out strength." Gabriel Jackson, *Civilization and Barbarity in 20th Century Europe* (Amherst, N.Y.: Humanity Books, 1999), 42. Rainer Maria Rilke completely agreed: "In 'Fünf Gesänge' Rilke, the leading lyric poet in the language, celebrated the resurrection of the god of war rather than a symbol of weak-minded

peace." Stanley Weintraub, *Silent Night: The Story of the World War I Christ-mas Truce* (New York: Free Press, 2001), 3–4. Rilke later repudiated this early enthusiasm for the war.

45 Chesterton, *Autobiography*, 254.

46 Margaret Canovan, *G. K. Chesterton: Radical Populist* (New York: Harcourt Brace Jovanovich, 1977), 110.

47 The mass manufacturer of high-powered explosives imagined nothing akin to their actual use. "Perhaps my factories will put an end to war even sooner than your congresses," Alfred Nobel wrote in 1892 to Baroness Bertha von Suttner, his friend who had founded the European antiwar movement and who had recently attended the fourth World Peace Conference in Bern. "On the day when two army corps may mutually annihilate each other in a second, probably all civilized nations will recoil with horror and disband their troops." Qtd. in Nicholson Baker, *Human Smoke: The Beginnings of World War II and the End of Civilization* (New York: Simon & Schuster, 2008), 1.

48 Even when the war that was supposed to be finished in three months stretched toward the end of its second year, Chesterton still had no doubt that the children of Christian light were destroying the agents of demonic darkness: "I confess that for me personally there was never anything unexpected about the prolongation of the war. I never thought Hell an easy city to take. The only legitimate effect that prolongation can have is ratification. As it reveals link after link of the chain of enslavement these [Germans] have wound round the world, it adds reason upon reason for unwinding it to its last coil." G. K. Chesterton, *Collected Works of G. K. Chesterton*, vol. 30, *Illustrated London News 1914–1916* (San Francisco: Ignatius, 1988), 108.

49 The *Golden Legend* celebrates Barbara as a woman of striking beauty whose pagan father Dioscurus locked her in a tower in order to discourage unworthy suitors. Finding that she had become a Christian, her father sought to kill her, but she was miraculously delivered from his grasp. Furious, he turned her over to the Roman imperial authorities. Their torture having failed to make her recant, they ordered Dioscurus himself to execute her. When he did so, he was struck by a bolt of lightning that calcined him to ashes. "From the ninth century her cultus became very widely spread; because of her father's fate she was invoked against danger from lightning, and by an extension of this idea she later became patron of gunners and miners, and is regarded as patron by the artillery companies of many countries, including Great Britain. Her special emblem is a tower." Donald Attwater, "Barbara, Martyr," in *The Penguin Dictionary of Saints*, 2nd ed. (New York: Penguin, 1983), 54.

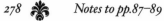

50 G. K. Chesterton, *Collected Poems of G. K. Chesterton* (New York: Dodd, Mead, 1932), 59, ellipsis in original.

51 G. K. Chesterton, "Arms and the Armistice," in *End of the Armistice*, 18–19.

52 Josef Pieper, in seeking to restore the lost importance of festivity in modern life, cites Roger Callois' contention that "in the present world it is . . . war that fulfills the function of the great festivals. In [latter-day] war, he says, all the attributes of festivals may be found (he considers festivals as essentially 'a time of excess'): the most drastic conversion and consumption of energies, the eruption of stored force, the merging of the individual in the totality, the squandering of resources ordinarily carefully husbanded, the wild breaking down of inhibitions—and so on." Pieper, *In Tune with the World: A Theory of Festivity*, trans. Richard and Clara Winston (South Bend, Ind.: St. Augustine's Press, 1999), 80.

53 The horrors of the First War shaped J. R. R. Tolkien's imagination even more decisively than Eliot's, perhaps because he was a combatant, as Chesterton and Eliot were not. Tolkien witnessed, firsthand, the awful futility and desolation of the Battle of the Somme. His memory of stepping onto the faces of rotting comrades submerged in the mud became the basis for "The Passage of the Marshes," a harrowing chapter in *The Lord of the Rings*. He may also have drawn upon his nightmarish memories in depicting the wasted landscape of Mordor: "The gasping pools were choked with ash and crawling muds, sickly white and grey, as if the mountains had vomited the filth of their entrails upon the lands about. High mounds of crushed and powdered rock, great cones of earth fireblasted and poison-stained, stood like an obscene graveyard in endless rows, slowly revealed in the reluctant light." Tolkien, *The Two Towers* (Boston: Houghton Mifflin, 1982), 239. Tolkien was no sort of pacifist, but he learned a lesson from the Great War that reappears throughout the *Rings* epic: it is virtually impossible to conquer an enemy such as Sauron without adopting his own evil tactics, and such "victory" becomes far worse than any defeat; hence the necessity of destroying rather than employing the One Ruling Ring.

54 Peter Taylor Forsyth, *The Justification of God: Lectures for War-Time on a Christian Theodicy* (1917; repr., London: Independent Press, 1957), 97. A British Catholic reviewer was also troubled that Chesterton's war poems, published in a collection from 1915, were wan and watery compared to the might of his religious poems, "The Church Militant" and "The Truce of Christmas." Katherine Brégy, "Straws—and Cannon Balls: Impressions of Some Recent Poetry and Drama," *Catholic World* 610 (1916): 471.

55 Chesterton, *Collected Poetry, Part 1*, 537–38.

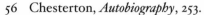

56 Chesterton, *Autobiography*, 253.

57 Chesterton, "Hiding an Earthquake," in *End of the Armistice*, 189. In this collection of late essays published after his death, GKC offered a clairvoyant prophecy of the strangling horror that approached Europe. He foresaw, for example, that Germany and Russia would become allies and that they would both crush Poland. Chesterton never denied that Christians have done monstrous things in the name of Christ, including war making of the worst kind. Yet he never confessed that, when Christians perpetrate such horrors, they violate fundamental Christian moral teaching. David Bentley Hart articulates the need for Christians to repent of such self-contradiction: "Christianity expressly forbids the various evils that have been done by Christians." Hart, *Atheist Delusions: The Christian Revolution and Its Fashionable Enemies* (New Haven, Conn.: Yale University Press, 2009), 13.

58 No mention of them appears in Chesterton's *Autobiography*. Instead, Chesterton was content to strike off witty lines, as when a lady supposedly asked him why he was not "out at the Front." He reportedly replied that, if she would view him from the side, she would discover that he was indeed "out at the front."

59 Wilfred Owen, *Wilfred Owen: War Poems and Others*, ed. Dominic Hibberd (London: Chatto & Windus, 1975), 79. Hibberd observes that Owen was hardly a Christian pacifist; on the contrary, he objected to what he perceived as Christ's "passivity" in the face of evil. In fact, Owen fought so valiantly that, only two months before his death, he was awarded the Military Cross. Yet Owen was temporarily unhinged when, in April 1917, "he took part in a successful attack on the village of Fayet and was in continuous action for twelve days, during which he was blown into the air by a shell and had to spend some days sheltering in a hole near the dismembered remains of a fellow-officer" (25). Though he eventually recovered from the resulting "shell-shock," as posttraumatic stress and nervous collapse were then called, Owen was haunted by war dreams for the remainder of his exceedingly brief life.

60 Tolkien regarded the noncommissioned officers of his company as raw youths forced to bear burdens that were meant, even at best, for seasoned adults. He thus describes certain members of Aragorn's army as being "unmanned" by their terror in preparing for the assault on the Black Gate of Mordor. It is noteworthy that, in clear contravention of pagan notions of courage, Tolkien has Aragorn show mercy toward those who had quailed. Like so many other war writers, Tolkien resorts to metaphors of nightmare to describe the piteous scene: "[T]hey walked like men in a

hideous dream made true, and they understood not this war nor why fate should lead them to such a pass." Tolkien, *The Return of the King* (Boston: Houghton Mifflin, 1982), 162.

61 Owen himself was killed less than a week before the armistice, on November 7, 1918. One of the many other ironies of the Great War is that it was the most sanitary of conflicts: "Generally speaking, the men lived in fear and boredom during the long months between infantry battles. They were well-clothed and well-fed, and hygiene was so much superior to that of past wars that, for the first time in history, more men were killed in wartime by bullets than by diseases." Jackson, *Civilization and Barbarity*, 38. Even so, there is no denying the squalor of the dugouts, on the German side as well as on the English: "Candle stubs lit the dripping, rotting sandbagged walls. Floors were foul-smelling, 'viscuous mush.' Sand-filled sacks hung from the ceilings not always successfully kept food from the reach of rats. Men deloused themselves by sizzling lice in the flame of a candle while others not so fortunate blew on their hands, seized rifles, and ascended for sentry duty. Relieved soldiers would stagger in, blinded by the candles, unbuckle and search for food." Weintraub, *Silent Night*, 2.

62 In his Ignatius Press edition of Part I of Chesterton's poetry, Aidan Mackey lists "The Truce of Christmas" as being from 1904, but he admits (in a personal conversation on August 3, 2009) that he offers only intelligent guesses about such dates, based as they are on the stages of GKC's handwriting, the condition of the manuscripts, etc.

63 Solemnity did not dominate all of the celebrations held up and down the line. There was a soccer match, for instance, in which "the Fritzes beat the Tommies 3–2. The Germans rolled barrels of beer across and swapped them for plum puddings. A German juggler entertained and a Tommy had his hair cut by a German barber." *The Christmas Reader*, comp. Godfrey Smith (Harmondsworth, UK: Penguin, 1986), 168.

64 Weintraub, *Silent Night*, 8.

65 *The Christmas Reader*, 169.

66 Chesterton is not sentimentally idealizing this scene. A German commander, Gustav Riebensahm, recalled it in almost exactly the same terms, as a sudden freeze turned the damp and dreary Niemandsland into "a hoarfrost of magic and beauty." Qtd. in Weintraub, *Silent Night*, 74.

67 Chesterton, *Collected Poetry, Part 1*, 181–82.

68 This was the precise position of Corporal Adolf Hitler concerning the English. Not only did he refuse to attend a chaplain's joint reading of the Christmas story to his unit in the cellar of the monastery at Messines; he vigorously opposed the truce itself. "Such a thing should not happen

in wartime," Hitler argued. "Have you no German sense of honor at all?" Weintraub, *Silent Night*, 71.

69 Chesterton is perhaps recalling the venerable English Christmas tradition that turned the social hierarchy upside down, as women and men would exchange roles, as a mere child would be declared bishop, and as a peasant or apprentice, acting as the "Lord of Misrule," would mock the Lord of the Manor by pretending to be an authentic "gentleman." Thus was the Magnificat given ritualized if also rowdy expression, for the mighty were indeed put down from their seat, while the meek and humble were exalted. Yet the celebration was not entirely symbolic: "Christmas was a time when peasants, servants, and apprentices exercised the right to demand that their wealthier neighbors and patrons treat them as if they were wealthy and powerful. The Lord of the Manor let the peasants in and feasted them. In return, the peasants offered something of true value . . . their *goodwill*." Stephen Nissenbaum, *The Battle for Christmas* (New York: Random House, 1996), 8–9, ellipsis and emphasis in original.

Chapter 4

1 It is significant that Huntington cites Dawson but not Chesterton as confirming his thesis about the basic religious kinship of the major civilizations. See Samuel P. Huntington, *The Clash of Civilizations and the Making of World Order* (New York: Simon & Schuster, 1996), 41, 47, emphasis in original.

2 Peter R. Demant observes the irony that while Islamism seems totally antimodern, it "grows in the most advanced Muslim countries—Egypt, Lebanon, Iraq, Iran, and Pakistan—where the dilemma of overlapping but incompatible collective identities is strongest, and where the impossibility of achieving a balance among them has been most painful. . . . [T]he failure of competing ideologies such as local patriotism, pan-Arabism, communism, and Western liberalism opened the door to radical religious alternatives." Demant, *Islam vs. Islamism: The Dilemma of the Muslim World* (New London, Conn.: Praeger, 2006), 193–94.

3 Huntington, *Clash of Civilizations*, 258, emphasis in original. In a footnote, Huntington remains adamant in defending his incendiary statement: "Quantitative evidence from every disinterested source demonstrates its validity."

4 Huntington, *Clash of Civilizations*, 33. Huntington uses "the West" as a metaphor for cultures that embrace modernization as against "the rest" that reject it, whereas Chesterton, of course, meant the Christian West versus its manifold pagan alternatives.

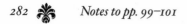

5   Hence the claim made by Chesterton's fictional character Evan MacIan: "The Church and the heresies always used to fight about words, because they are the only things worth fighting about." G. K. Chesterton, *The Ball and the Cross* (1910; repr., Mineola, N.Y.: Dover, 1995), 42.

6   G. K. Chesterton, *The Everlasting Man* (New York: Dodd, Mead, 1925), 361. Chesterton seems to ignore the profound indebtedness of both Thomas Aquinas and Moses Maimonides to the philosophical accomplishment of ibn-Sina (Avicenna). For fine treatments of the overlapping character of their work, see David B. Burrell's *Knowing the Unknowable God* (Notre Dame, Ind.: University of Notre Dame Press, 1986) as well as *Freedom and Creation in Three Traditions* (Notre Dame, Ind.: University of Notre Dame Press, 1993).

7   Hilaire Belloc, *The Great Heresies* (1938; repr., Manassas, Va.: Trinity Communications, 1987), 92, emphasis in original. Like Chesterton, Belloc regards the Crusades as "the major tragedy" of the West because they failed to confine Islam to Africa and Asia, thus allowing Muslims to establish a counter civilization as the "permanent rival" to Christianity. Like the Arians, the Muslims insist on the majestic unity of God at the expense of the Trinity. And like the Calvinists, they stress the omnipotence and omniscience of God without regard to human liberty. Such close but still deviant approximations of true Christianity prompt Belloc's dire prophecy: Islam "is, as a fact, the most formidable and persistent enemy which our civilization has had, and may at any moment become as large a menace in the future as it has been in the past" (66).

8   It is appropriate, I believe, to regard *The New Jerusalem* as Chesterton's deliberate compliment to Belloc's great book, *The Path to Rome*. G. K. Chesterton, *The New Jerusalem* (1920; repr., Champaign, Ill.: Book Jungle, 2007).

9   Chesterton, *New Jerusalem*. All references are to this printing and are indicated NJ.

10 I use the word *civilization* to entail the symbiotic interweaving of religion and politics through the formal establishment of a religious state or a state religion. Athens, Rome, and medieval Christendom are the obvious Western examples. The anthropologist Clifford Geertz defines culture, by contrast, as "an historically transmitted pattern of meanings embodied in symbols." These symbols are instantiated in the customs and the arts, the social institutions, and the technical achievements of a particular social group. Christian culture and Christian civilization are not coterminous. A Christian culture can exist within a non- or even an anti-Christian civilization. This is the condition in which the contemporary Church finds itself. As we shall see, Pope Benedict calls for the creation of a vigorous Christian

culture that might enhance the Church's witness to the pagan civilization of modern Europe and, increasingly, of modern America as well.

11   Strictly speaking, the word *paganism* is a Christian term usually applied to the non-Abrahamic religions, including ancient religions that may have preceded them.

12   As usual, Chesterton cares more about the truthfulness of legend than the accuracy of facts. The cave site of the Nativity was first "identified" by Justin Martyr, the second-century apologist. Begun perhaps in 326 by Constantine's mother, St. Helena, the Church of the Nativity was erected on a preexisting sacred site devoted to Adonis. It was destroyed in a Samaritan revolt during the sixth century and then rebuilt by Emperor Justinian around 529. The only remaining artifacts from the Constantinian era are the floor mosaics discovered in 1934. Yet these mere "data" do not deter GKC from probing the ultimate wonder of the star and the kings and the Light illumining the pagan darkness. As in our own time, so did the ancient darkness seem quite enlightened, though it was bound to the ever-repetitive, ever-circling wheel of cosmic necessity—an inversion of the late modern notion that we inhabit an entirely accidental, unsponsored, unguided universe.

13   Though Chesterton applauds the sign of the double eagle which signified the Christian *imperium* of both Byzantium and Rome, he has little regard for the Christian East as it subsequently developed: "In the East the continuity of culture has only been interrupted by negative things that Islam has done. In the West it has been interrupted by positive things that Christendom itself has done. In the West the past of Christendom has its perspective blocked up by its own creations; in the East it is a true perspective of interminable corridors, with round Byzantine arches and proud Byzantine pillars. That, I incline to fancy, is the real difference that a man come from the west of Europe feels in the east of Europe, it is a gap or void. . . . In the East the civilisation [of Byzantine-Roman Christianity] lived on, or if you will, lingered on; in the West it died and was reborn" (NJ, 142–43).

14   G. K. Chesterton, *The Common Man* (New York: Sheed & Ward, 1950), 275.

15   Charles Norris Cochrane, *Christianity and Classical Culture: A Study of Thought and Action from Augustus to Augustine* (New York: Oxford University Press, 1957), 113.

16   The work of John Howard Yoder is the most obvious instance; see *The Politics of Jesus* (Grand Rapids: Eerdmans, 1972).

17   This anti-Augustinian incorporation of society into the Church was to cause much mischief in the future, especially when it got turned upside

down in the modern notion of the independence of society from the Church. A misinterpretation of Luther's doctrine of the two kingdoms led to the notion that there are two autonomous "orders of creation," the sacred and the secular, so that life in one sphere can be utterly independent of the other. That Nazis of both Catholic and Protestant persuasion took heedless advantage of this division is not surprising.

18 Qtd. in Barry A. Harvey, *Another City: An Ecclesiological Primer for a Post-Christian World* (Harrisburg, Pa.: Trinity International, 1999), 24. That Christians "do not expose their offspring" was a key disjunction between the early Church and the late Roman Empire. Already by the end of the first century, the *Didache* ("The Teaching of the Twelve Apostles") commanded Christians that "you shall not murder a child by abortion nor kill that which is born." Hence the legitimacy of Harvey's large claim: "In general, the members of this other city expected to experience [the goods and hardships of life] in ways that were largely indistinguishable from those of their fellow subjects in the empire. Nevertheless, their identity as citizens of another *res publica* made them different, noticeably different, from their neighbors, for they saw themselves as constituting the mission sent to represent the one whom they worshiped as Lord and God" (Harvey, *Another City*, 26).

19 Augustine, *Concerning the City of God against the Pagans*, trans. Henry Bettenson (Baltimore: Penguin, 1972), XVIII, 54, 842.

20 "The Moslem had been checked," Chesterton adds, in Spain and France, "but he had not been checked enough. The whole story of what was called the Eastern Question, and three-quarters of the wars of the modern world, were due to the fact that he was not checked enough" (NJ, 174). Vartan Gregorian agrees that the Crusades had a huge enervating effect on Christendom, but far more decisively in the East than the West: "The Crusades rapidly degenerated into intra-Christian wars, for Europeans were just as eager to seize and plunder the lands of Christian Byzantium as the Muslim Turks had been. It is ironic that in doing so, the Christian West set the stage for the eventual collapse of the Byzantine empire and its loss to the Ottoman Turks" (Gregorian, *Islam: A Mosaic, Not a Monolith* [Washington, D.C.: Brookings Institution, 2003], 33).

21 Gregorian, *Islam*, 2, 112.

22 "In the space of a single decade [Muhammad] fought eight major battles, led eighteen raids, and planned another thirty-eight military operations where others were in command but operating under his orders and strategic direction. Wounded twice, he also twice experienced having his positions overrun by superior forces before he managed to turn

the tables on his enemies and rally his men to victory. More than a great field general and tactician, he was also a military theorist, organizational reformer, strategic thinker, operational-level combat commander, political-military leader, heroic soldier, and revolutionary. . . . He reportedly spent hours devising tactical and political stratagems, and once remarked that 'all war is cunning,' reminding modern analysts of Sun Tzu's dictum, 'all war is deception.' In his thinking and application of force Muhammad was a combination of Carl von Clausewitz and Niccolò Machiavelli, for he always employed force in the service of political goals. An astute grand strategist, he used nonmilitary methods (alliance building, political assassination, bribery, religious appeals, mercy, and calculated butchery) to strengthen his long-term position, sometimes even at the expense of short-term military considerations. Muhammad's belief in Islam and his own role as the 'Messenger of God' revolutionized Arabian warfare and resulted in the creation of the ancient world's first army motivated by a coherent system of ideological belief." Richard A. Gabriel, "Muhammad: The Warrior Prophet," *Military History Quarterly* 19, no. 4 (2007), www .historynet.com/muhammad-the-warrior-prophet.htm.

23   Chesterton, *Everlasting Man*, 319–20, emphasis in original.

24   In "The Sultan," an essay written roughly at the same time as *The Flying Inn*, Chesterton vituperates against the empty-headedness of Cecil Rhodes for helping to create the moral and religious vacancy that Eastern ideas could easily occupy: "For that very governing class which urges Occidental imperialism has been deeply discoloured with Oriental mysticism and Cosmology." He actually quotes Rhodes concerning the role he envisioned for himself in South Africa: "'It is inevitable fate that all this should be changed; and I should like to be the agent of fate.' This was Cecil Rhodes' one small genuine idea; and it is an Oriental idea." Chesterton, *A Miscellany of Men* (1912; repr., Philadelphia: Dufour, 1969), 135. Lord Ivywood will utter similar sentiments in *The Flying Inn*.

25   Vartan Gregorian describes the phenomenal growth of Islam as eastward no less than westward: "Within less than a century of Islam's birth [in 622], the Muslim community had grown by conquest into one of the largest empires ever—one that lasted longer and, indeed, was bigger than the Roman Empire. By 712, Muslim conquests extended from the Pyrenees to the Himalayas, from the Iberian Peninsula in the west to the Indus Valley and Central Asia in the east." Gregorian, *Islam*, 11.

26   "And slay them [i.e., unbelievers] wherever ye find them, and drive them out of the places whence they drove you out, for persecution [of Muslims] is worse than slaughter [of nonbelievers] . . . and fight them until

persecution is no more, and religion is for Allah [i.e., until all have become Muslim]" (Qur'an 2:191-93).

27   John L. Esposito, *Islam: The Straight Path*, expanded ed. (New York: Oxford University Press, 1991), 54. As the future biographer of Thomas Aquinas, Chesterton might have been expected to hail the Muslims for preserving not only the texts but also the thought of Aristotle, without which the Angelic Doctor could hardly have become the greatest theologian of the medieval Church.

28   G. K. Chesterton, *Orthodoxy* (1908; repr., San Francisco: Ignatius, 1995), 145.

29   In an infamous lecture delivered at the University of Virginia in 1933, T. S. Eliot similarly extolled the need for religious and ethnic uniformity in a so-called Christian civilization: "The population should be homogeneous; where two or more cultures exist in the same place they are likely either to be fiercely self-conscious or both to become adulterate. What is still more important is unity of religious background; and reasons of race and religion combine to make any large number of free-thinking Jews undesirable" (Eliot, *After Strange Gods: A Primer of Modern Heresy* [New York: Harcourt Brace, 1934], 20). Eliot later repudiated these sentiments and withdrew his book from further publication.

30   G. K. Chesterton, *Collected Works of G. K. Chesterton*, vol. 29, *Illustrated London News 1911–1913* (San Francisco: Ignatius, 1988), 184. Chesterton's judgments here are not true in the strict sense. The Qur'an forbids only the worship of images made to serve as idols. Islam shares the Jewish prohibition against graven images of God, and the *hadiths*—the later collection of Muhammad's words and deeds—show him as opposed to images. The tradition thus developed that painters and sculptors wrongly seek to supplant God's own creativity. Even so, images pervade Islamic culture: "Depictions of the Prophet are . . . found in accounts of his life. . . . Palaces were sometimes rife with figurative work in statuary and wall-paintings. Books were illustrated chiefly for princes and the well-to-do . . . representation extended through textiles, metalwork and pottery to the possessions of other levels of society." Barbara Brend, *Islamic Art* (London: British Museum Press, 1991), 19.

31   Rémi Brague, "Sin No More," *American Spectator* 41, no. 4 (2008): 28–35. As a professor of Arabic philosophy at the Sorbonne, Brague is no culture warrior in behalf of "the West against the rest." In fact, he has devised an acerbic term for those who advocate Christianity for mere instrumentalist reasons—namely, as a means for underwriting Western civilization, not as a Faith valued for its distinctive mission and absolute claims. As the mirror image of Islamists, Brague calls such pseudo-believers "Christianists."

"I would like to remind them," Brague explains, "that Christianity is not interested in itself. It's interested in Christ. And Christ is also not interested in His own self. He is interested in God, whom He calls in a unique way 'Father.' And in man, to whom He proposes a new access to God." "Christians and 'Christianists,'" an interview with Rémi Brague by Gianni Valente in *30Days* (October 2004): 2, http://www.30giorni.it/us/articolo.asp?id=5332.

32 This was also Charles Williams' chief objection to Islam, as C. S. Lewis explains: "Islam denies the Incarnation. It will not allow that God has descended into flesh or that Manhood has been exalted into Deity. It is [what Williams called]

the sharp curved line of the Prophet's blade
that cuts the Obedience from the Obeyed.

"[Islam] stands for all religions that are afraid of matter and afraid of mystery, for all misplaced reverences and misplaced purities that repudiate the body and shrink back from the glowing materialism of the Grail. It stands for what Williams called 'heavy morality'—the ethics of sheer duty and obedience against the shy yet (in the long run) shameless acceptance of heaven's courtesies flowing from the 'homely and courteous lord.'" Charles Williams and C. S. Lewis, *Arthurian Torso* (Grand Rapids: Eerdmans, 1974), 308.

33 John Coates, "The Philosophy and Religious Background of *The Flying Inn*," *Chesterton Review* 12, no. 3 (1986): 315. Coates also observes that Chesterton composed the novel during one of the darkest periods of his life. Chesterton had become disillusioned with the "New Liberalism" of Asquith and Lloyd George, who were enriching themselves at public expense. When his brother Cecil sought to expose the corruption, he was brought to trial on charges of criminal libel and barely escaped imprisonment. Chesterton was also in such ill health that he nearly died in the winter of 1914–1915. The failure of the *Daily News*—the paper with which GKC had been closely associated for more than a decade—to pursue the malfeasances of the Liberal government led to Chesterton's painful and permanent break with the journal. And for the first and last time in his entire life, his drinking went virtually unchecked. That *The Flying Inn* remains such an amusing book, despite its disjointedness, is remarkable: "If the reader contrasts the degree of that unhappiness known from other sources [with] the text of the novel, the extent of Chesterton's intellectual control and his capacity for aesthetic distances seem both amazing and admirable." John Coates, "Malaise at the Heart of *The Flying Inn*," *Seven: An Anglo American Literary Review* 8 (1987): 27.

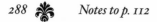

34 Perhaps the funniest figure in the novel is the journalist Hibbs However, a man who, as his name indicates, muddles everything with endless qualifiers. "If modern journalists have to state unpopular and unpleasant truths," Chesterton wrote in 1907, "if they have to admit something which does not fit in with the policy of their paper, they can always cloud the question with a swarm of bewildering conjunctions. Despite this, nevertheless that, and considering the third, consequently the other . . . until the brain of the reader reels under the mere number of parenthetical sentences. . . ." *Collected Works of G. K. Chesterton*, vol. 27, *Illustrated London News 1905–1907* (San Francisco: Ignatius, 1986), 519.

Chesterton's novel also takes witty swipes at sundry other evils, including the commercializing of food by grocers who, in marketing canned vegetables and fruits as well as ales and wines, encourage the Brits to sup solitarily at home rather than communally at their local inn. Hence Humphrey Pump's "Song against Grocers":

"God made the wicked Grocer,
    For a mystery and a sign,
That men might shun the awful shops,
    And go to inns to dine;
Where the bacon's on the rafter
And the wine is in the wood,
And God that made good laughter
    Has seen that they are good."

. . .

"The hell-instructed Grocer
    Has a temple made of tin,*   *a teetotalist chapel
And the ruin of good inn-keepers
    Is loudly urged therein;
But now the sands are running out
    From sugar* of a sort,   *perhaps for making rum
The grocer trembles; for his time
    Just like his weight is short." (FI, 72–73)

G. K. Chesterton, *The Flying Inn* (1914; repr., Mineola, N.Y.: Dover, 2001). All references to the novel are taken from this printing and are indicated by FI.

35 Lady Joan Brett, the woman whom Ivywood is seeking to convert to his new philosophy, wisely replies, "But perhaps the breaking of barriers might be the breaking of everything."

36 Coates notes that Nietzsche's work was first mediated to the Anglophone world, quite accurately, by A. R. Orage, a British intellectual and theosophist who, in 1908, had invited Chesterton to lecture at the Leeds Art

Club (Coates, "Philosophy and Religious Background," 311). In a passage reminiscent of Lord Ivywood's boast, Orage cites the three successive metamorphoses of the human animal (as Camel, Lion, and Child) that Nietzsche envisions in *Thus Spake Zarathustra*: "It is evident that the spirit of man is now only at the Camel stage. Man is a beast of burden. But, as one by one the camels are laden and go into the solitary desert, they become transformed into lions. And Nietzsche's description of his coming race of philosophers is 'laughing lions.' But the Superman is the child. In his nature all the wild forces of the lion are instinctive. He will not seek wisdom, for he will be wise." Orage, *Friedrich Nietzsche: The Dionysian Spirit of the Age* (Chicago: Lippincott, 1911), 74.

37 As his name suggests, Crooke clandestinely operates a pharmacy that is in fact a grog shop where legislators can purchase and consume alcohol when they have left off their legislative work of denying the same privilege to ordinary people. It was such gross injustice favoring the rich against the poor that Chesterton found most outrageous in Prohibition. He regarded it as a sanitized version of slavery, since wealthy owners and manufacturers were willing for their workmen to take exercise and have leisure, yet only in order that they might become more proficient workers. "But they are not in any way willing that workmen should have fun; for fun only increases the happiness and not the utility of the worker. Fun is freedom; and in that sense is an end in itself. It concerns the man not as a worker but as a citizen, or even as a soul; and the soul in that sense is an end in itself. That a man shall have a reasonable amount of comedy and poetry and even fantasy in his life is part of his spiritual health, which is for the service of God; and not merely for his mechanical health, which is now bound to the service of man. The very test adopted [i.e., Prohibition] has all the servile implication; the test of what we can get out of him, instead of the test of what he can get out of life." G. K. Chesterton, *What I Saw in America* (New York: Dodd, Mead, 1922), 146.

38 N. T. Wright, *Simply Christian: Why Christianity Makes Sense* (San Francisco: Harper, 2006), 65–66.

39 Among our nature poets, perhaps Wordsworth best evokes this Presence, especially in the sonnet "It Is a Beauteous Evening" as well as the following passage from "The Stolen Boat." The youthful speaker, his conscience stricken because of his thievery, rows with "troubled pleasure" until a "rocky Steep" rises up suddenly on the evening skyline, only to be followed by the appearance of something far more awesome and arraigning and inescapable. His guilt thus becomes not merely subjective and imaginary but objective and real. As the speaker oars desperately away

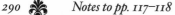

from the gigantic peak, the more fully it comes into view, and thus the larger the Presence looms:

> When from behind that craggy Steep, till then
> The bound of the horizon, a huge Cliff,
> As if with voluntary power instinct,
> Uprear'd its head. I struck, and struck again,
> And, growing still in stature, the huge Cliff
> Rose up between me and the stars, and still,
> With measur'd motion, like a living thing,
> Strode after me.

Wordsworth: Selected Poems, ed. H. M. Margoliouth (London: Collins, 1959), 86.

40 Max Beerbohm wrote GKC to commend the novel and its poems: "I think *The Flying Inn* is quite one of the very best of all your things. I constantly—though melodiously—sing snatches from the songs that are there." Beerbohm, "An Endearing Invitation: Max Beerbohm to G. K. Chesterton," http://vitalsignsblog.blogspot.com/2010/09/endearing-invitation-max-beerbohm-to-gk.html.

41 See the appendix to this chapter.

42 *Collected Works of G. K. Chesterton*, vol. 27, *Illustrated London News 1905–1907*, 75–76. Chesterton wished that the local public house might be frequented in the same way as are the post office and the railway station: "[I]f all types of people passed through it for all types of refreshment, you would have the same safeguard against a man behaving in a disgusting way in a tavern that you have at present against his behaving in a disgusting way in a post-office: simply the presence of his ordinary sensible neighbors. In such a place the kind of lunatic who wants to drink an unlimited number of whiskies would be treated with the same severity with which the Post Office authorities would treat an amiable lunatic who had an appetite for licking an unlimited number of stamps. . . . At least, the postmistress would not dangle a strip of tempting sixpenny stamps before the enthusiast's eyes as he was being dragged away with his tongue out" (446–47).

43 Chesterton does not sanction drunkenness—at least not when it affects others. On the contrary, he laments the vice of overindulgence in this song by Dalroy:

> "As for all the windy waters,
> They were rained like trumpets down,
> When good drink had been dishonoured
>   By the tipplers of the town.
> When red wine had brought red ruin,
>   And the death-dance of our times,

> Heaven sent us Soda Water
> As a torment for our crimes." (FI, 224)

44 Josef Pieper, *In Tune with the World: A Theory of Festivity,* trans. Richard and Clara Winston (South Bend, Ind.: St. Augustine's Press, 1999), 30, emphasis in original.

45 Pieper, *In Tune,* 71.

46 *Collected Works of G. K. Chesterton,* vol. 27, *Illustrated London News 1905–1907,* 445. Hence GKC's splendid aphorisms on the subject: "The dipsomaniac and the abstainer are not only both mistaken, but they both make the same mistake. They both regard wine as a drug and not as a drink." *Collected Works of G. K. Chesterton,* vol. 11, *Plays, Chesterton on Shaw* (San Francisco: Ignatius, 1986), 384. "Drink because you are happy, but never because you are miserable. Never drink when you are wretched without it, . . . but drink when you would be happy without it." G. K. Chesterton, *Heretics* (1905; repr., London: Bodley Head, 1960), 99.

47 It is almost impossible to overemphasize the Christian devotion to bodily life, even when, with St. Paul, it is being pummeled into subjection. That the soul is the form of the body is no idle Christian claim, as Hilaire Belloc makes clear: "[E]very pleasure I know comes from an intimate union between my body and my very human mind, which last receives, confirms, revives and can summon up what my body has experienced." Belloc, *The Path to Rome* (1902; repr., Washington, D.C.: Regnery Gateway, 1987), 118.

48 Chesterton praises George MacDonald as a Scots Calvinist who, miraculously, developed a sacramental imagination that made him akin to the holy man of Assisi: "In his particular type of literary work he did indeed realise the apparent paradox of a St. Francis of Aberdeen, seeing the same sort of halo round every flower and bird. It is not the same thing as any poet's appreciation of the beauty of the flower or bird. A heathen can feel that and remain heathen, or in other words, remain sad. It is a certain special sense of significance, which the tradition that most values it calls sacramental. To have got back to it, or forward to it, at one bound of boyhood, out of the Black Sabbath of a Calvinist town, was a miracle of imagination." G. K. Chesterton, "Introduction" to Greville MacDonald, *George MacDonald and His Wife* (London: George Allen & Unwin, 1924), republished in *Chesterton Review* 27, nos. 1–2 (2001): 7.

49 This isn't to say, of course, that analogies are never misleading, much less exhaustive. Metaphors are especially dangerous, Chesterton observes, because of what they omit—as in the familiar phrase "the ship of state." "To sail on the sea is a special departure and adventure even to seamen.

To live in a community is the only imaginable life for men. Life in a community covers the whole of a man's life; therefore life in a community must allow him a liberty and relaxation not allowable on a ship. A man in a community is like a man in a house that is his own. A man on a ship is a man in a house on fire. He must observe special discipline and promptitude because the situation is exceptional." *Collected Works of G. K. Chesterton*, vol. 27, *Illustrated London News 1905–1907*, 129.

50 Perhaps he also knew that he could not improve on Belloc's memorable "Heroic Poem in Praise of Wine," especially its final lines:

> But when the hour of mine adventure's near
> Just and benignant, let my youth appear
> Bearing a Chalice, open, golden, wide,
> With benediction graven on its side.
> So touch my dying lip: so bridge that deep:
> So pledge my waking from the gift of sleep,
> And, sacramental, raise me the Divine:
> Strong brother in God and last companion, Wine.

Hilaire Belloc: An Anthology of His Prose and Verse, comp. W. N. Roughead (New York: J. B. Lippincott, 1951), 20.

51 Chesterton, *Orthodoxy*, 42.

52 G. K. Chesterton, *Collected Works of G. K. Chesterton*, vol. 15, *Charles Dickens* (San Francisco: Ignatius, 1989), 208–9.

53 As young lovers, they had actually used a secret tunnel at Ivywood Hall as their trysting place. Still vying for Joan Brett's love many years later, Dalroy sings one of Chesterton's most affecting love lyrics near the end of the novel. Though he is hidden in the darkness below the high turreted window whence Dalroy's Juliet once listened to her Romeo, there is no Iago-like suspicion about this Desdemona's fallen handkerchief. The poem is imbued instead with a quiet Augustinian reminder that romantic love must also be ordered to the Love that lies beyond this life, so that it might embrace greater goods than contentment and delight:

> "Lady, the light is dying in the skies,
> Lady, and let us die when honour dies,
> Your dear, dropped glove was like a gauntlet flung,
>   When you and I were young.
> For something more than splendour stood; and ease was not the
>   only good
> About the woods in Ivywood when you and I were young.
>
> "Lady, the stars are falling pale and small,
> Lady, we will not live if life be all

Forgetting those good stars in heaven hung
    When all the world was young,
For more than gold was in a ring, and love was not a little thing
Between the trees in Ivywood when all the world was young."

               (FI, 314)

54 "The fairy tales said that the prince and princess lived happily ever after-wards: and so they did. They lived happily, although it is very likely that from time to time they threw the furniture at each other. Most marriages, I think, are happy marriages; but there is no such thing as a contented marriage. The whole pleasure of marriage is that it is a perpetual crisis." G. K. Chesterton, "Introduction to *David Copperfield*," in *Collected Works of G. K. Chesterton*, vol. 15, *Charles Dickens*, 333. "If Americans can be divorced for 'incompatibility of temper' I cannot conceive why they are not all divorced. I have known many happy marriages, but never a compatible one. The whole aim of marriage is to fight through and survive the instant when incompatibility becomes unquestionable. For a man and a woman, as such, are incompatible." G. K. Chesterton, *What's Wrong with the World*, in *Collected Works of G. K. Chesterton*, vol. 5 (San Francisco: Ignatius, 1986), 67–68.

Chapter 5

1 G. K. Chesterton, *Collected Works of G. K. Chesterton*, vol. 28, *Illustrated London News 1908–1910* (San Francisco: Ignatius, 1987), 194.

2 Chesterton, *The Everlasting Man* (New York: Dodd, Mead, 1925), 314.

3 This is not to deny that Chesterton had scorching things to say about such spurious modern notions "as that law is above right, or right outside reason, or things are only as we think them, or everything is relative to a reality that is not there." G. K. Chesterton, *Heretics* (1905; repr., London: Bodley Head, 1960), 146.

4 Qtd. in Kristen Deede Johnson, *Theology, Political Theory, and Pluralism* (New York: Cambridge University Press, 2007), 15.

5 All quotations from "A Letter Concerning Toleration" are taken from William Popple's 1689 translation of Locke's Latin original, *Epistola de Tolerantia*, http://www.constitution.org/jl/tolerati.htm. Voltaire translated it into French five years later, though not without showing his witty contempt for religion: "[England] is the country of sects. An Englishman, as a freeman, goes to Heaven by whatever road he pleases."

6 Thomas Jefferson agreed. "The legitimate powers of government," he would add a century later, "extend to such acts only as are injurious to others. But it does me no injury for my neighbor to say that there are

twenty Gods, or no God. It neither picks my pocket nor breaks my leg." "Notes on Virginia" (1782), www.nobeliefs.com/jefferson.htm.

7 Locke's thin notion of natural law has but faint resemblance to its rich medieval counterpart. Hence Lord Herbert of Cherbury's minimalist Lockean formulation of the five reasonable propositions that, according to him, all people of all times have held, without regard to race or religion, except when obscured by the distortions and accretions of so-called revealed truth: (1) that God exists, (2) that he ought to be worshipped, (3) that virtue and piety are the chief part of worship, (4) that there must be repentance for crimes and vices, (5) that there are rewards and punishments in the life to come based on the ways we have acquitted ourselves in this earthly life.

8 Locke denies even this authority to the churches, regarding them as purely voluntary organizations whose sovereignty resides solely in their individual members, not in their ministers or deacons, their presbyters or vestry, much less in their bishops and prelates who represent the authority of Christ himself. This Lockean doctrine led to much mischief in America. The principle of religious freedom, originally intended to protect the churches from the predations of the state, *was made to apply to the churches themselves.* Just as the state cannot mandate religious belief and practice, so it was argued that the churches could not require ethical and theological norms of their own members! Hence the gradual development of the risible idea of Christian freedom as believing and behaving however one wishes—whether, for example, as Unitarians in belief or snake-handlers in practice. This, despite the fact that every Christian body since the inception of the Church has held to basic requirements in both doctrines and deeds, whether they be formulated in creeds or covenants or other means of common affirmation.

9 Williams, the Separatist-turned-Baptist-turned-Seeker, is often regarded as the earliest advocate of American religious tolerance and thus of religious freedom of conscience. It is certainly true that Williams was ejected from Massachusetts and that he founded Rhode Island because he repudiated the Puritan insistence that the state exercise control over matters of Christian belief by punishing those who failed to conform. On the contrary, he held that governments must protect their citizens against any outward and bodily compulsion in religious matters. Yet Williams was no Jeffersonian advocate of religious equality, as if Christianity were one faith among others: "With a low opinion of the efficacy of human reason, his goal was not freedom of thought for its own sake: he did not think that one way of seeking God was as good as another. He wanted freedom

because it was the only way to reach the true God. Although few men would reach Him at best, only freedom of conscience would bring them to Him, because Christ had forsworn the use of force. And history had demonstrated, to Williams at least, that force always favored false religion." Edmund S. Morgan, *Roger Williams: The Church and the State* (New York: Norton, 1967), 141.

10 Harvey adds that when such secular institutions were eventually unified "with the ecclesiastical institutions of Protestantism," they then constituted "the goalless rationality embodied in the commercial republic of liberal democratic capitalism." Barry A. Harvey, "Re-Envisioning the Wall of Separation, or One and a Half Cheers for Secularization: Toward an Ecclesial Identity after Christendom" (unpublished essay)

11 For Christians (and others) rightly to order their loyalties so as not to make the nation-state into the supreme object of allegiance is no idle matter, as Karl Barth declared in his first lectures after returning to the post-war rubble of Bonn, the university from which the Nazis had ousted him: "A nation which . . . chooses itself and makes itself the basis and measure of everything—such a nation must sooner or later collide with the truly chosen people of God. In the proclamation of the idea of such an elect nationality, even before anti-Semitism is expressed, there is already involved a basic denial of Israel and therewith a denial of Jesus Christ and therefore, finally, of God himself. *Anti-Semitism is the form of godlessness beside which, what is usually called atheism . . . is quite innocuous.* For in anti-Semitic godlessness realities are involved irrespective of whether those who invented and worked this business were aware of them or not." Karl Barth, *Dogmatics in Outline* (New York: Harper & Row, 1959), 77, emphasis added.

12 I borrow this term from the late James Wm. McClendon, who held that Christians should welcome the pluralism that allows them to make their best case, both in deed and word, within the context of other competing metanarratives, including the case that God's self-identification in the Jews and Jesus and the Church is the world's one true Story—final, definitive, unsurpassable.

13 William T. Cavanaugh, "The City: Beyond Secular Parodies," in *Radical Orthodoxy*, ed. John Milbank, Catherine Pickstock, and Graham Ward (New York: Routledge, 1999), 191, 189, 190, 192. The rise of the modern nation-state is premised on the elevation of these isolated and autonomous individuals who are defined largely by their accumulation of privately owned goods. As essentially propertied creatures, individuals have relation to each other primarily by means of self-protecting contracts. These contracts have a temporal duration, moreover, even as they are contingent upon

the agreement of the contracting parties. Contracts can also be dissolved by limiting clauses or by mutual consent. No longer is there an unbreakable bond that unites the entire body politic in devotion to common ends. "It is not surprising," declares Cavanaugh, "that . . . Descartes placed 'among the [antique] excesses all of the promises by which one curtails something of one's freedom,' that Milton wrote a treatise on divorce, or that Kant condemned the covenants that bind one's descendants" (190).

14 See http://www.law.cornell.edu/supct/html/91-744.ZS.html. Consider, by contrast, Abraham Lincoln's sharp riposte to Stephen Douglas' insistence that Southerners should have the right to choose slavery if they so wished and so voted: "No one has the right to choose to do what is so fundamentally wrong." Qtd. in Wilson D. Miscamble, C.S.C., *Keeping the Faith, Making a Difference* (Notre Dame, Ind.: Ave Maria, 2000), 100.

15 This argument is made most convincingly by Michael Sandel in *Democracy's Discontents: America in Search of a Public Philosophy* (Cambridge, Mass.: Harvard University Press, 1996).

16 The epistemological results have been no less devastating, as the feminist political theorist Wendy Brown reveals: "[T]hat which is most vital to individuals qua individuals—personal belief or conscience—is not only that which is divorced from public life but that which is divorced from shared Truth. Tolerance of diverse beliefs in a community becomes possible to the extent that those beliefs are phrased as having no public importance; as being constitutive of a private individual whose private beliefs and commitments have minimal bearing on the structure and pursuits of political, social, or economic life; and as having no reference to settled common epistemological authority." Wendy Brown, *Regulating Aversion: Tolerance in the Age of Identity and Empire* (Princeton, N.J.: Princeton University Press, 2006), 32.

17 Alasdair MacIntyre argues that, precisely because the contemporary state cannot be "evaluatively neutral . . . it cannot be generally trusted to promote any worthwhile set of values, including those of autonomy and liberty." MacIntyre, "Toleration and the Goods of Conflict," in *The Tasks of Philosophy: Selected Essays on Ethics and Politics*, vol. 2 (New York: Cambridge University Press, 2006), 213–14.

18 Jeff Polet reminds me that keen political prudence must be exercised in the practice of hospitality, since it is also our Christian duty to protect the innocent. This means that the Church itself must remain the locus of such prudential judgments as well as the place where aliens and enemies are welcomed.

19 Among the most helpful studies of hospitality, I have relied primarily on the work of my former student, Elizabeth Newman, *Untamed Hospitality:*

Welcoming God and Other Strangers (Grand Rapids: Brazos, 2007). The works of Mennonite peacemakers in contemporary Iraq and Palestine and Israel are examples of such Christian hospitality. They live in the midst of Muslim and Jewish groups that are hostile not only to each other but also to Christians, offering them both shelter and friendship, thus demonstrating "a more excellent way."

20 Lest anyone fear that Chesterton is engaged in mere metaphor and trope, consider this altogether typical claim: "That the duel kills seems to me a comparatively trifling matter; football and fox-hunting and the London hospitals frequently do that. The only rational objection to the duel is that it invokes a most painful and sanguinary proceeding in order to settle a question, and does not settle it." Chesterton, "The Patriotic Idea," *Chesterton Review* 30, nos. 3–4 (2004): 229.

21 All quotations from *The Ball and the Cross* are taken from the Dover edition (1909; repr., Mineola, N.Y.: 1995) and are documented within the text as BC.

22 Alison Milbank, *Chesterton and Tolkien as Theologians: The Fantasy of the Real* (London: T&T Clark, 2007), 33.

23 Once again, Chesterton exhibits his orthodoxy, refusing any dualist notion of Satan as set over against Christ. The negative and entirely derivative character of evil means that Christians refuse to attribute divinity to the Devil. All of the Church's creeds affirm *Credo in Deus*, none affirms *Credo in Diabolus*. Hence C. S. Lewis' Chestertonian claim that Satan's adversarial opposite is not Christ but the archangel Michael. C. S. Lewis, *The Screwtape Letters* (New York: Simon & Schuster, 1996), 6.

24 G. K. Chesterton, "A Defence of Farce," in *The Defendant* (1901; repr., London: J. M. Dent, 1940), 124–25. Chesterton makes the surprising claim that, while "black and catastrophic" pain attracts the immature artist, "joy is a far more elusive and elvish matter, since it is our reason for existing, and a very feminine reason; it mingles with every breath we draw and every cup of tea we drink." Precisely because joy remains largely unrecognized in its invisible ubiquity, it requires extraordinary modes of expression.

25 *Compendium of the Catechism of the Catholic Church* (Washington, D.C.: United States Conference of Catholic Bishops, 2006), quest. 99, 32.

26 "It seemed to him that he had stepped through a high window that looked on a vanished world. A light was upon it for which his language had no name. All that he saw was shapely, but the shapes seemed at once clear cut, as they had been first conceived and drawn at the uncovering of his eyes, and ancient as if they had endured for ever. He saw no colour but those he knew, gold and white and blue and green, but they were fresh

and poignant, as if he had at that moment first perceived them and made them names new and wonderful. In winter here no heart could mourn for summer or for spring. No blemish of sickness or deformity could be seen in anything that grew upon the earth. On the land of Lórien there was no stain." J. R. R. Tolkien, *The Fellowship of the Ring*, 2nd ed. (Boston: Houghton Mifflin, 1993), 365.

27   It is evident that, for Chesterton, mystery does not mean mind-stopping conundrum or perplexity, but rather the ever wiser, ever more ignorant, knowledge of God.

28   "Never has there been so little discussion about the nature of men as now, when, for the first time, any one can discuss it. The old [authoritarian] restriction meant that only the orthodox were allowed to discuss religion. Modern liberty means that nobody is allowed to discuss it. Good taste, the last and vilest of human superstitions, has succeeded in silencing us where all the rest have failed." G. K. Chesterton, "Introduction" to *Heretics*, 7.

"The special mark of the modern world is not that it is sceptical, but that it is dogmatic without knowing it. It says, in mockery of old devotees, that they believed without knowing *why* they believed. But the moderns believe without knowing *what* they believe—and without even knowing that they do believe it. Their freedom consists in first freely assuming a creed, and then freely forgetting that they are assuming it. In short, they always have an unconscious dogma; and an unconscious dogma is the definition of a prejudice." *Illustrated London News*, March 15, 1919, qtd. in *The Man Who Was Orthodox: A Selection from the Uncollected Writings of G.K. Chesterton*, ed. A. L. Maycock (London: Dennis Dobson, 1963), 98, emphasis in original.

29   G. K. Chesterton, *Autobiography* (New York: Sheed & Ward, 1936), 229.

30   G. K. Chesterton, *Heretics*, 288–89.

31   Chesterton was early to discern that tolerance becomes impossible when belief no longer prevails, for then there is no transcendent Order which makes such tolerance possible: "A nation with a root religion will be tolerant. A nation with no religion will be bigoted." G. K. Chesterton, "The Sectarian Society," in *A Miscellany of Men* (1912; repr., Philadelphia: Dufour, 1969), 78.

32   It is noteworthy that Turnbull and MacIan's contest is based on mutual truth telling and thus on the common assumption of at least a minimal doctrine of axiomatic moral law. Neither hospitality nor friendship is possible when this most basic fundament of human existence is denied.

33   MacIan may be remembering the cry of the Psalmist: "Do I not hate them, O LORD, that hate thee! . . . I hate them with a perfect hatred: I count them mine enemies" (Ps 139:21-22).

34   The council "never actually met in full session," Brian Daley notes, "or
     issued an official decision." Instead, "subsequent negotiations between
     the two sides—the bishops, principally, of the Patriarchates of Antioch
     and Alexandria—resulted in a joint statement, a year and a half later, that
     has come down to us as 'the faith of Ephesus.'" Daley, "The Divinization
     of the Theotokos: Fifth-Century Christological Controversy and the Fig-
     ure of Mary," unpublished lecture, Villanova University, October 22, 2010.

     J. N. D. Kelly observes that "Probably the earliest allusion to Mary in
     Christian literature is the phrase 'born of woman' in Galatians 4:4, which
     was written before any of the Gospels. As parallels such as Job 14:1 and
     Matthew 11:11 suggest, the phrase is a Hebraic way of speaking about the
     essential humanity of a person. When applied to Jesus, therefore, 'born
     of woman' was intended to assert that he was a real man, in opposition to
     the attempt—later seen in various systems of Gnosticism, a 2nd-century
     dualistic religion—to deny that he had had a completely human life."
     The Synod of Ephesus sought not only to acknowledge Mary's exalted
     status in the economy of salvation, but also to resist the Nestorian insis-
     tence that Christ's divine and human natures were so loosely associated
     that they existed virtually as two persons. Such a notion, as Cyril of
     Alexandria made clear, denies "the reality of the incarnation and rep-
     resents Christ as a God-inspired man rather than as God-made-man."
     Kelly, "Nestorius," *Encyclopedia Britannica* (http://www.britannica.com/
     EBchecked/topic/409867/Nestorius).

35   John Henry Cardinal Newman, *Certain Difficulties Felt by Anglicans in Cath-
     olic Teaching Considered*, vol. II (London: Longmans, Green, 1920), 82–83.

36   Newman, *Certain Difficulties*, 55.

37   John Henry Newman, *An Essay on the Development of Doctrine* (Notre
     Dame, Ind.: University of Notre Dame Press, 1989), XI, 2, i, 426. New-
     man also links doctrine and science in ways that Chesterton's MacIan
     would endorse: "[T]he very first impulse of [the Christian's] faith is to try
     to express itself about the 'great sight' which is vouchsafed to it; and this
     seems to argue that a science there is, whether the mind is equal to its dis-
     covery or no. And, indeed, what science is open to every chance inquirer?
     which is not recondite in its principles? which requires not special gifts
     of mind for its just formation? All subject matters admit of true theories
     and false, and the false are no prejudice to the true. Why should this class
     of [theological] ideas be different from all other? Principles of philoso-
     phy, physics, ethics, politics, taste, admit both of implicit reception and
     explicit statement; why should not the ideas, which are the secret life
     of the Christian, be recognized also as . . . capable of scientific analysis?

Why should there not be a real connexion between science and its subject matter in religion, which exists in other departments of thought?" John Henry Newman, "The Theory of Developments in Religious Doctrine," in *Fifteen Sermons Preached before the University of Oxford* (Notre Dame, Ind.: University of Notre Dame Press, 1997), 327–28.

38 Henri de Lubac, *Catholicism: Christ and the Common Destiny of Man* (1938; repr., San Francisco: Ignatius, 1988), 18.

39 The absolute worth of human life is found not in its spiritual essence, but in the fact that its matter is susceptible of form, as Chesterton would later declare in his fine little book on St. Thomas:

> [The word] "formal" in Thomist language means actual, or possessing the real decisive quality that makes a thing itself. Roughly [speaking] when [St. Thomas] describes a thing as made out of Form and Matter, he very rightly recognizes that Matter is the more mysterious and indefinite and featureless element; and that what stamps anything with its own identity is its Form. Matter, so to speak, is not so much the solid as the liquid or gaseous thing in the cosmos; and in this [conviction] most modern scientists are beginning to agree with him.

Saint Thomas Aquinas: The Dumb Ox (1933; repr., Garden City, N.Y.: Doubleday Image, 1955), 158–59. Chesterton is alluding to the then-recent discoveries of Einstein.

Like St. Thomas, MacIan goes far beyond Aristotle. He puts his basic trust not in the inherent human capacity to form its own life, but in the all-decisive act of God to establish the final Form of the world in the Jews and Jesus and the Church.

40 It is tempting to wonder whether Chesterton might have just come from a fresh reading of Newman when he wrote *The Ball and the Cross*, so numerous are the echoes: "Nor is it any real objection [to the persistence of heresy] that the world is ever corrupt, and yet, in spite of this, evil does not fill up its measure and overflow; for this arises from the external counteractions of truth and virtue, which bear it back; *let the Church be removed, and the world will soon come to its end.*" Newman, *Development of Doctrine*, V, 7, ii, 204, emphasis added.

41 Newman again voices a conviction that is close to MacIan's. Blessed John Henry is inveighing against the proposal of Lord Brougham and Sir Robert Peel, made in 1841, to create "reading rooms" that would enable the lower classes to become moral and religious by encountering literature and the physical sciences as replacements for direct Christian instruction in the churches. For Newman, such well-meant humanism can give men mere opinions, not real convictions. It can enable them to entertain

probabilities and thus to tolerate counterproposals as having equal weight. It cannot convert consciences to convinced belief and behavior: "The heart is commonly reached, not through the reason, but through the imagination, by means of direct impressions, by the testimony of facts and events, by history, by description. Persons influence us, voices melt us, looks subdue us, deeds inflame us. Many a man will live and die upon a dogma: no man will be a martyr for a conclusion. A conclusion is but an opinion; it is not a thing which *is*, but which we are '*quite sure about*;' and it has often been observed, that we never say we are sure and certain without implying that we doubt. To say that a thing *must* be, is to admit that it *may* not be. No one, I say, will die for his own calculations: he dies for realities. This is why a literary religion is so little to be depended upon; it looks well in fair weather; but its doctrines are opinions, and, when called to suffer for them, it slips them between its folios, or burns them at its hearth. . . . [N]o religion has yet been a religion of physics or of philosophy. It has ever been synonymous with revelation. It never has been a deduction from what we know; it has ever been an assertion of what we are to believe. It has never lived in a conclusion; it has ever been a message, a history, or a vision." John Henry Newman, *The Grammar of Assent* (Garden City, N.Y.: Doubleday, 1955), 91–92, emphasis in original.

42 This is the salutary truth that MacIan has learned from Turnbull—that the cosmos cannot be readily explained by reference to the traditional and hierarchical ordering once known as the Great Chain of Being. A new kind of theology joined with a new kind of science will be necessary if nature is to be understood in a Christian rather than a physicalist fashion. In the meantime, Father Michael experiences something akin to Pascal's nightmarish "vertigo of the infinite" when he looks down from the dome of St. Paul's Cathedral into the interior, thinking it to be another realm entirely. Once again, Chesterton acknowledges the frightening truth of modern perspectivism—namely, that what one sees depends upon the stance from which one beholds it:

> He had stepped as it were into another infinity, out under the dome of another heaven. But this was a dome of heaven made by man. The gold and green and crimson of its sunset were not in the shapeless clouds but in shapes of cherubim and seraphim, awful human shapes with a passionate plumage. Its stars were not above but far below, like fallen stars still in unbroken constellations; the dome itself was full of darkness. And far below, lower even than the lights, could be seen creeping or motionless, great black masses of men. The tongue of a terrible organ seemed to shake the very air in the whole void; and

through it there came up to Michael the sound of a tongue more terrible; the dreadful everlasting voice of man, calling to his gods from the beginning to the end of the world. Michael felt almost as if he were a god, and all the voices were hurled at him. (BC, 10)

Lest the reader be too awestruck by Father Michael's metaphysical moment, we immediately learn that the man shouting up at him is a policeman ordering him to come down from the balustrade of the cathedral dome!

43 G. K. Chesterton, *Collected Works of G. K. Chesterton*, vol. 28, *Illustrated London News 1908–1910* (San Francisco: Ignatius, 1987), 392.

44 Stephen R. L. Clark, *G. K. Chesterton: Thinking Backward, Looking Forward* (Philadelphia: Templeton Foundation, 2006), 58.

45 G. K. Chesterton, *Collected Works of G. K. Chesterton*, vol. 3, *The Catholic Church and Conversion* (San Francisco: Ignatius, 1990), 70.

46 Chesterton, *Autobiography*, 88.

47 Chesterton employs the same metaphor in *Orthodoxy*: "I found this projecting feature of Christian theology, like a sort of hard spike, the dogmatic insistence that God was personal, and had made a world separate from Himself. The spike of dogma fitted exactly into the hole in the world—it had evidently been meant to go there. . . ." (84).

48 MacIan explains that an "apocalypse is the opposite of a dream. A dream is falser than the outer life. But the end of the world is more actual than the world it ends" (BC, 166). He means, I suspect, that an apocalypse brings the world to its true *telos*, the finality and completion toward which it has been aiming from the outset. Lacking any such *finis*, dreams falsify the real world by making it either better or worse than it is.

49 The novel's real complementarity may be found in the marriages that the adversaries are about to make: MacIan to a non-Christian and Turnbull to a Catholic. Yet there is little suggestion that opposites are necessary to each other even in conjugal life. The Catholic MacIan cannot marry an unbeliever with the Church's blessings, and so Beatrice will presumably become Catholic before their wedding. And since Turnbull is converted in the end, he and his new Catholic bride will surely share their Christianity as their deepest commonality.

50 Jean Daniélou, *Prayer as a Political Problem* (New York: Sheed & Ward, 1967), 87.

51 MacIan is not justifying evil ecclesial means used to accomplish "good" ecclesial ends, as he makes clear: "Torture should be violently stopped, though the Church is doing it" (BC, 167).

52 A Nobel laureate in physics, Steven Weinberg, reveals the inherent impossibility of such a task. Weinberg has offered the morally self-canceling judgment that is but another version of Turnbull's failed humanist physicalism: "The more the universe seems comprehensible," Weinberg has announced, "the more it also seems pointless." Weinberg urges his fellow physicalists, therefore, to take up arms against religion, routing all who would discern moral and spiritual order inherent in the universe: "Anything that we scientists can do to weaken the hold of religion should be done," Weinberg urges, "and may in the end be our greatest contribution to civilization." Weinberg fails to specify the moral authority under whose auspices he offers this plea, or the reason civilization is worth preserving, perhaps because he has none. Qtd. in James Glanz, "Physicist Ponders God, Truth, and 'a Final Theory,'" *The New York Times*, January 25, 2000.

53 If Chesterton had written his novel in 2009 instead of 1909, he surely would have had MacIan confess, "I am the pedophile priest of the European and American churches."

54 Once more, a conviction shared by Newman: "The political principles of Christianity, if it be right to use such words of a divine polity, are laid down for us in the Sermon on the Mount. Contrariwise to other empires, Christians conquer by yielding; they gain influence by shrinking from it; they possess the earth by renouncing it. Gibbon speaks of 'the vices of the clergy' as being 'to a philosophic eye far less dangerous than their virtues.'" Newman, *Development of Doctrine*, V, 2, v, 184.

55 The coronation ceremony assumes, of course, such a Church-state alliance. It thus specifies "the Delivery of the Orb" to the new monarch as follows: "Then shall the Orb with the Cross be brought from the Altar by the Dean of Westminster and delivered into the Queen's right hand by the Archbishop, saying:

> Receive this Orb set under the Cross,
> and remember that the whole world
> is subject to the Power and Empire
> of Christ our Redeemer.

"Then shall the Queen deliver the Orb to the Dean of Westminster, to be by him laid upon the Altar" (http://www.oremus.org/liturgy/coronation/cor1953b.html).

56 Pope Benedict XVI, *Salt of the Earth: The Church at the End of the Millennium,* an interview with Peter Seewald (San Francisco: Ignatius, 1997), 16, 164, 222.

Chapter 6

1   G. K. Chesterton, *William Cobbett* (1925; repr., London: House of Stratus, 2000), 19. There is also a good deal of autobiographical confession in his sketch of Cobbett: "He liked old customs and the continuity of family life to be found in the countryside; he loved England in a sense that was very real and unfortunately very rare. I mean that it was a positive love that looked inwards upon the beloved; and not merely a negative love that looked outwards for rivals or remote imitations" (26).

2   G. K. Chesterton, *Orthodoxy* (1908; repr., San Francisco: Ignatius, 1995), 155–56, emphasis in original. Lest Chesterton seem naïve in his belief that Europe would perpetually renew itself because of its Christian resources, we might remember that, two and a half centuries earlier, John Bunyan was even more convinced that England would remain not only permanently Christian but also permanently Protestant. The evils that beset Christian and Faithful on their quest for the Celestial City come chiefly from unconverted churchmen or else from secular temptations. The two grotto-dwelling giants, Pope and Pagan, pose no real danger, since their triumphs are irreversibly finished: "Pagan has been dead for many a day; and as for the other [i.e., Roman Catholicism], though he be yet alive, he is by reason of age, and also of the many shrewd brushes he met with in his younger days, grown so crazy and stiff in his joints, that he can now do little more than sit in his Caves mouth, grinning at Pilgrims as they go by, and biting his nails, because he cannot come at them." John Bunyan, *The Pilgrim's Progress*, ed. N. H. Keeble (Oxford: Oxford University Press, 1984), 54.

3   Qtd. in Robert Speight, *The Life of Hilaire Belloc* (New York: Farrar, Straus & Cudahy, 1957), 387.

4   Qtd. in Stanley Jaki, "Myopia about Islam, with an Eye on the Chesterbelloc," *Chesterton Review* 28, no. 4 (2002): 91–92. Much to the Tories' dismay, Belloc was elected.

5   Hilaire Belloc, *The Path to Rome* (1902; repr., Washington, D.C.: Regnery Gateway, 1987), 157.

6   G. K. Chesterton, *The New Jerusalem* (1920; repr., Champaign, Ill.: Book Jungle, 2007), 207.

7   Chesterton, *What's Wrong with the World* (New York: Dodd, Mead, 1910), 136.

8   Oddly enough, we have heard the atheist Turnbull expressing exactly this same sentiment in G. K. Chesterton, *The Ball and the Cross* (1910; repr., Mineola, N.Y.: Dover, 1995).

9   Chesterton, *What's Wrong with the World*, 253–54.

10 Richard L. Rubenstein, *The Cunning of History: The Holocaust and the*

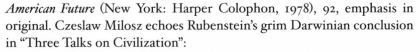

American Future (New York: Harper Colophon, 1978), 92, emphasis in original. Czeslaw Milosz echoes Rubenstein's grim Darwinian conclusion in "Three Talks on Civilization":

> We created a second Nature in the image of the first
> So as not to believe that we live in Paradise.
> It is possible that when Adam woke in the garden
> The beasts licked the air and yawned, friendly.
> While their fangs and their tails, lashing their backs,
> Were figurative and the red-backed shrike,
> Later, much later, named *Lanius collurio*,
> Did not impale caterpillars on spikes of the blackthorn.
> However, other than that moment, what we know of Nature
> Does not speak in its favor. Ours is no worse.
> So I beg of you, no more of those lamentations.

Czeslaw Milosz, *New and Collected Poems 1931–2001* (New York: Harper-Collins, 2003), 204. *Lanius collurio* means "thrush-like butcher."

11 George Steiner, "Remembering the Future," *Theology* 93 (1990): 439. It should be added that an overdetermined doctrine of "justification by faith alone" enabled many German Protestants both to sanction and to participate in the Nazi atrocities. Such "cheap grace," as Dietrich Bonhoeffer rightly labeled it—the notion, namely, that "faith" is entirely inward, focused either on private morality or else on the hope of postworldly rewards—ignores the costly grace of the Cross. In a paradox worthy of Chesterton, Bonhoeffer describes radical obedience *to* Christ's Cross as itself enabled *by* the Christ who is crucified there: "Only when we have really forgotten ourselves completely, when we really no longer know ourselves, only then are we ready to take up the cross for his sake. When we know only him, then we also no longer know the pain of our own cross. Then we see only him. If Jesus had not been so gracious in preparing us for this word, then we could not bear . . . this hard word as grace. It meets us in the joy of discipleship, and confirms us in it." Bonhoeffer, *Discipleship*, in *Dietrich Bonhoeffer Works*, vol. 4, ed. Geffrey B. Kelly and John D. Godsey (Minneapolis, Minn.: Fortress, 2001), 86.

12 G. K. Chesterton, *Tremendous Trifles* (1909; repr., Sandy, Utah: Quiet Vision, 2004), 98.

13 G. K. Chesterton, *Collected Works of G. K. Chesterton*, vol. 34, *Illustrated London News 1926–1928* (San Francisco: Ignatius, 1991), 588.

14 G. K. Chesterton, *The Common Man* (New York: Sheed & Ward, 1950), 95. Gilles de Rais was a fifteenth-century Breton knight and distinguished soldier who dabbled in the occult and who murdered scores, perhaps hundreds, of children.

15 "The Shape of Things to Come," *Daily News*, February 18, 1905, in *The Man Who Was Orthodox: A Selection from the Uncollected Writings of G. K. Chesterton*, ed. A. L. Maycock (London: Dennis Dobson, 1963), 123.

16 Friedrich Nietzsche, *The Gay Science*, trans. Walter Kaufmann (New York: Vintage, 1974), bk. 5, sec. 362, 318, emphasis in original.

17 Friedrich Nietzsche, *Human, All Too Human: A Book for Free Spirits*, trans. R. J. Hollingdale (Cambridge: Cambridge University Press, 1996), 355–56, emphasis in original.

18 After enduring a deadly snowstorm in Jerusalem that left more than a hundred dead, GKC wrote poignantly of the human suffering caused by the cruel visitations of nature: "It seemed as if a breath of the aimless destruction that wanders in the world had drifted across us; and no task remained for men but the weary rebuilding of ruins and the numbering of the dead." Chesterton, *New Jerusalem*, 77.

19 G. K. Chesterton, *The Ballad of the White Horse*, ed. Bernadette Sheridan, IHM, (1911; repr., San Francisco: Ignatius, 2001). All quotations from this poem are taken from this edition and indicated as BWH.

20 The first aphorism is voiced by the journalist Michael Moon in *Manalive* (1912; repr., Mineola, N.Y.: Dover, 2000), 112. The second is found in G. K. Chesterton *Alarms and Discursions* (New York: Dodd, Mead, 1912), 162. Surely the finest is to be located, like so many other Chestertonian gems, in his book on Dickens: "There is an apostolic injunction to suffer fools gladly. We always lay the stress on the word 'suffer,' and interpret the passage as one urging resignation. It might be better, perhaps, to lay the stress upon the word 'gladly,' and make our familiarity with fools a delight, and almost a dissipation. Nor is it necessary that our pleasure in fools (or at least in great and godlike fools) should be merely satiric or cruel. The great fool is he in whom we cannot tell which is the conscious and which the unconscious humour; we laugh with him and laugh at him at the same time. An obvious instance is that of ordinary and happy marriage. A man and a woman cannot live together without having against each other a kind of everlasting joke. Each has discovered that the other is a fool, but a great fool. This largeness, this grossness and gorgeousness of folly is the thing which we all find about those with whom we are in intimate contact; and it is the one enduring basis of affection, and even of respect." Chesterton, *Collected Works of G. K. Chesterton*, vol. 15, *Charles Dickens*, 187–88.

21 See Eugene H. Peterson, *A Long Obedience in the Same Direction: Discipleship in an Instant Society* (Downers Grove, Ill.: InterVarsity, 1980).

22 In retelling the legend of Alfred, Chesterton does not make the plot serve as the poem's chief interest. Instead, he ponders why the English won

against such overwhelming odds and what ultimate purposes they served. Thus does he announce the victory in advance, saying to Frances that, in her, he first discerned the sacramental marker that was also embraced by the defeated but converted Danish captain: "the sign [of the Cross] that Guthrum saw / When he let break his ships of awe, / And laid peace on the sea" (BWH, Dedication, 56–58). The poem's riveting interest lies not with the victorious outcome of the battle at Ethandune but with the surprising circumstances that enabled it.

23 These are the seven peoples who have constituted Chesterton's "Englands" as best I can reconstruct them: the prehistoric Celts, the Romans, the Saxons who followed them, the Celtic Christians who converted the Saxons, the pagan Danish invaders of the ninth century, the Saxon Christians who in turn converted them, and finally the Norman conquerors of the eleventh century.

24 Chesterton's rhyme scheme is often varied, but the chiming of the final line always rings true. His ballad meter also fluctuates in scansion, mixing the iambic with the anapestic, but also with consecutively stressed spondees and a rare double-feminine ending (see the dactylic "suddenly" below). So does the cadence vary, yet always with three or four pulsing beats per line. Readers of all persuasions may thus enjoy the poem (like *Lepanto*) with foot-tapping delight. Joseph Pearce reports that John Galsworthy praised its "splendid stir and thrum"; that the communist Douglas Hyde read it during a train journey "in rhythm with the wheels"; that C. S. Lewis could quote long stretches of it; and that Graham Greene embarrassedly compared it to the signature poem of the twentieth century: "Put *The Ballad of the White Horse* against *The Wasteland*. If I had to choose one of them, I'm not sure that . . . well, anyhow, let's just say I reread *The Ballad* more often!" Joseph Pearce, *Wisdom and Innocence: A Life of G. K. Chesterton* (San Francisco: Ignatius, 1996), 164–66, ellipsis in original.

Garry Wills also notes that Chesterton's metric alterations in the manuscripts "are all in the direction of irregularity, to keep the ballad's loose and vigorous form." Wills, *Chesterton: Man and Mask* (New York: Sheed & Ward, 1961), 229n11.

25 Stark statements of Chesterton's theme can be found almost everywhere in his work: "The meanest man is immortal and the mightiest movement is temporal, not to say temporary." *The Man Who Was Orthodox*, 40. *The Ballad of the White Horse* complicates such a Christian commonplace, however, by giving poetic embodiment to the fear that men do not *seem* immortal, and thus to the dread that the mightiest movements of both ancient tyrannies and modern nation-states, with their virtually untrammeled dominance, are the only things that *are* permanent.

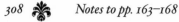

26 Friedrich Nietzsche, *On the Genealogy of Morality*, trans. Carol Diethe (New York: Cambridge University Press, 1994), I, 11, 26, emphasis in original.

27 See the appendix to this chapter for J. R. R. Tolkien's tart denial of this link.

28 Garry Wills observes that "Ogier of the stone and sling" here "expresses the nihilistic mystique in clear-etched lines which reveal the depths Chesterton's verse could reach" (*Chesterton*, 138). W. H. Auden agrees, declaring that there are no more succinct statements of unredeemed human sentiment than those expressed by Elf the minstrel, Ogier the warrior, and Guthrum the king: "what they sing could not be further condensed without loss." Auden, "The Gift of Wonder," in *G. K. Chesterton: A Century Appraisal*, ed. John Sullivan (New York: Harper & Row, 1974), 74.

29 Maisie Ward, *Gilbert Keith Chesterton* (London: Sheed & Ward, 1944), 243–44. Ward also mentions that Dorothy Thompson, the first American reporter expelled from Nazi Germany (in 1934), greeted Jacques Maritain with these same quatrains on the occasion of his sixtieth birthday in 1942, when the war was still raging. Knowing well the cultural and religious resonance that Chesterton's famous lines would carry, the Anglican priest and inveterate opponent of South African apartheid, Trevor Huddleston, chose its key phrase for his memoir about his twelve-year struggle against Afrikaner racialism. Like Chesterton, Huddleston believed that Christians must sometimes use force to overcome evil, yet only in order to preserve and enable what Huddleston called "this most precious human treasure, the opportunity of love itself. If I am mistaken, as well I may be, in the methods I have used, then I trust in the mercy of God for my forgiveness. For He, too, is a Person. And it is his Person that I have found in Africa, in the poverty of her homes, in the beauty and splendour of her children, in the patience and courtesy of her people. But above all I have found Him where every Christian should expect to find Him: in the darkness, in the fear, in the blinding weariness of Calvary.

    And Calvary is but one step from the Empty Tomb." Trevor Huddleston, *Naught for Your Comfort* (Garden City, N.Y.: Doubleday, 1956), 246.

30 Aidan Nichols, O.P., *G. K. Chesterton, Theologian* (Oxford, UK: Second Spring, 2009), 108–9.

31 The Danes had earlier pillaged and burned the monasteries at Ely, raping the nuns.

32 The most obvious example of this Christian practice is to be found in the Stoic ethics that pervades much of the New Testament, but also in the early Church's adoption of the four cardinal virtues (prudence, justice, fortitude, moderation) from Greco-Roman culture, even if these virtues

still require an "infusion" of divine grace to make them authentically Christian.

33   Bede's *Ecclesiastical History of the English People*, trans. Leo Sherley-Price, rev. R. E. Latham (London: Penguin, 1990), I, 30, 92. The Christian record was far from pristine, for many worthy pagan things were destroyed alongside the idols that new believers were always in danger of reclaiming for their worship. The Venerable Bede thus describes the razing of a shrine to the god Woden by the high priest Coifi who had once made sacrifices there, before he and King Edwin and their fellow Anglo-Saxons were converted to Christianity: "Girded with a sword and with a spear in his hand, [Coifi] mounted the king's stallion and rode up to the idols. When the crowd saw him, they thought he had gone mad; but without hesitation, as soon as he reached the shrine, he cast into it the spear and thus profaned it. Then, full of joy at his knowledge of the worship of the true God, he told his companions to set fire to the shrine and its enclosures and destroy them" (II, 13, 130).

34   "All the teachings of the pagans contain not only simulated and superstitious imaginings and grave burdens of unnecessary labor, . . . but also liberal disciplines more suited to the uses of truth, and some most useful precepts concerning morals. Even some truths concerning the worship of one God are found among them. These are, as it were, their gold and silver, which they did not institute themselves but dug up from certain mines of divine Providence, which is everywhere infused, and perversely and injuriously abused in the worship of demons [i.e., false gods]." Saint Augustine, *On Christian Doctrine*, trans. D. W. Robertson (Indianapolis: Bobbs Merrill Library of Liberal Arts, 1958), bk. II, sec. XL, 75.

35   Pope John Paul II adopted this latter phrase from the Second Vatican Council's "Pastoral Constitution on the Church in the Modern World," *Gaudium et Spes*, as his own motto. It lies near to the heart of the Christian humanism that Chesterton himself embraced and that Peter Candler explains: "To put this tradition in Thomistic terms, the *matter* of pagan antiquity—as of all human desire and reason—remains yet in a state of *potency* [as] to its form, which is realized in a unitive consummation in Christ. Yet here the hostility between God and the world is shown to be already removed—God, as Gregory of Nyssa says, has no opposite. Thus can Augustine say that 'the Church is the world, reconciled.'" Peter M. Candler Jr., "The Logic of Christian Humanism," *Communio* 36 (2009): 90, emphasis in original.

36   The Greek *poesis* lies at the root of our word "poetry," but its prime meaning is "making," so that all true makers are also poets, no matter the

media wherewith they make. The Scots word for poet (*makar*) reveals, even more obviously, the deep kinship between the two kinds of making.

37 Rémi Brague, *Eccentric Culture: A Theory of Western Civilization* (South Bend, Ind.: St. Augustine's Press, 2003), 91. Brague also argues that Islam is dangerously devoid of any such sense of cultural "inferiority" or "secondarity." This absence leads, Brague maintains, to cultural arrogance and contempt. According to Muslims, the Christian and Jewish revelations recorded in Scripture are either corrupted or fragmentary, and thus completely superseded by the Qur'an. Arabic becomes the ultimate language, the very tongue of God, so that while texts from other languages may be translated into Arabic, they need not be preserved. Nor do the linguistic and historical skills necessary for learning the cultures that produced these superseded texts need to be cultivated.

38 "[I]n that terrific tale of the Passion there is a distinct emotional suggestion that the author of all things (in some unthinkable way) went not only through agony, but through doubt. . . . In a garden Satan tempted man: and in a garden God tempted God." *Orthodoxy*, 145.

39 In nine previous encounters with the Danes, Alfred had lost seven of the battles.

40 Such repetitions are characteristic of the ballad form, whose refrains are often elaborated, thus carrying the main moral burden of the poem, as with the stern and oft-repeated Marian prophecy given to Alfred: "the sky grows darker yet, and the sea rises higher." Frequent dialogues are another ballad feature that Chesterton employs, while adding his own Anglo-Saxon note with the use of kennings; i.e., such word combinations as "throne-scramble" to describe the fury of those who sought to succeed Alfred as king.

41 Augustine, *Concerning the City of God against the Pagans*, trans. Henry Bettenson (Harmondsworth, UK: Penguin, 1984), bk. 1, chap. 35, 45–46.

42 G. K. Chesterton, *A Miscellany of Men* (1912; repr., Philadelphia: Dufour, 1969), 64.

43 He took the baptismal name of Athelstan (OE *ætheling* < *æthele*, "noble"), and in fact he kept the peace for the remainder of his life.

44 Bruce Marshall, *The World, the Flesh, and Father Smith* (Boston: Houghton Mifflin, 1945), 108.

45 Walker Percy, *Love in the Ruins: The Adventures of a Bad Catholic at a Time Near the End of the World* (New York: Farrar, Straus & Giroux, 1971), 21.

46 G. K. Chesterton, *Autobiography* (New York: Sheed & Ward, 1936), 253.

47 Chesterton, *Common Man*, 237.

48 Speaking of the tireless repetitions in nature—the endless rising of the sun, the constant change of the moon, the perpetual sameness of all

daisies—Chesterton observes that God may have "the eternal appetite of infancy; for we have sinned and grown old, and our Father is younger than we." *Orthodoxy*, 66.

49 Chesterton often remarked that ours may be the first age wherein men and women no longer sing at their labors, and that this silence marks a profound spiritual grimness in our souls.

50 I have sought to make the case for God's own erotic love in "Flannery O'Connor, Benedict XVI, and the Divine Eros," *Christianity and Literature* 60, no. 1 (2010): 35–64.

51 *Deus Caritas Est*, sec. 10, par. 2.

52 *Collected Works of G. K. Chesterton*, vol. 10, *Collected Poetry, Part 1* (San Francisco: Ignatius, 1994), 173–74.

Chapter 7

1 Flannery O'Connor, *Mystery and Manners*, sel. and ed. Robert and Sally Fitzgerald (New York: Farrar, Straus & Giroux, 1970), 71.

2 Qtd. in *Conserving Walt Whitman's Fame*, ed. Gary Schmidgall (Iowa City: University of Iowa Press), 158.

3 G. K. Chesterton, *The Annotated Thursday: G. K. Chesterton's Masterpiece "The Man Who Was Thursday,"* annotated by Martin Gardner (1907; repr., San Francisco: Ignatius, 1999). All citations are from this edition and are indicated MT.

4 At the outset of the novel, this seems especially to be the case. Once these two philosophical combatants promise not to reveal each other's true identity, the novel seems set for a neat up or down contest: "Don't you see we've checkmated each other?" cried Syme. "I can't tell the police you are an anarchist. You can't tell the anarchists I'm a policeman. I can only watch you, knowing what you are; you can only watch me, knowing what I am. In short, it's a lonely intellectual duel, my head against yours" (MT, 60).

5 "Now Solipsism simply means that a man believes in his own existence, but not in anybody or anything else." G. K. Chesterton, *Thomas Aquinas: The Dumb Ox* (1933; repr., New York: Doubleday, 1956), 149.

6 Aidan Nichols, O.P., *G. K. Chesterton, Theologian* (London: Darton, Longman & Todd, 2009), 61. Though he did not live to witness the emergence of Abstract Expressionism, Chesterton would not have been surprised by this further turning away from the external world.

7 G. K. Chesterton, *Autobiography* (New York: Sheed & Ward, 1936), 87–88. Chesterton was especially troubled that Whistler could depict his mother in coldly impersonal terms, as if she were just another model posing for a life study, so that he need not even attach her name to his painting. John

D. Coates observes that Chesterton objected to the Impressionism of George Moore, the author of *Modern Painters* and the chief artistic influence at the Slade School. Moore dissociated "the visionary moment of aesthetic delight from any kind of moral or emotional framework. . . . To deny an object visual relationship to an unseen background was hostile to imagination. . . . Chesterton sees [Impressionism] as flat and literal minded, a truncating of the process of imagination and of the kinetic relationship of one subject with another, of the seen to the unseen. . . . Chesterton felt an artist should not be concerned with an 'impression', a perfect moment, an aspect, but should attempt to engage the deepest levels of man's consciousness, providing a form for the vast unknown pattern of perception of knowledge which exists there." John D. Coates, *Chesterton and the Edwardian Cultural Crisis* (Hull, UK: Hull University Press, 1984), 197, 200, 201.

8   Ancient European folklore held that abortive animals or humans were the products of the moon's sinister influence on fetal development. By extension, the term "Mooncalf" came to refer to any grotesque or monstrous creature, including Caliban, the deformed servant of Prospero in Shakespeare's *The Tempest.*

9   G. K. Chesterton, "The Nightmare," in *Alarms and Discursions* (New York: Dodd, Mead, 1911), 29. The best guides to the autobiographical sources of *Thursday* are Adam Schwartz, *The Third Spring: G. K. Chesterton, Graham Greene, Christopher Dawson, and David Jones* (Washington, D.C.: Catholic University of America Press, 2005), 46–54; and David Leigh, "The Psychology of Conversion in Chesterton's and Lewis' Autobiographies," in *G.K. Chesterton and C.S. Lewis: The Riddle and the Joy*, ed. Michael Macdonald and Andrew Tadie (Grand Rapids: Eerdmans, 1989), 290–304.

10 Chesterton, "The Nightmare," 29.

11 W. R. Titterton, *G. K. Chesterton: A Portrait* (London: Douglas Organ, 1936), 92–93.

12 Saint Thomas similarly links providence with things going right: "For we observe among beings of nature that what is best comes to pass either always or most of the time. This would not be the case were not there some providence guiding such beings to an end, the good" (S.T., 1a, 103, 1). *St Thomas Aquinas: Summa Theologiae*, vol. 14, *Divine Government*, trans. T. C. O'Brien (London: Blackfriars, 1975), 5. Chesterton also admits that the natural order is riddled with chance, and that such fortuity may cause great pain and poverty. Even when it doesn't, there remain "those innumerable accidental limitations that are always falling across our path—bad

weather, confinement to this or that house or room, failure of appoint-
ments or arrangements, waiting at railway stations, missing posts, finding
unpunctuality when we want punctuality, or, what is worse, finding punctuality when we don't." G. K. Chesterton, "The Advantages of Having One
Leg," in *Tremendous Trifles* (1909; repr., Sandy, Utah: Quiet Vision, 2004), 21.

13 The narrator subverts the nobility of Syme's newfound resolve by calling
it "romantic," noting that "all his brain and body [were] throbbing with
romantic rhythm" (MT, 110). Syme's heroic determination proves bootless from the outset, even at the first meeting of the anarchist council.
Despite his pulsing fears, Syme himself is not exposed as the false insurrectionist in their midst; instead, Sunday ejects Gogol the faux Pole.

14 We are reminded that their one-legged table is mounted on a "screw," a
mechanical device for raising and lowering heavy objects. There is nothing necessarily preternatural about a trapdoor and circling table, and the
underground vault is depicted in thoroughly realistic terms.

15 The narrator virtually duplicates the personal confession we have heard
Chesterton making; i.e., that the prevailing pessimism of his era tempted
him with "a strong inward impulse to revolt" into optimism.

16 Booth does not sanction such a potentially infinite regress of confused
narrators and implied authors nestled inside each other like Russian dolls:
"When human actions are formed to make an art work, the form that is
made can never be divorced from the human meanings, including the
moral judgments, that are implicit wherever human beings act. And nothing the writer does can be finally understood in isolation from his effort
to make it all accessible to someone else—his peers, himself as an imagined reader, his audience. The novel comes into existence as something
communicable, and the means of communication are not shameful intru-
sions unless they are made with shameful ineptitude." Wayne C. Booth,
The Rhetoric of Fiction, 2nd ed. (Chicago: University of Chicago, 1983), 397.

17 "The anarchists sought to abolish the state," writes Tom Armitage, "and
put in its place a society based upon the voluntary organisation of individuals. Like Marxism, anarchism was an international movement, with
tentacles in a number of different countries. In the 1870s anarchists promoted the concept of 'propaganda by the deed'—the belief that a mass
uprising could be triggered by [violent] action. A spate of assassination
attempts was made on European heads of state: in 1881, Tsar Alexander
II of Russia was killed. Soon, the anarchists began targeting civilians as
well, and took to planting bombs in public places. Opera houses, stations,
town halls, government offices and private clubs all came under attack."

Tom Armitage, "Commentary," *New Statesman* 134, no. 4752 (2005), http://www.newstatesman.com/200508080038. The London attacks during the 1880s targeted mainly train stations, especially Charing Cross, Westminster, Paddington, and Ludgate Hill.

Alzina Stone Dale points out that during the decades prior to the Great War, "six heads of state were murdered by what has been called [by Barbara Tuchman] 'The Idea,' a dream of a stateless society without government, law, or property, where a man would be as free as God meant him to be. This idea had made established society sense violent revolution in the air, for those tried for these murders insisted they were only creating a better world." Dale, *The Outline of Sanity: A Biography of G. K. Chesterton* (Grand Rapids: Eerdmans, 1982), 114–15.

18 Chesterton describes his own early condition in almost identical terms. Responding to Schopenhauer's despairing estimate of the human condition, for example, he confesses that "the first movement of my mind was simply an impulse to say that being rotten was emphatically all rot." "I was merely a reactionary," he admits, "because my thought was merely a reaction." G. K. Chesterton, *Where All Roads Lead*, in *Collected Works of G. K. Chesterton*, vol. 3 (San Francisco: Ignatius, 1990), 48, 45.

19 Alzina Stone Dale is surely wrong to say that, while the atmosphere in the work of both Franz Kafka and H. G. Wells is truly portentous, in *Thursday* it is merely "absurd" (Dale, *Outline of Sanity*, 113). It would be better to say that the chillingly portentous alternates with the harmlessly absurd, and that such oscillation is at once more discomfiting and more credible than a steady regimen of pure horror or pure farce. Kingsley Amis thus declares that "because the nightmare is a controlled nightmare," it is "in its way believable." "Introduction" to *G. K. Chesterton, The Man Who Was Thursday* (New York: Penguin, 1986), 4.

20 Readers approaching the novel for the sixth or sixteenth perusal may, like Syme and his co-conspirators, have at first been mortified by the President's hair-raising revelation. Now we know, in retrospect, that the President is in fact Sunday himself. Ironically, the Supreme Anarch turns out to be the ultimate advocate of order; for at the end, he urges his recruits not to become anarchical in their opposition to anarchy!

21 Mark Knight, *Chesterton and Evil* (New York: Fordham University Press, 2004), 88–115.

22 Friedrich Nietzsche, *Daybreak: Thoughts on the Prejudices of Morality*, trans. R. J. Hollingdale (Cambridge: Cambridge University Press, 1997), 28.

23 G. K. Chesterton, *Orthodoxy* (1908; repr., San Francisco: Ignatius, 1995), 69.

24 Chesterton here as always is unfailingly Augustinian and Thomistic in his regard for evil as a privation or perversion of the good. Having refused its

proper ordering to the love of God, evil remains parasitic on the good it denies. "People are not described as thinking or speaking against God," Aquinas writes, "in the sense that they are in total opposition with the pattern of his government, *since even those sinning are intent upon some good*" (ST, 1a, 103, 8, emphasis added). *St Thomas Aquinas: Summa Theologiae*, vol. 14, *Divine Government*, 33.

25 Chesterton here envisions a future even more frightening than the one C. S. Lewis prophesied in 1943. "The Conditioners" are those philosophers and scientists whom Lewis describes as seeking to save humanity by conquering the harsh moral and natural conditions under which our species labors, while themselves remaining unaffected by such conditions. They succeed, alas, by conquering human neediness and destroying themselves:

> Man by eugenics, by pre-natal conditioning, and by an education and propaganda based on a perfect applied psychology, has obtained full control over himself. Human nature will be the last part of Nature to surrender to Man. . . . Nature, untrammeled by value, rules the Conditioners and, through them, all humanity. Man's conquest of Nature turns out, in the moment of its consummation, to be Nature's conquest of Man.

C. S. Lewis, *The Abolition of Man, or, Reflections on Education with Special Reference to the Teaching of English* (1943; repr., San Francisco: Harper, 2001), 69–70, 76. Chesterton's nihilists have gone a horrible step further: they believe it better for other human beings never to have existed at all, and thus as worthy only of extermination.

26 Secretary Buttons' likening of the brain to the bomb uncannily anticipates the resemblance of the atomic cloud to the cranial stem and bulb, as Henry Moore made hauntingly clear in his sculpture titled "Nuclear Energy." It somberly commemorates the first self-sustaining chain reaction of nuclear fission at the University of Chicago (http://physics.uchicago.edu/about/history/manhattan.html). The Secretary's discourse on dynamite is also remarkably accurate: "The anarchists [of the late nineteenth century] preferred bombs to firearms (perhaps because of their chaotic and unpredictable nature), and their explosive of choice was dynamite. Invented in 1866 by Alfred Nobel, dynamite was notable for being hugely powerful but also very stable." Armitage, "Commentary."

27 For Chesterton, such satanic bombast is not only foolish but also incoherent, since pure evil would constitute pure nothingness. In "The Diabolist," for example, Chesterton reports his encounter with a figure who, having indulged in every imaginable vice, contemplates a final denial of

virtue by discovering "in evil a life of its own." Yet this nameless diabolist also admits that such an endeavor would make his diabolism meaningless, since "I shan't know the difference between right and wrong." How would he even know when he is being diabolic? The man disappears as Chesterton contemplates the flames of Guy Fawkes Day, wondering whether the diabolist's confession had revealed "hell or the furious love of God." If the man persists in his denial of the good, he will end in Hell. If, by contrast, he confesses that the demonic has no significance apart from the prior and final reality of the divine, he will have been saved by the Hound of Heaven. "The Diabolist," in Chesterton, *Tremendous Trifles*, 104.

28 Chesterton, *Autobiography*, 77.

29 He is also a worshipper of havoc and mayhem as Nietzsche was not. Hence de Worms' quotation from Alexander Pope's *The Dunciad*, as he substitutes the alliterating word "life" in place of "spark" in the second line. What Pope intends as witty satire of gloomy eighteenth-century poets, de Worms takes as grisly eternal truth. Yet even in his mistaken nihilism, we are reminded that Chaos and Old Night may finally rule the world depicted in *Thursday*:

> "Nor public flame, nor private, dares to shine
> Nor human life is left, nor glimpse divine!
> Lo! thy dread Empire, Chaos, is restored;
> Light dies before thine uncreating word:
> Thy hand, great Anarch, lets the curtain fall;
> And universal darkness buries all." (MT, 214)

30 G. K. Chesterton, "Wishes," in *The Uses of Diversity* (New York: Dodd, Mead, 1921), 116. It would be better to call de Worms a spiritualist, as Chesterton was early to discern the link between nihilism and the faddish spiritualism of his day—an interest in psychic phenomena embraced perhaps most notably by Sir Arthur Conan Doyle but also by Lord Balfour and even William James. Not only does the reality of the material world remain generally dubious to de Worms; so does our most specifically human feature: the face. "I don't know whether your face, Bull, is a face or a combination in perspective. Perhaps one black disc of your beastly glasses is quite close and another fifty miles away. Oh, the doubts of a materialist are not worth a dump. Sunday has taught me the last and the worst doubts, the doubts of a spiritualist. I am a Buddhist, I suppose; and Buddhism is not a creed, it is a doubt. My poor dear Bull, I do not believe that you really have a face. I have not faith enough to believe in matter" (MT, 244–45).

31   Syme also reminds Dr. Bull that "[w]hen duty and religion are really destroyed, it will be by the rich" (MT, 210).

32   John Atkins suggests that such nearness of good and evil, truth and illusion, makes *Thursday* perhaps "the best spy book ever written." The reason, says Atkins, is that "it contains a deep-lying truth. It is that if you say quite openly that you are a spy or an anarchist, no one will believe you and you will be able to do pretty much as you please. Attempts to hide your identity lead to suspicion, and then everyone will know you are a spy (or an anarchist)." Atkins, "Styles in Treachery," in *G. K. Chesterton: A Half Century of Views*, ed. D. J. Conlon (New York: Oxford, 1987), 347.

33   Chesterton, "The Nightmare," 26. Authentic "Tales of Terrors," Chesterton adds, depend on a fundamental human certainty: "Man, the central pillar of the world, must be upright and straight; around him the trees and beasts and elements and devils may crook and curl like smoke if they choose. All really imaginative literature is only the contrast between the weird curves of Nature and the straightness of the soul" (28).

34   "An Atheistic Nightmare," *The Speaker*, August 10, 1901, in *The Man Who Was Orthodox: A Selection from the Uncollected Writings of G.K. Chesterton*, ed. A. L. Maycock (London: Dennis Dobson, 1963), 83–84. At one point in the novel, Syme is described as feeling "like a man who had dreamed all night of falling over precipices, and had woke up on the morning when he was to be hanged" (MT, 175). Only a year before his death, Chesterton was still obsessed with the subject, declaring that, in nightmares, "No is the same as Yes." Chesterton, "Reflections on a Rotten Apple," in *The Well and the Shallows* (1935), in *Collected Works of G. K. Chesterton*, vol. 3 (San Francisco: Ignatius, 1990), 496.

35   Qtd. in Martin Gardner, "Appendix" to *Annotated Thursday*, 277–78.

36   Martin Gardner, "*The Man Who Was Thursday*: Revisiting Chesterton's Masterpiece," *Books and Culture* (May–June 2000): 31.

37   Nichols, *G. K. Chesterton, Theologian*, 99.

38   It is important to remember that Sunday is an allegorical representation of God, not the God whom Milton impersonates in *Paradise Lost*. As Robert Sokolowski observes, "God himself, as God, does not appear in the world or in human experience. He is not the kind of being that can be present as a thing in the world. And yet, despite this necessary absence, he is believed to be that which gives the definitive sense to everything that does appear in the world and in experience." Sokolowski, *The God of Faith and Reason: Foundations of Christian Theology* (Notre Dame, Ind.: University of Notre Dame Press, 1982), 1.

39 The boar or hart, the fox or elk, "turns to bay" when it refuses any longer to flee; instead, it wildly attacks its pursuers until they kill it.

40 Gardner, "Appendix," 277–78.

41 "Aesop," in *G. K. C. as M. C.: Being a Collection of Thirty-Seven Introductions by G. K. Chesterton*, ed. J. de Fonseka (London: Methuen, 1929), 86–87. David Hume was one atheist who was not thus frightened. Man matters not to nature more than an oyster, he calmly declared. Our future nonexistence, he added, should trouble us no more than our previous nonexistence. Nor was Robert Frost frightened so much as appalled by a spider's devouring of a moth, a shock finely expressed in his poem titled "Design":

> I found a dimpled spider, fat and white,
> On a white heal-all, holding up a moth
> Like a white piece of rigid satin cloth—
> Assorted characters of death and blight
> Mixed ready to begin the morning right.
> Like the ingredients of a witches' broth—
> A snow-drop spider, a flower like a froth,
> And dead wings carried like a paper kite.
>
> What had that flower to do with being white,
> The wayside blue and innocent heal-all?
> What brought the kindred spider to that height,
> Then steered the white moth thither in the night?
> What but design of darkness to appall?—
> If design govern in a thing so small.

Robert Frost, *The Road Not Taken: A Selection of Robert Frost's Poems*, comp. Louis Untermeyer (New York: Henry Holt, 1971), 202.

42 http://www.nd.edu/~afreddos/courses/417/summa1,14-26.htm.

43 Alison Milbank, *Chesterton and Tolkien as Theologians: The Fantasy of the Real* (London: T&T Clark, 2007), 62, 67. Geoffrey Galt Harpam offers an especially lucid description of the grotesque and its various effects: "When we use the word 'grotesque' we record, among other things, the sense that though our attention has been arrested, our understanding is unsatisfied. Grotesqueries both require and defeat definition: they are neither so regular and rhythmical that they settle easily into our categories, nor so unprecedented that we do not recognize them at all. They stand at a margin of consciousness between the known and the unknown, the perceived and the unperceived, calling into question the adequacy of our ways of organizing the world, of dividing the continuum of experience into knowable particles." Harpam, *On the Grotesque: Strategies of Contradiction in Art and Literature* (Princeton, N.J.: Princeton University Press, 1982), 3.

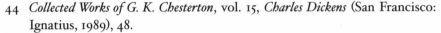

44 *Collected Works of G. K. Chesterton,* vol. 15, *Charles Dickens* (San Francisco: Ignatius, 1989), 48.

45 Nor do we pay sufficient attention to humanly created things, all of which bespeak their makers. After the masquerading anarchist Colonel Ducroix has fired on Syme—thinking him to be a true terrorist—but struck only his sword, Syme clubs his assailant to the ground with a single swing of his bull's-eye lamp. Though the whole charade is verging on total exposure as the farce it truly is, the poet continues to lecture the pseudo-dynamiter whom he has just bludgeoned:

> "Do you see this lantern?" cried Syme in a terrible voice. "Do you see the cross carved on it, and the flame inside? You did not make it. You did not light it. Better men than you, men who could believe and obey, twisted the entrails of iron and preserved the legend of fire. There is not a street you walk on, there is not a thread you wear, that was not made as this lantern was, by denying your philosophy of dirt and rats. You can make nothing. You can only destroy. You will destroy mankind; you will destroy the world. Let that suffice you. Yet this one old Christian lantern you shall not destroy. It shall go where your empire of apes will never have the wit to find it." (MT, 217)

Syme strikes the faux Frenchman with the sturdy lamp once more before flinging it into the sea.

46 Chesterton, *Thomas Aquinas,* 180–81.

47 G. K. Chesterton, "A Defense of Skeletons," in *The Defendant* (1901; repr., London: J. M. Dent, 1940), 49.

48 Milbank, *Chesterton and Tolkien,* 67. "That which is infinite is known only to itself," declared Tertullian sometime near the turn of the fourth century. "This it is which gives some notion of God, while yet beyond all our conceptions—our very incapacity of fully grasping Him affords us the idea of what He really is. He is presented to our minds in His transcendent greatness, as at once known and unknown." Tertullian, *Apology* (Cambridge, Mass.: Harvard University Press, 1977), 54–55. Hans Urs von Balthasar stresses the apophatic quality of all knowledge of God by adopting a phrase from the Fourth Lateran Council (1215) as his motto: *"The ever greater dissimilarity to God no matter how great the similarity."*

49 The tenanted Cross is the ultimately grotesque thing—unbalanced, out of kilter, ugly. Its occupant "hath no form nor comeliness; and when we shall see him, there is no beauty that we should desire him. He is despised and rejected of men; a man of sorrows, and acquainted with grief: and we hid as it were our faces from him; he was despised, and we esteemed him not" (Isa 53:2-3).

50 G. K. Chesterton, "Dickens' Christmas Tales," in *The Spirit of Christmas*, selected and arranged by Marie Smith (New York: Dodd, Mead, 1985), 25. "The highest and most valuable quality in nature is not her beauty, but her generous and defiant ugliness. . . . The croaking noise of the rooks is, in itself, as hideous as the whole hell of sounds in a London railway tunnel. Yet it lifts us like a trumpet with its coarse kindliness and honesty. . . . Has the poet, for whom nature means only lilies and roses, ever heard a pig grunting? It is a noise that does a man good—a strong, snorting, imprisoned noise, breaking its way out of unfathomable dungeons through every possible outlet and organ. It might be the voice of the earth itself, snoring in its mighty sleep. This is the deepest, the oldest, the most wholesome and religious sense of the value of nature—the value which comes from her immense babyishness. She is as top-heavy, as grotesque, as solemn, and as happy as a child." Chesterton, *The Defendant*, 48.

51 Graham Greene, *The Power and the Glory* (New York: Penguin, 1991), 130–31, ellipsis in original.

52 My friend Sarah Gordon wisely observes that she has never met a stutterer who wasn't also a kind person. Though they fumble grotesquely at our most distinctively human act, stammerers suffer a disability that is not wholly evil. Pretentious claims do not often issue from stumbling tongues.

53 Chesterton believed that such lightheartedness could also be found in the Lord who is recorded as having wept but never as having laughed. As he contends in the final paragraph of his most famous book, Christ "restrained something. I say it with reverence; there was in that shattering personality a thread that must be called shyness. There was something that He hid from men when He went up to pray. There was something that He covered constantly by abrupt silence or impetuous isolation. There was some one thing that was too great for God to show us when He walked upon our earth; and I have sometimes fancied that it was His mirth." *Orthodoxy*, 167–68.

54 G. K. Chesterton, *Heretics*, in *Collected Works of G. K. Chesterton*, vol. 1 (San Francisco: Ignatius, 1986), 166.

55 Only two years later, Chesterton would grant the Bulgarian monk named Michael a similar vision of life's theonomous oneness despite its heteronomous opposites. Yet he is reminded that complacency can be its inadvertent result: "It seems almost as if there were some equality among things, some balance in all possible contingencies which we are not permitted to know lest we should learn *indifference to good and evil*, but which is sometimes shown to us for an instant as a last aid in our last agony." Chesterton, *The Ball and the Cross* (1910; repr., Mineola, N.Y.: Dover, 1995), 9, emphasis added.

56   Though there can hardly be imagined two more contradictory charac-
     ters, Chesterton's basic conviction about suffering is similar to Simone
     Weil's notion of *malheur*, a word usually translated "affliction" but also
     connoting "inevitability" and "doom." Affliction means for Weil, as it does
     also for Chesterton, much more than physical suffering alone. *Malheur*
     names the encounter with all of those inexorable forces, both without
     and within, that make for oppression and evil, whether they take the form
     of war, disease, human degradation, or natural disaster. Affliction serves
     to thrust us out of an otherwise bestial existence and into the anguishing
     (though also potentially joyful) contradiction of living in abject, naked
     dependence on God. "The extreme affliction which overtakes human
     beings," writes Weil, "does not create human misery, it merely reveals
     [human misery]." "Evil," she declares in a staggering paradox, "is the form
     which God's mercy takes in this world." Simone Weil, *Gravity and Grace*
     (London: Routledge, 2003), 78, 145. Yet a huge difference remains. Unlike
     Chesterton, Weil is exceedingly loath to find anything redemptive, much
     less comforting, in *malheur*:

   > A blind mechanism, heedless of degrees of spiritual perfection, con-
   > tinually tosses men about and throws some of them at the very foot
   > of the Cross. It rests with them to keep or not to keep their eyes
   > turned toward God through all the jolting. It does not mean that
   > God's Providence is lacking. It is in his Providence that God has
   > willed that necessity should be like a blind mechanism.
   >
   > If the mechanism were not blind there would not be any affliction.
   > Affliction is anonymous before all things; it deprives its victims of
   > their personality and makes them into things. It is indifferent; and it
   > is the coldness of this indifference—a metallic coldness—that freezes
   > all those it touches right to the depths of their souls. They will never
   > find warmth again. They will never believe any more that they are
   > anyone.

     Simone Weil, "The Love of God and Affliction," in *Waiting for God* (New
     York: Harper & Row, 1973), 124–25.
57   Chesterton, "The Book of Job," in Chesterton, *G. K. C. as M. C.*, 46.
58   John Paul II, *Salvifici Doloris*, par. 2, 7 (http://www.vatican.va/holy_father/
     john_paul_ii/apost_letters/documents/hf_jp-ii_apl_11021984_salvifici
     _doloris_en.html), emphasis in original. The Greco-Roman ideal of "edu-
     cation through suffering" is widespread in Eastern cultures as well. In the
     Christian world, this perennial moral appeal is radically recast. The One
     who asked that the cup of rejection might be removed from his lips is
     not appealing for God to grant his followers the courage to turn natural

affliction into human understanding. Nor does he speak from the dread of his own unjust death so much as from his solicitude for his disciples that his Kingdom might come by some other means than persecution and martyrdom. Yet in a wretchedly disordered world, there is no other way, as Jesus finally embraces the divine silence that constitutes the decisive answer to his urgent desire: "Nevertheless not my will, but thine, be done" (Luke 22:42).

59 Chesterton, "The Book of Job," 51.

60 Chesterton, "The Book of Job," 52.

61 The boy would have seen the huge granite head at the British Museum, where it was brought from Thebes in 1821. It depicts Pharaoh Ramesses II. Eight feet tall as well as seven wide, and weighing seven and a quarter tons, the statue is topped by a cobra diadem that surely would have frightened a child.

62 Chesterton is perhaps recalling Moses' encounter with God in the thunder and lightning and thick clouds of smoke atop Sinai, as well as the shroud of night that covered the earth at the hour of Christ's death.

63 "Whatever else human evil is, it is—considered apart from any religious doctrine—a cosmic constant, ceaselessly pouring forth from hidden springs of brute impulse and aimless will, driven by some deep prompting of nature as we know it, and so it raises all the same questions concerning the world and its maker that are raised by natural disasters: *Unde hoc malum*—Whence this evil? And what sort of God permits it?" David Bentley Hart, *The Doors of the Sea: Where Was God in the Tsunami?* (Grand Rapids: Eerdmans, 2003), 37.

64 Sunday is of course repeating the question posed by Jesus to his disciples James and John, after they have foolishly asked about their standing in Paradise (Matt 26:42; Mark 10:38).

65 This is not to say that Chesterton makes the serious theological mistake of regarding God as passible. A suffering God would differ from us only qualitatively, and thus would remain utterly unable to heal our wounds, whether those suffered or self-inflicted. Instead, Chesterton remains thoroughly orthodox in having only the incarnate Christ suffer. As Thomas Weinandy explains, "God does not grieve because he himself experiences some injury or the loss of some good, nor that he has been affected, within his inner being, by some evil outside cause, but rather he grieves or sorrows only in the sense that he knows that human persons experience some injury or loss of some good, and so embraces them in love." Thomas G. Weinandy, *Does God Suffer?* (Notre Dame, Ind.: University of Notre Dame Press, 2000), 169.

66 Albert Raboteau describes his reversion to the faith of his childhood, after a desert wandering of his own, as having come by way of an exhibition of Russian icons at the Princeton University Art Museum. He visited it three times, returning to one particular "icon of the Theotokos with [her] sad loving eyes. She seemed to hold all the hurt of the world with those eyes. I stood in front of her for a long time. I gazed at her and she gazed at me." He found in her face and eyes the essential quality of the Christian life: a "sad joyfulness, a sense that life in a minor key is life as it is. Christianity is a religion of suffering. The suffering of Christ and the martyrs is at the center of the Christian tradition and suffering grounds the Christian to the suffering of the world. As the old [African-American] slaves knew, suffering can't be evaded, it is the mark of authentic faith." Albert J. Raboteau, *A Sorrowful Joy* (Mahwah, N.J.: Paulist, 2002), 41–42, 50.

Appendix to Chapter 1

1 Qtd. in Philipp Blom, *The Vertigo Years: Europe, 1900–1914* (New York: Basic Books, 2008), 358.

2 Christine Rosen observes that it was not secularists and humanists alone who supported eugenics, but that numerous Protestant clergy and even a few Catholic priests joined the movement as well. Oddly, the latter took Pope Leo XIII's encyclical, *Rerum Novarum*, as a call to social reform and thus to race improvement. Father John M. Cooper (1881–1949) was an anthropologist and professor of sacred theology at Catholic University who also belonged to the American Eugenics Society. From the pulpit of St. Matthew's Catholic Church in Washington, D.C., Fr. Cooper declared to the congregation assembled for High Mass that the Church "has made and is making great contributions to the betterment of humanity through the [eugenic] betterment of parents." Christine Rosen, *Preaching Eugenics: Religious Leaders and the American Eugenics Movement* (New York: Oxford University Press, 2004), 143.

3 Holmes, who served as a justice of the U.S. Supreme Court from 1902 to 1932, was unsatisfied with the sterilizing of "imbeciles." He advocated the actual killing of "unfit" infants, eliminating "at once with instant execution what now is left for nature to destroy." "I believe," he added, "that the wholesale regeneration [of our culture] which so many now seem to expect, if it can be helped by conscious, coordinated human effort, cannot be affected appreciably by tinkering with the institution of property, but only by taking in hand life and trying to build a race." Qtd. in Albert Alschuler, *Law without Values: The Life, Work, and Legacy of Justice Holmes* (Chicago: University of Chicago Press, 2000), 27.

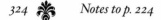

4   Qtd. in Harry Bruinius, *Better for All the World: The Secret History of Forced Sterilization and America's Quest for Racial Purity* (New York: Knopf, 2006), 6. Daniel Kevles notes that, in a book published in 1891 and titled *The Rapid Multiplication of the Unfit*, Victoria Woodhull had made what would soon become a commonplace claim: "The best minds of today have accepted the fact that if superior people are desired, they must be bred; and if imbeciles, criminals, paupers, and [the] otherwise unfit are undesirable citizens they must not be bred." Daniel J. Kevles, *In the Name of Eugenics: Genetics and the Uses of Human Heredity* (New York: Knopf, 1985), 85.

5   The Mental Deficiency Act (not repealed until 1959) established "four classes of 'mental defectives': idiots, imbeciles, the feeble minded, and moral defectives." Stephen R. L. Clark, *G. K. Chesterton: Thinking Forward, Looking Backward* (West Conshohocken, Pa.: Templeton Foundation Press, 2006), 215n20. The bill was prompted largely by public alarm over "the feebleness of English troops during the Boer War." Adam Schwartz, "G. K. C.'s Methodical Madness: Sanity and Social Control in Chesterton," *Renascence* 49, no. 1 (1996): 31. Schwartz offers the most thorough study of Chesterton's fierce opposition to eugenics, especially the effort to rid England of those who were deemed insane. Schwartz shows the remarkable similarity, despite their antithetical viewpoints on other matters, between Chesterton and Michel Foucault.

6   Churchill could at least claim the small if foolish and hobgoblin virtue of consistency regarding the wanton disregard for human life, as in his description of the British naval quarantine of Germany in 1914: "The British blockade treated the whole of Germany," Churchill later wrote, "as if it were a beleaguered fortress, and avowedly sought to starve the whole population—men, women, and children, old and young, wounded and sound—into submission." Qtd. in Nicholson Baker, *Human Smoke: The Beginnings of World War II and the End of Civilization* (New York: Simon & Schuster, 2008), 3.

7   G. K. Chesterton, *Eugenics and Other Evils* (London: Cassell, 1922), 21. Such foul physicalism has not died during the century since Churchill first introduced the Mental Deficiency Act. In his desire to rid the world of the "unworthy," Justice Holmes was joined by other prominent Americans such as Clarence Darrow and Calvin Coolidge. "America must be kept American," Coolidge wrote in 1921. "Biological laws show that Nordics deteriorate when mixed with other races." Qtd. in Bruinius, *Better for All the World*, 266.

       Walker Percy registered the subtle ways in which the incubus of the eugenics legacy continues to grip this nation's moral life. The national "newspaper of record," the *New York Times*, declined to print Percy's letter from 1988:

> The most influential book published in German in the first quarter of [the twentieth] century was entitled *The Justification of the Destruction of Life Devoid of Value*. Its co-authors were the distinguished jurist Karl Binding and the prominent psychiatrist Alfred Hoche. Neither Binding nor Hoche had ever heard of Hitler or the Nazis. Nor, in all likelihood, did Hitler ever read the book. He didn't have to. . . .
>
> I would not wish to be understood as implying that the respected American institutions I have named [the *New York Times*, the United States Supreme Court, the American Civil Liberties Union, the National Organization of Women] are similar or corresponding to pre-Nazi institutions.
>
> But I do suggest that once the line is crossed, once the principle gains acceptance—juridically, medically, socially—[that] innocent human life can be destroyed for whatever reason, for the most admirable socioeconomic, medical, or social reasons—then it does not take a prophet to predict what will happen next, or if not next, then sooner or later. At any rate, a warning is in order. Depending on the disposition of the majority and the opinion polls—now in favor of allowing women to get rid of unborn and unwanted babies—it is not difficult to imagine an electorate or a court ten years, fifty years from now, who would favor getting rid of useless old people, retarded children, anti-social blacks, illegal Hispanics, gypsies, Jews. . . .

Walker Percy, *Signposts in a Strange Land*, ed. Patrick Samway (New York: Farrar, Straus & Giroux, 1991), 350–51.

8   Don M. Shipley Jr., "Chesterton and His Interlocutors: Dialogical Style and Ethical Debate on Eugenics" (Ph.D. diss., Baylor University, 2007), 40. As Shipley explains, "race-suicide" referred to the fear of the middle and upper classes that their ranks were being decimated while the poor and working classes were proliferating. Their superior Nordic stock was being threatened by the influx of Jewish and Catholic immigrants, the former from Poland and the Slavic nations, the latter from Ireland.

9   Chesterton, *Eugenics and Other Evils*, 14.

10 G. K. Chesterton, *What's Wrong with the World* (1910; repr., San Francisco: Ignatius, 1994), 180.

11 Henri de Lubac, *Catholicism: Christ and the Common Destiny of Man* (1938; repr., San Francisco: Ignatius, 1988), 37–38.

Appendix to Chapter 4

1   John J. Mulloy is a typical representative of those who discern no serious divide between the two Englishmen. See his "Christopher Dawson and G. K. Chesterton," *Chesterton Review* 9, no. 3 (1983): 226–32.

2   Christopher Dawson, "The Historic Reality of Christian Culture," in *Christianity and European Culture: Selections from the Work of Christopher Dawson*, ed. Gerald J. Russello (Washington, D.C.: Catholic University of America Press, 1998), 15, 27. Emerson was wrong, at least in this context, to declare that "when half-gods go, the gods arrive." Dawson blames Christians for allowing the atrophy of their own tradition and thus for the replacement of holiness with benevolence: "The improvement of social conditions—one might almost say the civilizing of our industrial society—has coincided with the secularization of English culture" (11). He also insists that most people do not reject authentic Christianity so much as they are repulsed by its perversions: "the dread of moral rigorism, of alcoholic prohibition or the censorship of books and films or of the fundamentalist banning of the teaching of biological evolution" (31).

3   Dawson, "Historic Reality of Christian Culture," 67.

4   Christopher Dawson, "Man and Civilization," *The Listener*, August 23, 1933, 281. Hence Dawson's still prophetic caveat from 1929 against any attempt to recapture Western culture by adopting secular means to achieve religious ends: "I do not think that Christianity can ever compete with these forms of mass culture on their own ground. If it does so, it runs the danger of becoming commercialized and politicized and thus of sacrificing its own distinctive values. . . . Christians stand to gain more in the long run by accepting their minority position and looking for quality rather than quantity." Qtd. in Adam Schwartz, *The Third Spring: G. K. Chesterton, Graham Greene, Christopher Dawson, and David Jones* (Washington, D.C.: Catholic University of America Press, 2005), 233.

5   Dawson speaks of three "psychological" levels of human life: (1) the subrational instincts and unconscious drives that often govern humankind in the mass, (2) the rational and conscious activity whereby people free themselves from their primordial dependence on the natural order by creating the artificial social world of culture, and (3) "the super-rational level of spiritual experience, which is the sphere not only of religion but of the highest creative forces of cultural achievement—the intuitions of the artist, the poet and the philosopher—and also of certain forms of scientific intuition which seem to transcend the sphere of rational calculation and research." Dawson, "Historic Reality of Christian Culture," 77.

6   Dawson, "Historic Reality of Christian Culture," 49, 31, 66, emphasis

added. This is not to make Dawson into a Toynbeean pluralist who refuses to adjudicate among the differences in civilizations, much less an adherent of Toynbee's conviction that civilizations produce religions rather than the reverse. Yet Dawson seems naïve in his belief that there is a neutral and nontraditioned viewpoint from which one can assess the different civilizations: "[P]hilosophy and science . . . involve objective values and it is difficult to see how these are to be reconciled with a thoroughgoing historical relativism . . ." (88). Dawson seems not to recognize that, if there is anything akin to a late modern consensus concerning these matters, it is that neither philosophy nor science can lay claim to "objective values," since all sciences and philosophies are deeply grounded in and deeply dependent upon particular historical traditions of thought and practice. The work of Alasdair MacIntyre is most instructive here, especially *Three Rival Versions of Moral Inquiry* (Notre Dame, Ind.: University of Notre Dame Press, 1990) and *Whose Justice? Which Rationality?* (Notre Dame, Ind.: University of Notre Dame Press, 1988).

7   Adam Schwartz, "Sitting Still with Christopher Dawson," a review of *Eternity in Time: Christopher Dawson and the Catholic Idea of History*, ed. Stratford Caldecott and John Morrill, *Touchstone*, March–April 1999, http://touchstonemag.com/archives/article.php?id=12-02-046-b.

8   Chesterton does not deny, of course, the differences in degree, although he insists that they derive from differences in kind: "Of those courageous and invigorating conceptions, the conceptions that make life possible to live, Christendom has infinitely more than any other culture; more of the idea of free-will; more of the idea of personal chivalry and charity; more of the clean wind of hope. The metaphysics and morals of those things have been worked out by our fathers fully as deeply and delicately as any of the dark and disenchanted metaphysics of Asia." G. K. Chesterton, *Generally Speaking* (New York: Dodd, Mead, 1929), 27. Though he penned these words well after he had been received into the Roman Catholic Church in 1922, Chesterton still assumed that such virtues were so inherently strong, indeed so undying, that they would be self-sustaining, when in fact they will also disappear, or at least go underground, apart from the sacramental and prophetic life of the Church.

9   Dawson regards the Hebrew Torah as demonstrating the proper relation between religion and culture: "[H]ere the unity of religion, ethics, law, rites and ceremonies is made peculiarly clear and we see how this sacred law is also regarded as the foundation of the national culture and the very essence of people's being." Israel is for Dawson no longer God's special if often stiff-necked and rebellious people whom he nonetheless is molding,

by means of its rightly fulfilled law, into his unique nation meant for the blessing of the whole world. She is, instead, a particular instance of a pattern to be found in "the great world cultures" ("Historic Reality of Christian Culture," 22),

10 Dawson, "Historic Reality of Christian Culture," 16, 79, 78. Nowhere does Dawson explain how such a Christian culture might be politically installed, given that Christians will remain, barring a miraculous turnabout, the significant minority at best.

11 Dawson, "Historic Reality of Christian Culture," 97, 32. Dawson was not alone in desiring a restored, if radically modified, version of Christendom. Jacques Maritain and Jean Daniélou promote a similar transformation of modern political life by infusing it with a so-called Christian spirit. Daniélou thus urges believers "to *penetrate* civilization with the spirit of the Gospel" (*Prayer as a Political Problem*, trans. J. R. Kirwan [New York: Sheed & Ward, 1967], 48, emphasis added). Maritain adopted the same metaphor: "Such a [theocentric] humanism would recognize all that is irrational in man, in order to tame it to reason, and all that is supra-rational, in order to have reason vivified by it and to open man to the descent of the divine into him. Its main work would be to cause the Gospel leaven and inspiration to *penetrate* the secular structures of life—a work of the sanctification of the temporal order" (Maritain, *The Range of Reason* [New York: Scribner, 1952), 194, emphasis added).

In similar fashion, Maritain called for the creation of a new humanism "in which man must regain his lost unity by taking himself in hand again under the instinct of grace, to progress toward God." This, Maritain concludes, "will be, it seems above all, to prepare man for the terrestrial conditions of a life into which sovereign love can descend and make in man and with him a work divinely human" (Maritain, *Integral Humanism: Temporal and Spiritual Problems of a New Christendom*, trans. Joseph W. Evans [1936; repr., South Bend, Ind.: University of Notre Dame Press, 1973], 74). In both Maritain and Daniélou, the Church becomes an instrument for this larger project of a restored cultural (though not an ecclesial) Christendom. It is noteworthy that Maritain worked toward that end by helping to draft the United Nations Universal Declaration of Human Rights in 1948.

12 The absence of any real sense of the Christian *skandalon* in Dawson's work may explain why William Inge, the eugenicist "Gloomy Dean" of St. Paul's, held Dawson in high regard while scorning Chesterton. The anathema was mutual, not only concerning eugenics but also the Eucharist. "[T]he Dean uttered an unconscious truth when he said that the sacramentalists must

be 'natural idolators.' He shrinks from [the Blessed Sacrament] not only because it is idolatrous, but also because it is natural. He cannot bear to think how natural is the craving for the supernatural. He cannot tolerate the idea of it actually working through the elements of nature. . . . The Manichean horror of matter is the only *intelligent* reason for such sweeping refusal of supernatural and sacramental wonders." G. K. Chesterton, "Inge versus Barnes," in *The Thing: Why I Am a Catholic,* in *Collected Works of G. K. Chesterton,* vol. 3 (San Francisco: Ignatius, 1990), 295–96.

13 Georges Bernanos, *The Last Essays of Georges Bernanos,* trans. Joan and Barry Ulanov (Chicago: Henry Regnery, 1955), 28. Further quotations from this volume are indicated *LE*.

14 Bernanos is capable of exceedingly acerbic and prophetic wit: "The day a new miracle of technology permits some physicist to manufacture in his laboratory some kind of matter which disintegrates easily, thus placing the destruction of an entire city at the mercy of the firstcomer, I think police troops will constitute nine-tenths of the population and a citizen will no longer be able to cross the street from one side to the other without twice taking off his pants in front of a policeman anxious to be assured that he isn't hiding a single milligram of the precious stuff" (LE, 115).

15 At this writing, the U.S. war in Afghanistan drags into its tenth year, the longest in the nation's history.

16 Between 1946 and 1958, twenty-three nuclear devices were detonated at Bikini Atoll, an archipelago located within the Marshall Islands of Micronesia. Bernanos lived long enough to learn about only the first of these peacetime hydrogen bomb tests. If he had known that Castle Bravo, the thermonuclear paroxysm of 1954, employed explosives with a force equal to one thousand bombs of the kind used at Hiroshima and Nagasaki, and that nearly seventy acres of the Bikini Atoll were eventually vaporized, he might have described our time not as the Nightmare of Hands but as the Wraith-Age of Ashes.

17 Here is perhaps Bernanos' most chilling description of this subhuman creature: "Totalitarian man makes an excellent instrument of work or of war; he has enormous efficiency for a while, but he cannot serve long. The existence of totalitarian man, masterpiece of a soulless technology, will never be anything but an accident in the history of mankind; and this historical accident may even be the last one. Before attaining the imaginary paradise of universal comfort for perfected animals, totalitarian man will die of thirst while crossing a spiritual desert where there will be nothing to quench his thirst except the blood of his fellowmen. They will all drink the blood, they will lap it up like dogs, because they have exhausted the

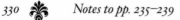

sources of the living waters. They will die of thirst; they will chew the last clots of black blood, their ears glued to the soil so that, while dying, they may try to hear the sound of subterranean waters" (LE, 171–72).

18 Hans Urs von Balthasar, *Bernanos: An Ecclesial Existence*, trans. Erasmo Leiva-Merikakis (San Francisco: Ignatius, 1996), 253.

19 G. K. Chesterton, *The Catholic Church and Conversion*, in *Collected Works of G. K. Chesterton*, vol. 3 (1928; repr., San Francisco: Ignatius, 1990), 68.

20 Chesterton, *Catholic Church and Conversion*, 100.

21 This claim is largely but not completely true: "The emergence of the ulama, the 'learned scholars of the faith,' as a distinctive grouping within Islamic society, and the development of the great schools of Islamic law in a way independent of government control were important parts of the early Islamic experience. Later, great mystic brotherhoods developed as an important foundation for popular religious life. These institutions and social structures were not 'churches,' but they were autonomous and separate from the state, and sometimes in conflict with state institutions." John L. Esposito and John O. Voll, *Islam and Democracy* (New York: Oxford University Press, 1996), 4.

22 G. K. Chesterton, *Where All Roads Lead*, in *Collected Works of G. K. Chesterton*, vol. 3 (1922; repr., San Francisco: Ignatius, 1990), 52.

23 Chesterton, *Catholic Church and Conversion*, 95.

24 G. K. Chesterton, *The Thing*, 127.

Appendix to Chapter 6

1 *Letters of J. R. R. Tolkien*, comp. and ed. Humphrey Carpenter (Boston: Houghton Mifflin, 1981), 92.

2 I owe this important insight to David Wilmington.

3 J. R. R. Tolkien, *"The Monsters and the Critics" and Other Essays*, ed. Christopher Tolkien (London: George Allen & Unwin, 1983), 21–23. Hans Urs von Balthasar offers a similar affirmation of the Anglo-Saxon capacity to receive the scandalous Gospel of God's unbreakable fidelity to his people. The Angles and Saxons understood the radical significance of steadfast fidelity and obedience to their feudal lord. Hence also their understanding of Christ as the true and final Lord. For despite their abysmal abandonment of him, he had nonetheless restored their capacity for true loyalty by refusing to break trust with them: "It was possible for this unique, unfathomable thing to seem almost normal, almost obvious even to the barbarian Germanic tribes, when the Savior presented to them the faith of the apostles as the fidelity of loyal followers to a glorious leader." Hans Urs von Balthasar, *A Theology of History* (San Francisco: Ignatius, 1963), 50.

4 John Henry Newman, "The Theory of Developments in Religious Doctrine," in *Fifteen Sermons Preached before the University of Oxford* (London: Longmans, Green, 1918), 343. Nicholas Berdyaev confirms this argument a good deal more chastely: "Historical myths have a profound significance for the act of historical remembrance. A myth contains the story that is preserved in popular memory and that helps to bring to life some deep stratum buried in the depths of the human spirit." Berdyaev, *The Meaning of History*, trans. George Reavey (Cleveland, Ohio: Meridian, 1962), 33. In *The Flying Inn*, Patrick Dalroy comically protests against mere realism when Humphrey Pump offers a drinking song that strives for a comprehensive account of English roads: "Don't be exhaustive! Don't be a scientist, Hump, and lay waste fairyland! . . . What you want is legends. What you want is lies, especially at this time of night, and on rum like this" (G. K. Chesterton, *The Flying Inn* [1914; repr., Mineola, N.Y.: Dover, 2001], 275).

5 Chesterton envisions King Alfred and his captains, not as seizing the spoils of the Danes, but as anticipating the chivalric tradition whose modern loss he never tired of lamenting. Like figures as far removed from each other as Dante and Hopkins, he too regarded chivalry as a worldly manifestation of Christian virtue.

6 There is no more astute definition of nihilism as Chesterton understands it than this one from Dietrich Bonhoeffer, written in the last years before his arrest in April 1943 and his subsequent execution by hanging in April 1945, twenty-three days before the Nazi surrender:

> This nothingness into which the West is sliding is not the natural end, the dying, the sinking of a flourishing community of peoples. Instead, it is again a specifically Western nothingness: a nothingness that is rebellious, violent, anti-God, and antihuman. Breaking away from all that is established, it is the utmost manifestation of all the forces opposed to God. It is nothingness as God; no one knows its goal or its measure. Its rule is absolute. It is a creative nothingness that blows its anti-God breath in all that exists, creates the illusion of waking it to new life, and at the same time sucks out its true essence until it soon disintegrates into an empty husk and is discarded. Life, history, family, people, language, faith—the list could go on forever because nothingness spares nothing—all fall victim to nothingness.
>
> Faced with the abyss of nothingness, the question about a historical heritage that we must make our own, use in the present, and pass on to the future is snuffed out. There is no future and no past. There remains only the present moment rescued from nothingness and the

desire to grasp the next moment. Already yesterday's concerns are consigned to forgetfulness, and tomorrow's are too far away to obligate us today.

Bonhoeffer, *Ethics*, in *Dietrich Bonhoeffer Works*, vol. 6, trans. Reinhard Krauss, Charles C. West, and Douglas W. Stott (Minneapolis: Fortress, 2005), 128.

INDEX TO THE WORKS OF CHESTERTON

Index of Names

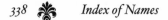

Subject Index